Impossible
Beyond This Point

By Virgil, Marcella and Joel Horn

Publisher	Horn Family
Editor/Proofreader	Crystal Marie
Cover Photos/Design	Karen Balvin-Horn
Production	Gaines Horn
TechnoGeek	Kelly Horn

ISBN-13: 978-1492756699
ISBN-10: 1492756695

www.ImpossibleBeyondThisPoint.com

Table of Contents

Note from Joel

This is the actual story of my family's adventure in the wilderness. At an age when most couples are settled down to a comfortable suburban lifestyle, my parents, both on the brink of middle age, challenged themselves to a hard and risky life adventure. Most of the names herein are real, with just a few exceptions. In fact, despite the relatively few key players in our story, among the first handful of people we met after moving to Trinity County, two were named Red.

This story combines parts of *We Walked the Tall Grass* by Marcella Horn, my mother's self-published book about the adventure, with much of *Hooray the Wilderness* by Virgil Horn, an earlier unpublished manuscript written by my father. In addition to these combined works by my parents, I've written sections, giving the perspective of three different people; a man and father, a woman and mother, and a child growing up to be a man in the wilderness. I've also added technical detail to give a fuller picture of how we accomplished what we did.

Although this is a true story and I've worked hard to be as accurate as possible, I did have to compromise between the memories of all the original witnesses when developing the narrative. There may be slight inaccuracies due to faulty memory after the passage of so much time or just the different perceptions of the same event common when two or more people share any experience. I've also taken the liberty of condensing the story in places and developing some dialogue, when necessary, based on my knowledge of the people herein and what they would likely say. This work contains my best effort given the practical constraints under which I wrote this book.

Also, both *Hooray the Wilderness*, written in 1972, and *We Walked the Tall Grass*, written 25 years later, were written in first person narrative. In order to bring the story together smoothly, I converted Virgil and Marcella's works to third person narrative and wrote my portions in third person, as well. I chose not to identify the different viewpoints, leaving it up to the readers to ponder which perspective they might be reading. Also, *Impossible Beyond This Point* covers just the first 15 years. The adventure spans several more decades and continues today, but that is for a different time and a different book.

Acknowledgements

Putting these manuscripts together into one book was a long and arduous process. Many timeline and duplicate event accounts had to be caught and corrected. I gave the manuscript to my wife, Crystal, to polish when I thought I had the faults all worked out. Apparently I didn't. She worked a number of months editing and finding incongruities I had missed.

One of the early timeline errors she caught was when some puppies were born after they were given away. As she went over this problem with the family, it was laughingly mentioned that she had to go back and "kill some puppies." For the rest of the manuscript editing, Crystal would head to the computer in the morning saying, "I'm off to kill more puppies."

I would like to thank my dear wife for all her months of hard work. I would also like to thank my sister-in-law, Karen, for the hours she spent scanning old worn photos and editing out the cracks, dust, thumbprints and yellowing. I also thank my brother, Gaines, who spent hours correcting computer glitches that occurred throughout the entire process and in doing so, took the brunt of the tears when paragraphs and pages vanished into some inaccessible portion of a hard drive. And last but not least, I thank my brother, Kelly. Once you read the book, you will know how indispensable he is to our life on the Flat.

There are many folks who aided in our adventure and enriched our lives. We received much encouragement from numerous visitors, some just passing through and some who became regulars. There's quite an extensive list of these people and the biggest gift they gave us is the knowledge that people are really good.

In particular, I wish to thank Gary and Lonie Anderson for their help in obtaining the patent to the mine, for without it, the adventure would have ended. And I'd also like to thank them for all the fun times we had together during their visits.

Also in this, I'd like to thank Grandma, Aunt Emy and Uncle Gary for all their help and support over the decades.

And finally, thanks to Maxine, Marjie, Donna, Debbie and Rhonda for their time spent proofreading and for providing invaluable feedback and corrections.

Joel Horn, 2013

Dedication

This book is dedicated to Doug Horn and to Raymond C. Cooper.

To Doug for his steadfast moral and at times financial support, and for his optimism and encouragement over the many years of this story.

To Ray for his light heartedness, his concern and care for all of us, and his thoughtful and very useful items that helped us build and survive on the Flat.

In days when the people are demanding more and more from their government and yet decrying their children for making the same demands on them; when, for a large part of the people, the greatest goal is an easy job or total government support; when that same government tries to be all things to all people at whatever cost; then someone has to reassert the evident truth that the individual is the basis for a free society.

It is for this reason that we have come to the wilderness and through continuing hard work and enterprise show that the American dream of freedom of the individual is worth much more than security of the masses.

~ Virgil Horn, 1972

1 - A New Beginning

A cool breeze drifted through tall Douglas fir and ponderosa pine and fluttered the leaves in clumps of black oak as they sat on rocks amongst their scattered possessions on the red clay dust of Backbone Ridge in the far Northern California wilds of Trinity County. The blue Ford station wagon would go no further, for from this point on, two miles of treacherous trail picked its way down to a lonesome canyon where a shell of a shack stood waiting. This would be their home. Virgil and Marcy, along with their three young sons, came to this juncture through an untamed notion to find a way of life that would give them independence, dignity and contentment.

Virgil sat across from Marcy and his blue eyes twinkled. "I hope we made the right move, Ma. There's no returning now."

"Yes," she whispered. "We made the right move."

It was the beginning of June and the year was 1967.

"Well, Ma, we accomplished our dream," he stated, as thrilled as she to be starting their adventure. He yanked his beret down on top of his blond hair and over one ear, the true image of a poet, sculptor and jewelry artist.

Prior to setting off for this untamed wilderness, they had lived several years in a charming old adobe house on five acres in southern California. Marcy was thrilled when she first saw the magnificent living room with its huge fireplace and large beams. They both had immediately seen the potential to convert it into a jewelry shop and custom picture framing business, with the courtyard walls used to show the work of local artists, many of whom were friends.

Besides making jewelry, Marcy raised organic vegetables, which sold easily because she specialized in unusual varieties. 'Organic' gardening was new in the '60s and people stopped at her stand out of curiosity. She raised yard-long beans, elephant garlic and a round cucumber that came from Italy. Her bestselling item was a sweet meaty winter squash, fondly called Mama Squash after her mother who had brought the seeds back from Mexico but had forgotten the name. Another bestseller was spaghetti squash, a nutritious substitute for pasta.

Virgil and Marcy lived in the adobe house for many happy years. Friends dropped by often and engaged in lively discussions while enjoying an abundance of wine. Thinking back, however, Marcy realized that the words spoken under the spell of wine lacked wisdom.

During the Cuban Missile Crisis in 1962, Virgil and Marcy pondered moving somewhere far away. Both wanted their sons to have a life free of fear.

The time to move finally came some years later when neighbors started reporting the huge piles of chicken manure that Marcy used for her gardens to the health department. She'd tried to keep them covered up but the piles were invariably a breeding ground for flies.

Gaines, the eldest son at eight years old, stared at his parents with serious blue eyes. "Are we really going to move?" he asked.

"If we can find a suitable place we will," Virgil replied.

Kelly, six years of age with a budding talent for all things electric, simply lowered uncertain brown eyes and ran his hand across hair that never seemed to stay in place.

At just four, little black haired, blue-eyed Joel had known no other home. "Can I take my trucks?" was his only question about a possible move.

"Of course," Marcy smiled.

"I hope I can take all my books," Gaines said.

"Yes, and also Kelly can take some of his electrical things. But remember, we haven't found a place to move to yet," Virgil said.

Virgil and Marcy were considering a small seaport town near Tamales Bay when a friend, Larry Fullerton, told them about a remote gold mine in Northern California.

"My aunt and uncle answered an ad for this mine in a Sacramento paper," he told them. "Beings they're adventurous, they decided to hike in to see it. Trouble is, it was a 10-mile hike into the canyon. According to them, they saw a small log cabin and an old apple orchard. Also plenty of bear sign everywhere." He grinned as the anticipated look of fear crossed Marcy's face. "They lost interest because my aunt didn't think she could hike the trail if they decided to live there."

The part about bears worried Marcy. Bears at the zoo had an uncanny habit of eyeballing her and she didn't know if they thought she was a kindred spirit or something to eat, but they were undeniably attracted to her.

Virgil perked up. "Is there any gold on it?"

"I'm not sure," Larry said. "Wouldn't you think in such a remote place that the miners wouldn't have mined it all out?"

Mountains held an almost fey emotion for Marcy. Even as a child, she loved them. Virgil had similar feelings although he loved the ocean and desert, too.

"You guys can create your jewelry out of the gold you mine and have a mail-order business to boot!" Larry's enthusiasm was contagious. "I don't have the address or the name of the man who owns it, but I'll try to get the information for you later."

They hadn't heard from Larry by early September so Virgil and Marcy loaded up the 1955 blue Ford station wagon with kids, clothes and blankets, ready to drive to Tamales Bay. As they walked out the door of the adobe house, the phone rang.

"Larry just stopped by and left the name and address of some gold mine owner for you," said Virgil's sister, Fran. "Do you want it?"

"It's like an omen!" Virgil told Marcy.

"You're right! Let's check it first and if it doesn't pan out, we'll go on to Tamales Bay," Marcy replied.

They drove over to Fran's to pick up the address and she cheerfully waved them off. Their destination was Junction City, California, over 600 miles away.

Reaching Redding late that evening, they spent the night in a motel. The following morning, they drove west over Buckhorn Summit on State Route 299, a notoriously narrow, twisty highway. Marcy held her breath every time the station wagon encountered a logging truck while rounding the steep bends.

At last, they came to Weaverville, a charming town where trees shaded the sidewalks and buildings old and new lined both sides of the street. Situated in a high valley with mountains all around, it looked like a village nestled in the Swiss Alps. They were enchanted.

"It's just as I imagined it," Virgil said, eyes aglow as he surveyed the only town of any significance near Junction City.

On Main Street, a grocery store attached to a feed store looked gray and very old, as though built during the early mining days of California. A weathered sign read *Ryan's Store* and they decided to stop and pick up something for lunch.

Upon entering the store, their footsteps clumped stridently across the bare wood floorboards made from narrow planks of Douglas fir. As the clerk sliced a chunk of bologna into rounds and wrapped it in white butcher paper, Virgil asked for directions.

"Do you know how far Junction City is?"

"Sure do. Just drive west over Oregon Mountain and you can't miss it. Or maybe I should say you might, it's so small," the clerk chuckled.

Entering Junction City eight miles later, they saw just how small it was. On the left side of the highway sat a gas station, a grocery store with a wooden bench in front displaying a few old timers, and a few other buildings scattered around to one side. Across the highway, the restaurant looked as if it belonged in a Bavarian village. That was the whole town and Marcy loved it.

They parked the station wagon in front of the store. Under the careful scrutiny of the old timers, they walked inside to ask directions to Al Garedo's place. The storeowner, Mr. Dixon, was glad to help.

"Just drive a mile or so down the road until you come to an apple orchard. Al Garedo owns the orchard and runs a fruit stand there so I'm sure you'll find him home."

Although Mr. Dixon looked at them questioningly, they kept quiet about the mine and returned to the car. As they drove away from the store, Gaines spied flowing riffles of murky green river and leaned out the left rear window.

"Look at the river!" he exclaimed.

"That's the Trinity River," Virgil replied.

Shortly, an orchard appeared to the right of the highway and they saw a small man with curly blond hair eating an apple, one foot propped against a fruit stand. He studied them as they drove in. As Virgil got out of the Ford, the man threw down his apple core and walked jauntily toward him.

Marcy couldn't hear the conversation but a big smile stretched across the man's face and he reached into his pocket, retrieved a scrap of paper, wrote something down and then handed it to Virgil. Before opening the door of the Ford, Virgil took a long draw on his pipe and studied the paper. Once inside, he laid the scribbled scrap on the dashboard.

"That's Al Garedo and the claim is still for sale. He said to continue driving down this road until we come to a bridge. Right after the bridge, we'll turn right off the highway. We should come to a ghost town and then a few miles beyond that, we'll take a left onto a dirt road called Hobo Gulch. The trail is a hard left off Hobo Gulch Road," Virgil explained. "Oh yes, and he marked the trail with orange parachute ribbons and it's only a two-mile hike down to the claim."

"Thank goodness for that!" Marcy had expected a 10-mile hike and had wondered how long it would take going at a slower pace with the boys.

The highway closely followed the flowing waters of the Trinity River until a steel I-beam truss bridge crossed the clear emerald green waters of a small tributary. The limpid waters blended with the murky green of the Trinity in picturesque swirls of emerald.

"What river is that?" Gaines wanted to know.

"North Fork of the Trinity, according to the sign just before this bridge," Virgil said.

A one-lane tar and gravel road intersected the highway just beyond the bridge. Virgil turned right, drove past a *Primitive Area 12 mi.* sign and continued a short distance to the ghost town that Al had mentioned.

The first faded red brick building stood just off the right side of the road on the steep banks of the North Fork and looked as though it was ready to fall into the river. Driving on, another brick building stood in front of houses hidden like ghosts behind veils of wild roses and feathery Queen Anne's lace. The homes had the natural gray patina of aged wood and some stood under unkempt fruit trees. Old walnut trees shaded the street and recently fallen nuts littered the road.

"Ouch, we're crunching them! Think of all the cookies they'd make," Marcy laughed as Virgil drove over the walnuts. "Virg, wouldn't this make a wonderful art colony?"

"Yes, but would you like to live so close to the artists?" Virgil inquired.

"No, not really," Marcy replied.

Walnuts continued to crunch under their tires and Marcy asked Virgil to stop so she could pick some up. As Virgil looked for a turnout, they saw a trailer parked next to a fine old house that was undergoing repairs.

"Here's a good spot to stop," Marcy pointed.

"I really think not," Virgil replied.

Marcy followed his gaze to a frightening man leaning on a rifle by the side of the road, scowling at them.

"You're right. Keep driving," she said.

Shortly beyond the ghost town of Helena, the tar and gravel surface ended and the road dropped steeply into the North Fork gorge, where it crossed a bridge made of large logs. At this point, the North Fork branched, with the main arm passing under the bridge. This main branch disappeared into a wild gorge on the left, while the road followed the smaller tributary on the right. The road climbed back up and became tar and gravel once again.

Kelly, though only six years old, took notice of odd things like this and posed a question. "Hey, Virg, why did the gravel disappear and then come back like that?"

Virgil slowed and surveyed the oddness of the road in the rearview mirror. Finally, he answered. "See those big concrete pillars? There used to be a bridge there, a higher bridge, but it was taken out by a flood. That's a temporary bridge and section of road."

As they continued along the narrow road, hammered-on signs bearing the names of gold mining claims decorated trees in front of steep winding roads that disappeared into the deepening ravine where the smaller river branch flowed. Cozy, well-built cabins were visible now and again along the banks of the stream.

Following his older brother's river-name quest, Joel asked, "What river is this?"

"I believe it's the East Fork of the North Fork," Virgil replied. "This road is called East Fork Road."

Suddenly, Virgil slammed on the brakes. "I think this is the road we take," he said as he read his scrap of paper. "Yep, this is Hobo Gulch Road."

Virgil grinned as he turned the station wagon onto a narrow rocky red dirt track that forked upwards from East Fork Road. Virgil and Marcy both got a kick out of the name, thinking that perhaps they would be like hobos if they moved there.

The shrubbery along Hobo Gulch Road was covered with dust and more settled on the foliage as brown clouds billowed behind and around the Ford, forcing them to roll up the windows. With every mile, the road climbed and became narrower. Thickets of dense shrubbery leaned out over the road and obscured their view around every curve.

Marcy worried that they'd smash into another car or, heaven forbid, a logging truck coming from the opposite direction. Most places were only wide enough for one car to pass and all signs of civilization had disappeared. Virgil glanced over and grinned at Marcy's reaction.

"Gee, it's so far," she commented. "I don't know if it's the twisty road or what, but it seems like more than the five miles shown on Garedo's map."

"It seems that way to me, too, but we have to drive so slow it's giving us the illusion that it's longer. Did you notice how nervous Al was?" Virgil asked to divert Marcy's thoughts from the lonely road. "He looked shocked when I told him we were interested in his gold mine."

"Yes, but I also saw him smiling," Marcy replied.

"Well, you'll certainly have an exciting birthday today, sweetie," Virgil said.

"Today is September sixth, my birthday for sure, and I wondered how my day would turn out," Marcy said.

"There it is, Dodo, the road!" Gaines shouted using the nickname he'd devised when unable to say Daddy as a toddler.

Hanging vegetation partially obscured the turnoff and a barely visible, broken sign read *Road Ends 1/2 mi.* Virgil pressed the brake pedal and turned the Ford sharply left onto this steeper, almost non-existent road. The Ford lunged and bounced in washouts from previous rains and crunched over pinecones and pine needles while low hanging branches scratched the sides of the station wagon.

"Boy, oh boy, no one has used this road for a long time." Virgil grunted between each lunge and swerved to miss a big dead branch lying in the middle of the lane.

"Is this the trail?" Kelly asked.

"I don't think so," Virgil said. "Al said we park on top of a ridge."

"What's a ridge?" Kelly wanted to know.

"A long narrow mountain top," Virgil replied.

Passing through a grove of younger Douglas fir trees interspersed with larger ponderosa pines, they came to a wide flat area bulldozed on the ridge top. Stepping out of the Ford, they saw the mountains encircling them and forgot the long drive. A soft breeze brushed their faces and the scent of sunbaked fir and pine needles engulfed them. A silver snag with twisted branches towered above.

"Oh, this is heaven," Marcy sighed, sniffing the air and stretching the kinks out of her back.

"I bet that's the trailhead over that hump, Ma. Come on boys, time for hiking!" Virgil exclaimed.

Marcy considered taking their lunch and soft drinks down the trail but assumed they'd be back in time to have a picnic on the tailgate. All were anxious for the adventure so they set off without delay.

They found what appeared to be the trail marked with a weather-beaten Forest Service sign that read *Impassable Beyond This Point.* The trail was wide enough for a car but descended steeply down to the north, cut in the hard outcroppings of sedimentary rock on the precipitous ridge flank.

"This is great! Maybe we could clean all these rocks and branches off and drive down," Marcy proposed.

About a quarter-mile down, they came to a large timber structure presumably left over from an old mining operation.

"I wonder what that was," Virgil commented as they gazed at odd-angled decaying poles. "Looks like they never finished it but it might have been a stamp mill."

The wide trail ended abruptly and pinched down to a steep narrow path littered with slippery dead leaves and waxy pine needles. On both sides were thickets of oak, madrone and various other shrubs.

A hundred yards down from the old mill structure, the trail leveled and followed the flank of a spur ridge to a rocky spine where the forest thinned out to a few towering gnarled sugar pines clinging to shallow pockets of poor soil between the rough outcroppings. A small clump of manzanita brush baked in the hot afternoon sun, its roots set into a shelf on the top of a rocky bluff.

Below the bluff, treetops fell away before giving way to an even steeper rock gorge that contained the tiny sparkling ripples of a thread of river water. The coiling silver thread appeared and disappeared several times before finally vanishing into the enfolding clutches of heavily timbered green ridges.

A large high ridge rose from the distant riverbank and climbed to an elevation far above them. Covered in heavy stands of timber broken intermittently by patches of talus, brush and rock outcroppings, steep angling slopes of spur ridges extended from the large ridge. A tall dead sugar pine just turning silver stood in another patch of wild manzanita immediately below them to the right.

Watching the wind gracefully bend the treetops, Marcy got a strange nostalgic feeling, as though she'd been there before. As she looked far down into the canyon, she was sure that Gaines and Kelly would have no problem but wondered if little Joel could make it.

Dropping steeply after the promontory point, the trail became nothing more than a collection of foot-sized shelves of soil held in place by large tree roots that grew over the surface rocks in their search for nutrients.

"We're crawling over a hogback," Virgil muttered.

"What's a hogback?" Kelly asked.

"It's a rocky outcropping formed along the top of a ridge," Virgil explained.

They found the first orange ribbon trail marker tied to a branch on an old fallen snag about a hundred feet further down the path. As they climbed over the fallen tree, Marcy was pleased to see Joel and Kelly scramble over the downed snag like monkeys.

"There's another orange ribbon!" Kelly shouted and it became a game to see who could spot the ribbons first.

One ribbon dangled from a branch overhanging a cliff. Virgil and the boys climbed over with ease but Marcy followed more slowly as her shoes slipped on small round dried sticks. The trail veered straight down to where another ribbon adorned a live oak branch and they had to sidestep to keep from sliding too fast down the loose shale.

Dead branches scratched Marcy's arms and she ripped her pants climbing over another fallen tree with sharp stubby points. Marcy's smooth-soled shoes were suited only for flat land, but luckily Virgil wore work boots and the boys each had sturdy shoes with heels.

Having previously lived a year in Arkansas, Virgil cautioned the family about timber rattlers. "They like to hide beneath fallen logs where it's cool, so watch where you put your feet."

The last ribbon lay on a boulder with the remains of the parachute stuffed under a log beside it. They couldn't hear the river so they knew it was still a ways down.

"It's on the river, right?" Marcy asked.

"That's what Al Garedo said," Virgil shrugged. "We'll have to follow the trail as best as we can and mark our own way now." Virgil draped the remaining parachute cloth around his neck. "I wonder why Al stopped here."

The path they followed gave way to just a network of intersecting game trails. The boys forged ahead but stopped at each crossing until Virgil determined which one to take. Since the hogback, the going had all been under heavy timber forest but suddenly they broke out onto an open, relatively level chaparral covered bench.

"Is this it?" Marcy wondered as the boys ran to look over a wall of rock outcroppings.

"The river is right down there!" Joel yelled.

Joel's 'right down there' was actually a 500-foot open slope of rock and talus that formed the east wall of the river gorge and supported only a few clumps of buckbrush in its steepness. Though not any steeper than the hogback, no trees grew here to hide the height of a potential plunge. Virgil tied a ribbon torn from the parachute on a branch at the edge of the cliff.

"Virg, the boys and I can't climb down that; I'll get height fright!" Marcy protested in horror.

"Sure you can, Ma," Gaines encouraged." See? There's a trail around it."

Marcy dug her fingers into cracks in the cliff as her shoes slid on the waxy needles shed on the incline by a silvery green digger pine that leaned out from the top of the bluff. Slipping constantly with her smooth soles, she sat down to remove her shoes. Years of going barefoot around the adobe house had callused her feet and she thought she'd do better with nothing on them.

"Stop everyone! I'm going to take off my shoes!" she shouted.

Laces tied together and the shoes draped around her neck, Marcy started down the cliff again but quickly realized that removing her shoes was a mistake. With each step, sharp rocks and pine needles cut into the soles of her feet. Hordes of tiny black gnats obscured her vision and the shoes around her neck slapped her across both cheeks as she lurched down the rocky face.

"Stop again! I have to put my shoes back on. I cut my foot! My God, do you think we'll make it?" Marcy looked at their red faces, black flies gyrating around four sets of eyes.

"Listen," Gaines said, cupping his hand over his ear. "Do you hear the river now, Ma?"

Just 100 yards away, the waters of the North Fork poured over a jumbled dam of boulders before plunging into white foam under one edge of a whitened boulder nearly the size of a house. Around the far edge and downstream of the boulder, a deep emerald pool formed. The water was so clear that the rounded boulders on the bottom were vividly sharp, except tinted a beautiful green. At the edge of the sparkling foam, the green darkened to deep green-black and the boulders faded into the depth.

The sound of the cataract ascended on the hot up-sloping breeze. A series of near vertical moss-covered cliffs formed the far wall of the gorge, which the afternoon sun painted with a pattern of shade and bright sunlight. Directly across from the pool, a recent slide exposed the ocher of fresh rock streaked with deep blood-red mineral stains. On the far bank below the slide, jagged mineral-stained rock slabs littered the whitened river rock. Upstream, ancient Douglas fir trees with roots exposed in an eroding river bar held up jagged dead tops. The leaves of the willows and cottonwood trees flickered like silver tinsel in the wind.

"Okay, it's up to you guys if we decide to stay, but I can't see us crawling out every time we want to go to town," Marcy declared.

They reached the river and Gaines immediately set off rock hopping down the banks, followed by his younger brothers. The boys found a shallow quiet spot to swim and Marcy sat down to wash off the trail dust and soak her feet to clean and soothe the scratches.

"Since it's my 35th birthday, I'm going swimming in my birthday suit," she announced.

Virgil sat on a big flat boulder and smiled when she ducked under water. "September Morn," he quoted.

Little hopping water oozles dove into the white foaming waterfalls. Unafraid, they'd probably not seen humans before. The icy cold river left a delightful tingle and Marcy splashed a handful on Virgil. But like a cat, he shunned cold water.

"I'm going to check downriver to see if I can locate the cabin," Virgil decided.

After he left, Marcy slipped into her clothes. A while later, the boys came out of the cold water covered with goose bumps.

"You'd better get your clothes back on in a hurry," Marcy advised.

Far up on the east wall, Marcy watched the last ribbon waving in the breeze. It was their link to finding the way back; it would be easy to get lost in this canyon.

Virgil came back shaking his head. "There's not a sign of any cabin or even a trail."

The steep west wall already blocked the sun, giving Marcy visions of bears coming out in the evening. The thought urged her to rush them to leave although she was thoroughly enchanted with this boulder strewn wild gorge and wasn't ready.

"Drink a lot of water before we start up," she instructed the boys.

They took a last look around and headed back up. After the chilling river water, the sun felt good for the first 100 yards. But the building heat on the west facing canyon wall plus the exertion of the dusty climb across talus slides soon had them all sweating.

They found a slight trail to the right of the last ribbon so decided to skirt around the cliff. It was very steep but the boys didn't complain. Even little four-year-old Joel kept going up over boulders, crawling on hands and knees and grabbing dead branches to pull himself up.

Gasping for breath, Marcy made them stop to rest. The whole family was sweaty and plagued with black flies that rimmed their eyelashes like thick mascara, but even worse, a horrible thirst set in. Joel whined a bit but soon grasped that no matter how much he wanted a drink, his parents weren't able to help and so he struggled on in silence.

At last they emerged on the main trail were Al Garedo had quit marking the way but they all remembered that they still had a lot of climbing to do to reach the top where the station wagon was parked. Kelly walked ahead, followed by Joel and Marcy, while Gaines and Virgil brought up the rear. Kelly disappeared around a bend in the trail and then suddenly raced back.

"Ma, there was a scary noise ahead!" he rasped, mouth parched.

Virgil went to investigate and there, coiled in an indentation on the trail, was a timber rattler. Woven like an Indian basket with its triangular designs, its tail stood straight up, rattling fiercely. Virgil couldn't find a stout stick to kill it with, so they threw rocks until it slithered down over the side of the trail.

Dusk was settling in and still they climbed.

"What greenhorns we are for not bringing water," Marcy remarked.

"Come back here!" Virgil yelled.

Marcy and the younger boys looked back to see Virgil and Gaines perched upon the root of a giant madrone tree. They climbed up to where the two sat and saw a tiny pool of water filled by a trickle seeping out of the rocks and roots at the very base of the tree. Mosquito wigglers swam around in the pool and Virgil dipped them out with a madrone leaf.

"How did you find it?" Marcy gasped.

"I looked up and saw green grass growing up here, so I decided to check it out," Virgil replied.

They each got a leaf and very carefully, so as not to disturb the sediment, got their drinks. The water tasted cold, pure and delicious, even with the mosquito larvae. They named their savior spring the Drinking Tree.

Shedding its bark, large brown scrolls like giant cinnamon sticks were scattered beneath the tree. The new bark showed through and Virgil commented on the pistachio green hue. Marcy lay under the tree gazing up at the big glossy leaves and forgot the time.

"Hey, it's getting late. We'd better get going," Virgil urged.

Bears! she thought and jumped up.

In the waning evening sun, they dragged themselves to the top, exhausted. They ate their belated lunch of warm drinks and dry bologna sandwiches on the tailgate of the Ford. Marcy never dreamed that it would take them all day to hike down to the claim and then back up.

"Obviously that wasn't the right place," Virgil said, the orange parachute still wrapped around his neck and his eyes twinkling. "We'd better stop and see what Al says about that before we find a camping spot."

The lights were still on at the Garedo's. Al's wife, a heavyset woman with a tired smile, greeted them at the door. Al jumped up when he saw who was there.

"Alvarita, these are the people who are interested in the gold mine," Al explained. "Come on and have dinner with us," he offered, scraping several chairs out from the table.

"Well, we don't have much because I just got back from work," Alvarita apologized, offering a plate of bologna, a jug of milk and a big bowl of crisp, juicy fresh apples.

"Thanks for the offer but we just ate. But an apple will taste real good," Marcy said.

After hearing about their trip into the canyon and how they got lost, Alvarita shook her head.

"The old hermit that lives down there probably moved the ribbons. He doesn't want anyone invading his territory," Al said. "How did those little guys make it? Boy, they sure must be strong. That trail is steep!"

"I give them Tiger's Milk," Marcy explained. "It's a health food drink that has brewer's yeast in it."

Al jumped out of his chair. "Alvarita! Do you still have any brewer's yeast left? Maybe I should go back to taking some again."

Virgil and Marcy chatted a bit with Al about the claim. Suddenly, he asked if he could play his electric organ for them. He played hymns suited to a funeral and turned around on the bench between songs to tell bear stories, each more frightening than the last.

"Do we have to crawl and climb all the way down to the claim?" Marcy interrupted.

"Oh no, you can walk upright all the way," Al replied. "I don't know what shape the trail is in…we haven't cleaned it this year. Why not come back tomorrow and I'll have a map ready for you?"

Agreeing to stop back by in the morning, they said good-bye and Virgil drove the Ford down a side road to the Trinity River. Marcy made the boys a bed in the back of the station wagon and she and Virgil decided to sleep in the front seat. Thanks to Al's stories, Virgil thought he saw a bear moving across the river.

The next morning, Al was waiting outside his fruit stand. Alvarita had gone to work and Al had decided he would lead Marcy and Virgil to the claim himself. He grabbed a sack of apples and Marcy had drinks and sandwiches for a picnic. Once on top, they made good time down to the trailhead.

"What's this old pole structure?" Virgil inquired.

"That's what's left of the old stamp mill. The guy had a big operation going here but a truckload of gold concentrates disappeared one night and he went broke. His son and daughter own it now. It's still a good hard rock mine."

When the party reached the last ribbon, Al yelled, "Ah ha! Someone has moved them, all right. You're supposed to walk straight ahead, not down."

The trail was very narrow but nowhere was it like the path they'd taken the day before, although they did have to crawl over several fallen trees.

"Where does that hermit live?" Virgil asked.

"You mean Red Barnes? He lives about where you guys ended up yesterday."

"Oh no! I was skinny dipping down there!" Marcy cried.

"I wouldn't worry about that. He's been living down there for so long he wouldn't have recognized you as being a woman. Probably thought you were some hairless animal," Al chuckled. "He could have shot you, too."

"Does he live there all year round?" Virgil asked.

"Yeah, most of the year. But he's getting old and someone saw him sneaking aboard a bus last November. Guess he still wants the image of being the tough old mountain man. Don't get me wrong though, he is tough for a man his age. That trail's mighty steep. Lots of times he walks all the way to town." Al shook his head.

"That's a 10-mile hike to Junction City," Virgil remarked.

"Yep, and he's close to being 65 years old. Some guy was telling me that Red shot a coyote but it had just eaten a skunk, so it wasn't fit to eat," Al confided. "He brags about eating anything that crawls or walks on four legs in this canyon."

The trail traversed down through mostly heavy timber and then the group walked up a hill, around a jutting promontory spur ridge and came to the base of a cliff with blocks of limestone stacked like giant books in disarray. Dwarfed oak trees with gnarled roots twined in and out of the blocks and vine maples with a hint of yellow hung from above the area.

"Well, here's an Elfin Dell," Virgil pronounced.

They crossed a tall talus slide formed at the base of a cliff that baked in the hot September sun. Everyone was puffing and sweating after crossing the hot slide but nobody complained, not even little Joel.

"Is there any gold on this claim?" Virgil asked.

"There sure is," Al answered. "Me and Alvarita come down here with my sister and her husband all the time and pan for gold. I'll prove to you that you can get enough gold out for your jewelry and make a good profit, too."

After crossing the talus, the trail narrowed. "Watch this part of the trail," Al warned.

The next section of trail was so narrow and steep that Virgil and Marcy held the boys' hands until it widened again and opened into a relatively flat clearing covered with blue bunch grass crowned with tall golden seed stalks. The clearing was rimmed with digger pine trees, narrow leaf buckbrush and manzanita bushes. A cool sighing breeze from the north undulated through the golden stalks in a flowing dance.

"You know, there's always a cool breeze up here even in the hottest of summers," Al said, wiping his face with his shirt sleeve.

"Wind Dance Lookout," Marcy said and Al did a little jig.

"Come over here," Al said. "I want you to see the Flat from the lookout."

Below the rugged mossy cliffs, they could see the river curving through a broad white gravel bar 500 yards away and 600 feet below. Above the bare gravel bar, a fair-sized flat covered with open forest nestled inside the crescent bend of the river. The wide breadth of the white gravel gave Marcy the impression of a desert. Virgil tugged the hairs on his eyebrow as he stared down.

"I want it!" Marcy whooped.

Al and Virgil laughed as the group started down the last leg of the trail. Nearing the bottom, the steep mountainside moderated and an old apple orchard in slightly sloping ocher soil came into view. The top branches of the trees were dead and snapped over, the tips touching the ground. With a little imagination, the orchard looked like a small village of teepee frames.

"By golly, the bears and the snow almost ruined every tree in that orchard but a little water and a lot of pruning will bring them back," Al commented.

Next to the river stood a 10-by-12-foot vertical board and batten shell of a shack. Tarpaper covered only half of the steep gable roof and a plastic tarp draped over the exposed side. The ravages of weather and time had stained the wall of the shack in streaks of sienna and dirty burnt umber. A small pine tree no higher than Joel grew beside the door and a scraggly climbing rose grew out of a boulder in front. Out the rear of the cabin, a small window had been cut through the boards. Remnants of clear plastic film, once stapled over the window, now framed the opening like cracking film ice. *So this is the log cabin I envisioned,* Marcy thought.

Virgil stared in dismay at the large hole gnawed out of the bottom of the door. When he pushed the door open, the smell of mildew and animal dung assaulted them and they could see an eerie darkness through the gaps between the uneven floorboards.

A board table with two broken legs stood against the wall and rusty cans with no labels lay in disarray on shelves. A stove made from an old oilcan stood in the middle of the room and what was left of the window adorned the back wall.

A crossbar over the window was broken inward and Marcy imagined some big animal had made brutal entry into the cabin. Scores of paper wasp nests hung under the eaves and the wasps buzzed loudly about their heads as the group made a hasty exit.

"We can't live in there, Ma," Virgil determined.

"Maybe it could be fixed temporarily until we can build something else," Marcy replied. "We can line the floor with some of our floor tile."

The surrounding area was almost as bad as the shack. On the fine dusty silt lay cans, dirty clothes and other rubbish. Most disgusting were several deer carcasses with only the choice backstraps cut away, crawling with blue bottle flies and giving off a nauseating stench. Regardless of this, Marcy could visualize grapes, vegetable gardens and flowers.

"There's been some poachers using this cabin," Al frowned. "What a waste of deer meat. Come on, I'll show you the swimming hole," Al offered. "Now that's real pretty."

They followed Al down to the river, passing another makeshift table hammered between a cedar, a pine and an oak that was better made than the one in the shack.

"That used to be Dan Raymond's blacksmith table," Al said. "He's the guy that owned this claim before I bought it. See, you can still see pieces of iron rods." Al reached down and picked up a couple. "Dan Raymond lived here with his wife and small son many years ago."

Virgil pointed to silver planks lying along the distant riverbank. "What are those boards across the river?"

"That used to be the flume that fed water to the Schlomer Mine some 10 miles downriver at the old ghost town," Al explained. "There was a fairly large log crib dam here, as well, to supply the water to the flume. They cut down an old Model T Ford to fit wooden rails secured to the top of the flume frame and they drove it all the way to the mountain above Helena. They even strung telephone wire into here. The flume was in good shape until the '55 and '64 floods ripped the first sections away. Then a fire burned the lower sections. The dam tender lived in a house across the river but it burned down years ago."

Al pointed to a darkened spot covered with blackened stove parts, twisted bed frames and the sparkle of melted bottles atop the 30-foot bluff that formed the far riverbank. "That's all that's left," Al sighed. "Sure was a lively place until President Roosevelt made it against the law to own gold. Most of the mines were shut down for the war effort and the miners drafted into the army."

When the group came to the swimming hole, Marcy thought of the looking glass pool in the Raggedy Ann and Andy book she'd been reading to the boys. The emerald water reflected the tawny colored willows and there was scarcely a ripple until a fish made a gentle splash.

Joel plopped down on a patch of sand and started digging, and Kelly and Gaines joined him. A ridge of bedrock encircled an oak tree and made a table for lunch. In the lazy spirit of the afternoon, they watched dragonflies bouncing on the surface of the pool laying their eggs.

Suddenly, Al jumped up. "I want to show you the Rock of Gibraltar," Al said.

"No, Dodo. I'm not going another step," Joel protested, so Virgil went with Al and Marcy stayed with the boys.

"Do you boys like it here?" Marcy asked.

"Oh yes, it's beautiful," Gaines answered, and Joel and Kelly nodded in agreement. "This is better than the irrigation ditches to play in. We never have to worry about the water bill and we can play forever," Gaines said.

When Virgil and Al came back, Al was pointing down the river and Marcy heard him telling Virgil that the inside curves of the river were the best places to mine for gold.

"We'd better start packing because I don't know how fast the boys will make it up trail and we don't want to be stuck down here in the dark," Al said. "There's another trail that will take us to the upper stream. It's on the way out anyway and it's pretty."

Joel frowned. The group moved slower uphill but perked up when they saw the stream.

"By gosh, it's been a dry summer and the stream is still running. I never saw this stream go dry yet," Al stated.

Virgil looked pleased. "It's a long drop to the Flat. I'm sure it would run a water power system."

Vine maples, cascara trees and soft green shrubs flanked both banks and the stream flowed through a patch of wild blackberries. A remnant of an old reservoir filled with leaves and other debris stood above it.

"All I have to do is ditch the water from further upstream down to this reservoir and then pipe it down to the Flat below. I suspect the old timers used this to sluice their mines," Virgil said, pointing to a faint ditch.

"Yes, most likely they did," Al agreed, "but it sure was a long time ago."

Leaving the stream, they started back up a steep path to get to the original trail. It was slow walking but Al encouraged the group. "Don't let on that the trail is tiring you. Just stop and comment on the beautiful scenery," he advised.

Virgil and Marcy dropped Al off at his house. From the savings Marcy had made at her vegetable stand, they counted out a down payment on the claim and Al accepted the money with a broad smile. Returning to the same camp spot by the river, the family flopped down and fell asleep almost immediately.

Around midnight, a small voice woke Marcy. "I can't sleep, Ma," Joel groaned. "My legs hurt."

We overdid it with the little tike by going down the second time, Marcy thought as she rubbed Joel's legs until he relaxed. "You can handle it," she soothed.

Joel nodded and drifted back to sleep.

Virgil back up at trailhead with
orange parachute around his neck

2 - Prepping for an Adventure

Virgil and Marcy agreed not to tell anyone about their plans when they got back to southern California. They wanted to avoid the onslaught of pessimistic comments from relatives and friends alike that they'd experienced when sharing their ideas and dreams in the past.

They set a date to make the move in two years, but one afternoon while sitting under the Chinese Locust tree with the Santa Ana winds blowing blossoms all around them, Virgil slowly brushed the petals from his pant leg, deep in thought.

"Marcy, I know we decided to move in two years but I don't think I'll have the nerve to do it if we wait that long," Virgil admitted. "Most guys at age 40 are well settled into their careers and are already thinking about retirement."

"Well, let's move next spring," Marcy suggested. "We can leave in February."

"The snow won't even be melted at that time of year," Virgil replied.

Marcy was ready to leave immediately. "Well, how about March?"

"June is a good time; we'll go then," Virgil decided.

"June it is then," Marcy agreed, beaming with happiness.

Full of enthusiasm, they clandestinely packed all their belongings in cardboard boxes that they stacked behind a screen in the big living room of the adobe house. Virgil kept a meticulous list of all the things they'd need. For many years, he'd been collecting nails, motors and equipment that they would now use for the gold mine.

They kept to their agreement not to tell anyone until their friend and Virgil's part-time employer, Ray Cooper, came to visit. Ray owned a hardware store down the boulevard and frequently helped Marcy with her organic garden. He had brought her great bundles of palm fronds for the roof of her stand, and when things were slow at the jewelry and picture frame shop, he called on Virgil to help him with window glazing. Ray eyed all the boxes suspiciously.

"Looks like you're packing. What's going on here?" Ray demanded.

Virgil looked questioningly at Marcy.

"Heck, let's tell Ray!" she said.

They went into detail about the gold mine, and the more they told him, the redder Ray's face got. It even turned a shade of purple before he exploded.

"You can't do that! You won't make it! You'll starve!" he shouted. "Virg, for gosh sakes, are you mad exposing your kids and wife to a life like that? The Forest Service doesn't want people on the claims. They're running them out and burning their cabins down." He swung around and looked right at Marcy. "There are bears down there, too, you know."

Ray jumped to his feet and slammed out the door. After that outburst, Virgil and Marcy were glad they hadn't yet told anyone else. Gaines was unusually quiet after Ray left.

"What's wrong, Gaines?" Marcy asked.

"Remember that movie we saw with the dog and the forest ranger?" he whispered.

"You mean Lassie?" Marcy inquired.

"I wasn't going to be scared of the bears because I thought the rangers were going to save us," Gaines said. "Why are they burning cabins down?"

"I don't know, Gaines. This is the first I've heard of it," Marcy said.

"When I was a park ranger at Lake Mead one summer, people filed claims just to have lakefront cabins and never planned to do any mining. Ray's been reading a mining journal and they're probably just overdramatizing things," Virgil speculated.

The next day, Ray had recovered and wanted to know the location of the claim so he could take his wife, Sue, to see it. Virgil drew Ray a map and gave him Al Garedo's address.

After breaking their agreement not to tell people, Marcy told many customers that stopped at her stand. The men were envious but most of the women thought they were nuts for moving to a shack.

"I see you're going to Bigfoot country," one customer commented.

"What's that?" Marcy fretted.

"Oh, some people saw big gorilla-type humans running around in the mountains there," the customer replied. "They even found huge footprints in the snow."

First bears, now huge gorillas…what next? Marcy thought.

Marcy dreaded the day when she'd have to tell her mother, a tiny woman with blue eyes and an iron disposition who often nagged in her deep east European accent, 'Vhy don't you tell Virgil to get a goot government job? Vhy do you always vant to start your own business?'

Although Marcy's mother had believed in the free enterprise system of the United States when she first came from Czechoslovakia, she and Marcy's dad had failed in several businesses before finally succeeding with an egg ranch and she felt it was her motherly duty to spare Marcy similar heartache by discouraging any financial project that didn't seem to provide security.

Ray and Sue returned four days later and both were exuberant. "We were going to spend the night in the shack until we saw it, ugh! Besides, we got scared of the bears and decided to hike back up the trail. I had to push this big lug all the way up," Sue said as she punched Ray's bulging stomach.

At six-foot-two and nearly 300 pounds, Ray looked like a giant when standing next to petite Sue. "Very funny," he replied.

Ray was now enthused about their move and decided to join in the adventure by helping them out. He brought Marcy a roll of thick plastic sheeting to sew into big bags with zippers to keep beans, rice and flour dry. Another time, he took Marcy out to his truck to show her a beautiful new wood-burning kitchen stove, which was something she'd really wanted.

"Virg traded me the old Volkswagen for it," Ray said.

Marcy was thrilled. "But we must still owe you more money!" she exclaimed.

"Well, I want to eat when I come down," Ray replied.

Ray also gave Virgil a new 30-30 Marlin rifle and found them two dogs. "To chase the bears away and to shoot the ones that don't run!" he laughed.

The female Australian shepherd had pale blue eyes and gray and white mottled fur; Marcy named her Tissy. Gaines had been reading Huckleberry Fin and named the male Border collie Hucky. To their chagrin, Tissy got pregnant. They already had a mother cat with two kittens, two geese, a dozen laying hens and three roosters that they intended to take with them.

Virgil and Marcy started trying to sell off things they wouldn't need. Virgil was counting on being able to raise about $2,000 but as the days went by and the moving time got nearer, the cash wasn't coming in at all. They ran more newspaper ads offering lower prices and still had no takers. Virgil was beginning to have doubts but Marcy kept adding to their stores and packing.

Virgil and Ray spent many days rummaging through thrift shops and secondhand stores looking for materials that would help at the mine. They bought gold pans and screening for the sluice boxes and even came home with a pipe organ blower cover, a big clumsy hollow shell to use as a cover for a water wheel that Virgil intended to make for a power system.

All of the jewelry equipment had to be taken apart, oiled and stored carefully. They sold all of their picture frames, mats and equipment to the highest bidder.

A neighbor advised them to wear baggy pants so that the rattlesnakes would strike the oversize pant legs rather than their legs. She even gave them a snakebite kit. "Why are you going to expose the boys to so much danger?" she scowled.

Marcy was getting nervous with all the attention on snakes and wished she had kept their agreement and not told the neighbor about the move.

The day finally came when Marcy knew she had to tell her mother, so she decided to phone rather than confront her in person. But upon hearing where they planned to move, her mom was delighted. "That is vonderful! Vhere is it located exactly?" she asked in her heavy Bohemian accent.

When Marcy told her the claim was at the bottom of a canyon deep in the Trinity Alps, she was thrilled. Marcy's dad had died of cancer three years earlier but had spent some time on a mining expedition in Mexico himself; maybe she was thinking about that. To Marcy, it made things so much easier that she approved.

One morning, Ray told Virgil that he'd talked to someone who wanted to get rid of a small house trailer. Virgil went to see it and decided that he and Ray could convert it into a hauling trailer. They peeled the top off and added sides. Ray planned to pull it with his truck while Virgil pulled a horse trailer that belonged to Ray's brother, David.

The days passed quickly and a group of friends gave them a going away party. As gifts, they received fencing, a posthole digger and many useful tools, and Ray came to the party with a big old-fashioned galvanized tub filled with multicolored bars of soap.

Toward the end of May, Virgil scooped up Marcy's enormous piles of ripe chicken manure with the big Ford tractor and plowed them under. Windows around the neighborhood slammed shut in response to the atrocious smell. Marcy raked all around the adobe and the only thing left in the gardens was a 100-foot row of elephant garlic.

"They aren't done yet but maybe whoever rents the place will let you dig them up," Marcy told Ray.

Virgil and Marcy wanted to be out of the adobe on the first of the month so they wouldn't have to pay rent in June. The house had rented immediately and the new tenant showed up before breakfast and started moving in on that rainy morning, mixing his things in with theirs. He put his television set on one side of the living room and his recliner chair on the other and then shouted at Virgil and Ray to quit obstructing his view as they carried boxes out of the house.

Friends and relatives began showing up to help them, to worry for them and to worry them. 'My God. How are you going to make a living?' one asked. 'Where will the boys go to school?' inquired another. 'How 'bout wild animals?' chimed in a third. 'What if you get sick?' fretted a fourth.

Virgil turned to answer one of these questions and didn't watch as he hooked the trailer lights into the Ford station wagon. Soon, blue wisps of smoke encircled the trailer and before he could find the short, all the wiring was gone. It took about three hours to rewire and Ray had decided on some last minute modifications to his trailer, as well.

All the while, the drizzles kept drizzling and five cowhides that they'd scraped and salted were getting soaked and beginning to stink. Their helpers ran in and out of the house carrying things to stack in the trailers. Every few articles, the new tenant ran out in the driveway hollering 'That's mine! That's mine!' and then returned to his chair and watched his TV, complaining as each person carried something through the puddle that was now the living room floor.

Marcy's dear friend, Vicki, followed her to the back of the house where Marcy had a few slabs of marble. Being an artist, Vicki thought she could use the slabs in some of her art.

The new tenant noticed them in the backyard, left his television and followed them around. "That's mine now, you can't give that away!" he growled.

Finally fed up with his rudeness and interference, Marcy screamed at him and he slunk off like a dog with its tail between its legs.

A misty rain fell as Ray and Virgil finished packing the trailers. Kelly, their little electrician, wanted to take along a 12-plug electric bar. "No way, Kell!" Virgil shouted. "There just isn't enough room."

But Kelly sneaked around to the backside and slipped his '12-plugger' into the trailer anyway.

One man carried several boxes out of the house. Everyone thought he was a friend of Ray's so none of the moving party paid much attention to him until Virgil saw him put a box in the back of his truck and drive away.

"Who was that guy?" Virgil shouted from the top of the trailer. "I saw a lot of boxes in the back of his truck."

Everyone shrugged. No one had ever seen him before. Apparently, he was just some stranger helping himself, and he did it so proficiently that there was little doubt he'd perfected this gig on others, using his own version of party crashing.

Virgil threw the rolled up cowhides on the very top of the trailer.

"What are you taking those for?" someone shouted.

"Who knows when baby needs shoes?" Virgil countered, poking fun at one of the recurrent themes used to try to discourage them. "One cowhide in hand is worth two buckskins in the bush," he said for he had serious doubts about his ability as Boone and Crockett, not having shot a gun since World War II.

Ray and Sue, with their baby, Sean, planned to go ahead in their truck with the made-over house trailer hooked behind. Sue got Sean settled in while Ray tied a big wire cage with two geese and the flock of chickens on the back of his truck in front of the trailer, his new pickup looking incongruous hitched to the conglomerate mass of the homemade trailer behind him.

"We're on our way now. When will you be ready to take off?" Ray asked, backing out of the driveway.

"Right behind you!" Virgil shouted after him.

At last, Virgil, Marcy and the boys climbed in the station wagon with the loaded trailer secured in back. The odor of rain-drenched cowhide filled the air as friends and relatives waved good-bye and Virgil's sister, Fran, wiped her eyes. The hood of the station wagon pointed skyward like a surface to air missile as they pulled out of the driveway in the waning light and headed toward their new life.

Climbing the Grapevine over the Tehachapi Mountains on Highway 99, the '55 Ford's headlights illuminated Ray's trailer. Like white snowflakes, feathers flew out of the cage, plucked from the geese and chickens by the wind. Marcy's birds were getting a beating!

Virgil tried to pull up next to Ray so that Marcy could signal him to pull over and take care of the birds but acrid fumes and white smoke suddenly poured out from under the hood, obscuring the highway. Virgil fought to steer the station wagon to a narrow dirt shoulder and bring it safely to a stop.

"Shit, we're separated from Ray now!" Virgil snapped as he kicked the door open.

Disobeying Marcy's orders to stay in the car, Kelly scrambled out of the back seat to be at Virgil's side as he opened the hood to find the cause of the smoke. Fluid forced out by the extra burden placed on the automatic transmission when trying to pass Ray flowed over the hot engine manifold.

Headlights coming from the opposite direction suddenly veered toward them and pulled up in front of the Ford. Ray appeared in the headlights. "Now what?" Ray's nasal voice demanded as he saw the hood up on the Ford.

"Damned transmission fluid is blowing out on the manifold," Virgil replied.

"Well, this Joad rig is killing me." Ray waved contemptuously toward the converted house trailer. "It's too much load and unstable as a drunken witch. I can't pull this trailer. I'm jeopardizing Sue and Sean's lives," he declared. "And from the looks of this rig, you'll not make it another 600 yards, let alone that many miles."

Virgil nodded slowly and took out his pipe. "You're right. I'll tear out my transmission if I try to go any further."

"But we've got no place to go," Marcy sobbed. "We don't have a home at all now."

"Come and stay at our place for the night. We got beds. We'll figure something out tomorrow," Ray told her gently.

Virgil was up as soon as it got light and the drizzle of the day and night before had passed on. All the hills were green, flowers were blooming and it was one very beautiful day. But no matter how they reloaded Ray's trailer, when he tried it out around the block, it didn't track right.

"I know you haven't got much money, Virg," Ray said. "I'll rent a truck, you drive it up."

"Thanks for the offer, Ray, but you've done enough," Virgil answered. "Let's find out if we can get one and how much. If it's not too steep, we'll get it."

Marcy slept late and awoke to find Virgil, the kids and Ray gone.

"They went to rent a moving truck," Sue explained. "Why didn't you think of that earlier?"

"I guess we just didn't," Marcy fibbed, not wanting to admit how little money they really had and that they were trying to save as much as they could.

Marcy phoned her mom, her sister, Emy, and Fran to tell them what had happened.

"I cried last night for you guys and I'm not going to cry for you again," Fran declared, but Marcy's mom and Emy came over to say goodbye once more.

"Your uncle Chale sent you this, Marcella," Mama said as she slipped her $200. "It vill help pay for the rented truck."

Chale was Marcy's bachelor uncle who had lived with them all the time she was growing up. Marcy loved him almost as much as she loved her father. He always made her birdhouses and bought dolls for her and her sisters, and if they angered him, he never stayed mad long.

As Marcy hugged Mama, the big yellow rental truck came down the street. They stacked everything from the horse trailer and half the stuff from Ray's trailer inside the rental truck and Marcy thought of all the things that she'd had to sell and give away due to lack of transport space. One luxury she had made room for was a big, wall-to-wall braided wool rug that a woman had traded Virgil in exchange for painting her cabinets. Marcy planned to put the rug on the floor of the shack and up the walls, if necessary.

Virgil loaded the station wagon with the chickens, the pair of geese and both dogs, and hooked it to the rear of the rental truck. Everyone squeezed onto the single bench seat in the U-Haul and Emy hugged Marcy again through the window.

"Good-bye, Auntie Emy and Grandma!" the boys yelled.

"Good-bye, my darlings. Ve vill come to see you later," Grandma promised.

Virgil and Ray had decided it was too hard to convoy and agreed to rendezvous at the trailhead, some 600 miles to the north. Virgil clumsily got the unfamiliar truck into gear and they flapped off on the frazzled wings of adventure.

⤙⥽⤚

The day was unusually clear of smog and big billowing clouds floated across the blue sky. Marcy had her first tinge of sadness as she watched Mama's tiny figure waving back at them as they drove away. She was leaving this part of California for good, the place she'd been born and where she'd lived most of her life. Although they were only moving to the northern part of the state, it felt so far away.

Shortly after leaving Ray's, a highway patrolman stopped Virgil and told him to put a taillight on the back of the Ford being towed behind the U-Haul. Later that day, they were stopped again and held up for more than an hour because the rental agency had the wrong license plate on the truck.

The truck used gallons of gas and took great bites out of their cash. The large basket of fried chicken that one of the neighbors had given them kept the family fed.

Virgil could only go 45 miles per hour while pulling the station wagon and after many hours of driving, they finally reached Redding. It had been a long stressful drive so Virgil and Marcy decided to use some of the money from Uncle Chale to stay at a motel and get a good night's rest.

The next morning, they all felt that subdued excitement of meeting an unknown. Even the beginnings of clouds and drizzle didn't bother them. They found the U-Haul rental center, stuffed the dogs, chickens and geese into the back of the truck, and left the station wagon there for Virgil to pick up when he returned the rental. With growing excitement, they all climbed back into the cab of the big yellow truck.

The adventure was fun for the boys. They waved at every trucker they met all the way to Trinity County. After all, they were truckers now.

They stopped to get gas at Junction City and it started to shower. Virgil had on his usual green beret, snagged from one of the boys' Halloween costumes, pulled over one ear.

"Moving to Eureka?" the filling station owner asked as he pumped their fuel.

"Nope, we're going to the North Fork to our gold mining claim," Virgil smiled.

"What did you say?"

"We're moving to our mining claim up on the North Fork," Virgil repeated.

Mouth agape, the man stared at Virgil in disbelief. "You don't mean the same area where that old hermit lives?"

"That's right!" Virgil said merrily as he drove away.

Gaines, Joel and Kelly -
shortly before moving to the North Fork

Vigil at the organic produce stand - Sylmar 1966

3 - Camp Desperation

A drooping vine maple lifted out of the mud as their fender hit it, swiped a red smear across the yellow hood and windshield, and then broke and skittered along the thin aluminum side of the van. Fir limbs scraped along the other side and Virgil and Marcy worried about having to pay extra for damages to the truck. But Virgil should have worried more about the road. It's one thing to drive a car on a narrow mountain road, quite another to wrestle a moving van up one in the mud.

In the darkness of the forest, the road shrank to just a narrow path in the lights of the truck. The turns became sharper and the trees bigger and thicker for the next few grindingly slow miles. Virgil was relieved when they saw the broken sign saying *Road Ends 1/2 mi.*

Virgil had to stop and back up three times to maneuver the truck around the sharp turn. He shifted into the lowest gear and started up the steepest, muddiest, slickest, narrowest stretch yet. Marcy climbed out several times to drag deadfall limbs out of the way. Finally, they came out on the small flat spot that served as the trailhead.

On the top of the mountain, out of the shadows of the forest, there was still light. They'd expected to find Ray and Sue already camped but had seen no tracks and they were nowhere in sight.

For the first time, Virgil saw clearly what they had done in leaving a comfortable city routine where they had firemen, policemen, streetlights, libraries, gasoline stations and friends, for the unknown, unprotected, isolated wilderness. Yet here they were, euphoric.

The clouds from the afternoon showers were being torn to shreds of high fog on the peaks of the great ridge to the northwest. Below them to the west lay a tiny trickle of silver-green reflecting the lonesome evening sky. It looked small, but it was a long ways down. And somewhere down there in the wrinkles of the ribs of Backbone and Limestone ridges was a new neighbor, of whom they had only heard, the only other person in over 100 square miles.

But they had no time to breathe in the atmosphere as adventurers often do, for they had to unload the truck and get it back to the rental agency before noon the next day or more of their money would be gone. They'd counted at the last stop on the highway and were down to less than $500, not much to last until they got all the tools and equipment down the trail, the garden planted, a house built, their jewelry business set up and their mine producing.

Virgil backed the truck into the flat area with the help of the boys and their flashlights. He then opened the rear door and both dogs jumped out. They eased the big cage of chickens and geese out onto the ground and Virgil reached in and grabbed the chain saw. "Who the hell put those chickens on top of my chain saw?" he growled. With a look of disgust, he tried to find a rag to wipe the chicken droppings from his hands.

It was getting too dark to see anything but Marcy found some Kleenex in her purse. "Here," she grinned.

Virgil was not grinning. He pulled out his pipe and lit it, deep in thought.

"Dodo, when's Ray coming?" Gaines asked.

"Is he lost?" Joel wondered.

"Why isn't he here yet?" Kelly added.

Although it was just a nickname, Virgil was beginning to feel like a Dodo, not only in the matter of possible extinction but also in the sudden comparison with the size of the job he confronted. "How am I going to get that 800-pound generator off this truck?" Virgil mused.

His passive acceptance of dependence on Ray's help crumbled like a dry clod. Then he remembered that the truck had a hydraulic lift, but he still had to move the generator to the tail of the truck to lift it out.

He tied a rope around a tree, then around the generator, much like trying to pull an aching tooth by tying a string around it and a doorknob, then falling over backwards. Virgil hoped to pull the truck far enough forward without the front wheels going over the edge.

Virgil pulled forward, easy and slow. The headlights were bright enough, but in the clear air, there wasn't sufficient diffusion to light up the area, and there wasn't anything for them to reflect on either. The lights shone out over the edge of a 1,400-foot canyon and made the black night blacker with the sharp whiteness.

"Hold it! Just a little more," Marcy called. "Ok. It's on the platform. What do I do now?"

"Wait for me," Virgil instructed.

He got out, lowered the tailgate with the generator on it, retied the rope tautly, got back behind the steering wheel and eased the truck forward until the 'thump' of the generator hitting the damp ground signaled that the tailgate was free, just as the front wheels started sagging over the edge of the dark maw.

The rest was easy. They put the pipe organ blower, which would one day be the heart of their waterpower supply, under a tree. They placed their other belongings where they could, bracing each box on the down side, for if one started rolling, they would never be able to catch it.

By the light of the truck headlights, they assembled the little tin stove that Virgil named Hot Rock. Joel, Kelly and Marcy stuffed in pinecones and dead branches and had the stove crackling in a short while. Gaines helped Virgil pull the queen box springs and mattress out of the truck and carry it to a flat spot. Marcy brought cushions for the boys' bed and started to line the bottom of the truck.

"Be careful of the chicken poop, Ma," Gaines warned.

Kelly found the Coleman lantern, which Virgil lit. Marcy opened some canned stew and set it on Hot Rock to heat. She filled the coffeepot and then put the rest of the water in an enamel wash pan, which she handed to Virgil while pointing to the soap on one of the boxes. They opened some folding chairs and plopped down.

"This is Camp Desperation," Marcy announced.

"That it is," Virgil agreed.

Marcy's fear of being eaten by bears while they slept subsided since she knew the dogs would warn them and they could run to the truck if something came near. She tucked the boys into bed in the back of the truck. Outside, Virgil and Marcy collapsed onto their mattress under the stars.

After a while, Virgil broke the silence. "Sleep, Marcy?" he asked.

"No," she replied.

A little later, Marcy broke the silence. "You asleep, Virg?"

"Not yet," he answered.

There was no wind. The black patches of pine needles didn't move against the background of stars, nor did the leaves rustle with the passage of small animals. It was not until later in the night, when a wind brought the faint roar of the river up the canyon sides, that they were able to go to sleep. Insignificant in itself, this showed them how deeply conditioned they were to the never-ending noise of the city.

In the faint light of dawn, Virgil hurriedly drank a cup of coffee and ate an egg with a few strips of bacon. Boxes were everywhere and there was no room left to turn the truck around. After dragging around and restacking everything so he could get the truck out, Marcy wiped the red dirt smears from the doors so the fresh scratches would be less noticeable and Virgil left to return the truck and retrieve their station wagon from the rental agency.

Marcy and the boys surveyed their new domain. Marcy's wool rug sat in the shelter of a tree, securely wrapped in a plastic tarp so that it wouldn't get wet or dirty. She stuck the staff of their American flag into the big pipe organ blower case and the stars and stripes waved gently in the breeze.

At one time, Camp Desperation had served as a work area and black-smithy for building the ore mill just down the trail and there were still two old planks nailed between two trees. They put the cans of food on the makeshift workbench and the mother cat and her babies made a home in an old hollow black oak that supported one end of their newfound kitchen table.

They let the geese and chickens out of the wire cage, which Marcy quickly realized was a mistake. Tissy leaped at one of the geese, tearing out some feathers and making the goose squawk. Yelling, Marcy kicked at her but Tissy wouldn't let go. In sheer desperation, she hit Tissy with a stick. Marcy was thankful that the other dog, Hucky, didn't get into the ruckus. When Tissy finally let go, the goose, minus tail and neck feathers, ran squawking over the side of the mountain.

Marcy chained Tissy after that. With her face resting on her paws, Tissy glared at Marcy. She had been Marcy's faithful dog, following her everywhere in southern California. After the goose incident, Tissy abandoned Marcy and became Virgil's dog.

The sun was hot, but best of all, there wasn't any smog to dilute the rays. Putting on their shorts and tee shirts, the boys took their toy trucks up on the side of a mountain to make roads.

Kelly soon returned and motioned for Marcy to follow. "Be real quiet," Kelly warned, pointing to several wild quail taking dust baths on the sunny side of the bank. "See, Ma? They look like your donuts taking sugar baths," Kelly said, referring to the donuts Marcy always rolled in sugar and cinnamon.

"They sure do," Marcy laughed.

As the morning went by, Marcy wondered what had happened to Ray, Sue and Sean. She decided to lie on the bed and glory in the solitude while watching the crested Stellar Jays play hide and seek in the oak branches. Occasionally they gave off loud raspy squawks and a couple flew close over her head. Marcy was sure that she felt feather dust land on her face.

The boys were making noises like trucks way up the mountain when Marcy thought she heard a real motor coming up the road. "Here comes Ray and Sue!" Marcy yelled.

The boys came running down but instead of Ray and Sue, a car filled with gawking people appeared. Behind that car came another one filled with more gawkers. Both vehicles inched past their scattered belongings and turned around at the dead end. One woman smiled and nodded as she passed back by.

Soon after they had driven off, a green Forest Service truck drove up. Marcy immediately thought of Ray telling them that the Forest Service wasn't letting anyone move onto the claims. *How in the world did he find out about us so soon and what will I say to him?* Marcy wondered.

The forest ranger glanced around and then got out of his truck. "Hi. I heard you folks were up here so I thought I'd get acquainted," said the heavy-set, jovial man.

Marcy still had some coffee in the pot so she offered him a cup. "How in the world did you hear that?" she asked.

"Well, I heard it in Junction City," he smiled. "Word's out."

"Junction City?" she gasped, then remembered the incredulous look from the filling station attendant the day before and realized he must have spread it all over. This was certainly a small town filled with curious people, probably busybodies to boot. "What did you hear about us?" Marcy asked, cocking her head to one side.

He lowered his glance and a shy smile spread across his face. "That the first hippies have arrived."

Marcy thought of Virgil with his mustache and green felt beret pulled over one ear. They weren't hippies but maybe they looked like they were. Virgil had once told Marcy that the name hippie came from Harry the Hipster, who glorified drug use through his music. She was indignant because they certainly didn't use drugs.

Gaines and Marcy waited to see if the ranger was going to tell them they couldn't live at the mine but he didn't say anything about it. Instead, he wanted to know where they were going to stay. He was friendly and likable, so she told him the name of their claim.

He finished his cup of coffee, walked back to his truck and waved good-bye. As he drove off, Gaines smiled. Marcy figured Ray had told them the horror story about the Forest Service to keep them from moving.

In Redding, Virgil got the truck back to the rental agency just one hour late. The agent was going by the book until Virgil explained their situation. He smiled a smile that Virgil didn't know how to interpret and whether he thought Virgil a great liar or felt sorry for a fool was unclear but he didn't charge for the extra day that he could have. Virgil felt free and suddenly rich so he stopped by a market and bought several gallon cans of things he thought they might need.

He got all the way to the *Road Ends* sign before the station wagon quit completely, having threatened to do so most of the way home.

His good physical condition that he'd imagined was just that, imaginary, for when he reached the top of the mountain with his load of groceries, he was beat. After a long day, Virgil walked into Camp Desperation singing 'Zippity-do-dah' and carrying two large cans, one of tomato sauce and the other stew.

"Why are you walking? Where's the station wagon?" Marcy asked.

"It quit on me down at the road. Probably just vapor locked or overheated, or it's rebelling at these rough roads. I'll go down and try again when it's cooled off," Virgil replied. "Look what I brought!"

"Gallon cans? Virg, how can we keep them after they're opened without a refrigerator?" Marcy shook her head and sighed.

"I never thought about that," Virgil admitted. "I even bought some meat. It's sure going to take some getting used to up here."

"Well, we'll eat the meat tonight," Marcy said. "What did the rental guy say about the scratched truck?"

"He looked like he thought I was crazy when I told him where we were moving. He didn't charge me extra though."

Smiling at Virgil, Marcy poured him a fresh cup of coffee. "Well, my dear, we're home."

<hr>

Before dusk, Virgil walked back down to the Ford, got it started and drove it up to Camp Desperation. A nervous hush that spreads through the forest before a storm had settled all around them while the heavy clouds had flattened the setting sun against the mountaintops. Lightning bolts stayed hidden, only their flashes lighting the upper rims of the clouds.

They hurriedly searched out the bed frame, a ponderous thing made to resemble a wagon wheel and an ox yoke, put it together with poles tied at the four corners and stretched a striped awning between them. Marcy and Virgil now had a place to sleep out of the rain in a contraption that looked like the deserted wreck of a Conestoga wagon. Virgil placed the .22 rifle under his pillow.

With the coming of deep dusk, the boys were fed and put to bed in the station wagon. The lightning now cracked closer and grey white mist hid Limestone Ridge across the valley. Marcy and Virgil covered everything they could and sat by Hot Rock in lantern light until the first drops sent them under the shelter of the awning.

The rain fell gently and made sleepy sounds on their camp style four-poster. Virgil would have gone quickly to sleep but for the discomfort of the rifle under his pillow. It wasn't long before he felt and heard a pat-pat on the blankets. It was raining harder and he imagined in the dark that something had come to bed with them to keep warm. In the light of the flashlight, he saw that the awning had developed a bad case of Sag-osis. It was a beautiful striped thing made for drier climates and hadn't been waterproofed, so they pulled a plastic drop cloth over the awning.

"Are you asleep?" Marcy asked a while later.

"Not quite," Virgil replied, reaching over to kiss her.

"I need a poem," she said.

A brief silence followed, and then Virgil recited:

TONIGHT INSPIRATION

There is a mystery of a lost, green hill.
Fog shrouded cool-dim-
Time shunned, it lies waiting
For tired feet to feel free and
Let the strength yet gentle
Peace, flow upward
I see you now-arms lifted-hair lifted
And the wind touches lightly
Your neck-as if making
Sure you are there.

By morning, the rain was over and a new day in June on top of a wilderness mountain is like a new gold coin to spend. Virgil had planned on this first whole day for a long time and was now ready to splurge.

He'd spent several days while still in L.A. building a rack to fit on a power garden hoe that was to be their gas-powered burro. He dug out all the parts and looked happier than Marcy had seen him in a long time as he put together his modified Roto-Hoe tiller. It could haul 300 pounds on flat land and 150 across a plowed field and Virgil planned to use it to carry all the equipment down the trail.

While Virgil was gone the previous day, the boys and Marcy had found a trickle of water seeping out of the ground by the old stamp mill 200 yards down the trail from camp. Marcy had placed her big canning pan under it and used a stiff madrone leaf as a spigot.

"Can you bring up that pot of water?" Marcy asked.

"Ok, it's as good as here!" Virgil jauntily waved his beret to her as he putted out of sight, rattling over rocks and sticks with his little gasoline burro.

After a while, Marcy heard the Roto-Hoe coming slowly up the hill. Virgil, his pipe stuck in his mouth, fought with the machine, trying to keep it from tipping over in the ruts and on debris that littered the mill road. Water splashed out of the pan. With a grimace, he brought Marcy the pot with just an inch of water remaining.

"Is that all the water there was?" Marcy asked. "I'll need more than that today."

"We'll have to carry it then," Virgil said. "Darn, this thing worked perfectly on flat ground but it will never work to get any of this stuff down to the cabin with all those rocks, roots and ruts. Maybe after we clean the trail," he frowned.

"When are we going to the cabin?" Gaines asked.

"I don't want to go until Ray and Sue get here," Marcy said.

"He's probably bored with the whole thing and has gone on home. You know how he is," Virgil said. "We won't see them again for quite a while."

"They'll be here. Ray wouldn't leave us up here without a bigger gun than a .22, not with bears around," Marcy said.

"The bears won't bother anything," Virgil said with an assurance born of living several hours in the wilderness.

"What about the window down in the cabin? It wasn't a mouse that broke it up. I'll feel better when we have the 30-30," Marcy replied.

"They won't bother," Virgil repeated, reassuring himself and the boys who were sitting quietly among their forgotten toys.

For lunch, Marcy made flour tortillas in her cast iron skillet on Hot Rock. She was anxious to try out her new wood cook stove but that would have to wait until they were at the Flat. Marcy brought out her flat board to roll the dough on and made some nice, tender tortillas. Then she rose up, put her hand in the small of her back to ease the ache, looked at the peacefulness amid the confusion, then out across the valley to the mountains.

"I don't ever want to go back. I don't care what happens," she declared.

"We won't if I can help it," Virgil said, glancing up at Marcy and seeing a look of contentment that he hadn't seen in several years.

These were brave words, for Virgil was just beginning to realize how deep in the wilderness they were and the tremendous amount of work they had before them. The year before, when they had decided to buy, it had taken three hours to come up the trail from the Flat. In the interval, he had forgotten how rough the trail really was.

He also realized that the gas burro was a waste of time and the backpack he'd bought for 95 cents was beginning to look less like a joke than he'd meant it to be. Virgil reached down for the steel-framed backpack and started rubbing Neatsfoot oil into the cowhide straps. The boys came over to watch.

"What's that thing for?" Gaines asked.

"It's a backpack. To carry things on," Virgil replied.

"How's it work?" Kelly asked.

"I'll show you," Virgil said and put the pack on the makeshift table.

Virgil loaded the pack with about 60 pounds and got his shoulders into the straps. They cut and pinched as he tried to lift the load.

"What you gonna do now," Joel asked.

"You're supposed to lift it off the table and carry it down the trail," Virgil grumbled, embarrassed that he couldn't lift the pack an inch.

Marcy came over to watch. "What do you suppose a packer would cost us?"

"I don't know but I'm sure whatever it is, it would be too much. We haven't enough money to live on and we haven't even got a shovel down the trail to spade a spot for a tomato patch!" Virgil growled.

Marcy had started tomato plants in her greenhouse in February and with great care had gotten them this far. Suddenly, she noticed them on top of the Ford where she'd put them for safekeeping. The sun had gotten to them and they looked cooked.

"Oh my God! They're the last of that seed I had. Bring me some water," she said and Gaines ran to get it while Virgil struggled out of his straps.

If anyone could save a wilted plant, Marcy could. The biggest part of their success the first year depended on her and her ability to make things grow for they didn't have supplies or money to buy them.

After lunch, Virgil took the chain saw and hiked down the hill to cut some fallen trees off the trail. The boys were playing with their trucks again so decided not to go with him.

Later that evening as the sun started to set, Virgil hadn't returned and Marcy began to worry even though Tissy was with him. She had no idea how many bears or cougars were around and decided to go look for him. "Come on guys, let's go find Dodo!" she hollered.

The boys raced down from the mountain with their shorts and tee shirts streaked with red clay and then raced past her down the trail. "Hey! Hold off there! Wait for me!"

They saw where Virgil had cut several dead trees, making the trail easier to walk. A ways down the trail, they met him loaded with the chainsaw, fuel and bar oil under his arms. His face was red and perspiration dripped off his nose. The boys took the cans of gas and oil from him.

"Oh boy, oh boy, am I glad you guys came. I'm pooped!"

"Why did you bring all the stuff back up, Virg? Couldn't you have left it behind a tree or something?" Marcy asked.

"Someone might steal it," Virgil answered automatically. "Well, I guess this isn't southern California," he said sheepishly.

They were all a little subdued around the stove that evening, but the beans, biscuits and coffee tasted good. The sun had set in various colors of red and orange and darkness crept up the sides of Backbone Ridge, filling the valley with a bluish hue.

The ultra-quiet of the evening was disturbed with just the suggestion of a hum at first, but a little later came the unmistakable sound of a car. "I bet it's Ray," Kelly said.

"I know it's Ray," Marcy replied.

"It could be a fisherman," Virgil suggested.

Ray drove up. Sue looked beat but she was grinning. Ray didn't grin but backed carefully into the one clear spot and began unloading his camping gear. Virgil went over to help him.

"What happened, Ray? I thought you'd given up on us."

"Almost," his said, and went on unloading.

Virgil wouldn't have blamed Ray if he had given up. He'd said he'd help them move and he'd done much more than that. If Ray thought they would need something, he spent his time to get it, even finding them a book on how to build a log cabin.

"You've been back to L.A." Virgil observed when they took out the last of Ray's gear and underneath everything, cut into manageable lengths, lay all the galvanized water pipe that they'd had to leave behind.

"Thought you might need it," was all Ray said.

"How come? All the way back?" Virgil asked.

"When we got here, we went on to a campground. Then we came looking for you guys. We asked the guy you bought the claim from and he hadn't heard from you. We got worried that you'd had trouble, packed up and started back down the highway looking for you," he answered.

"We could only go 45 and were held up twice by the Highway Patrol, once for no brake lights on the station wagon and again for a wrong license on the truck. We were on the East Alternate," Virgil explained.

"Seanie wasn't feeling good so we took him to Grandma," Sue said.

Marcy offered them some biscuits with beans but Sue shook her head.

"Thanks, no. I have my supply. Here, join me in an Oreo," Ray said, offering a package of cookies.

"Ray, you can't live on candy bars and Oreo cookies," Marcy teased.

"I'm doing pretty good," he grinned, patting his belly where his tee shirt failed to cover it by about six inches. Then Ray set up his tent, lit his catalytic heater, checked his 270 Magnum, handed Virgil the 30-30 carbine and said good night.

Roto-Hoe before being outfitted as a mule

Virgil and Ray - 1975

4 - The Hermit

The next morning was chilly and foggy. Just a hint of the mountains showed through the mist and a mystic feeling hung over the mountaintop. Virgil and Marcy were up and had a good fire going, coffee pot hot and were enjoying their second cup, when a tap-scritch, tap-scritch, tap-scritch came from down the mill road.

Then, like Lazarus rising, an old cloth hat followed by white curls, faded blue eyes and a denture-less mouth almost hidden in a scraggly white beard seemed to rise from the earth. A moment later proved that the head was on top of a long, black raincoat worn by a man in his middle sixties. "Howdy all," he called.

Penetrating blue eyes emphasized by long bushy eyebrows surveyed the scene, taking in three youthful faces peering curiously out of the station wagon, Ray's tent pitched off to one side and Hot Rock warming the morning coffee. Inside his open raincoat, the stranger's chest hair grew right through his gray undershirt. He turned and frowned at all the equipment lying around. His fingers, tipped with long dirty nails, fidgeted around his wooden staff.

"You must be Red Barnes," Marcy said.

He turned to Marcy and his eyes gentled. "Might be. You folks camping here?"

"No, we're going to be your neighbors," Virgil answered. "We bought the old mine above your place and are moving to the Flat."

"For the summer?"

"No. Permanently. Here, sit down. Have some coffee," Marcy said.

He sat down and glared around again. Then he leaned his walking stick against his side, accepted the coffee cup in both hands and slowly turned to Virgil. "Got an income?"

"No. We're going to mine gold and make it into jewelry," Virgil answered.

"Ain't no gold," he replied.

"Well, we hope to mine, and some fish and game will help," Marcy answered.

"We hope, we hope," the stranger mocked. "Ain't no fish; ain't no deer; ain't no bear. Gov'ment ordered 'em all destroyed in '45."

"What'd they do that for?" Virgil inquired.

"So's a man can't live in the mountains. So's he has to move to town. Be controlled by Washington Dirty City and have the mark of the beast tattooed on his forehead like a good citizen. It's all written down!" he bellowed.

"What about gold mining?" Marcy challenged.

He looked her up and down. "You look strong enough to handle the digging but what I'm getting at, there ain't no gold. They plan to turn the water off too so's people can be controlled."

"Where did you hear that, Red?" Virgil asked.

"I'm trying to tell you. It is all written down in the World War I Plan that started in 300 B.C."

"We'll grow a garden," Marcy said, ignoring his outburst.

"And get the old apple trees in shape," Virgil added.

"What'll you use for dirt? Nothing here but bedrock."

"We can build soil," they both replied.

"As for them apple trees, if the bears don't eat 'em when they're green, you might get some nubbins every seven years," Red continued in the ringing voice of a prophet.

"What's going on?" Ray crawled out of his tent, rubbing sleep from his eyes with the back of a hand filled with Oreos.

"I'm John Barnes. John S. Barnes," the old man said, getting to his feet. "Well, I got to get going. Get into town. Ain't been in but once since November."

"Would you like some bacon and eggs, Red?" Marcy asked.

"Nope, just 'et." He pulled out a can of Copenhagen and delicately put a pinch in his mouth, carefully sucking the snoose from under his dirty black fingernails.

"Want a lift to town?" Ray offered.

"Thanks for the offer of the buggy ride, but nope."

Red picked up his pack and walked toward a barely noticeable trail. Placing a coffee can with a candle inside behind a large ponderosa pine, he disappeared into the thinning fog.

"Hopeful old boy, isn't he?" Virgil commented.

"It can't be that bad," Marcy replied with just a tinge of anxiety.

They were used to people seeing plots and doom in everything, and also those who didn't see at all. But this man, whom they knew had lived on the river nearly 40 years, did shake them because they thought that maybe he did know and that they knew next to nothing.

Other than Virgil's failed demonstration for the boys the previous day, none of them had ever worn a backpack. But Ray had a couple in the truck and handed one each to Sue and Marcy.

Marcy started to load hers with canned goods when Ray told her not to bother because he and Sue had left plenty in the shack the past fall. So Marcy packed a light pan, margarine, popcorn and some dirty clothes.

They loaded a few things into a burlap sack and a pillowcase for Joel and Kelly to throw over their shoulders. Gaines carried oil for the chainsaw in his knapsack and Virgil gathered some tools to carry in his backpack. Ray's pack was full of fishing gear and Sue filled hers with summer shoes and shorts.

They came to the spot where Virgil had hidden the chainsaw under the huge trunk of an uprooted Douglas fir that blocked the trail. Virgil started the new Remington Super 754 and lifted it high over his head to start cutting through the massive tree trunk. The bar barely reached past half way, and after completing that cut, Virgil fought his way up the hillside, around the giant root ball and worked his way back down to the other side opposite the cut.

"Here, catch the saw!" Ray yelled and shoved the Remington over the top of the log into Virgil's hands.

Virgil started the second cut by following directions bellowed by Ray but it was nearly impossible to hear the words, only the yelling, over the extremely loud saw. Visual cues were out as neither could see the other over the log. Finally, Virgil cut through but the log stayed solid.

"Gimme the saw, Virg," Ray yelled. "I don't think you got it cut all the way through on this side."

Virgil passed the Remington back over the log and Ray started cutting furiously in the first cut. Suddenly, the log shifted and the high-speed snarl of the saw lugged to a groan. Ray let up on the throttle.

"It's pinched," he yelled above the rumble of the idling saw.

"I can hear that," Virgil's dry reply came over the log. "We need the wedges."

"Where are they?" Ray asked.

"On top," Virgil replied.

"Sue, you and Marcy run up and get them," Ray ordered.

"Where are they?" Sue grumbled, envisioning the quarter mile and 500 foot climb back up to Camp Desperation followed by a search through the piles of equipment there.

"I know where they are," Marcy said, and the two women left.

Ray shut off the saw and sat heavily on the moss-covered rocks, brushing away sawdust stuck to his sweat-soaked white tee shirt as best he could. The boys watched from a short distance away where Virgil told them to stay, out of harm's way if the log shifted.

Suddenly, Ray got up impatiently and started the saw. Quickly, he squeezed the throttle, and again the saw made the slow groaning noise. Ray let the throttle back to idle. "It's still pinched," he informed Virgil again.

"I know. We need the wedges."

"It'll eat its way out," Ray muttered and squeezed down the throttle again. The saw groaned and soon acrid smoke streamed from the clutch housing. "It's burning its way out!" he yelled.

"No, it's burning up the clutch. The chain isn't even moving," Virgil told him.

"Oh." Ray shut off the saw and sat down, panting, but impatience got the best of him again and he grabbed an ax and disappeared up into the forest above the trail. The sound of furious chopping rang out and soon Virgil and the boys heard him crashing heavily down toward them, dragging a large section of pole.

"What's that?" Joel asked.

"Pry pole, Joey," he laughed. "Hey Virg! Hold onto that saw hanging out of the log."

Ray worked the pole under the log and heaved. The pole slipped and Ray lost his balance and nearly fell off the trail. Scrambling to recover, his fancy footwork sent a cascade of debris down the mountainside. The boys laughed and Ray joined in. "Like my new dance steps?" Ray teased.

Ray repositioned the pry pole and threw his full 280 pounds against the lever. The log shifted and Virgil pulled the saw free. Twenty minutes later, a section of the tree trunk fell away into the trail. Ray seized his pry pole and started to fight the log off the trail.

"Hold on, Ray. Let me get a pry pole, too," Virgil called.

But there was no stopping Ray as he worked until the sweat poured off his face. Kelly grabbed a block of wood and shoved it under the log to keep it from rolling back after Ray had rolled it forward with his pry pole. The other boys joined in to help.

"If you guys will just hold on, I'll have a pry pole and be down to help you," Virgil called from where he was chopping on a downed sapling.

"Ray just wants to see this log roll down the mountainside," Kelly said.

"I'm trying to get this thing off the trail," Ray panted and gave a great heave. The log teetered on the edge for a second, and then rolled 30 feet down into the bottom of the draw. Ray climbed down to it and tried to get the log rolling again.

"It's not on the trail anymore, Ray," Kelly called.

Ray grinned as he continued to work on rolling the log section but it stubbornly stayed where it had come to rest, as it would for the next 39 years until it burned up in a forest fire. Sue and Marcy reappeared, none too happy when they discovered that the wedges weren't needed, and Clutch Tree became another trail marker.

In the afternoon, they came out on the high point of rock that overlooked the Flat. The sun had gotten hot as soon as the fog lifted and they rested in the shade of the few cedar trees that had filled in the places between the rocks. There at Wind Dance Lookout, the dogs panted in the shade of the bigger rocks, their noses pointed down the path.

Suddenly, Hucky jumped up, barking at something down the trail toward the Flat. Tissy, who was born with poor eyesight and her hearing 180 degrees out, ran off barking down the other side of the point toward Red Barnes' place.

"Must be several bears," Ray said.

Concern etched Marcy's face. *Our first bear,* she thought.

Gaines grabbed Hucky by the collar as he started down the trail. A man in a black hat on a black horse rode out of a dense stand of fir trees below, followed shortly by a man on a roan horse.

"Bear. Ha!" Virgil scowled at Ray, feeling the pretty pictures they had painted for themselves all winter beginning to be chewed to pieces by a growing monster of doubt. There are two popular views of Nature; one holds her to be a big, bountiful, all-protecting mother while the other holds her to be an enemy to be subdued. Their view was beginning to change from the former toward the latter, and since man is an integral part of that very nature, they were suspicious of the men riding up on their horses.

"My God! What's going on here?" the taller man on the roan asked, taking off his white cattleman's hat and hanging it on the pommel of his saddle.

"What are you doing on this place," Virgil asked, remembering old stories of claim jumping in Western movies.

"We're cuttin' through a government trail. I'm Shotgun. This is Wiley." He looked at Ray. "Bet you're one of these college guys in here looking for minerals."

"No," Ray answered. "They're moving in."

"Sure. We're moving down to that flat there," Virgil said with more confidence than he felt.

"File or buy? Claim or patented?" Shotgun asked.

Growing suspicious of all the questions, Virgil took out his pipe and slowly lit it before answering. "Claim. Bought," he finally said. "We intend to mine it."

"Hope you don't lose your money," Shotgun replied.

"I'm going down to scout something for lunch," Ray announced and marched on down the trail.

"Hope he has luck," Shotgun said. "We haven't seen a thing alive except rattlesnakes in the last seven miles. Sure is a surprise to find a bunch of women and kids out here. Thought there wasn't anybody for a hundred miles." He looked over their little packs. "If you folks are going to eat, you'd better have brought it. There's no hamburger stands here."

"Well, we have to get on down to the Flat so we can get back out before dark," Virgil said. "It was good meeting you."

They moved aside so the horses could get by. As they passed, Wiley turned back. "I hope you know what you're doing bringing in three small boys. Mining for gold could be damn skimpy," he quipped.

"Yeah, well, thanks for the advice," Virgil shot back as the two rode on down the other side of the point. "Boy! Everybody around here is sure optimistic. Let's get on down, ok?"

Wind Dance Lookout bore patches of yellow wildflowers nodding in the hills and gullies. The maroon blossoms of Farewell to Spring hid under chaparral bushes. They shouldered their sacks and packs and walked over to the edge of the cliff to look down.

"There she is," Virgil grinned.

The river was green and white in the June sun, making an emerald and silver tracery through the rock bar in front of the tiny black-brown square of the cabin. Two bleached deadfall trees made an 'X marks the spot' on the grass-spotted red dirt below. A feeling of peaceful adventure flowed up the hill with the sound of the river and they started on with renewed hope.

"It's so far yet to go," Sue groaned.

It was a true statement, but not in distance. It was only a quarter mile to the Flat, but a monumental undertaking awaited them there. Instead of a log cabin with a picturesque fireplace chimney and snug windows, they had a plank box with a decaying roof and window opening covered in rotted plastic sheeting.

Down the trail a ways, they came to the stand of firs where they'd first spotted Shotgun and Wiley. Virgil looked up and stopped the group. Stripes of golden sunshine filtering through the tall trees played across their faces and the treetops swirled with strands of rainbow colored webs. "This is Cathedral Way," Virgil declared jubilantly and another trail point was named.

At the Flat, the deer carcasses from the previous fall were gone and green grass sprouted around the cans and rubbish. Marcy spread a tablecloth over the blacksmith table constructed of heavy boards and hammered between the cedar, fir and oak trees. "Come on, Sue. Let's go open the door to the shack and see what the weather did to it," Marcy suggested.

Peering inside, both women were surprised to find the shack was relatively clean. A picture of a nude girl hung on the door and some new cans stood on the table, which was propped more solidly against the wall. A brown sleeping bag hung on a nail in the corner.

"Did you and Ray clean up in here?" Marcy asked. "I don't remember that picture or sleeping bag being there."

"Those new cans are the ones Ray and I brought down," Sue said. "But we sure didn't put that picture there."

"I guess some hunters broke in and were using the cabin," Marcy said, yanking the picture off the door.

They carried the cans to the outside table and Virgil opened them with his pocketknife. Ray refused the canned goods and headed downriver with his fishing pole, an Oreo cookie stuck in his mouth. Marcy found kindling sticks and lit a small fire to pop some corn while Sue sliced canned Boston brown bread.

After they ate, they walked down to the river and found a whirlpool that Virgil called Charybdis. "It's a giant whirlpool Homer wrote about," Virgil explained. "It was supposed to be near eastern Sicily and every ship that had the misfortune of getting caught in it would disappear."

Virgil thought the whirlpool might be a good place to put the dirty clothes to let the river wash them clean. Marcy tied the batch of clothing from her backpack together with a rope, put them into the pool and tied the other end of the rope to a tree. The clothes swirled around just like in a washing machine.

Virgil walked towards Rock of Gibraltar while Sue and Marcy took the boys to the swimming hole. Back at the adobe, Marcy often thought about this wonderful swimming hole. Now the sunbathed willows were the color of fresh lime and the oak tree sported ruffles of green moss. They sat down under the oak and lazily enjoyed the afternoon sun.

Later, Virgil joined them at the swimming hole and had just started to speak when Ray returned empty handed and interrupted him. "Get your things together, Sue, we're going. Red was right; there ain't no fish and there ain't no game. This is a dead place. I'm going to Alaska."

Startled, Sue walked off with him and Marcy stared after them in disbelief as they went up the trail. "Why did they leave us like that?" she asked.

"Ma, Ray's tired. Don't blame him too much. He's driven from L.A. twice. And you know he never stays long." Virgil took Marcy's hand. "Sweetie, we chose a sward that was seldom scythed and from now on we walk the tall grass."

"Exactly what do you mean?"

"Well, the tall grass can be a place to hide in or it can be a wild and free place with hidden risks, but in the end, more rewarding," he explained. "Come, I have something to show you."

Marcy and the boys followed Virgil to Rock of Gibraltar, a large rectangular outcropping of rock next to the river that had 20-foot high vertical walls. About 20 feet wide by 30 feet long, the top was roughly flat and a small stunted live oak grew from one corner, accompanied by a sarvisberry and several manzanita bushes scattered across the top.

The cliffs above were laced with three different shades of moss and pink lewisia, and yellow hen and chicks poked their blossoms from the outcroppings. Purple and scarlet larkspur kept company with the pale blue brodiaea growing in the crumbly shale. The wild azalea across the river perfumed the erratic winds that swirled down the canyon with a sweet honeysuckle fragrance.

They crawled down a rock face and walked over river boulders until they came to a sandy spot where Virgil pointed up a brush-choked stream. "Look up there."

Dazzling in the sun and haloed by rainbows was a waterfall. Garlands of fragrant yellow monkey flowers cascaded down the wet sides. Ferns, white fawn lilies and Solomon's seal nodded in the mist. They forgot the disappointment of Ray and Sue and all the other negative things people had said and were thankful that they were going to live in this lovely canyon.

When they hiked back up to Camp Desperation, Ray and Sue had everything packed and were just about to drive away.

"Are you leaving, Ray?" Gaines asked.

"We have to go and check on the baby," Sue said.

"I gotta get back to work," Ray said, starting his engine.

Having worked with Ray, Virgil knew better than to try to change his mind. "Thanks for everything," he said.

"You didn't see it all," Marcy sighed.

"I've seen enough," Ray hollered as he drove off. "You'll be back to L.A. in a year. Your old job will be waiting for you, Virg."

"He could have said anything but that," Virgil stated as Marcy gathered fuel for Hot Rock.

"What a sendoff," Marcy groaned.

"Ma, you know how if you stay in the groove you will spin on acceptance but if you get out of it, people will squash you because they don't have the guts to do it themselves," Virgil consoled.

Marcy stuffed the stove with pinecones and dry sticks and lit it to boil water for coffee. They were all tired and sad. Marcy made some biscuits in her heavy cast iron pan and put a pot of lentils on to cook.

After their meal, the boys went to bed in the back of the Ford. Virgil and Marcy sat quietly and looked at the sparks shooting out of Hot Rock's lid, both lost in thought. Marcy wondered if Virgil felt uncertain about the move. She hoped not. Off down the Hobo road, they heard a car. "Darn, who's that now? It's getting to be as busy as Grand Central Station," Marcy groaned.

The boys leaped out of the station wagon. "Maybe Ray and Sue decided to come back," Gaines said.

"No chance, Gaines," Virgil replied.

"Howdy all!" Red Barnes yelled as he stumbled out of the car with a half-empty bottle of wine and a box of groceries in his arms. The driver, the owner of one of the little country stores found along the Trinity River, got out of the car and Red put some bills in his hand. "He knew about you before I got there, even," Red slurred, looking at Virgil.

The storekeeper shook his head. "Everybody down along the river has heard about you folks."

"What's the head shaking for?" Virgil asked.

"Why, everybody knows that you can't make a living in these mines anymore, not with the price of gold," he answered. "Well, glad to meet you. Got to get back. Miss my TV program if I don't." He hurriedly turned his car around and roared down the road out of sight.

"That's what's wrong with people these days; they try to live in two worlds at once with their TV sets. Say how about a drink of doodle juice?" Red muttered, handing Virgil the bottle.

"No thanks, Red. I quit drinking."

"Hummpf!" Red grunted as he pawed through his supplies, found a can of beer and popped the top. "That's another one."

"That's another what?" Virgil asked.

"Fool," he replied. "Thinks he can crawl in that tube and make things the way he thinks they used to be. You can't live in two worlds at the same time, just the same as there ain't no Garden of Eden. People think they can go to the Naaational Forest and live like Adam. It's a desert and will be worse in 2033. Like it's written in the World War I Plan."

He drained his beer and tossed the empty can over the side just as Marcy handed him a bowl of lentil soup and a biscuit. "No! Can't eat a thing. Just 'et breakfast. Got a load to get down the mountain tonight," he said, accepting the bowl.

He plopped down on one of the chairs, putting the lentil bowl on one knee and the biscuit on the other. As he rambled on about the World War I Plan, Marcy's black and white hen, Betty Boop, shared his bread. Each time Red took a bite out of the biscuit and let his hand drop, Betty Boop picked off a piece. But Red didn't even notice; he was mumbling about an argument he'd had at the bar. "I told him we're all children of Israel," Red declared, then got up, placed his bowl and a bit of biscuit on the ground, stumbled over to get his wine bottle and started down the trail.

"I hope he doesn't fall over the edge in his condition," Marcy worried.

"Nah, he's had 40 years of practice, probably knows every rut in the trail," Virgil reassured.

As Red shuffled and staggered around the corner and disappeared down the road to the mill, Virgil stared after him for a long moment.

"What are you staring at?" Marcy asked.

"I was looking at that Forest Service sign over there, *Impassable Beyond This Point*, and thinking of changing the A to an O.

"Oh! Impossible Beyond This Point. Aren't there any positive people left in this country? I'm sick and tired of hearing that you can't do this or can't do that," Marcy grumbled.

"Boy, we sure had it today, didn't we? If we get much more encouragement like that, we'll go slinking back to L.A.," Virgil said.

"We won't!" Marcy declared and Virgil knew it was true.

5 - The Move to the Flat

"We've been here a week and haven't moved hardly anything down yet," Marcy groaned. "Couldn't we hire a packer?"

"They cost cold, hard cash and we haven't got it. We'll just have to take more down every time we go," Virgil replied.

"I'm carrying all I can," Marcy protested.

"Look, there's only about five tons. If we can get down a hundred pounds a day, then that's only a hundred trips. That's only…" Virgil took out his pocketknife and scraped the inside of his pipe, and then shook out the debris before he continued. "Maybe we can get a packer for the heaviest stuff," he finished.

"That sounds like a great idea," Marcy sighed.

That evening, they counted their cash again and decided that they could spend $100, and the next morning, Virgil took the boys and Tissy off down the mountain looking for help.

"Will you be ok here all by yourself, Ma?" Gaines asked as they pulled away.

"Sure. I have Hucky here to run the bears off," Marcy replied.

Anticipating the pack mules, Marcy began sorting and organizing their belongings as soon as Virgil and the boys drove away. Suddenly, Hucky announced an intruder. She was frantically looking for a tree to climb when she heard 'Howdy, all!' and saw Red coming up the trail shirtless, his trousers cut above his ankles with a rope woven through the belt loops and tied around his waist. He sat down and Marcy poured him a cup of coffee. Hucky bristled and she yanked him down beside her.

"You know, Marcy… your name is Marcy, isn't it?"

"Yes, it is."

"Dan Raymond used to get good gold down there hydraulic mining. By the way, I used to own this mine." Red waved his arm around, indicating Camp Desperation. "I was coming back from town when my shoestring broke and I bent to tie it. I was still bending over tying it together when I saw a flash in the corner of my eye. It was a vein of gold running along the side of the mountain down by that old stamp mill. Soooo, I named it the Busted Shoestring Mine. I worked it until I saw that the vein was pinching out and then sold it to some guy named Hazley.

"He made that stamp mill and hired workers but he didn't get much gold because someone stole all his concentrates. He told me once that I'd better not stick my snoot around him because I looked an awful lot like a deer. I guess he thought I cheated him on the mine. I also guessed that he thought I stole his concentrates, which I didn't. Gold veins in this country tend to pinch out and then form again somewhere else. I didn't have the money or equipment to look for it, so I sold it."

"I heard that Dan Raymond lived down there with his wife and son," Marcy said, changing the subject.

"Yes, he had a wife and son. He tended the dam gate and got five dollars a week. He loved it down there but his old lady sure didn't. I saw their son a while back and asked about Dan and his wife and all he did was point both thumbs down."

With a shy grin, Red reached for his snoose can and continued reminiscing about the old days. "Dan used to have mules and cattle that he let run free. His prize bull never liked me and every time I came to visit, he'd charge me. Dan had to keep him locked up when I stopped by. One time that bull showed up on my trail but I saw him coming."

Before continuing his story, Red pried his snoose can open and put a tiny pinch in his mouth. Then he tapped on the inside of the lid until all the tobacco fell out of his fingernails and he dumped that back in the can.

"Soooo, I climbed up the side of a hill, picked up a hundred pound boulder and threw it down on him. It bounced off his head and he fell to his knees. After a while, he woke up and started shaking his head. When his senses came back, he stuck his tail straight in the air and took off like the devil was chasing him. Every time he saw me after that, he stuck his tail straight in the air and went bawling home. Heh."

"Would you like more coffee?" Marcy offered.

"No. I guess I better head on down the trail." Red glanced around. "I left my groceries around here someplace," he muttered. "When are you folks going to move down there?" he added.

"Soon as we can get our things down. Virg and the boys are looking for a packer now."

"Well, as soon as you do, I'll come down and see you on Sundays." Red found his groceries and stuffed them into his homemade backpack, a gunnysack with fire hose shoulder straps. "Yes, I'm glad you folks are moving here," he mused and walked down the trail.

Marcy boiled rice to mix with the beans and bacon grease, sliced up leftover biscuits and opened peaches that she'd canned the previous summer. It was hard to cook many dishes on the little stove. At last, she heard the Ford coming up the road.

"Well, Ma, I think we have our problems solved! I found two packers who are willing to haul our stuff down as soon as they finish some trail work in the Yolla Bolly Mountains. They want to see our things to estimate how much it will cost. We'd better start hauling the lighter stuff down on our backs."

Marcy was anxious to get her spindly tomato plants into the ground and wanted to clean the shack. "Oh that really suits me!" she exclaimed.

In the evenings at Camp Desperation, Virgil had made a little backpack out of wood for Gaines to carry small loads. On this first trip packing things down to the Flat, Kelly and Joel would alternate carrying a small red lard can with a wire bail handle and the old knapsack Gaines had been using.

Marcy loaded the backpack Ray had left for her with some pots and pans, silverware and her tomato plants. Virgil filled his pack with beans, dried milk and rice. Gaines tied blankets and canned peaches to his pack frame.

Carrying the lard bucket was not fun for Joel and Kelly. The wire handle cut into their hands and before long, they were arguing about who'd had it the longest and whose turn it was to carry it. By the time they'd reached the open area just above Cathedral Way, Marcy couldn't take the arguing anymore. "Give it to me if you guys are going to argue!" Marcy snapped, taking the lard bucket from Joel.

Joel gladly relinquished the bucket and started to pass her when Marcy slipped and fell on her butt in a cloud of dust. The lard can ripped from her hand and rolled down the steep section of trail, then crossed over the edge, gathering ever more speed as it did.

Kelly threw himself down on the trail. "Joel tripped Ma! He got the handle sweaty and slick with his hands!" Kelly wailed.

By the time the can was a hundred feet down the mountain, it no longer rolled but bounded. And just before disappearing, it struck a boulder, made a huge bound and released a great arc of soft lard, which left a grease trail and earned that section of footpath the name Grease Mountain.

When they reached the Flat, a wonderful fragrance greeted them. Marcy placed her tomato plants in a sunny spot until they could dig a proper garden for them and sniffed the air. "Ah, what plant is that?"

"Whatever it is, it sure does smell sweet," Virgil answered.

Some years later, to Marcy's horror, she found it to be the smell of poison oak in bloom.

Suddenly, Marcy remembered Charybdis. "Oh my clothes!" she exclaimed running to the river. When she pulled them out, green slime covered the clothes and the twisting river currents had tied them into complex knots.

"How did the clothes turn out?" Virgil asked when she returned.

"Not good," Marcy groaned. "I left them in too long and they're slimy and tied in knots."

"Why, that slime is algae," Virgil said.

Marcy thought about the big galvanized tub Ray had given them at their going away party. He'd also given her a hand plunger to agitate the laundry and a roll of rope. "Here's your automatic clothes dryer," Ray had said, handing her the rope. "Just string it between two trees."

"I guess we'd better bring the washtub down soon," she said.

Marcy opened the shack door to let the sun bake out the stale odors. She found a well-used broom left by hunters and swept the cobwebs off the rafters. While the boys and Marcy gathered dry wood, Virgil found some webbed wire and flat stones and made a makeshift camp stove. Sitting on an old oil drum stove, Marcy found a big gray enamel pot that made an excellent container for boiling water. Then she made lunch from the canned goods left by Ray and Sue.

"As soon as we rest up a bit, do you all want to come with me up to the upper stream?" Virgil asked. "I want to see how much water is in it."

"Can you remember where the trail is that Al took us on?" Marcy asked.

They explored until they found a remnant of a path that they thought was the right one. Following it, they came to a deep forest where their feet sank beneath the layers of decomposed fir and pine needles. "I think it went over this way," Virgil said.

The stream was wider and deeper now, and the water was clear. The rocks and sand that lined the streambed were like painted pictures. Scattered rocks along the banks wore hats of soft, slightly moist moss that they used as seats. The faint coffee scent of a civet cat drifted in the breeze, and wake-robins and hound's tongue violets grew in cool, shady places. Vines of fox grapes hung like hairy ropes from cedar trees, and the boys grabbed the vines and swung on them, yelling like three Tarzans.

Catching the scent of some animal, the dogs shot past them like arrows, barking furiously. "I hope they don't chase a bear over here," Marcy fretted. "Maybe we'd better go back to the cabin."

Back down at the Flat, Virgil and Marcy went to the swimming hole and watched the boys swim. The water was icy cold and they shivered when they came out, but warmed up when they buried their legs and stomachs in the hot clean sand. The slabs of bedrock were covered with flimsy skins from stonefly larva that looked like Indian petroglyphs. They stayed at the swimming hole until after the last golden sunlight left the fir and ponderosa pine high on Backbone Ridge and a cold breeze crept up the river.

After the sun had baked it out, the cabin smelled decidedly fresher. Marcy gathered a bundle of dry pine needles and spread them on the floor, and then laid one of Virgil's paint drop cloths over them before she put all the blankets down. It was going to be a community bed until Virgil could get bunks built for the boys.

Marcy examined the gaping hole where the window had been and worried that a bear might come in. She searched the dump until she found some old string and cans that she tied together and hung around the hole. *I'll wake up if anything tries to get in*, she thought.

Virgil laughed when he saw her contraption. "As soon as the mules bring down the glass, I'll put in a couple windows for you, Ma."

That night Marcy heard the cans rattling and sat up in bed, petrified. "The bears are coming in!" she screamed.

Virgil awoke in a flash but discovered no bear. Instead, in her sleep, the end of the string had tangled in Marcy's bedclothes and she was the one rattling the cans.

After breakfast the next morning, they all hiked up to Camp Desperation to get the geese. They chased and cornered the geese and stuffed them into gunnysacks. Tissy's hackles started to rise, so Virgil grabbed her collar just in case she jumped them.

At the Flat, they dumped the geese out of the gunnysacks into the swimming hole. Obviously, these geese were not born with a natural instinct attracting them to a body of water for they flew out and raced honking straight up the trail with outstretched wings. Virgil shook his head sadly. "Well, they just signed their death warrant."

None of the family had the energy to follow them. Without the dogs and humans around to keep watch at night, some predator got the geese and they found scattered feathers at Camp Desperation the next time they went up. Marcy suspected that Tissy had sneaked back up there and killed them. The chickens had roosted in the trees, however, and were spared.

One thing Virgil and Marcy discovered during the move from Camp Desperation to the Flat is that they had more ability than they'd previously given themselves credit for. Over the next few days, they were up and down the mountain carrying flour, sugar, blankets, nails, knives and other tools they'd need before the packers came. Every trip exhausted them so much that they would have preferred to lie around for the rest of the afternoon and not do anything else. "We sure are out of condition, Virg," Marcy observed.

Often, however, a project on the Flat needed something from the top or a project on top needed something already taken down to the Flat. They made many more trips than they would have ever thought possible, but by finally arriving where they'd intended to go, their moods improved and the boys were happy playing in the shallows of the river when they got down from a trip to the top.

It was a good feeling to sit on a flat rock by the river and eat pancakes each morning. The temporary kitchen was under the cedar tree where a cool breeze blew upriver in the afternoons, and they could rest on a sandy spot not far from the kitchen. They were in the longest days of the year, and as long as it was light, they worked. When they finally did lie down, they were so full of plans that sleep was a long time coming.

Some days later, Virgil and Marcy decided that they'd go up the trail to Camp Desperation at least every other day and haul the lighter stuff down so that it would be cheaper when the mules came. They told the boys to watch the place and always watch each other. Kelly and Joel never tired of running their toy trucks and making roads all over.

Virgil and Marcy were carrying increasingly heavier loads and were getting their mountain legs. After yet another trip to the top, they had just plopped down when Red gave off his 'Howdy, all!' from up the trail.

"Where does that old buzzard get his energy?" Virgil wondered.

"Maybe we'll get that way after a while," Marcy grinned.

Gaines wanted to go fishing so Marcy tied a string around a willow stick and put a safety pin on the end like she'd seen in a Tom Sawyer book. Red watched intently.

"What are you doing, Pantywaist?"

"I hope to catch a fish," Gaines answered for Marcy.

"We hope, we hope, don't we?" Red muttered.

Gaines' shoulders sagged slightly.

"Be careful where you fish," Red advised. "If I hear a brass band playing by a fishing hole, I know I won't have any luck. If I hear some beautiful music playing, I always catch a fish."

Gaines and Virgil left on Gaines' first fishing trip while Marcy entertained Red. Later, proud and grinning, Gaines and Virgil walked into the kitchen area. The Coleman lantern flared on Red's white whiskers as Gaines ran up to him with his fish.

"That ain't no fish. Before the gov'ment ordered 'em all killed, there was 300 steelhead in that hole down yonder. That's right, by gov'ment count, 300. The fish are gone. The bear are gone. The deer are gone."

Gaines politely ignored Red. "I never tried fish but I think I'll try this one," he declared and the fresh clean flavor made a fish eater out of him.

"Do you have a flashlight, Red?" Virgil asked pointedly as the evening wore on.

"Nooo. Looky here." Red pulled a contraption out of his backpack and handed it to Virgil. It was an empty two-pound coffee can with a handle bent from the remnants of the galvanized iron telephone wire that had once followed the flume from the dam tender's cabin to the Schlomer hydraulic mine above the ghost town of Helena.

Holding this wire handle suspended the can horizontally. Opposite the handle, an asterisk-shaped pattern of knife slits punctured the side of the can with the points bent inward. In this opening, a candle pressed inward held securely, prevented from backing out by the metal spines formed by the asterisk-patterned opening. "Candle bug," Red said. "Never use a flashlight and have the batteries always going dead. Candles last longer and are cheaper." He pointed a dirty fingernail into the open end of the candle bug. "Bottom's gots to be new and shiny to reflect the light out."

"The candle doesn't heat the can up enough to melt the candle out of the holder?" Virgil asked.

"Nope," Red said taking the candle bug back. "Never push the candle up so the wick is higher than half way, otherwise she'll melt it." Red fumbled in the pocket of his dirty jeans, retrieved a strike-anywhere match, struck it on his long fingernail and lit the candle. The open end cast a soft beam of light and Red stepped off into the darkness. When his presence was only tangible by the moving beam of light, he offered them one last piece of advice. "Never forget to keep pushing the candle up. Otherwise, when it burns down, it'll drop out and start a forest fire!" he bellowed.

Virgil made a candle bug just like Red's for each member of the family and one particularly warm June night, they came down the trail watching for rattlesnakes with their lit candle bugs. Ahead of them, they saw a tiny light.

On closer inspection, they found the light was a caterpillar with red and green luminous designs that looked incredibly like windows on both sides of its pale blue body. They stood transfixed, enchanted as it crawled like a tiny train across the trail, up a piece of bedrock and into a crack.

With a little imagination, you could almost hear the 'toot toot' of this tiny magical insect. What wonderful butterfly would emerge from it, they wondered. It was to be only on this one midsummer's night, however, for they never saw another like it. Like a lone flower on a craggy cliff, it can only be captured in a person's soul.

One day while exploring, Joel and Marcy found wild gooseberries. The wild gooseberry is a wicked little berry in the western wilderness, a spherical ball of fruit inside bristling needlelike thorns that puncture fingers on contact. Marcy got them both a pair of gloves. "Maybe I can make some jelly out of these to cut down on our craving for oranges," Marcy explained.

They gathered a couple quart jars full of gooseberries. Marcy boiled the berries, mashed them with a potato masher and ran them through a sieve, but the stickers still came through. Finally, she strained them through a pair of nylon hose and made pancake syrup that everyone loved.

When Joel tired of picking gooseberries, Marcy went with Hucky. The hazards she endured were in direct proportion to her enthusiasm to make more syrup. Across the river where the old dam tender's cabin had burned, she found some of the best berries hanging over the cliff of the west riverbank. One of the bushes even had a rattlesnake coiled under it as the self-appointed guardian that she chased away with a stick. Still, she managed to can two dozen pints of syrup that summer.

6 - The Packers

The day they expected the packers, the whole family decided to go up to Camp Desperation and wait for them. The packers, Marvin Whitney and Red Cockroff, came as they said they would. Red was about Marcy's age, with red hair in a butch cut, a missing front tooth or two, and about four days' growth of beard. He was a big jovial man who volunteered lots of general information. "Haw! Haw! Haw!" he laughed when Virgil told him about the near mishaps with the two trailers when they first left Sylmar.

Marvin, a tall thin man with washed-out blue eyes who always wore a white western hat, surveyed the equipment and the family. His eyes rested briefly on Marcy's torn blue sweater and the tattered clothing worn by Virgil and the boys. He looked over at Red inquiringly. They walked around the equipment and huddled together for a while. "How about $60?" Marvin said.

"That's great!" Virgil beamed.

"Clean the old trail to the Flat," Marvin said. "You have to make it wide enough for a mule and his pack."

"How wide is that?" Virgil asked.

"Wide enough that a man can stretch out both arms and not touch anything," Marvin replied. "And high enough that a tall man with a tall hat on a tall horse on a dark night don't have to worry about knocking his hat off. Let us know when you have it done and we'll bring in the mules."

"Thanks, Marv," Virgil said.

"And don't forget to make the tread wide enough for the mules to put both feet down side by side," Red added.

"How wide is that?" Virgil asked.

"About 18 inches."

The next morning, the boys and Virgil loaded up with rakes, hoes and the chainsaw. Joel took his small toy rake, which turned out to be just the width of the trail. By noon, they had broken the toy hoe Joel got for Christmas and one shovel had only half the handle left.

With a four-pound hammer and a chisel, Virgil chipped away on the rock spur of the hogback that would knock a pack from a mule. The boys stacked brush on the lower side of the trail and leveled the tread, all the time making noise like bulldozers and graders. One old madrone tree had a limb growing out over the trail that they couldn't bear to cut. Virgil could barely get under it, let alone a tall horse, so they drove stakes in the slippery talus, piled brush against them and built the trail lower.

While Virgil and the boys worked on the upper part of the trail, Marcy set up camp on top again so they wouldn't have to hike all the way up from the Flat each morning. That evening as they ate beans and bread at Camp Desperation, Gaines asked how far they had gone that day. "I'll guess we've made about a quarter of a mile," Virgil said.

"Boy, that's a lot!" Gaines exclaimed. "We'll be all done in three or four days, won't we?"

"Or done in," Virgil answered as Marcy handed him another bowl of beans. With hands swelled and bruised, Virgil wondered whether he'd even be able to make jewelry again.

Knowing that the packers were going to bring all their belongings to the Flat, Virgil went to sleep before sundown that evening with the weight of the tons of equipment off his back for the first time since he'd discovered his Roto-Hoe turned gasoline burro to be useless. The next morning, they counted the paces down to where they'd stopped work the day before. "Two hundred multiplied by three gives 600 feet," Virgil announced.

"Is that a quarter mile?" Kelly asked.

"Not even an eighth," Virgil replied, the weight of the load of the equipment still at Camp Desperation resting heavier than ever on his back.

Below the hogback, they discovered that the tread was a thin fill between tree roots that had made a net over the face of bedrock, which tilted just a few degrees off vertical. They did what they could to widen it, and after going up and down several times with a six-foot stick held horizontally just below his waist, Virgil thought it would do. No other section of the trail was as hard as that one, yet it still took them a number of days to reach the Flat.

They planned a trip to town to inform the packers that the trail was ready and everyone settled in the Ford. Virgil turned the key but the engine did not turn over. "Damned starter motor," Virgil swore under his breath.

"Can we push-start it?" Marcy asked.

"It's an automatic transmission so we'll have to get it rolling down the hill at 30 miles an hour before it'll start," Virgil explained.

The Hazley road, named for the owner of the Busted Shoestring Mine, was not a road that could be traveled much faster than five miles per hour, so Virgil warned the family to hang on while he got the Ford rolling. With a rumbling crescendo, the Ford gathered speed as Virgil pushed against the doorjamb of the open driver's doorway. As soon as he was sure the station wagon would keep rolling, he jumped in and slammed the door.

When the Ford made a flying leap at the bottom of the first hill and crashed loudly back to the roadbed, Virgil applied the brakes, which was a mistake; near the middle of the Hazley road was a short but steep hill and the Ford rolled to a stop partway up. Virgil tried pushing the heavy station wagon but it wouldn't move and soon the rest of the family joined him. Still, it stubbornly refused to move up the grade.

Virgil pulled the bumper jack out of the trunk and positioned it under the rear bumper, then raised the Ford high on the jack until it slid forward and rolled a foot or two. One of the boys slid a block behind the wheel to keep it from rolling backward again. For two hours, they inched the Ford forward, until the station wagon finally went over the hump. Once over, it was a mad rush for the family to get aboard as the Ford took off like a roller coaster. The station wagon bounced over bumps and skidded around corners as sheets of gravel and dust sprayed from beneath the tires, until enough fluid poured through the torque converter to start the V8 engine.

"That starter needs to be fixed so we don't have to do that again," Virgil stated calmly despite the hair-raising ride.

The packers were home and said they'd bring the mules and start packing things down the next day. "Could they bring the bed and the mattress and the boys' cushions down first?" Marcy asked.

The next morning, Virgil disassembled the bed and piled the cushions on the mattress, and then filled the little stove with flour and oranges before tying it on his backpack. Marcy removed the plastic from her beautiful wool rug and discovered to her utter dismay that it was rotten with mold. Tiny teeth marks dotted the plastic where some little animal had bitten through it, and moisture and the hot summer sun caused the rot to take over.

The first packer arrived at the Flat with his mule, Bridget, loaded down with all the cushions, some heavy equipment and tools. Marvin's face dripped sweat. Marcy opened a jar of home-canned gooseberry syrup, diluted it with water and handed it to him. Marvin eagerly drained the glass. "What kind of drink is this?" he asked. "It's the best drink I've ever tasted!"

"I made it with wild gooseberries."

"No kidding? Who would've thought those prickly berries would taste this good?"

"Is Red Cockroff coming down, too?" Virgil asked.

"He got stuck on the hogback; it's too darn treacherous for the mules. She almost went over the side," Marvin replied, pointing to Bridget. "Red had to leave your mattress just below that hogback and take the mule back up. Is there another way to come down here?"

"Yes, but it's four miles longer," Virgil said.

"I guess you're going to have to move your stuff to that trailhead to get it down." Marvin rubbed his chin. "I still have more trail jobs to do so it'll be a while before we can get to it."

Marcy refilled his gooseberry drink and after draining the glass, he mounted his mule. "Thanks for the drink, Marcy," Marvin said, and headed up the trail.

"Well, I guess we've got Mattress Point as another trail marker now. At least he got my tools and the cushions down," Virgil said.

7 - Gardens and Water

By the last week of June, getting a garden in became the top priority. Near the upper stream that would eventually power their waterwheel, remnants of an old ditch and reservoir led them to a small flat and two badly wrecked walnut trees. Here they decided to plant and it was a good feeling to spade the soil for a garden on the small flat 200 feet above the river.

Bracken fern and chaparral had almost taken over. In the early mornings and evenings, they worked the earth, making terraces. Although easy at first, the soil dried and they could no longer get a shovel to penetrate it. The small tractor they'd brought from southern California was still at Camp Desperation so Virgil and Marcy spaded and shoveled until they felt their backs would break.

"We have to get this water system working," Virgil said one morning after he broke a tine off a potato fork in the hardened ground. "This soil looks pretty black and rich so I think we can grow plenty of stuff if we get the water to it."

"There's not much humus in it," Marcy observed. "It wouldn't bake this hard otherwise."

"Well, I'll start the reservoir. I hate to cut all those little firs but it can't be helped. In this case, it's either them or us."

"But they're Christmas trees," Gaines protested.

"I know, I know! But we won't be here at Christmas to use one unless we have a garden," Virgil said.

"I'll dig them out and replant them," Gaines offered and started digging.

A sharp ridge of rock and clay separated the garden spot from the water gulch. The old reservoir had been dug in a U shape where the ridge made a small gap. The water was supposed to run from a small diversion dam 700 feet back up the gulch, along the side of the ridge and into the reservoir. It hadn't been used in many years and the ditch had completely disappeared in several places. In addition, termites and black ants had eaten the sluice gates and wooden dam.

"How long do you think this is going to take?" Marcy asked.

Virgil planned to use a Granberg Alaskan chainsaw mill attachment to cut lumber for the dam, which according to the advertising claims, was just the thing to zip out a few boards as needed or cut enough lumber for a two-story house in a week or two. "About a week. We ought to be able to mill some boards for a dam in a couple of days. But first, I'll have to make a log frame across the stream to hang the boards on," he replied.

They walked along the ditch to the remains of the old dam where the spring-fed stream made a shallow pool. The flanks of the gulch rose so steeply on each side that, although it was nearly noon, the sun's rays had not yet reached the water. Vine maple and water alder lined the pool. Two great pines rose on each bank, while blackberry vines bloomed on tiny flats down along the stream. Many unfamiliar plants were crowded almost into the water by shoulders of bedrock and the steep sides.

The first tree Virgil felled missed its mark by about two feet, which is not bad but was enough to hang it in a maple. Virgil cut part of the maple and both trees fell with a prolonged crash into the pool, flinging gobs of sand and rotted leaves over the surrounding shrubs. By dark, they had the trunk of the tree laid across the stream and leveled. It was a great effort for two people with only pry bars and a three-sheave block and tackle, but the mosquitoes helped too. After being disturbed during their afternoon slumber, thousands of the hungry bloodsuckers swarmed Marcy and Virgil as they worked. Anger gives the body greater strength, and between scratches, the infuriated duo rushed to finish the job they'd started.

The next morning, they were shocked to see the pool dry. They were also dismayed to see the water rush in to what had been the upper end of the pool and disappear, then reappear in another pool some 200 feet farther down, completely bypassing the dam site.

"Well, what do we do now?" Marcy sighed.

"Get down to the bedrock that I thought we were on. I think the leaves were the only bottom the pool had. Now that we broke the seal, we have a sieve," Virgil answered.

"Got any ideas of how far that might be?" she asked.

"Your guess is as good as mine, but I might as well get started," Virgil replied and slid down to the dry stream to start shoveling.

It took until the end of June for them to realize that they weren't going to get a diversion dam built to water the garden; the mill attachment cut the boards too slow and the gas needed to run it was too expensive. But the tomato plants had been moved from their temporary spot near the shack to the upper garden, so they carried water over the ridge each day to keep them alive.

⚡

Glorious June slipped away and their favorite holiday, the Fourth of July, arrived. It was Independence Day and independence was why they were there.

Their two favorite treats were old-fashioned homemade ice cream and watermelon. Marcy had brought her mother's antique crank-style ice cream maker with them, the same one her family had used when she was a child. Virgil backpacked in a big block of ice rolled in newspaper. They chipped off enough ice for the ice cream maker and buried the rest in leaves. They put the watermelon in the cold river to chill for later.

With their mouths watering in anticipation of the rich cream that they hadn't had for such a long time, they took turns cranking the ice cream maker. Suddenly, the dogs started barking. "Naturally, now that we're going to have ice cream, we'll have to share it," Marcy grumbled.

Red Cockroff, one of the packers, appeared. Bent almost double, sweat ran down over a soaked handkerchief into his eyes. "I couldn't get the four-legged mules to do this but I guess I'm better than they are. Where you want this thing?" he grunted.

"Put it down where you're standing," Virgil said, recognizing the heavy stator coils for their electric generator. "Let me help you out."

"I can manage. Here ok?" he asked, and as Virgil put some boards under it, Red let the pack slide to the ground. "We're through on the trail. Gotta wait a few days for our money. Thought I'd come on down and give you folks a hand."

"Well thanks," Virgil and Marcy answered with more enthusiasm than they felt. While they appreciated the offer, their place in Sylmar had gotten the name El Refugio Para Las Almas Perdidas, or Refuge of the Lost Souls, and they didn't wish to have the same name here, especially since they'd had trouble getting those lost souls moved out again. But you don't say 'no thanks' to someone who has just hauled 80 pounds of steel and copper two miles down a mountain for you, so Virgil said, "Marcy, do you have a bowl of ice cream ready for this man?"

"Haw! Haw! Haw! I never thought I'd eat ice cream in this canyon. What a treat!" Red pulled a huge boulder out from under a tree, rolled it flat side up, placed it where it still sits nearly a half-century later, and plopped down. After he finished his ice cream, Marcy poured him a cup of coffee and he scooped in a teaspoon of sugar. As she watched in disbelief, he scooped in three more. *Coffee syrup,* she thought.

When it was time to bed down, Red looked hurt when Marcy gave him two blankets and pointed to a sandy place under the cedar tree. But the family was packed like sardines on the floor of the little shack and there was no room for another body. Red spread one blanket under his sleeping bag and laid the other over the top and was soon fast asleep.

The next morning, Virgil told Red about the failed dam project. "Haw! Haw! Haw! You don't know much about rivers and streams in Trinity County, do you? When a flood comes, poof, it's all gone!" he roared.

Virgil pulled out his pipe and his eyes narrowed. "Well, that's our misfortune now, isn't it? Anyway, I decided to run a ditch over to the old miner's reservoir and pipe the water to the upper flat. Marcy and I think that would be a good garden spot."

"Well, I'd like to see it!" Red exclaimed. "What are we waiting for?"

They each grabbed a tool, including the boys, and set off up the hill with shovels, rakes and hoes. Virgil showed Red the old ditch that he wanted to clean out. Wasting no time, they started scraping and shoveling the old leaves and debris from the ditch. Red's size and the hardening process of building trails since early May enabled him to produce a lot of change in a short time.

Marcy left them working and went down to start lunch. She decided to make shepherd's bread from dough she'd had rising all morning in a cast iron pan. As the cook stove was still on top, she dug a big hole in the sand and started a fire in it. Piling on river driftwood, she let it burn down to coals.

She gently placed the covered pot on some of the coals, covered it with aluminum foil and put the rest of the coals on top before heaping sand over the pot. She also had beans heating on one side of Hot Rock with the aluminum coffeepot on the other. Marcy had been down at the Flat almost an hour when Red, starved as a bear, appeared. "What's for lunch?" he roared.

"I've got shepherd's bread cooking in that mound," she said, pointing to the hump in the sand.

"Well, I'll be darned. Haw! Haw! Haw! Let's open it up and see how it's doing!"

"No way!" Marcy snapped. "It's the first time I've done this so I don't know how long it's going to take, but I just put it in and it can't be done yet. Where are Virg and the kids?" she asked, pouring Red a cup of coffee that he sweetened with his usual four heaping teaspoons of sugar.

"Oh, they're still up there on the ditch. They'll be coming down before long."

Red kept bugging Marcy to open the sand oven but she was determined to wait until Virgil and the boys came down, despite her curiosity. When they finally arrived, Red anxiously helped her. He carefully scooped the sand off the top and lifted the cast iron pot out with potholders. He then blew the sand from the aluminum foil before taking it off the pot. When he opened the lid, a big brown steaming loaf appeared and slipped out of the pan, perfectly baked. "Well, haw, haw! How about that?"

"Ma, that bread is beautiful," Virgil smiled.

Over the years, Marcy tried many more times to make the sand-baked bread but it never turned out as nice. The only ingredient she lacked was Red bugging her.

During Red's two-week stay, he helped Virgil and Marcy get water to the upper garden. He also told them that they could make maple syrup out of the bigleaf maple trees in the winter when the nights were freezing and the days were sunny. "The syrup is better than that Vermont type," he declared.

The ditch ran across bedrock in several places, and the bedrock was cracked and porous. Where they'd finally channeled water from the stream into the ditch with pieces of stovepipe, downspouts, kerosene tins and pie pans, they had a full six inches of water. But by the time it got to the reservoir, there was only about as much as comes out of a small garden hose. It took all night to fill the pond, but it emptied in less than 10 minutes with only half of the garden space irrigated. Either Marcy or Virgil had to irrigate what they could every day, and one of them had to make the trip up trail every other day to feed the chickens still up top in their makeshift pen.

During these trips, they noticed an increase in traffic at Camp Desperation. Due to the confusion there, it was difficult to tell whether things were missing, but they started to worry and decided to break the mule-sized loads down into loads they could carry. Red proved to be an eager helper with this task, as well, and hauled down many loads.

On one trip he and Virgil made up trail to get more of their belongings, Red became weak with hunger. "Virg, do you have anything up here to eat? I've got to have something to eat when I feel weak like this."

Virgil looked through all the boxes and found just a can of lard and a jar of mustard. After eating the combo like it was ice cream with banana topping, Red seemed satisfied and suffered no ill effects from his impromptu snack.

On one of her trips, Marcy stopped just past Mattress Point to catch her breath on the only level stretch of trail. Something moved on the trail ahead of her and Hucky took off after it like a shot. Marcy realized that Hucky was chasing a small bear and that he might be back in a moment with a very angry mother bear after him. Without bothering to rid herself of the pack, she scrambled down the mountain to the Flat, breaking every trail safety rule Virgil had established. "I brought some parts for the cook stove and the last of the beans," she announced when she finally caught her breath and could talk again.

"We didn't order them express," Virgil teased. "But I wish you'd had the whole cook stove with you. Then we could've built a cabin around it. That little stove isn't going to last much longer."

Red saw that they were getting low on food and rolled up his sleeping bag. "I've overstayed my usefulness so I won't last much longer either," he said as he started up the trail.

"Whenever you're around this part of Trinity, drop by and see us," Virgil urged.

Purring and humming like various machines, the boys ran up and down the empty reservoir digging in their toes and heels like a sheepsfoot roller to compact the ground while Virgil and Marcy tended the garden. "With them doing that, it'll help seal it so the water won't leak out," Virgil said.

The boys came back happy but exhausted and plopped down under an old walnut tree next to the garden. Virgil and Marcy joined them, and they all lay down and watched the summer sun shimmer on the oak leaves as the pine and fir needles sewed silver stitches in the bluest of skies.

Suddenly, the serene mood was broken. "What the horse feathers are you doing? Daydreaming? Work to be done!" Red Barnes hollered as he walked toward them with a sack on his back. "Here's something I brought you. Road apples."

Marcy's mouth watered. The boys huddled around Red as he emptied his gunnysack and round clods of horse manure fell out. Virgil already knew about road apples and doubled up with laughter.

"The trail men's horses were very generous," Red said as he crumbled the manure with his bare hands. "This soil is too alkaline because of the lime ridges and it needs acid. Ammonium sulfide is the only thing that will dissolve the lime."

"No chemicals on my garden!" Marcy objected.

Virgil leaned back against the old walnut tree and took out his pipe. He scraped the inside of the bowl with his pocketknife and knocked the debris out on a rock, as usual, and then settled in to enjoy the show.

"I'm from the school of putting compost instead of chemicals on my garden," Marcy declared.

"Ha! You'd better go back to school because you'll never get enough compost to put around this big garden. Are you going to use human manure like the Chinese?"

"No, I'm not! Human manure causes diseases."

"Well, you got that right, Pantywaist. I didn't think you wanted to spread hepatitis."

Marcy looked at her sickly tomato plants.

"Looky here," Red said. "Like I've been trying to tell ya, it was too late to plant anything but rutabagas or turnips."

"Maybe I'll get something," Marcy replied. "I'll plant some crookneck squash seeds. They grow fast."

As the sun climbed higher in the sky, the heat drove Red and Marcy under the walnut tree with Virgil and the boys.

"Once I planted some watermelon seeds," Red began. "I got one plant to survive with one watermelon that set. It really grew with ammonium sulfate." He grinned at Marcy. "I gave it the scratch test, which means to run your thumbnail across it and if the skin slips, it's ripe. I knew it was on the verge of being done. When I was on my way down to it, I ran into a fisherman. When he saw me, he doubled over. 'I'm sick. Oh God, I'm sick!' he howled. I didn't know what to do for him but after a while, he felt better and went on up the trail. When I reached my patch, I knew why he was sick. He'd eaten the whole watermelon."

Hot Rock's thin metal middle began to buckle from the weight of the bean pot, like a little old man getting ready for retirement, so they started looking for a place to build a permanent cabin. It seemed dangerous to build by the river with three little kids and they knew nothing about the possibilities of floods.

Near the upper garden, on a knob of land that stuck out at right angles to the ridge that bordered the reservoir, two worm-eaten cherry trees and some old split boards suggested that there had been a building there at one time or another. They began digging around in the bracken and seedling pines and soon discovered parts of a cedar shingle roof and six cast iron stove legs. With a little further digging and raking, they uncovered a depression that could have been a cellar and dug out old whiskey bottles, dynamite caps and a tube of artist's oil color. Here they would build the house.

Three very large pines would frame the southeast corner of a cabin, a cherry tree would stand just outside the kitchen window and four large oaks would provide shade over the back porch. They could see the cabin in their minds, the cherry tree blooming near an open window, a small spot of grass, and then small terraces with strawberry plants making steps to the edge of the eroded gulch that they would fill with debris from the tree trimmings and the remainder of the old cabin. They would hand split shingles for the roof and have big windows on the south and west. The eaves would be long and low and the logs would turn silver-brown with age.

They began the building by stacking quarter-kegs of nails under the oaks and digging out more worm-eaten timbers, rusty kerosene tins and shake shingle wood rats' nests, and carrying them to the gulch. They used the best boards and timbers to build a platform to put the cook stove on. They could start bringing more of it down now that they knew where they were going to build.

Before the move, Marcy had carefully taken apart the cook stove, removing the enameled doors, stove lids and anything else that was easily detached, and had packed these smaller parts in shredded paper and cardboard boxes. That left three big pieces too heavy to carry. In one morning, they took out every nut and bolt from these three large pieces until they were left with 29 separate parts. Joel's five-year-old legs could support the little pieces, and with the other parts apportioned according to strength and ability, they got the remainder of the stove down in three more days.

It was over a week before they had a pot of beans cooking on their shiny, black and white enamel stove gleaming under the oaks in the wilderness. The beautiful stove proved mostly useless, however, since the main camp was still down near the river and they only used the stove when they worked in the garden.

They'd planted only those things they thought would mature in what was left of the growing season. The squash had come up and turned a pale yellow-green. The radishes didn't come up at all. The blue jays ate the lettuce. The tomatoes had started growing but the stems were thin and almost white. Where the black rich soil had dried out, it turned the color of cement but was harder.

Fruit was at the top of the list of the many foods they craved that first summer. Each time they went to the store, always parking on a hill in case they had to roll start the car, they spent money that they couldn't afford on oranges. On one trip home, they almost cried as they watched the half-full pillowcase Kelly carried spit open. First one orange slipped out, and in ever faster and larger bounces, sailed through the tops of the trees below the trail and was gone. They yelled and Kelly desperately tried to grab the sack, but in his hurry, the pillowcase ripped and all the oranges went down the mountain and were gone.

The old apple trees at the Flat were broken, starved and insect-ridden. When there had been apples in previous years, bears had climbed the trees, breaking the limbs, and then eaten the apples in comfort on the ground. The result was a stunted growth that looked more like shrubs than 40-year-old trees. There were a few apples that first year but so few that they could count them individually. Each day, they watched and counted the apples and ate the little nubbins that fell because of worms. The old cherry trees were in the same condition, so they trimmed out the dead wood and filled the gulch with the trimmings.

Virgil - 1956

Marcella - 1950

8 - Life at the Flat

Virgil and Marcy had several nagging worries. Their shoes were wearing out and everywhere they looked, from the top of the mountain to the Flat, they had some unfinished project that was vital to their survival that first winter. The only luxury they had started was slabbing a board out of the old deadfalls on the Flat for a privy.

Building the privy was almost a necessity. Someone had stolen their portable toilet seat and an old cooking pot with the bottom rusted out had such sharp edges that Kelly named it Butt Cutter and the name had stuck. Virgil grew up in cold country before indoor plumbing and was acutely aware of what happens to tender skin in zero degree weather in contact with metal, but the pot worked all right in July.

With most of his tools down at the Flat, Virgil was in his element. From one of the deadfall snags that littered the Flat, he cut a section to make a table for the outdoor kitchen. With Gaines' help, he sawed the big log in half with the chainsaw mill and used one side for the tabletop. As Virgil drilled holes for the table legs with his wood bit, Shotgun and Wiley showed up with Shotgun's son and nephew who were helping with the trail work.

"We're going to camp here by the river," Wiley announced.

"You can't do that," Virgil replied. "Don't you see, we have our camp and kitchen set up here?"

"Too bad. This is where we intend to camp," Wiley answered. "We saw it when scouting earlier."

Marcy stared at them in disbelief while Shotgun surveyed their setup. "Don't worry, we'll find another place not so close to you," Shotgun said.

Virgil showed them a place between four trees where they could hang their tarp, and they got up early every morning to work on the trail. When they returned late each afternoon, with loud yells, the two boys leaped in a swimming hole downriver from the main camp and Shotgun came to visit and tell tales and give advice.

"We have to move the river trail down to your trail," Shotgun told Virgil and Marcy one afternoon.

"Couldn't you find the original?" Virgil asked incredulously.

"Oh no!" Marcy groaned. "We'll have people walking all over the Flat."

"Well, Wiley thinks the old river trail didn't come down this far and figures it went straight across the mountainside up higher. He's half Indian and knows all about trails," Shotgun explained.

"You know, I was scouting around one morning looking for an easier trail higher up and I think I found the old river trail," Virgil said.

"Well, take me to it and I'll have a look."

When they came back, disappointment shadowed Virgil's eyes. Once found, then lost, then lost again. He couldn't find the trail and they both wiped perspiration from their faces.

July was unbelievably hot and Marcy and the boys swam in the swimming hole every day. The water had finally warmed up and they even talked Virgil into coming with them.

One afternoon when it was too hot to do anything else, Shotgun asked if he could fish in the swimming hole. He had a huge red plastic ornament with silver balls hanging off his pole. Virgil and Marcy both laughed wondering how he could catch anything with all those hanging colored doodads that would scare the fish away. Returning to camp with a string of pan-sized trout on a peeled branch, Shotgun gave them half and sat down for a cup of coffee.

"How's the trail work going, Shotgun?" Virgil asked,

"It's doing well. Faster than I thought."

"Red said there's a place by the pond so choked with berries and trees that you'll never open it," Marcy said.

"Oh, that place. We went through it in half an hour. Just ripped through it with the chainsaw and that was that." Shotgun took a sip of his coffee and looked at a pile of firewood Virgil had cut and stacked near the camp kitchen. "You know, you should never cut firewood so close in when you're young," he said with a little humor turning up the corners of his mouth. "Save that stuff for when you're too old and decrepit to go any distance for your wood. And for heaven sakes, don't ever make anything temporary, because it'll always stay that way."

"Ma! You look like a huge ripe melon!" Kelly gasped one morning when he got up and saw Marcy's face.

"It's poison oak," she replied mournfully.

Kelly took a step back, afraid of catching it. This day it was doubly bad as her arms were covered with poison oak rash, as well. It took all Marcy's willpower not to scream when the pus ran down her cheeks. It itched terribly and she couldn't sleep because her face stuck to the pillowcase.

Red Barnes showed up, took one look at Marcy and laughed. "Pantywaist, you need to pee in a cup and rub it on that rash."

She glared at him through swollen slits.

Marcy and Kelly were the most susceptible to poison oak. They had bouts of it almost all that first summer and off and on for the next decade and a half until an old miner told them to drink a teaspoon of cream of tartar in a glass of water at the first sign of an outbreak.

Evening fishing trips gave them the chance to explore the river. A quarter mile above the Flat, the river flowed through a steep-walled gorge later known as Paradise Gorge by class-five-level kayakers. Below the moss-covered walls to the west and the steep brush-covered hillside to the east, the whitened walls of the gorge were sculpted with many deep smooth potholes created by an untold number of floods. At the point where the waters of the North Fork entered the upper gorge, an unnamed steep flowing tributary joined from the west. Above this, they found a deep pool formed where the narrow canyon forced the river around a giant boulder that had rolled down the mountain and restricted the flow.

They stared in disbelief at a huge steelhead trout motionless in the clear green water on the bottom of this deep pool. So much bigger than the small rainbow trout they were used to seeing and catching, the presence of this fish was a major shock. The thought of eating this fish was deeply on Gaines and Virgil's minds as they cast their bait and lures into the pool. The steelhead seemed to wake with a start when Gaines dropped his lure and disturbed the smooth surface of the water. The lure slowly crossed in front of the fish and he briefly moved to investigate, then drifted under a dark ledge and refused to look again.

"There's a reason that guy got so big. He's too smart to be caught and is the granddaddy of all the fish in this river," Virgil declared.

Many times Gaines returned to Granddaddy Hole to catch Granddaddy for dinner but the fish remained free.

Red Barnes was a frequent guest and told stories about his life during every visit. In one story, he shared how he had worked for the C.C.C. camps and was required to send a set portion of his earnings back to his family. "Heck! I didn't stay long at that work. My family had enough money of their own. Instead, I decided to do some mining and that's when I found the Broken Shoestring Mine.

"After I sold the mine, I worked below it, hoping to find the vein at its origin. I finally ended down by the river and built my original cabin out of slabs of cedar bark. Cedar makes great insulation for winter and summer, you know. I hired a mule to haul my 400-pound cook stove to the top of the mountain. Hobo Road wasn't built yet. From there, I hauled it down on a wooden sled I made. It took me two days to maneuver it down to the shack.

"I had strawberries, too, and they did wonderful that year. Fish and game were plentiful. The gold I mined was worth something then because everything was much cheaper during the depression. I lived like a champ then," he smiled. "Before the road was built, I used to run across big herds of deer. They weren't used to people at that time but that was before the hunters came. The bucks would stare at me and shake their antlers and scrape the ground. I knew better than to stick around because it was rutting season and they are dangerous then."

Virgil lit his pipe and Red took out his snoose box.

"I shot a bear one time." Red smiled shyly at Marcy. "She looked like a beautiful woman."

The old guy has been living alone too long, Marcy thought.

"I rendered so much fat out of her that I decided to drink a cupful, it looked so good. Quick energy! I could feel my strength coming back through my veins." Red paused remembering better days. "But like always happens when you're the happiest, things will change and go downhill just as fast. President Roosevelt made it against the law to own or trade gold. Then the war came and he closed all the mines. I did my time and then came back here. I had a beautiful garden and things were good. Then the '64 floods came. I could still pick blackberries in December that year, but then it started to snow. When the canyons and mountains were full of it, the rains came. They were so warm they felt like a warm shower.

"Of course, all the snow melted down here and at the upper elevations, too. The river raised so high it reached my cabin, but then it receded. Later in the night, I heard an eerie silence and lit my old rusty candle bug just in time to see a wall of water come surging down on me. I ran out and reached high ground just in time. My whole cabin was swept away and with it my stove." He looked at the ground for a while before he continued. "I found shelter in the little dog house I'd built when I first came here. It didn't get this cabin though," he said looking at their shack. "It's a good cabin but it did have 18 inches of water in it."

"Where did you live after that?" Virgil inquired.

"I stayed right here until I built another boar's nest."

Red finished his stay with a tale about one of his friends walking the 10 miles to see him. "You see, I was picking tomatoes at the time, when my friend, Freddy, decided to come to see me. He had two gallons of wine tied around his neck and a brand new rifle he wanted to show me. But he slipped and rolled down the mountain, breaking his bottles on rocks, and finally landing beside a boulder with his rifle bent into a U shape. I heard him lambasting and screeching so loud I thought a cougar was eating someone.

"I brought a gallon can of tomatoes up with me in case someone might need the moisture in them. There was Freddy sitting in the weeds with only two bottlenecks hanging from his neck with his bent rifle across his knees, crying like a baby. He knew I'd been dry for months and he was going to surprise me. He did get his rifle bent back in shape by the blacksmith in Weaverville. Heh."

Red got up abruptly. "I need to get some Oregon grape root and Balm-of-Gilead. One's good for the heart and the other is good for everything that ails you. Did you know Balm-of-Gilead is a sacred herb mentioned in the Bible? I find it at Donk Heaven," he said, pointing up the steep mountain to the north. "The old-time miners used to let their donkeys loose and they all headed up there. It had a lot of bear grass before the trees got so big. There's still some but now the bears have it for themselves."

During one of Red's visits, Marcy noticed a strong odor. "Why do you smell like kerosene?" she sniffed.

"I want to discourage the brown spiders that bite me at night!" he snapped. "You wait and see when they find you, Pantywaist, and I'll bring you a bottle to keep them away."

"No, thank you!" she answered quickly.

One Sunday, Red arrived as promised, giving his usual 'Howdy, all!' from up the trail. Accepting a cup of coffee and honey cookies Marcy had baked in a frying pan, Red sat down and watched Marcy finish cutting Virgil's hair. He reached up and touched his hat. "I didn't know you could cut hair," he said.

"Would you like me to give you a trim, Red?" Marcy offered.

"I sure would like that," he replied, removing his hat.

Hucky snarled at Red but settled down when Gaines scolded him. Marcy set to work on Red's hair, the scissors grating against the strands with each cut. By the time she finished, her fingers were black. "This is the last time I'm going to cut your hair until you wash the filthy dirt out of it," Marcy declared.

"That's clean dirt!" Red shouted.

Hucky walked over to Red's hair lying on the ground, sniffed and started rolling. "Look there, Red," Marcy pointed. "Beings dogs usually only roll in rotten carrion, is that clean dirt?"

After the haircut, Red stayed his usual two hours preaching, prophesying about dissension between men and women. "Men will turn to other men and the world will become a robot world. The Bear, the Eagle and the Dragon will have a terrible war and the Bear will be the victor," Red declared. "What I'm trying to tell you, Jarusabel will come again and he will be the last elected president of the United States. It's all written down if you took the trouble to read it.

"Saint John's clock tells when all this will come about, Pantywaist. You're strong and could live to be a hundred if you stay on beans and chicken scratch. Also, to live longer you have to make a concerted effort to kick your fat can out and hike the mountain even if your mind rebels. You could see it all if you study the clock; it gives you the secret on when it's going to happen. The year will be 2029."

Red started to put on his backpack when he remembered that he'd brought something for Marcy. Reaching in, he took out a packet wrapped in layers of newspaper. Opening it after he left, the stench overwhelmed her. Inside the folded newspaper was part of a rotten fish.

"Actually," Virgil said, "I think Red thought that fish was good enough to eat."

Early one morning in late July, they heard Red bellowing down the trail to let them know he was coming again. He'd started showing up in the middle of the week as well as on Sundays, geared up to preach to them from the Bible.

"I brought you this," Red said as he thumped his backpack on the ground and untied a roll of thin building paper. "It'll cover up the holes inside the cabin but you'll need a roof. Don't you know the Trinities have unpredictable weather and we could get a general rain in August?" He looked directly at Virgil. "You'd better get up trail and bring down that heavy-duty tarpaper you have on top," he declared.

"I can't go now!" Virgil snapped. "I've been interrupted enough and have a million things to do before winter," he said and went back to working on his current project.

"Come on, Pantywaist," Red said to Marcy. "You're good and strong. We'll bring it down ourselves."

Marcy was also busy but figured that since he'd lived in the canyon close to 40 years, he should know more about the weather than they did. As they headed up the trail, Red told her he'd already brought two rolls down to Clutch Tree. "You could haul those down and I'll bring the other two from on top."

As they pushed up the trail, Marcy asked Red why he came to live alone in this beautiful canyon. "Acheron, the river of woe," he lamented. "I have no other place to go but stay in this miserable place."

What a joke, she thought, disappointed. She'd believed that Red loved the canyon and had expected him to say something like 'This canyon is God's country.' "Were you ever married?" she asked and he gave her a shy smile.

"Well, I used to know an old Chinese scholar who told me that a woman will give you pleasure only for a little while but if you grow a garden, you'll have pleasure for years. Heh. I did know a gal in my youth that cared for me. She wasn't pretty, but she was a good cook and a Christian lady. I should've married her."

As they walked up the trail, Marcy was touched by Red's surprising kindness. He was truly concerned for them and it was especially nice that he went out of his way to bring them the building paper and get the tarpaper from the top. Red went on up to Camp Desperation to retrieve the remaining two rolls and bring them to the Drinking Tree and one at a time, Marcy packed the tarpaper rolls down to the Flat.

Red took full advantage of having neighbors with a vehicle and often rode into town with them. On one particularly hot day, they stayed in town longer than usual. They were getting to know many people who were curious about them and wanted to talk.

When they reached the trailhead, Marcy started down immediately with her usual 50-pound load to get the evening meal started. Going down the trail after twelve-noon is foolhardy and dangerous but they hadn't learned that lesson yet. She left hatless with her heavy load and headed for home while Virgil and the boys secured the car and got their packs ready.

Red laid his pack under a tree and snuggled up to his beer can. "I'm going to stay here until it gets cool," he said.

It was two o'clock in the afternoon when Marcy came to the talus-covered section of trail below Elfin Dell that slants toward the sun and became known as The Oven due to built-up heat. The relentless sun beat down and Marcy realized she wasn't perspiring, which was unusual.

When she reached the Flat, her face felt like a living torch. She splashed cold water all over herself but still felt like she was burning up. When Virgil and the boys arrived, margarine lay in puddles on the table where she'd dropped it and they found her with a washcloth dripping on her head, her face beet red. Although she recovered, for a long time after that she had to wear a hat while in the sun and always tried to avoid going up or down in summer except in the early morning or late evening when the sun was off the trail.

Virgil bought parts for the Ford's starter, which brought their cash reserves down to just $100. The next day, he and Kelly were up on the mountain at daylight. Even at seven years old, Kelly could hand Virgil the right wrench while he worked under the car.

Had Virgil been in town when they got the starter apart, he would have gotten a new one. The commutator was badly burned, so badly in fact, that it was almost square. At the very least, it was a job for a machinist, but at Camp Desperation, they did what they could with what they had. They filed and sanded, then filed some more, until they had it as round as they could make it, using a jar lid ring for a gauge. After soldering in some new leads and brushes, they were ready to put the starter back in.

The ground was hot by this time, even under the car, and dirt and grease kept falling in Virgil's face and sticking in the sweat. Virgil was just about at his cussing point when they heard a car coming up the hill. "I suppose it's some more tourists to look us over," Virgil said to Kelly, who was under the car with him by this time.

The car pulled up and stopped. "There's a box that says dirty clothes. Bet they're still dirty. It's their place all right," a male voice said.

"Horseshit, John! If you think they ought to be washed, wash 'em yourself!" Virgil hollered from under the Ford, recognizing the voice of a friend from Los Angeles.

"Ghosts!" John said. "They must have died and are haunting this place."

"No, John," Virgil said as he squirmed from under the car and wiped what dirt he could from his face with his sleeve. "Get out, and welcome to Camp Desperation."

"Is this where you live? Where's the cabin? Where's the river?" one of the four teenage kids asked from the back of their big station wagon.

They started piling out. The three girls sported magazine fashions of what to wear in the mountains and a semi-sneer of disdain at the confused mess of stuff that littered Camp Desperation. Gene, taller than his dad, jumped out with a fishing rod in his hand. "Which way to the river," Gene asked.

Vicki rolled out of her side of the car and John rolled out of the other, both a little rounder than when they'd helped load the trailers two months before. John wore shorts, a yellow nylon shirt and highly polished black oxfords. His black curly hair was damp with perspiration but his brown eyes sparkled with the good humor that seldom ever deserted him.

"Virg, you're skinnier than when you left," Vicki said.

"You'll be this skinny, too, after you've been up and down the trail a couple hundred times," Virgil replied. "Where's your camping gear?"

"We're just here for the afternoon," John said. "We have a campsite down near the highway and left all our stuff there."

"You can't go down to the Flat now and come back up in the afternoon heat. You better go back and get your stuff and then we can go down in the evening," Virgil said. "We got caught on this mountain yesterday and Marcy almost had sunstroke and the sausage fried on the way down."

"But we can't stay down there," the oldest girl said. "We're too much in Hicksville as it is."

"Let's go and get it over with and get back to the beach," another girl said.

"Ok," Virgil said. "But let me try this starter first. I'd like to know whether I've got wheels. Sorta scary to feel you haven't."

"The girls and I will go on down and surprise Marcy," Vicki said.

"You'd better wait for us so we can show you the way," Virgil cautioned but then glanced at Kelly leaning over the open hood of the Ford. "Kelly, you go and show them the way."

"I want to watch the starter," Kelly said, sliding even further into the engine compartment while the three girls giggled at his reluctance.

"Just tell us how to get there. We're not babes in the woods," Vicki chirped.

"All right," Virgil said pointing to the mill road. "Go on down the hill until you hit a narrower trail and follow that for about two miles. Don't turn left until after you've seen the cabin from a high point above the river. Always follow the most worn trail," Virgil directed.

"Got it," Vicki said and shouldered a big bag. "See you later!"

"I'll go, too." Gene grabbed his fishing rod and followed along with the girls.

After they were gone, John retrieved a can of beer from an ice chest in the back of the car. "I don't know how I could stand the rigors of a vacation without this stuff," he said as he sat down on a packing box and popped the top.

"I hope you brought a good supply. The only thing we keep to drink on the Flat is water," Virgil said as he finished hooking the wires to the starter and turned the key.

"It works! It works!" Kelly cried

"Well, Kell, we're shade tree mechanics now. You ready to go down?"

By the time Virgil and Kelly had picked up and put away the tools, John had gotten his camera, light meter and accessory pack hung from his neck and a six-pack under one arm.

"Got more than that?" Virgil asked. "I'll put another one on my pack frame if you have."

"This is all the camera equipment I brought," he replied.

"No, another six-pack," Virgil clarified. "You and Vicki will probably want it."

"This'll do us this afternoon," John said.

It was already a little past noon. The sun burned down from a completely cloud-free sky and the heat waves eddied and swirled around the outcrops of rock. The only sounds in the forest were an occasional grasshopper beating his wings against the solid stillness of the August heat and the scritch of John's slick shoes on the trail.

Virgil thought John was probably one of the world's best photographers. No risk was too great if he could get a better picture, even to standing directly over an angry rattlesnake to get a shot of the head about to strike or clambering out on narrow spines of rock for a better viewpoint.

At the Drinking Tree, John squeezed his girth flat on the trail to take a shot up through the limbs of the madrone, which was beginning to lose its yellow leaves with its red-brown skin splitting in long scrolls to show pistachio green underneath, while Virgil and Kelly drank from the spring that welled up between the roots. Then John rested on the trail with another can of beer.

They were resting again at Wind Dance Lookout, talking, when a wavering bleat came from down the trail to their left. "Joh-h-h-n. Joh-h-h-n!"

"Sounds like Vicki," John said.

"Couldn't be," Virgil said. "I told her to keep to the right until after she saw the cabin. You can see it from right over there." Virgil got up and inspected the dust on the trail toward the cabin. "See, here's some sneaker tracks."

"John, Joh-h-h-n!" the bleat came again, but closer.

"That's Vicki! Ve be here on der mountain, Ma Ma," John yodeled.

"Virg, is that you up there?" Marcy called from the trail on the other side. "We've got to find Vicki. Carol and Lisa have been down on the Flat for over an hour. Vicki and the others were supposed to be right behind them."

"There's a voice wailing in the wilderness down towards Red's," Virgil answered as Marcy came up. "I'll go see if they need some help."

"Here they come," Kelly said as Vicki and the two kids staggered into sight on the wrong side of Wind Dance Lookout.

"We got this far but turned down there," Vicki pointed. "We almost died of thirst," she said with tears in her eyes. "We must have walked a mile and then heard some noise in the bushes, so we turned around and skedaddled back. Then we heard voices and I recognized John's so I started screaming and here we are."

Vicki could go no farther. A drop of sweat hung from her nose and her drip-dry clothes hung about her, dripping. The two kids flopped limply on the ground. "John, have you got any beer left?" Vicky asked hopefully.

"Just a couple. I guess I can let you have one to save your life, but this stuff is expensive to get this far," he teased.

"I would have already died if we hadn't found a spring back there," she said as she popped the top and drained the can in two great gulps. "There! I'm gonna live."

"You've had a long trip," Virgil said after a while of silence. "Do you think you can make it another quarter of a mile?"

"If the legs are willing, the spirit can ride along," Vicki said and groaned herself to her feet.

The girls thought little of the Flat but Gene headed for the river with his fishing rod and they heard no more from him until the mosquitoes drove him in at dark. Marcy took Vicki skinny-dipping while John tried in vain to get someone to pose on Butt Cutter.

"John, if you want to go back up that trail, ok. But I'm not going," Vicki said when she came up from the swimming hole.

"But Mama! All our food. I can't keep up my front without it," he said, patting his belly.

"We have enough beans," Marcy offered.

"Too much protein. I've got to have my starch."

"Well, go get it then. I'm not going back up that trail for a least a week," Vicki declared.

The next morning, John recruited Virgil and Gene to help go get the camping gear they'd left at the campground. But most importantly, all the beer and whisky was gone. They started early enough but it took them nearly three hours just to get to Camp Desperation. It was well after noon before they got the gear, and by the time they'd driven to the nearest large market in Weaverville to replenish both the liquid and starch parts of John's diet, it was dark when they started back down the trail.

With one flashlight for the three of them, a bit overloaded with supplies and bedding, they made poor time. Down from Mattress Point, a section of trail had earned the name Question Mark because of its shape and questionable footing. In daylight, you could pick out the more solid spots and with lug-soled boots, still rarely make it without falling down. John, with his oxfords, slid all the way to the bottom. "Gene, Gene!" he hollered. "Shine the light down here."

The glare of the flashlight showed John sitting on the trail in a cloud of dust, like the round dot of the question mark. "Ah, thank God! It's only blood," he gasped, looking at his hand.

"You hurt?" Gene asked.

"Just a scratch, but I was sure scared there for a minute when I felt the blood. Thought I'd broke my pint!" John said with evident relief.

While the men and Gene went to town, Vicki and the girls stayed with Marcy and the boys, planning to spend the day down at the river. Walking to the swimming hole, they heard a roar from across the river. They froze. "My God, that sounded like a lion!" Vicki whispered.

"I'm not sleeping outside!" Carol declared.

"We aren't either!" Lisa and Michele yelled.

That evening, they piled all the blankets and sleeping bags in the shack and made a wall-to-wall bed. No one was brave enough to sleep outside.

Darkness fell and Virgil, John and Gene still hadn't arrived. Ray had scared Marcy by telling her wild animals hunt at night and she passed this information on to the others. They all sat in the cabin listening to every sound, jumping every time the dogs barked.

One of the baby kittens leaped on Lisa, playfully scratching her cheek, and she let out a screech. She'd had enough and snuggled down into her bedding only to lift her head and stare at an extra-large crack in the floor near her pillow. She reached out and placed her hand over the crack.

"Why are you doing that?" Gaines asked.

"A snake might crawl in!" she declared.

"Well, don't put your hand over the crack or it will just bite you. Put your shoe on it," Gaines advised.

Lisa jerked her hand away and then proceeded to put not just her shoe over the crack, but every other shoe that she could get her hands on, as well. Eventually, the dogs barked again and this time it was Virgil, John and Gene. With a sigh of relief, Marcy opened the door.

John and Vicki planned to leave the next day, which was Sunday. Of course, Red came over to preach. John immediately saw a great subject to photograph and had Red pose, fingers dipping in his snoose can and putting some on his tongue.

Red mentioned the 'sky pilot' and Marcy knew he was starting to preach to John. "What kind of plane does this sky pilot fly?" John asked.

"No! A sky pilot is a preacher!" Red bellowed.

"Red's such a nice looking man," Vicki commented after he left. "And he sure is in good shape for his age.

Marcy agreed with Vicki. "I know he needs a bath but he does have a good physique."

Virgil, Marcy and the boys helped John and Vicki get their things back up the trail and waved them off after the four-day impromptu visit.

View of Flat from Wind Dance Lookout

Rock of Gibraltar

Marcella, Virgil and Red Barnes

9 - Visitors

Chicken scratch was important to them that first summer. They could buy 100 pounds for $4, and it fed the chickens and it fed them. Soaked overnight, the wheat, milo and cracked corn made an excellent breakfast. Added to beans, they ate a fine succotash. Cooked with tomatoes, onions and spices, they had a meal like spaghetti and sauce. And when visitors left most of it in their bowls or on their plates, they knew that they'd begun to eat for the purpose of living rather than living for the purpose of eating.

But they were beginning to wonder about eating at all during the winter. They knew their garden wasn't going to make it, and what was left of it, Marcy could water by herself. So Virgil devoted most of his time to the problem of getting the kids to school. He planned to make a trail four feet wide that would accommodate a three wheel, seven-horsepower cart for the boys to drive to the school bus stop that he thought was no farther than five miles.

Virgil and the boys surveyed a grade that he knew a cart could make and as long as they were digging among the pines where there was still some moisture in the ground, the work went quickly. Virgil could already see the three boys in their coats and caps chugging up the trail in the frosty, but snowless, autumn mornings. As they worked farther up the hill, ribs of serpentine lay just underneath the surface, and instead of rakes and shovels, they picked their way through.

They had just three weeks left before school started when Virgil got a letter from his brother saying that he'd be up to help them out. He arrived with a heavy case of worries and a case of oranges. After listening to the horror stories from relatives back home, he feared they'd either starve to death or die of exposure since they had neither food nor shelter. So he quit his job as a nightclub pianist and came to give his older, but idiot, brother a hand.

With black hair and blue eyes, Doug had the craggy good looks seen in some tall thin men. He lit a cigarette and inhaled deeply. "This is the only one I have left and then that's it. No more," he vowed. When he finished smoking that final cigarette, he threw the butt in the sand and dug his heel in on it. "I've come to help, so where do we start?"

"Let's go pick berries and I'll make some Trinity Tarts," Marcy said.

"Trinity Tarts?"

"Oh, they're one of my cooking inventions," Marcy said. "I roll out small flat rounds of soft bread dough, put a spoonful of thickened cooked blackberries in the center, fold them over and seal the edges, and then deep-fry them. Last I roll them in sugar and cinnamon."

Virgil listened to the berry picking plans but told them to go ahead and pick without him so he could finish peeling poles for the boys' three-tiered bunk bed. With buckets made from two-pound coffee cans with the ever-useful scavenged galvanized iron telephone wire as handles, Doug and Marcy followed the boys who said they'd found a shortcut to the good berry patch at the upper stream. "Okay, lead the way," Doug said.

The boys took them up a talus slide that terminated at a steeply inclined slab of bedrock. About half way up, Marcy froze in terror, unable to force her body to go forward or backward. Just below her, Doug saw her shaking legs cause her feet to slide on the talus and quickly braced himself, afraid she might fall and send them both rolling down the mountain.

"Now Marcy, take it easy," Doug said in a slow, calm voice. "Put your foot right here." He scraped a step in the loose rock above her and pulled stout branches from a nearby bush. "Grab onto this and put your foot over here," he said softly. "I'll catch you if you fall."

Cautiously, Marcy tried to grab the bush but her foot wouldn't move to the crevice Doug had made for her.

"Look Marcy, I'm going to make a deeper step closer to you." He scraped a groove on the side of the hill right beside her. "Don't look down and take a deep breath."

Doing what he asked, she finally got her foot to move and then pulled herself to the other groove with the stout branch. It was slow going and her heart pounded with every step. The boys waited impatiently at the top of the slope. "Hurry up! That's not steep!" Joel shouted.

Doug shot Joel a dirty look and continued to help Marcy. After scraping a half-dozen steps, they reached the top and Marcy took a deep breath. "Do you want to go up through the woods or take this old trail and switchback up the creek?" Marcy asked Doug cheerily.

Doug's face went red, the calm reassuring tones of moments before forgotten. He reached for the pack of cigarettes no longer in his front pocket. "We're going that way! Right back to the Flat!"

"Come on, Doug. I'm all right now. Let's go get the berries," Marcy coaxed.

"This is the easy part now. Ma can make it with no problems," Kelly promised, echoed by Gaines and Joel.

Having just come up a recommended 'easy way', Doug was doubtful but reluctantly agreed to continue the expedition. Shortly, they came to the stream crisscrossed with thorny vines and soon spread out picking the deep purple berries. Marcy had picked berries as a child and was fast and efficient. She quickly moved through the heavy tall green vines, fending off the wicked thorns with a dead fir branch. Occasionally the boys yelped and Doug cussed as they cautiously picked through the patch.

The stream had cut a four-foot deep ravine and the berries were thriving on moist loam near the creek. The vines towered over Marcy and the berries, some as big as her thumb in this particularly lush section, hung in great clusters. But the ravine was hidden and the mesmerizing clusters of berries held Marcy's full attention as she stepped into the void and fell backwards, coming to rest on a gently swaying hammock of thick, thorny vines. Unable to move, with thorns piercing her arms and back, she screamed for help.

The sudden shrill shrieks echoed in the gulch, startling Doug and the boys, and they thrashed through the vines in the general direction of the screams. "What in the hell is wrong now?" Doug demanded, exasperated and afraid.

"I'm stuck!" Marcy screeched. She hung there helpless, not daring to move. She had no clue how far she'd fall should the vines break, and even the slightest shift drove the thorns deeper into her flesh. "Can't you see? I can't move!" she wailed.

What Doug could see was jagged sharp points in the rocky streambed beneath the vines and he worked carefully to get her out. She yelped every time a thorn stabbed her. "Easy, easy you're about out," Doug soothed.

Finally, she stood on her own feet again and rubbed the jabs and scratches that stung as only blackberry thorns can.

"Are you okay?" Doug inquired.

"Yes, I think so." She pointed to the heavy clusters of berries. "Look how big those berries are!"

"I don't give a damn how big they are! That's it; we're going back to the Flat right now and you're going to stay there so you don't kill yourself!" he exploded, grabbing for his cigarette packet again.

Back down at the Flat, Doug headed straight for the sandbar. Seeing the boys' swimming trunks lying on the ground, he exploded. "You people will never survive down here if you don't keep care of your clothes!" he yelled as he rummaged through the sand until he found and lit his discarded cigarette butt.

During his visit, Doug did everything he could but it's difficult to help people who are trying to do everything at once and aren't organized enough to tell someone else what to do. Before the week was out, he told Virgil that he was eating more than he was worth, so he was going back home.

Doug's leaving left them feeling alone and discouraged, with a feeling of failed hospitality, which Virgil thought was a feeling synonymous with failure. They were so down for the rest of the day after seeing Doug to the top that they sat in the shade by the river. Their supplies were almost gone, their money was almost gone, the time before school started was almost gone…and winter was an unknown thing hiding somewhere in the mountains to the north.

It was hard to believe in winter. Virgil hadn't seen one in 17 years and Marcy had never experienced a winter, except for the southern California kind. Some stories from old timers indicated very mild winters, but others told of snow covering a 40-foot stovepipe. The length of winter was another unknown, for the same sources claimed either they wouldn't be snowed in or they'd better have enough supplies to last six months. At this point, six weeks would be too long.

The sun sank, its antique gold light just about gone from the western face of Backbone Ridge. The mosquitoes and no-see-ums had joined forces and just about accomplished a rout when the family heard a lonesome bellow from somewhere up near Wind Dance Lookout. "My God! What is that?" Marcy asked.

"Someone's hurt," Virgil replied and ran to get the carbine from the cabin, fearing he'd find a bear or cougar attack.

"Something's moving on the trail," Marcy said, staring up the mountain. "Pretty big and black. There's a person right in front of it. Oh God! It's a bear chasing someone down the trail!"

"Virgil Horn! Virgil Hoorn! Virgil Hooooorn!

"They're yelling for you, Virg!" Joel cried.

Virgil lit out up the trail, rifle ready, half expecting to shoot a bear mauling someone they knew. Virgil jumped the gulch at a dead run with Gaines right behind him. "Virg, that's Ray!" Gaines hollered.

In the evening gloom, Ray came through the trees, a rag tied around his head, sweat dripping across the folds of his belly. Two of his goats, Clementine and Fawn, tripped daintily down the trail behind him.

"Can't stay long," he announced. "Just came up here to get a drink of genuine water."

"You're welcome to the whole river," Virgil replied. "Come on down."

"Thought you might need these," he said, pointing to the goats. "You can have Clementine and I'll loan you Fawn."

"We're happy to see you, Ray. We thought you'd gone to Alaska," Marcy said, remembering Ray's pronouncement in June.

"Nah," Ray replied. "I've got a truckload of beans and rice up at Camp Desperation."

That night when everyone was asleep in the shack, Marcy awakened to a sound. When she heard it again, the hair on her neck bristled. "Virg, wake up! There's a rattler in here," she whispered. "I think it's under Kelly."

"Nah. Go back to sleep. It's just a locust," he grumbled.

"At night?" Marcy demanded as she grabbed Kelly by the arm and with a quick jerk, had a sleepy, frightened boy on their blankets.

More awake now, Virgil heard the unmistakable whirr from Kelly's corner and jumped straight up. He grabbed the .22 and started poking among the blankets on Kelly's bed, but found no snake. Yet the whirr grew angrier.

Virgil stood in the decrepit shack full of cracks and holes, shoeless and pantless with only the light of a small flashlight, while cold sweat ran down his backbone. Suddenly, a flicker of white through a crack in the floor under the bunk caught his eye.

Tissy had given birth to a litter of pups under the shack several weeks before and in the light that shone through the crack, a tiny puppy wiggled closer and closer to a big rattler. The snake was scared enough to strike and the bunk was too low to get the gun into position to fire.

Awakened by the excited voices, Ray came in to investigate. "What're you doin' in your underwear, Virg?"

"Snake under there. 'Bout to strike a pup!" Virgil said trying to poke the rifle barrel through the crack with one hand while holding the dim light with the other.

"Here, use this." Ray handed Virgil his pistol, and for the first time, willingly handed over a job.

Virgil grabbed, pointed and fired in the same instant. The snake must have moved just then for when the neck laid across the pup, there was no head on it. Virgil then flashed the light all around under the shed to see if there were any more.

After everyone settled down again, Marcy glimpsed a light coming through the cracks in the shack. Looking outside, she saw Ray flashing his light all around. "What's wrong, Ray? Another snake?" Marcy called.

Ray looked up. "I haven't found one yet but there sure are a lot of crooked sticks around here."

In the next couple weeks, snakes started showing up everywhere; at the reservoir, the apple orchard, the sandbar where the boys played, in the kitchen area, and just about everywhere else they were working. They killed every snake they found in their work areas and the boys collected the rattles. By the end of the season, they had collected 29.

After Ray left the next evening, Marcy went out to milk the goats and Fawn was gone. She'd torn her tether loose and gone up trail after Ray. Virgil followed her tracks to the top. "I didn't find her but saw where a truck had backed up. She may have been stolen," he said when he got back to the Flat.

"She may come back in the morning," Marcy said. "She'll be full of milk and that'll be painful."

The next morning she was still gone. Virgil and the boys went up to look for her again and saw fresh tracks going up the trail, followed by tiny tracks. They found her at Wind Dance Lookout, her udder full and leaking. "I guess maybe some orphan baby deer followed her," Virgil said as he tied her to a tree. "I checked to see if she was suckled but she wasn't."

According to all the books, in the mountains, a goat is worth its weight in gold nuggets. They'll eat what a mule won't, they can climb where a cow can't, and they're charming, sweet, lovable creatures. Maybe some are but Clementine was not able to, or would not, read the books. Clementine was a spoiled old goat, sneaky and stubborn. Fawn might have lived up to the good goat reputation if she hadn't fallen in with bad company, but Fawn had no initiative and followed Clementine's lead on everything.

Never once did the goats go to the berry patch to pick berries, but waited until Marcy and the boys had all the berries picked and washed on the table. If she thought no one was watching, Clementine would quietly sneak over the riverbank, up along the river out of sight, climb on the table and eat the berries. Finally, Marcy put the berries high on a shelf nailed between a cedar and oak tree, forcing Clementine and Fawn to pick their own. In doing so, the beasts scratched their udders until they bled.

Clementine loved to play King of the Mountain with Tissy and Hucky, and she'd badger them until they played. Her horns kept them from getting too close, but the horns had no effect on the hornets the day she chose their log to be her mountain. She danced and pranced back and forth on the log, stomping her front feet until the yellow jackets had had enough. They swarmed out, not caring who or what was there. The dogs ran toward the family and the family ran toward the river. Clementine and Fawn made flying leaps from the log and ran nonstop 300 yards to the apple orchard.

That didn't calm her down. Shortly after, she hooked her udder on a fishhook attached to a fishing pole leaning against the cedar tree. Virgil had to pry it out with his pocketknife and Marcy rubbed her with Bag Balm until she healed. With all her faults, Clementine was a city goat to boot. Used to chlorinated water, she wouldn't drink from the river but drank up the rinse water Marcy treated with bleach when washing dishes.

But the goat milk was good and Marcy frequently made goat cheese and sour milk biscuits. She wondered, however, wondered what would happen to the goats when winter came. "I wonder if they're worth all the berries they ate," Marcy said grimly. "And we'll have to have them bred. Do you know who has a Billy?"

"No clue," Virgil shrugged.

Ray had brought news that Marcy's sister, brother-in-law and mother were coming for a visit and Marcy was thrilled. She was anxious to see her family and knew her mother would love the swimming hole. On the day before they were to arrive, Virgil and Marcy cleaned the camp extra well, scrubbed the boys and themselves to a shiny surface, then tethered the goats and hiked to the top of the mountain early the next morning. "Now keep clean," Marcy kept insisting. "You want to look nice for Grandma."

Virgil spent his time stacking and straightening some of the confused mess their goods had gotten into in the past two months. He even went so far as to wipe some of the red dust off the old Ford in hopes that by creating a more favorable first impression with Marcy's mom, they would at least get her approval of their project.

While they waited on top for Emy, Gary and Mama, Red showed up to haul down some of his groceries. Soon an overheated, overloaded new car steamed into the clearing at Camp Desperation. "Ist ok to open my eyes now?" they heard Mama ask.

"Sure, Mama. We're here," Gary said.

The guests piled out but the car still sagged heavily toward the rear. Mama dug in the back seat and proudly held up a pair of lug-soled boots, but because of the long trip, her feet had swelled too much to get them on. All the while, she kept muttering. "The road ist awful…so high…I couldn't look. Ist vas awful," she said repeatedly.

"Did you break a spring on the road, Gary," Virgil asked, concerned about the noticeable slant of the car.

"Naw, Virg. You know Mama. She had to bring half the market," he replied and started unloading box after box of food.

"We'll have to make two or three trips for all that stuff," Virgil said, forgetting his manners.

Mama was like that. Her background as a little girl in Czechoslovakia, and a much leaner time in the Pampas of Argentina had made her think in terms of a full cupboard. She'd had every kind of fruit, from apricots to mulberries, on her little ranch near Los Angeles and didn't see this raw forest as a fit place to raise a family.

Marcy introduced her visitors to Red and could tell that her mother liked him. "I am Marie," she said, shaking his hand with both of hers.

"Do you like the mountains, Marie?" Red asked.

"Yes, but I am a beich woman," Mama answered in her thick Bohemian accent.

With eyes wide, Red was momentarily silent. Then he realized she'd meant 'beach' and they had a good laugh when he told her what he thought she had said. "Well, Marie, I'll be over to see you Sunday," Red promised.

Tissy sniffed Mama. "Oh, you still have the ugly dog with the blue eyes, I see."

"Mama, her eyes look like yours," Marcy laughed.

"You saying I look like her? Vhat a bad thing to say, Marcella."

They loaded up as much food as they could pack and started down the trail. Mama wore beach shoes without heels since the trail boots she'd borrowed were now too small. She assured Marcy she'd be fine when questioned about the suitability of the flat soles but Emy and Mama both paled as they edged slowly down the first steep 50 feet until the trail flattened out.

From the viewpoint above the hogback, surrounded by the beautiful mountainous panorama, Mama was silent as she looked at the tiny river still 1,000 feet below and weighed the 50 feet she'd just struggled down against the thousand yet to come. When they reached the Drinking Tree, she still hadn't said a word, leaving Virgil and Marcy disappointed by her silence.

At Wind Dance Lookout, Marcy showed Mama the view of the Flat. "What do you think of that?" Virgil asked brightly.

"Yes, ist beautiful but vhat goot ist it? Ist not real property."

They all started down the trail again and suddenly Mama slipped and fell over the edge. Virgil dropped his pack and jumped down the side to stop her but she'd grabbed a branch and was holding on with all she had. Her yell brought Marcy back at a run and between them all they got Mama back on the trail. Her slacks ripped and dirty and her sandal twisted to one side, she jerked the sandal off and got to her feet.

"Oh, you poor thing!" Emy cried.

"Can you stand on it, Mama? Is it broke?" Gary asked.

"Goot Got in himmel! Probably ist broke but I am going down," she muttered and started to hobble down the trail.

"Hold on, Mama! Gary and I will hold a couple of branches between us and you can walk between them," Virgil said.

Gaines was already dragging two sapling deadfalls from above the trail for Virgil and Gary to use as a moving banister. Mama stood in the middle, hobbling and hanging on to the two poles for dear life. She moaned all the way down, no longer interested in any view. They got Mama to the Flat and sat her down under the cedar trees. "Get me some hot vater, Marcella, so I can soak my foot."

Mama's ankle swelled and turned a sickly purple so Marcy wrapped it up with torn sheets. "While Mama rests, let's go down to the river to wash these dirty dishes," Marcy suggested to Emy.

"Isn't this a fun way to wash dishes?" Marcy cooed, rubbing clean sand on the dishes and rinsing them in the river.

"Ugh! You'll soon tire of that," Emy predicted.

After Mama rested awhile, Marcy got a makeshift cane and coaxed her down to the river. When she got to the swimming hole, Mama put her foot in the water, slipped on the slimy algae and fell in, landing on her side on some rocks. "Oh my Got! Das place ist going to kill me yet."

Marcy helped Mama up and took her to the bed in the cabin to rest.

That night, Gary, Virgil and the boys slept under a tree. Marcy found a patch of soft-looking sand and threw a blanket over it so she and Emy could sleep comfortably. The next morning, Marcy was so stiff and sore she could barely move. She didn't want to admit to her sister that she was such a wimp until she heard Emy moaning. "Never, never did I have such a terrible night!" Emy cried.

"Me either," Marcy said, holding her sore back.

It was Sunday and Marcy knew Red would want to talk with Mama. Placing a soft pillow on their most comfortable chair, Marcy helped Mama hobble over to sit under the cedar trees. When Red arrived, Marcy told him to cheer Mama up. An hour later, Marcy walked past and heard Red droning on about Saint John's Clock and the World

War I Plan. Polite but not overly religious and unable to get away due to her swollen ankle, Mama kept looking at Marcy to save her. "Vhy did you leave me alone with him? He kept jabbering and jabbering," she said after Red left.

As the end of the visit neared, Marcy felt she hadn't shown Emy all the things she had wanted her to see, whereas Gary, Virgil and the boys were off exploring all the time. Mama had complained of constipation so Marcy brewed her some tea from cascara tree bark, which Red had told her was good for that problem. As they loaded the backpacks for the hike out, Marcy wrapped Mama's ankle and loaned her P.F. Flyers, the only shoes she had that laced up above the ankle. Red always called the high-top sneakers 'Poor Fanny Flyers' when he saw Marcy wearing them. Marcy then pulled Emy aside and handed her one of the Tissy's puppies. "Will you take Tissy's puppies with you and give them away?" Marcy pleaded.

"Oh no. We can't. Poor things would be miserable on the long trip back." Emy frowned.

"They'll starve here and Virg will just have to drown them," Marcy sighed, the first option highly probable but the second not at all.

"That's awful!" Emy gasped. "Okay. But don't tell Gary until we're on top and it is too late for him to say no," Emy agreed as the puppy licked her face. "You aren't going to be drowned, Snoopy," she crooned and slipped the puppy into her pack.

Gary and Virgil put Mama between the two poles again and she grasped them with hands like claws. Emy and Marcy went ahead with the puppies hidden in their packs and could hear Mama praying in Czech, German, Spanish and English. As they rounded a bend on the trail, they heard an extra loud bleat. "I wish she'd quit complaining so much," Emy declared.

Marcy agreed but then saw Clementine coming up behind them. The sisters stared at each other and laughed. "We'd better not ever tell Mama we thought she was bleating like a goat," Marcy said.

Emy wrote later and shared that Mama's woes continued after they left Camp Desperation. When they stopped for the night, Mama decided to sleep in the car to keep the pups quiet at the motel, all the while plagued by Marcy's cascara tonic. After reading the letter, Marcy wondered if Mama would ever come back to visit.

"Shedding season is upon us!" Red declared in mid-August and solemnly lifted his undershirt to display puncture scars on his stomach. "This is where a snake bit me many years ago. I was on the trail and it was getting too dark to go any farther, so I laid down and fell asleep on a timber rattler. I got bitten seventeen times there and didn't even feel him strike me."

"How much booze did you drink, Red?" Virgil laughed.

"I don't drink booze. I drink Christian Brothers brandy and that isn't booze, it's a good Christian drink. Soooo, like I'm trying to tell you, I knew I had to get down to the cabin before the poison spread in my bloodstream. I barely got there when I started seeing stars and circles. I soaked the wounds in baking soda and lay as quietly as I could.

"I don't know how long it was when I felt something snap in my stomach. I thought my appendix split. I was pretty sick and didn't dare move until the next morning. When I opened my eyes, I saw a foreign man with a funny looking flat hat standing in the doorway. He reached down and touched my wound and said 'I know how you feel for I have been there, too, old-timer.'

"It quit hurting immediately and then he walked out. I got up without any pain and looked outside but he was gone. Anyway, what I'm getting' at, on August 23rd, 24th and 25th, it's shedding time for the rattlers. That's when they're completely blind and strike out at any noise. I was a fool to have left my cabin at that time."

The next time Ray showed up, they told him Red's shedding season story. Ray's eyes sparkled. "I can see all the snakes in a line and the sergeant snake hollers, 'All right, men. Shed! It's August 23rd!'" he chuckled.

Enjoying the swimming hole

Marcella's mother, Marie

10 - Schooling Dilemma

With all their visitors, Virgil couldn't possibly get the trail widened and the cart built to get the boys to school. He also realized it would be useless if he could. In talks with old timers, they'd discovered two distinct local climates, one down along the main river with very little snow and the other, their Flat. They could expect their road and trail to be filled with snow from November until March or April. With a last sad look at their new trail, Virgil and the boys picked up their tools and carried them back down to the Flat.

So with a short trail going nowhere, Virgil went to town to see the County Superintendent of Schools to ask permission to home school the kids. It was dusk when he finally returned to the Flat. "There are none so blind as those who will not see," he declared, sagging onto a chair. "I tried to tell him how far we lived and what a hardship it would be to get them up trail every morning but the answer is no. You know what that guy said?" Virgil clenched his pipe between his teeth. "We should live in a tent at the campground!"

Not one to break the rules even though they exist only in the head of officialdom, Virgil registered the boys in the nearest school only to find that they were some thousand feet to the wrong side of the district line. Their school, Cox Bar, was eight miles further west from where they met the main road compared to five miles toward town to reach Junction City School. With helpful suggestions from the teachers at Junction City, and several trips and letters later, they were allowed to keep the boys in the nearest school.

The day after Labor Day, they got up before dawn, lit the lantern, scrubbed, dressed and ate. At five in the morning, Virgil, Gaines and Kelly lit their candle bugs and walked up the trail in the dark with paper bag lunches. Virgil drove the boys to school at Junction City while Joel and Marcy stayed home.

When he picked Kelly up that first day, the teacher pulled Virgil aside. "Kelly slept all day in class and only woke up when school was over," she said. "Are you getting him to bed on time?"

"It's not that he didn't go to bed on time, it's because he got up at four in the morning," Virgil replied.

"Why so early?" she frowned.

"We live on the North Fork and have to get up that early to get here on time," Virgil stated.

For a week, they continued to drag themselves up the trail each morning and Kelly continued to sleep his way through school. Gaines and Kelly had different schedules so Virgil and Kelly had to wait two hours longer for Gaines to get out of class, and they arrived home a little after dark each evening. Every night, both boys dropped on their beds exhausted.

Since the rattlesnake incident, Kelly insisted on sleeping on the top of the triple bunk that Virgil had built against the south wall of the shack. One night, Marcy awoke and saw him going up and down the ladder. "What are you doing, Kelly?"

"I have to get up this trail, Ma," he answered, still asleep.

Virgil tried coming back to the Flat to work but found he only had a half hour before it was time to leave again to get Kelly. All work stopped at the Flat and Virgil worried about the first snows. *Maybe they'll see the stupidity by then and let me teach the boys at home*, he thought.

On Friday that first week, Virgil went to Cox Bar School and asked if the school bus could meet him half way. "No," the clerk of the board answered. "Can't be done."

"Why not?" Virgil asked, vaguely remembering something about required school-provided transportation for all students in California.

"Well, you're off the county roads and our bus insurance is void under those conditions," he answered. "You'd have to meet the bus down at the highway."

"Isn't there some other way?" Virgil persisted.

"Why don't you come to the next board meeting and maybe we can arrange in lieu payments, that is, so much a mile for each mile you drive...something like five or six cents a mile."

"When?" Virgil asked.

"First Tuesday of every month," the clerk replied.

"Over three weeks from now?"

"That's right," the clerk confirmed, obviously relieved to have that settled.

Virgil wasn't relieved. In three weeks, I won't have a dime left or any shoes either, he thought. Gaines and Kelly probably won't be able to get out of bed and the old Ford will probably die of cirrhosis of the carburetor.

The teacher at the one-room school overheard the conversation. "I've heard you have a college degree, Mr. Horn. Why don't you apply for the teaching job that's open in Denny?" she suggested. "They need a teacher awfully bad."

"Me! A teacher!" Virgil laughed and was still laughing when they got back down to the Flat that night.

While Virgil picked up the boys from school that day, friends from southern California arrived at the Flat. Diane and Cecil Beatty and their two boys, Kurt and Keith had been visiting family in Oregon and stopped by on their way home. "Well..." Cecil said as Virgil walked into the light of the lantern. "You look like you won that round."

"Noooo. I'd still have to take the kids at least to the highway, but they may be able to pay me 50 cents a day. Funniest part is the teacher suggested I apply for the teaching job in Denny and..."

"Wonderful!" Diane interrupted. "I always told you, you should be a teacher!"

"Virg, do you think you should?" Marcy asked.

"Right now, I don't see any other way out. I could apply," Virgil said, opening his billfold to show her their last two dollars.

"Why not? We'll drive you over there tomorrow," Diane said.

Marcy was devastated by the prospect of leaving the Flat but knew they couldn't keep up the pace on the trail any longer. "It will destroy something down here if we leave," she whispered to Virgil later that night.

"I agree," Virgil said. "But what else can I do?"

As the crow flies, Denny School was less than 17 miles from the Flat, but by road, it was over 60 miles. To talk in term of miles gives a false picture of the area, however, and using terms of hours or days is much better. The county seat, for instance, was about an eight-hour trip from the Flat yet the distance round trip was only 50 miles. Going to the post office and back took four hours if they hurried and it was only 24 miles. But it was difficult to convince Cecil and Diane that they should start soon after dawn if the group was to make the trip in one day.

The next morning, they set out to talk to the head of the school board at Denny. The Beattys were anxious to see the country on the other side of the mountain and everyone piled into Cecil's station wagon for the trip. They got to the Denny Road turnoff a little after noon. The road twisted and turned up out of one river drainage over into another. Fir trees got bigger and darker as they went over the top, and the road got narrower. From the high places, they could see ridge after ridge of forested mountains sawing their way into a yellow-green sky. A few of the highest peaks showed snow, even that early in September.

When they drove lower, Himalaya berries grew in the gullies next to the roadside, all evenly coated with a heavy layer of dust that curled in and behind the station wagon, choking them. The five little boys in the back complained about the long, dry ride. The road twisted back upon itself like a worm track in a dead log until they came around one of the sharp turns and found themselves on an oiled road.

The sudden sunshine after the dark in the forest surprised them. Aluminum roofs gleamed on log ranch buildings perched on steep hills. Brown grass covered the lower places and golden walnut trees stood in rows all the way up to the timberline. They looked closely at each building to find a store or schoolhouse but didn't see either, so Diane pulled out a map. "This is the Dailey Ranch. Denny isn't for another five miles."

But it wasn't until 50 minutes later that they pulled into another little settlement that consisted of several log buildings, a couple of framed houses and fenced-in horses. Cecil parked in front of a building of mortared rock and log walls, with 1920 vintage gas pumps and post office sign hanging above the door. Inside, a woman told them her husband was a member of the school board but wouldn't be home until after dark. "Do you want to wait?" she asked.

"We can't hardly do that. We've got a couple miles of trail to go tonight," Virgil answered. "I do need to see some of the board, though. Is there anybody else?"

"The board is having a special meeting tomorrow afternoon," she offered. "You want to enroll those boys in school?" she asked, noticing the five boys sticking their heads out of the station wagon windows in hopes of being let out to blow off dust and energy. "We can sure use them."

"No," Virgil answered. "I want to apply for the teacher's job."

"Oh!" she frowned, taking in his sweat-stained beret, worn out trail shoes and untrimmed mustache. Virgil obviously didn't match her mental picture of a teacher. "Well, you can see them all tomorrow," she said and turned back to sorting the mail.

"Where's the school house?" Diane asked.

"Take this road on upriver to the county dump sign, turn right and you're there," the woman answered.

The schoolhouse Virgil expected and the one he saw were 50 years apart in time. This was no little country schoolhouse, but an ultra-modern, tinted glass, acoustic tile sort of thing plunked down on raw, red earth bulldozed over the remains of an old dump. It was saved from utter disgrace in its nakedness by a lone madrone tree left standing near one corner of the building, and that only by the grace of its being a property corner marker on the county maps.

"This is beautiful. It even has a kitchen," Diane said.

"And its own light plant," observed Cecil, the engineer.

"And no grass or flowers," sighed Marcy, the gardener.

The boys said nothing, for to them it was just another jail.

The prospective teacher was also silent. Virgil's degree had been in the bottom of a box for 17 years, a long time to be away from the halls of academe, which hadn't been particularly pleasant to him. He was especially critical of the faculty's ignorance of the real world, having been through four years of war before getting there. He also felt that he had just been through a tough course in pragmatism, and wasn't sure his newer outlook would prove compatible with the governing board.

They arrived back at Camp Desperation in the late evening. The Beattys walked down to the Flat with them but left early the next morning, and Virgil went to the special school board meeting while Marcy stayed home with the boys. As she watched the mist rise from rocks and ferns warmed by the morning sun, she dreaded leaving.

"I'm sure I'll get the job," Virgil informed Marcy when he got home that evening. "We'd better start organizing the things we're going to need and haul them back up the trail."

They worked at a frantic pace. Virgil tacked boards over the windows in the shack and stored all the jewelry equipment under cover. Marcy put her gooseberry syrup, canned apples and pears from the Garedos in stout boxes and stored the beans, rice and other grains in gallon jars with tight fitting lids so bears wouldn't smell them and the food would be there when the family came back on weekends

Marcy's cast iron pots and pans went everywhere with her so back up the trail they went along with clothes and other essential items. They had been so proud of the shrinking piles at Camp Desperation and now, with each trip up, the piles started growing again.

They knew they couldn't leave the stuff they wouldn't need in Denny up top much longer. The boxes at Camp Desperation began to look emptier each time they checked. They looked for a barn or shed to rent to store the stuff in until the next summer but no space was available. They ended up by getting Marvin to agree to haul the stuff down to the Flat from the Blue Ridge Trailhead, which they thought they could afford now that they'd have some money coming in.

Each day, they carried something up the trail that they'd need in Denny and then took two or three carloads of stuff they wouldn't need up to the little campground at Blue Ridge. They made quite a dent in the piles before Virgil received a card in the mail later that week stating that the school board had approved him for the teaching position and had found them a temporary cabin to live in. The board had also put in a bid with the Forest Service to see if they could live in the summer ranger's cabin after fire season.

On Saturday, a frosty morning with the air so clear that sound travels unimpeded down the canyons on the colder currents, they walked up the trail to get the Ford ready for the trip to Denny. As they reached the station wagon, they heard a bellow way down by the river. "That's Red! He must be hurt!" Marcy exclaimed.

"Maybe a tree fell on him or he fell down. Gaines, get the come-along and some rope!" Virgil yelled.

"I've got coffee in this thermos. We'll take that," Marcy said.

"You stay here. If Marv comes, we might need his help," Virgil said.

"No, I'm going," Marcy insisted. "He'll need my help if he is hurt."

The bellow became a cry when it came up the mountain again. By now, Gaines and Kelly had the come-along and 100 feet of rope and they all started down the mountain on Red's trail. *It must take 40 years of practice to enable a man his age to go up and down this,* Virgil thought.

The trail was so steep in places that Red had hacked out steps to keep from sliding down. They were almost running as the cries grew fainter. When they reached the Hobo Bench trail that Shotgun and his crew had built that summer along the ridge 400 feet above the river, they couldn't find the trail that led down to Red's cabin. Marcy searched one end of the trail and the boys and Virgil searched the chaparral bushes. One of them found faint tracks going down a game trail. They were sure the tracks were Red's as he'd been wearing one paratrooper boot with pieces of automobile tire for a sole and heel and one smooth soled rubber boot the last time they'd seen him.

Virgil and Gaines followed the tracks almost to the river and finally came to a shed perched like a swallow's nest on the side of a cliff. They saw no sign of Red. Huffing and puffing they came back up to where Kelly, Joel and Marcy waited. "I hope he hasn't fainted," Marcy said as Virgil gulped down a swallow of her coffee.

"I do, too. We'll never find him if he doesn't holler," Virgil said.

"I saw some tracks going towards the Flat," Marcy told Virgil. "Do you suppose he's tried to come to our place for help?"

"We'll go look," Virgil said. "Come on, Gaines. Look over the side at all the steep places. If he's down below, we can haul him up if he isn't too badly hurt."

"I'll wait here with Joel and Kelly," Marcy said. "Maybe we'll hear him again."

As they raced down the trail, Virgil tried to figure out how to get the sheriff's rescue squad in. Virgil and Gaines were almost to Wind Dance Lookout when they heard singing. Virgil frowned as he recalled his grandpa singing just before he died. "What song is that, Gaines?"

"I don't know, but he doesn't sound like he's hurt," Gaines replied.

With a sack on his back and a beer in his hand, Red rounded a bend and ambled toward them bellowing the words of *Down by the Old Mill Stream*. "What are you doing with that junk?" he asked, pointing at the come-along and rope with his beer can. "Is someone hurt?"

"We thought you were. What was all that bellowing?" Virgil replied.

"I was answering the kids. What were they doing across the river? You're a fool to let two little boys run loose in the wilderness."

"They weren't across the river! They're up the trail looking for you!" Virgil answered.

"I heard 'em across there. I've been up to your place to see if you'd fallen off the roof. Thought you'd sent the kids to get me." Red looked as if he was sorry to find Virgil in one piece.

Virgil and Gaines hiked back up to the top, getting Marcy, Kelly and Joel on the way. Their mountain rescue team was pretty tired when they got down to the Flat after finishing up with the Ford at Camp Desperation.

"What are we going to do with Clementine and Fawn," Marcy asked after the evening milking.

"Maybe we could come back for them later," Virgil suggested.

"You know they won't survive without a pen, Virg."

Suddenly, they heard Ray's distinctive bellow and looked through the trees up toward Wind Dance Lookout where they could see Ray struggling with a huge pack. Virgil and the boys ran up to help but when they met Ray, his 'pack' was a full bale of alfalfa. "Hiya, Gang. Thought you might need this for the goats. More on top. Barley, too."

"We're movin' Ray," the boys said.

"Movin'? Where to?" Ray asked as he plopped down heavily on the trail.

"Can't teach the kids here. Had to take a job. I'm teaching over at Denny this winter."

"You a teacher!" Ray laughed.

"Well, I admit they were desperate," Virgil grinned and helped Ray to his feet and down to the Flat with the bale of alfalfa.

"We can't take the goats with us. Do you want them back?" Marcy asked.

"Eat 'em," Ray replied but Fawn nudged his hand. "Okay. I'll take them back. I read that goats make good pack animals. I'll make some saddles and they can take up part of the load."

The next morning, Ray hammered together a packsaddle from loose boards and soon had Clementine packed with the rope he had used to carry the bale of hay. But Clementine hadn't read Ray's book and with a contemptuous toss of her horns, bolted up through the brush. Fawn followed behind jumping over hurtling objects flying off the pack. At Wind Dance Lookout, they caught up with Clementine and Fawn grazing at Red's feet.

"You'll be tired, Pantywaist, and fish are fast to cook," Red said, handing Marcy a fresh steelhead for their first meal in Denny.

"Thanks, Red. I appreciate it."

"I wish I could catch one like that," Ray sighed.

Red shoved something in Virgil's pocket as he helped him with his pack. Once he got steadied, Virgil fished in his pocket and held up a crumpled $50 bill. "I can't take this, Red. You've got to get supplies for winter."

"I can get by. You're gonna need it."

"Thanks, Red, but no. I'll be getting a regular paycheck and have enough money to tide us over until then.

END OF SUMMER

Summer left today, I saw her
Run along a bare brown hill
To cross a shadowed valley
Where everything was still
Except the crickets in the drying grass.
They sang "Farewell, Beloved"
As they saw her pass.

Summer left today. She watched us part.
"Farewell, Beloved" echoes in my heart.

Frances Morlan, Virgil's sister

They loaded as much as they could in the back of the station wagon and put the rest in the bed of Ray's truck with the goats. Arriving in Denny late that afternoon, they stopped by the store for directions to their new home.

"Go around behind the schoolhouse and follow the only road. You come to a bridge. It's ok, you can cross, and follow that road 'til you come to a big, red bulldozer. That's the place," Mrs. Holland told them. "And don't be afraid to drive across the bridge; a D7 Cat made it across all right."

Stopping by the new cement block schoolhouse, they stacked books onto shelves next to the teacher's desk and chair that dominated an alcove off the main classroom. The fluorescent lights gleamed brightly on the freshly waxed floor.

"I'm sure going to miss coming to the Flat," Ray grumbled. "It really did something for me."

"We're going back!" Virgil declared.

"I don't know. It's pretty hard to cut loose from all this." Ray spread his arms and looked around the classroom.

"We're not staying! It's only temporary," Virgil affirmed as he rushed out to get another box of books from the truck.

Ray finished unloading the truck and then left to return home.

"I hope I convinced him," Virgil said.

"He didn't even want to stay long enough to see where we're going to live," Marcy protested.

"Well, Marcy, you know Ray. He never stays long."

They arrived at the bridge, six huge fir logs held together by deeply rusted cables with the cracks between the logs partly filled with dirt and the ends resting in niches blasted out of granite on either side of the New River. The approach was bedrock covered with a thin layer of decomposed granite. Just to one side of the landing, a little gray locked building perched atop a small platform hung above the river. A metal box of the same color as the building was mounted to one of the logs that formed the edge of the bridge.

With brakes locked, the Ford slid down toward the end of the bridge and a small, flat place just wide enough to turn on to the logs. Suspended about 40 feet above the water on each end, the logs sagged to about 35 feet in the middle. It was necessary to drive close to one edge, for the holes in the dirt between the logs would allow a car wheel to fall in. There was no railing or banister on either side.

"She said we could cross, so it must be safe." Virgil eyed the decrepit bridge. "But why don't you and the boys walk over after I drive across?"

"Maybe we'd better walk across before you drive. It doesn't look like it will hold even the dogs," Marcy said.

"Oh, come on! It'll hold." Virgil gestured toward the bridge. "See, there's tracks in the dirt."

"Sure, and I see where someone has fallen through," Marcy said, pointing to a hole where the tire burn marks were still visible on the sides of the crack.

Marcy and the boys waited while Virgil eased across, keeping one set of wheels on the side log and the other set as near the middle as he could. He felt a slow ponderous sway, like a gently swinging hammock, near mid-span. "That was absolutely the longest drive I ever had. Now I know what the storekeeper meant by the way she said it was ok to cross," Virgil said as Marcy and the boys climbed in the car on the other side.

They drove through a forest of madrone, maple, fir and oak for another mile, the soft dampness of the narrow road silencing even the sound of the Ford, and came out in a junk yard. A broken down bulldozer, at one time bright red but now many shades of rust, squatted in front of a shack. Off to the left, another shack seemed to be scrabbling for a foothold on the side of the slope to keep from falling into a refuse pile of old car and truck parts.

The original cabin was built of sawn boards and bats with a hand-split shake roof. An addition had been built on to one side with scraps of siding and gables finished with pieces of corrugated fiberglass and corrugated tin roofing that had lost most of its zinc coating. The roof of the addition was of the same type of corrugated iron, but was more of the odds and ends fashion. A rust-spotted refrigerator leaned against the wall next to the front door as if to hold the shack upright. The front wall of the house sunk several inches down in the dirt, and the rear wall was supported about four feet above the slope on miscellaneous pieces of rock, automobile parts and rotting posts.

Several other buildings in various stages of completion and dilapidation were scattered about the flat and an old school bus body, still in its high visibility yellow, sat in the middle of a stagnant pool of water near a large pile of crushed rock. Below the pile of ore, a rusty conveyor ran into another corrugated tin structure filled with broken pipes and machinery. The wood supply was large bolts of fir about three feet across lying haphazardly all over the space not already filled by pieces of junk. A nostalgia for bygone mining days hung heavy in the air as they surveyed what used to be a big operation.

"I sure hope we can get the summer ranger's cabin. Can you imagine this place on a rainy day? I don't think I could take it," Marcy told Virgil.

The boys spilled out of the car and raced for the bulldozer.

"Let's get out and look in the house," Virgil suggested. "If the inside is anything like the outside, we'll camp out until something else turns up."

"Might as well, since we're here," Marcy agreed.

"That madrone leaning over the cabin is pretty, isn't it?" Virgil asked.

"'Bout the only pretty thing here," Marcy said. "I could plant some flowers along the front."

"Couldn't water too much, the water would go into the house," Virgil said, pointing at the doorstep below ground level.

"The curtains are clean," Marcy said as she peeked in the kitchen window at the sink and a huge gas refrigerator so heavy that the floor sagged beneath it.

Virgil looked through another window just as the afternoon sun shone through into what was a living room-library-bedroom combination. A lumpy mattress covered with a clean blue spread lay on the floor and a low bookshelf made a stunted room divider. After camping out all summer with their mattress leaning against a tree on the trail, the sunshiny room looked comfortable to Virgil. "We can have a ball here, Ma."

It sure looks better inside than the cabin we just left, Marcy thought.

The door opened with a creak to reveal a big oil heater on one wall. In the kitchen stood a wood and gas cook stove with a trash burner and a small table with four chairs adorned the middle of the room. From the window, they saw log buildings across the river bathed in sunshine and horses grazing contentedly in green fields. Their side of the river, on the north side of the mountain, was cold and damp. As Marcy stared across at the sunny scene, she sighed and determined to make the best of it.

Virgil lit the Coleman lantern and Marcy opened a squeaky door at the rear of the cabin to reveal a room with walls covered in old newspapers. Three cots, side by side, lined one wall and Marcy made them up for the boys with blankets they'd brought from Camp Desperation. "I wish we had our bed," Marcy sighed, but it was still leaning against a tree on the hogback where the packers had left it.

Virgil lit the oil stove and Marcy put some water on for hot chocolate and coffee. For now, this was home.

The next morning when she awoke, Marcy squinted in the bright light from a single overhead bulb. Virgil sat hunched over papers trying to get his school schedule in order. "It's the big day, sweetie. Who would have guessed that you'd be teaching school? Boy, Virg, just think how happy you're going to make Mama with a good steady job," Marcy teased.

Virgil didn't answer and didn't look happy at all.

"You boys are not to call me Dodo, Virgil or daddy in school," Virgil said when the boys got up. "You'll call me Mr. Horn. That's what all the other students will be calling me and if I let you call me otherwise, they'll think I'm showing favoritism."

"How 'bout if I call you Mr. Hornytoad?" Kelly grinned.

"No, that won't do," Virgil said.

With Tissy in the lead, Virgil opened the school and started the gas generator for lights and heat. Tissy made herself at home under Virgil's desk and growled at the kids as they arrived.

11 – Settling in at Denny

The flag rose slowly in the late September sun and 10 voices solemnly pledged allegiance in the cool morning air, each with a hand placed somewhere in the vicinity of a heart. Virgil's first days as a new schoolteacher were not unlike the experiences of other new teachers but due to his long absence from formal education, the first weeks were like trying to play a full concert by ear.

All the pamphlets he'd been given on how to teach in a small community didn't seem to deal with the same world Virgil had come to know in 40 years, and when he tried to use the well-meant instructions, they came out as phony as a three dollar bill. The deep insight into human behavior gleaned from psychologists and carefully selected, controlled and slanted experiments at some university had no relevance in Denny, as people who chose to live in a hostile environment, 90 miles from a city at the very end of a very bad road were unlikely to fit assumed standards. Virgil's highly intellectual public relations program flopped.

Also, rather than being a fresh-faced, enthusiastic young graduate of Unknown U. Teacher's College, Virgil was a middle-aged war veteran with an English degree and a couple decades of real-life experience. Behind his back, some of his students described him as a sour-looking scrawny old goat.

No doubt, his fumbling was duly reported at homes each evening, for his official hostess for the week brought a visitor into his alcove one afternoon. He was a small man, and immediately likable, who wore a blue Navy stocking cap in all seasons, and between trips to the veterans hospital, cut wood to supplement his inadequate pension for wounds suffered at Guadalcanal.

Virgil and his guest exchanged stories about their hitches during World War II for a while with frequent interruptions from the students. When Virgil had to change from silent to oral reading, Doug McGimski got up to go. "Whatever happens, Mr. Horn, I'm on your side." He winked and was out the door before a surprised Virgil could ask what he meant.

Virgil's 10 students included Joel who was only five and a half but wanted to go to school with his brothers, so Virgil enrolled him in first grade. With Virgil and all three boys at school, Marcy was alone for the first time since Gaines was born. She called Hucky over and hugged him.

In this period of aloneness, Marcy enjoyed long walks in the woods with Hucky and explored many beautiful areas. On one such outing, she stumbled upon an ancient dump overgrown with trees and shrubs. A charming little hand-blown bottle lay on the ground, awaiting discovery. After finding this treasure, she enthusiastically dug around with a stout stick and unearthed several more old bottles. The neck of an especially fine bottle protruded from the soil beneath some spindly bushes. She dug all afternoon until it was getting time to start dinner. The next day, her leg started itching. *Oh no*, Marcy thought, *I got poison oak in that old dump.*

Over the next few days, Marcy tried every ointment she could find, including what was in the school janitor's closet. Virgil heard of a woman upriver who had a surefire poison oak cure so they drove farther up the Denny road after school. Hacked into the steep canyon walls, the narrow road snaked along the New River. Eventually, they came across some miners and Virgil rolled down his window. "We're looking for Blanche Day," he said.

"What do you want to see her for?" one asked, suspiciously eyeing Virgil in his teacher's clothes.

"My wife has poison oak and Blanche has a cure."

"Are you the school teacher that has a gold claim?"

"Yes, I am."

"Okay then," the man replied, his face softening. "She lives across the river. Just cross that footbridge and go on up the creek a quarter mile."

There were no rails on the footbridge, and after several experimental starts, they managed to find a pace that allowed them to walk across in dignity rather than crawling. Blanche lived with her brother, Charley, and when they arrived, she was canning peaches.

"Soak your leg with manzanita bush tea," Blanche advised. "It works for me every bloomin' time." She continued pouring boiling peaches into several canning jars. "I can't stop to talk now. These peaches are ready to can and if I don't can them, I don't eat."

Although Marcy's poison oak didn't completely heal, it subsided to an occasional itch.

~~~~~~

It was hard for Marcy to adjust to leaving the Flat. Although Denny had beautiful scenery, it just wasn't the Flat on the North Fork. She was busy cleaning the shack when she heard a knock. A small girl in her early twenties with curly blond hair and bespectacled blue eyes stood at the door. "I'm Gay, the Holland's daughter. I heard a rifle shot from this direction. Is everything ok?"

Marcy had never fired the 30-30 because Ray told her it would bruise her shoulder when it kicked back. "Yes, everything's fine. I didn't hear a shot so it didn't come from here," Marcy said.

"Well, it sounded like it," Gay said, glancing at the rifle leaning against the wall. "My dad's deputized and we like to know who fires their rifles. They might need help or something," she explained. "Beings you're new to the area, would you like to hike around and see Denny?"

"Sure," Marcy agreed, not relishing the idea of staying in the house alone and happy to make a friend.

Marcy told Gay about her poison oak and learned that Gay wrote a column for the weekly newspaper about the happenings in Denny. They walked down toward the bridge and passed an open meadow above the road near the old school bus.

"Look at those shaggy manes!" Gay exclaimed. Rushing over, she broke off mushrooms that looked like shaggy white thumbs protruding out of the ground. "These are delicious fried in butter. This is the first time I've found them this tender."

Gay's youthful energy and enthusiasm were contagious and Marcy felt lucky to have found a kindred spirit in such a remote place. They continued to hunt mushrooms and Gay showed Marcy which were edible and which were poisonous. "These are coral mushrooms," Gay said pointing to yellow spikes poking out of decomposed fir needles.

"They sure do look like coral," Marcy agreed as they gently snapped them off and stuffed the mushrooms in plastic bags. Marcy also knew some wild plants and told Gay the names of the ones she recognized as being edible.

When Virgil came home that night, Marcy told him about meeting Gay and all the fun she'd had exploring with her new friend. She also told him about the rifle shot that brought Gay to their door. "Oh boy, small town," he laughed.

Virgil had wondered about the polished log lying across from the store and soon learned that it was the Judges' Bench. While awaiting the thrice-weekly mail delivery, locals gathered there and nothing, especially the new teacher, escaped solemn, beer-tainted judgment. The court deliberated, arranging and rearranging the affairs of the community, and polished the log as they waited for the mail to arrive.

The oldest boy in school felt he had to challenge Virgil and three evenings a week, he reported to the judges. The latest case before the log bench arose because Virgil had rushed the boy out the front door by the seat of the pants and the scruff of the neck and refused to let him come back to school unless he promised to stop creating confusion in the classroom and war on the playground. The next morning before school opened, the boy's father confronted Virgil in the classroom. "Now look, Horn, you let my boy back in. We're tired of flatlanders lordin' it over us. We don't put up with it. We've run out four before like you and we'll do it again. If my boy needs a beatin', then beat him, but don't you go sendin' him home again. The boys up on the log won't stand it."

Standing just inside the door of the schoolhouse during this harangue, Virgil pulled his ear lobe and rubbed his neck, which kept getting hotter and hotter. After a pause, Virgil took a deep breath. "I'm not hired to beat anyone; I'm hired to teach them. Your responsibility is to send your kid to me in a teachable frame of mind. That bunch on the log and you, if you're all so hot and fired up to run this school, are a damned poor example of what your kind of educational principles produces. When your boy settles down, he can come back, not before. I've never run before and I won't start now. Good day to you, Sir," Virgil said and opened the door.

Virgil half expected a bashing but the man turned, strode to his car and roared off, splattering gravel against the school's tinted glass windows. Virgil walked to his desk, grabbed all his mealy-mouthed pamphlets, dumped them in the wastebasket and had no more trouble with the judges that year.

But that other world of professional education kept intruding by law. Mandates kept pouring in to the county superintendent's office from the state, and of course, down to Virgil. As an example: *'Each child shall have at least forty minutes of Physical Education a day.'* Virgil felt his job was to create a desire to read, foster enjoyment for manipulating figures and help the students learn to write clearly. Then, from those basics and through the kids' curiosity, all else would fall in place. All his students walked at least one mile to school each day, chopped wood, did chores and played hard at recess, yet each afternoon they dutifully scrambled around in the dry red dirt among the star thistle after a softball or volleyball. Then, at the end of educational play, they all trudged home to cut wood and haul it in or do any one of the hundreds of things necessary to do when you live in the woods.

Virgil and Marcy soon found that the Denny residents were divided. The majority of those who regularly sat on the big log across from the store and drank while awaiting the mail were miners. If the real property owners drank, they usually did so in the comfort of their own homes. The miners were generally against the authorities and the property owners were overly for them. Marcy often stood in front of the log listening to the inebriated jokes and laughter, glad she had quit all drinking years earlier.

One regular who sat and drank on the log with the other miners was an old gal named Marge. Whenever someone asked where she lived, she'd answer vaguely about hiking a trail and turning left at Old Hanging Rock. She repeated the instructions so often that the name stuck and she was called Old Hanging Rock behind her back.

One day, a scraggly bearded miner staggered to his feet and stood swaying a moment. "In case any of you yahoos don't know, I'm a licensed certified minister," he announced. "Does anyone want to get married?"

"We do," Old Hanging Rock piped up, grabbing her boyfriend, Luke.

With the utmost dignity, the log preacher immediately went through the motions of a wedding ceremony and then pronounced them man and wife. Tears ran down Old Hanging Rock's cheeks while Luke's face turned red. A raucous cheer arose from the log dwellers, and beer cans and whisky bottles clinked and sloshed in toasts.

The toasting would have gone on but the mailman pulled up in his old pickup truck. "Heeere comes Ernie Neal with the mail," one stated dramatically. With much laughter and straining groans, the group fought their way to their feet and drifted toward the post office.

Ernie the mailman was also the local druggist, bottle-gas distributor, school janitor, plumber, garage man, and during the rainy season, miner. He was a big man and was bigger-hearted. Every morning that he made the mail run, he reported in at the schoolhouse for messages to the principal, whose office was at Burnt Ranch School in another valley 19 miles over the mountain. This messenger service was invaluable since the school had no telephone and sending written messages was the only way Virgil could keep in touch with the county superintendent's office.

Emy and Marcella - Hixson Place, Denny 1968

Marcella's friend in Denny

12 - *Life in Denny*

"I have a surprise for you, Ma! I ordered a 'Wife Saver' from Morris Hardware in Weaverville," Virgil announced. The Wife Saver was a gas powered, wringer-type clothes washer. Up to this time, Marcy had been doing all the laundry by hand in a large oval tin tub using a washboard to scrub the clothing clean.

When they got the wringer washer home, Virgil and the boys carried it under a big fir tree that mostly protected it from the elements. Marcy was thrilled and the mountains rang with the song of her new machine. She hung the clothes on a line between two trees but they never dried completely, so she had to bring them inside at night and hang them on clothesline strung by the heater.

Marvin stopped by in mid-October with their mattress and box spring in his truck. He'd carried them up the trail by himself from where Red Cockroff had left them during the failed pack trip. "I have to tell you, when I got back up to Camp Desperation, I caught someone stealing your electric motors. I couldn't believe they'd do that. I made them put everything back," he declared. "I really can't abide thievery."

Virgil asked Marvin to bring some of their equipment to Denny when he had time and then Virgil would take it all to the trailhead on Blue Ridge later. Marvin said that he still had to do the trail at Yolla Bolly but readily agreed and promised he'd pack their belongings already at Blue Ridge down to the Flat before the snow got too deep that winter.

～✦～

"I am not giving up my bed for anyone!" Virgil declared as he read a letter from his brother, Doug. Their cousin, Noah, his wife, Margie, and their twelve-year-old son, David, were bringing Doug to Denny to visit. Virgil and Marcy had been sleeping on the uncomfortable lumpy mattress and were just now enjoying their bed for the first time since they left Camp Desperation.

"I'll see if I can borrow some more blankets from Ernie," Marcy replied. "They can sleep on the air mattresses Ray left us."

When their visitors arrived, they met them at the bridge. The three adults had been drinking since they turned off the highway at Hawkins Bar and were happy as jaybirds. Despite Virgil's warning about the bridge, Noah drove right across. Doug slouched in the back seat with a cigarette dangling between two fingers and a big smile on his face. "Are you still mad at me, Marcy?" he asked, referring to his attempt to quit smoking during his summer visit to the Flat.

Marcy watched the smoke curl around him and smiled. "Nope. Not as long as you have your cigarettes."

Margie, ever glamorous, wore high heels with black lace stockings that looked out of place in the mountains. Noah, a navigator for the Flying Tiger Line airfreight company, was dignified in a tweed cap with his copper hair and mustache. "Could you teach David here?" Noah asked once they'd all settled at the kitchen table. "Margie and I thought a small town like this would get him away from the bad influences of the city."

Virgil looked around the tiny shack and sighed. "Noah, I know how you feel but can you honestly think we can all fit in this shack?"

Noah looked around the small house. "No, I guess not. There really isn't room."

At bedtime, Virgil handed each guest an air mattress and blankets borrowed from Ernie and pointed to the floor. David took his air mattress to the boys' room. "Don't worry about us," Margie said. "The air mattresses will be just fine."

With glasses of whiskey sours sitting beside them, they sat on the floor and blew up the mattresses. The sound of hissing air filled the room. Doug hooted with glee. "Hey, dig these crazy musicians!" he said, which brought laughter all around.

The trio awoke with loud groans the next morning and Margie sat shivering on the floor, her mattress deflated. "Virgil's starting the heater and I'll get the coffee on. You'll be warm in no time," Marcy assured her.

Margie pulled a fluffy sweatshirt from her suitcase and slipped it over her head. "Ah, happiness is a sweat shirt," she cooed.

Virgil and Marcy wanted to show their company the sights in Denny. When they stopped in at the store, Marcy mentioned how cold Doug, Noah and Margie had slept and Mrs. Holland offered them the bunkhouse, which provided sleeping quarters for loggers who came to Denny each summer.

Loud piano music and singing greeted Virgil, Marcy and the boys the next morning when they arrived at the Holland's place to see how their guests had slept. Doug played a piano that had been idle for years and lively tunes rang through the small community. Neighbors opened their windows and doors to enjoy the music as Margie lead the singing. "We slept fine until the bats came out of the loft and started bombarding Margie," Noah laughed. "She got scared that they were going to build nests in her hair."

Shortly after Doug and his group left, a letter arrived from Emy saying that she and Gary were coming to Denny within the week. Marcy was reading *Stalking the Wild Asparagus*, a book on wild edible plants by Euell Gibbons, and decided to surprise them with a complete meal made from wild plants and acorns. She immediately began leaching acorns in several changes of boiling water to flush out the bitter taste and planned to use chopped acorns in place of meat in a spaghetti main dish and as nuts in steamed bread served with wild berry syrup for dessert.

At the scheduled arrival time, Virgil and the boys drove down and met Gary and Emy at the bridge. "Don't drive across the bridge," Virgil cautioned. "It's weak."

"Don't worry," Gary said. "Emy almost had a fit when she saw it."

Emy leaned across Gary from the passenger side of the car. "I'm scared to even walk across it!" she declared.

Virgil and the boys helped them get their luggage across the bridge and they all loaded into the Ford station wagon for the short drive. When they reached the cabin, Gary and Emy both stared in shocked silence for several moments. "This is almost as bad as the shack at the Flat," Emy observed.

"Yes, but I still wish we were there instead of here," Marcy sighed.

Despite the early hour, Marcy served her wild meal by candlelight and each dish was a huge success. In addition to acorns as a meat substitute in the spaghetti, she'd found watercress for a salad and cooked wild mushrooms in butter. The steamed bread, laden with acorns and topped with berry syrup, completed the meal. Afterward, Emy and Marcy relaxed and enjoyed wild spearmint tea.

Anxious to take pictures with his new camera, Gary asked Kelly and Joel to show him around the area. "What do you want to see?" Kelly asked, rubbing one bare foot on top of the other.

Gary's eyes widened as he looked at Kelly's bare feet. "Your feet aren't cold?"

"No, my feet are tough."

Noticing that Joel's feet were also bare, Gary let out a small whistle. "You, too!" he exclaimed. "You mountain men are tougher than me!" Gary looked down the mountain toward the river. "I'd like to see the river. How do we get there?"

"Easy," Kelly said. "There's a road that cuts down to the river from the road to the bridge."

"Well, lead on, soldiers. I want to see the river."

The boys spent their free time exploring and were happy to show Gary around. Once they left the main road, they picked their way through overgrown saplings and soon reached the river. Slightly larger than the North Fork, the New River had the same beautiful clear green water. Upstream, the river flowed from a steep-walled gorge. And hanging ominously above this gorge was the bridge. From the vantage point of the riverbank, it was easy to see that one of the bottom logs was busted and partly hanging down. "Holy Smokes!" Gary exclaimed. "Is that broken log new?"

"No, that's old. I think that log broke when they drove the D7 Cat across," Joel informed him.

Kelly examined the road they'd come down, the river bar on the other side and a road cut up the far bank. "They didn't *ever* drive that cat across the bridge like Mrs. Holland says! They brought it across right here!" he stated, emphatically pointing to his evidence.

"Holy smoke, you're right," Gary said.

Joel's sharp eyes caught the faint outline of tracks crossing the river bar on the far side. Although washed over by high water each winter, the tracks were unmistakable. "Look!" Joel pointed. "You can see where they drove right down to the river's edge!" Joel couldn't wait to tell Virgil about their discovery. Despite repeated assurance from both Gay and Mrs. Holland that the bridge was strong enough for a D7 Caterpillar tractor to cross, Virgil had always been skeptical.

"You're right, Joey," Gary said. "I see it plain as day." But Gary wasn't quite as interested in this discovery as the boys and turned to look back the way they had come. "That was a long walk. Is there a shortcut out of here?" he asked.

"Sure," Joel said. "The house is right up there." He pointed straight up a hill covered in dense brush

"How far?"

"Not very far at all. It's a shortcut," Kelly said, backing up Joel's assertion.

"Let's do it!" Gary agreed.

Right up 'there' was only 500 feet but was on an incline greater than 45 degrees. In excellent shape from months of exploring, the boys forged ahead. Although Gary was in good shape, as well, he was soon puffing hard. "Hold up, you mountain goats," he gasped.

"Hurry up! Hurry up!" Kelly and Joel cried repeatedly while they waited for Gary.

As Gary caught up with them, they moved out through the heavy brush.

"Ouch!" Kelly suddenly cried from the lead.

"What?" Gary shouted, startled by Kelly's shriek.

"Stickers! My feet!"

Fearing a far worse catastrophe than stickers, Gary heaved a sigh of relief. "Well, get out of there and I'll pick them out."

Kelly did a careful step down, followed by a little panicky dance. "Ouch. Ouch! Ouch!! OUCH!!"

"Ok, ok! Stay there. I'll come up and get you." Gary quickly climbed to Kelly, lifted him up and carefully pulled out the stickers. "Ok," he panted, trying to catch his breath. "Let's go back to the road and go home that way."

"But we're almost there!" Joel protested, pointing up the hill where the cabin's roof was faintly visible through the brush.

Gary looked up and down the slope trying to gauge the shorter distance. Finally, he took a deep breath. "Ok," he agreed and carried Kelly up past the raspberry bush and set him on a patch of bare ground. "Can you walk from here?"

"I think so," Kelly said timidly.

From the brush below came a shrill, "Oww!"

"Gol' dang it! Hold on, I'll come get you." Gary turned and thrashed down the slope, catching a vine with his toe. He nearly flew head first down the hill but caught himself just short of where Joel stood pathetically on one foot. Catching Joel under one arm, Gary made his way up to where he'd left Kelly.

Kelly had disappeared but there was some rather loud yelping coming from a great raspberry vine a few feet up the slope. "Holy smokes," Gary wheezed. He put Joel down where Kelly had been and set off to rescue Kelly.

Joel didn't stay where Gary had left him either, but tried to make a transverse path around the raspberry bush, ending his progress on a Himalayan blackberry vine. Well, when a small boy steps on a large blackberry vine, he shrieks. And that's exactly what Joel did.

In a panic, Gary dropped Kelly where he was and leaped down the slope, slipped on a wet patch of grass and slid on his back, coming to rest where he thought he had left Joel. "Where the hell are you?"

"Here, in the blackberry patch," came a meek voice from his left.

"What the heck is a blackberry?"

"Right here," Joel said.

"Oh. Well, next time stay where I leave you. Don't try and walk!"

For the better part of an hour, Gary played a modified game of leapfrog, carrying first one boy and then the other, until they reached the cabin. Gary stepped through the front door trailed by two small limping boys.

"Holy cow!" Emy gasped.

His arms scratched and bleeding, his face and shirt soaked with sweat, Gary wheezed hard. "If these little rascals *ever* say they're taking you on a shortcut, *don't* take it!"

"I'll bet I know who wanted to take you on a shortcut," Marcy laughed, recalling the shortcut the kids took her and Doug on to pick blackberries.

"Joel suggested it," Gary said.

"Ah, I knew it."

The next morning, Emy and Gary were not inside the shack. Marcy walked outside and saw Gary bent at the waist vomiting under a big fir tree. "What in the world is wrong, Gary?" Marcy asked.

"I think you damned-well poisoned me with some weed or mushroom you fed us last night!" he gasped.

"Emy, did you get sick?" Marcy worried.

"No, I feel fine."

Everyone else felt fine, too. Marcy was certain she'd only used edible plants in the meal but still she worried that maybe one leaf of something poisonous had slipped through. Marcy was relieved when Gary started feeling better but he and Emy decided to leave early. "He probably thought I was going to make him another 'wild' meal," Marcy told Virgil. "I hope it wasn't that."

Later, she got a letter from Emy saying that Gary had seen his doctor and found he'd had a reaction to a medication he was taking.

"Let's try and get away to the North Fork this weekend," Virgil suggested one morning in late October.

"Oh yes! I need my Flat to rejuvenate me," Marcy agreed.

On the drive out of Denny, they passed the Dailey Ranch and saw a lone ranch hand in a white western hat bent over fixing a break in the fence next to the road. "That's Shotgun!" Gaines exclaimed.

"No. It can't be," Virgil said.

"I'm sure of it," Gaines insisted.

Virgil stopped the Ford and backed up. The ranch hand looked up and recognition brightened his face. "What are you folks doing here?" he asked, stiffly straightening up. "You're in the wrong drainage, you know."

"Virgil's teaching at the Denny school," Marcy explained.

"Well, I'll be darned! Would never have believed that when I saw you last summer."

"Is this where you live?" Marcy asked.

"Just the winter. I'm maintaining part of the ranch in exchange for wintering some cattle here. I'm glad to hear you'll be here for the winter. I was wondering about you folks," Shotgun said. "This is the Dailey Ranch and it's pretty run down. I'd love to jaw with you but I really can't until I catch up on my work."

"Well, nice seeing you, Shotgun. Stop by our place if you get time," Virgil said and drove away.

Over on the North Fork, Marvin had hauled the loads from Blue Ridge down to the Flat and had everything stacked out in the open near where they were to build their permanent house. Virgil was anxious to make some kind of shelter for their belongings before winter set in and everyone was thrilled to be going home for the weekend.

As they drove up Hobo Gulch Road, the dogwood trees were turning pastel pink, purple and mauve. It was a glorious fall day but their euphoria and enthusiasm suffered a shock when they came to the top of the ridge and found a couple trucks parked at Camp Desperation. "Oh no," Marcy groaned. "I'd forgotten hunting season."

She began throwing food and supplies into her backpack as soon as the station wagon stopped and headed down the trail with Kelly and Hucky close behind. "Hold on!" Virgil yelled as they disappeared from view.

When the trio arrived at the Flat, Marcy found the door of the shack wide open with a man standing beside it. Marcy held tightly to Hucky who had gotten mean from being tied up all the time. When he realized she was one of the owners, the man picked up his rifle and fired into the air to alert his partners.

Virgil, Gaines, Joel and Tissy hurried to catch up, walking as fast as Joel's short legs would go. At Wind Dance Lookout, they stopped dead in their tracks when they heard the shots. Then Virgil began running as well as he could, his loaded backpack nearly jerking him off the trail on the turns while he checked the 30-30 carbine for cartridges. "Empty!" he exclaimed, remembering that he'd unloaded it before they left Denny. "Gaines, do you have the shells for the gun?"

"No, they're in the glove compartment."

"Ok, you guys, stay behind me. We'll sneak over the side and try to get to the cabin without being seen and get some of the cartridges we left there."

They left the trail and as quiet as a bear with his tail singed in a fire, they crashed through the hazel brush and redbud. With each tree Virgil dodged behind, he got madder and madder, and by the time he dodged around the corner of the shack and saw Marcy and Kelly talking to a young man with a rifle in his hands, he was ready to blow.

Sleeping bags and camping equipment littered the cabin. A greasy substance ran down over the little stove legs onto the floor. Worst of all, Virgil's best axe stood in the corner, the cutting edge flattened like a hammer head after being abused while chopping wood on the big rock just outside the door. But the box of cartridges was undisturbed.

Virgil hurriedly jammed three bullets in the carbine, told the two boys to stay inside and with his gun at the ready, went out to rescue Marcy and Kelly. As Virgil approached, he overheard the young man complaining to Marcy. "The other guys said it was all right. They said they'd been told that you folks would be teaching somewhere and wouldn't be around. I didn't know."

"What are you doing here?" Virgil demanded, holding his rifle steady.

"We thought this was an open cabin for anyone to use," the young man gulped.

"What was that shot?" Virgil growled, sitting down on a bolt of wood.

"He was just signaling his buddies to come back," Marcy explained. "There are four more of them."

"Go check the cabin," Virgil told Marcy. "And bring back my axe," he called as she turned to leave. Virgil thought he'd confront the culprits with the evidence, for to him ruining an axe in the wilderness was a heinous crime, more so than breaking and entering. He sat with the carbine across his knees while the young hunter scraped up piles of dirt with first one boot, then the other, to be leveled off and started over.

In a short while, the other hunters arrived from different directions, all looking puzzled. The young hunter explained briefly. "Why, old Ferris said he knowed you folks real good and it was perfectly all right to use this place," a baby face half-hidden in a runty growth of whiskers said. "Why, he come in last year and was here again two weeks ago."

"Oh! So old Ferris, whoever he is, was our visitor last year and again this. Nice of him to give you permission to break the lock on the cabin. Well, that's sour owl shit! Didn't you see the lock on the door and the private property sign there? I suppose he amused himself in the long evenings by reading personal papers since he knew that we'd be in Denny," Virgil roared.

"Honest, Mister, we didn't break that lock. It was already broken. Besides, I thought that people in the wilderness didn't mind someone using their cabin," another hunter spoke up.

"I don't know what grade of wilderness literature you've been reading, or the other wilderness wanderers either for that matter, but our sheriff has made the remark that if we find two-legged bears in our cabins, shoot 'em and kick the remains over the side, no questions asked. You guys must be awfully brave or awfully stupid," Virgil said so insultingly that he half expected to have to use the carbine.

"We've got as much right here as you have," the youngest said, his courage having come up with his reinforcements. "This is our National Forest, and…"

"Yours and 200 million others," Virgil interrupted. "But only outside the corner markers of this place. We pay our taxes on this just as you do outside. Give me your address and I'll come down and build a campfire on your front lawn."

Marcy returned from the shack where she'd seen all her gooseberry syrup jars lying empty on the floor. "And while we're there, we'll see what you have to eat in your kitchen," she said to the men as she handed Virgil his axe. "If you're in the mood, you might come down and help me pick gooseberries. They make awfully good syrup, don't they?"

The men shifted uncomfortably, looking embarrassed. "Well, can we camp by the table under that cedar and fir?"

"No!" Virgil told them flatly. "I want to let my dog loose and I can't guarantee he won't bite you." Virgil examined his axe. "You know, you guys have just enough daylight left to make it up to your trucks."

Quietly and quickly, the men packed up and left.

Virgil turned to Marcy. "What got into you to run down here with Kelly and confront those men? You could have gotten shot!"

"I don't know, Virg, but I wasn't scared," Marcy insisted. "Look at those empty jars. They didn't even leave us one. They ate up all my summer's work!"

"I would've let them camp down here if they hadn't broken the lock," Virgil said. "But considering what they did to my new axe, I'm glad I didn't."

Everything else seemed to be in order so they put away their supplies and went to check the upper garden to see how it had fared without attention and water. They were surprised to find small tomatoes and tiny squash, which they picked to mix with their other food. Virgil built a makeshift shelter for the things Marvin had packed in while Joel and Kelly made roads in the sand with their trucks and Gaines spent time at the river fishing. They were all sad to see the weekend over when they finally started up trail in the early afternoon. "I hate to go back," Marcy sighed. "Good-bye, North Fork," she said, glancing around sadly.

It had been raining nearly every day and the roof on the house leaked badly. Every time Ernie showed up in the evening to clean the school, Virgil asked if there was any word about the Forest Service cabin.

"Nope," Ernie always answered.

"What's holding it up?"

"Just bureaucracy. Just bureaucrats."

"I was so sure about getting that cabin. It's a shame for it to sit there empty and molding when we could use it. It's been almost two months since we filled out the request forms in quadruplicate and not a word!" Virgil fumed.

Finally one evening Ernie rushed in and handed Virgil a letter, water dripping from his rain clothes, his truck standing in the lake that served for a front schoolyard now. "I think that's it," Ernie grinned. "I'll help you move in my truck. Help you get up some wood, too."

Virgil tore open the letter. "Due to the high danger of fire, we regret that permission to use the Denny ranger cabin must be denied. Regional Forester's Office, San Francisco," Virgil read and then handed the letter to Ernie.

"Well, diddly damn darn! If that don't take the fur-lined pot to beat all!" Ernie exclaimed and then stomped back across the lake to his 1939 Ford pick-up.

In mid-November, they received a letter from Virgil's sister, Fran. "We're in for more company," Marcy told Virgil as she read the letter. "She's coming with Leta and Bonnie for Thanksgiving."

"It'll be good to see both of my sisters," Virgil said. "And I'll bet Bonnie has really grown."

Dick and Marietta Holland invited them all for Thanksgiving dinner and also invited Virgil's sisters and Bonnie to sleep at their place. Dick planned to roast the turkey and Marcy mentioned that she'd heard roasting a turkey in a greased paper sack eliminates the need for basting, so he decided to try that method.

When Fran, Leta, and Bonnie arrived the day before Thanksgiving, they stopped at the store for directions and Marietta told them they could stay in the bunkhouse. Further up the road, they took one horrified look at the bridge and decided they wouldn't dare drive across and went straight back to the Holland's. So Dick drove over in his red and white Scout to let the family know their guests had arrived and Virgil drove Marcy and the boys to the Holland's.

Gay took the women to all her secret mushroom haunts and all afternoon they poked under different varieties of trees up and down the mountain. When they finally came back, they had a big bag full of mushrooms that they cleaned and fried. "Wouldn't it be awful if we died from eating these?" Marcy asked.

"What's the difference?" Leta stated in her dry pan way. "You almost killed me anyway, hiking me up and down these mountains!"

When they got to the Holland's the next day for Thanksgiving dinner, Dick met them at the door and scolded Marcy for telling him to use a sack on the turkey. "The darn thing was still raw, so I took the sack off and it's finally cooking."

Several other couples came for dinner, including an old friend of the Holland's from the Bay Area. After dinner, Fran took out her guitar and started singing folk songs. In a clear strong voice, she sang about a young girl who had gotten pregnant out of wedlock. "What will my father say?" Fran crooned.

At that exact moment, Gay opened the door with her two ducks quacking loudly under her arms. Dick turned around in his chair to look at Fran. "That's what her father would say!"

Gay let Bonnie and Gaines ride her horse while everyone else went for a walk and enjoyed the beautiful autumn. The weather was mild that day and the trees, with their many changing colors, were especially gorgeous that year. The next morning, Fran, Leta and Bonnie said their good-byes and headed back to southern California.

Dailey Ranch - Denny

13 - A New Home

The temperature dropped after Thanksgiving and it got bitterly cold in the poorly insulated cabin. In the early morning on a drizzly Saturday, a clanging and rattling came up the road through the forest and Marcy wiped the steamy window and looked out. "It's Ernie. I wonder what he wants."

Ernie walked across the room to the combination trash burner, gas cook stove sighing away on its load of soggy wood, his steps bending the floor down enough that the unwashed breakfast dishes rattled in the sink. "Figured you might be able to use the gas part of this stove if I hooked it up," he said. He glanced into the lean-to bedroom where the patchwork roof seemed to act as a funnel. "What's that doing on the bed?" he asked just as a stream of water poured through the plywood ceiling into a large tub Marcy had put on the bed.

"I can't find the leaks," Virgil said defensively.

"Well, that tears it," Ernie said, moving to the stove and finding the disconnected gas pipes. "Kelly, let's get this hooked up."

All morning long, Ernie and Kelly, who wanted to be a 'fresh water only' plumber at that time, cut, threaded and fit pipe. Kelly, at seven, being small enough to crawl under the shack and work where Ernie couldn't, did much of the work.

Early the next morning, Ernie showed up again and stood warming his hands over the heater. "An old man left for the winter and told me that you guys could use his house if you keep the thieves out. He'll be gone all winter and spring, so it should be all right to move in."

Later that day at the Denny store, Marcy told Marietta about the move. "Do you really want to move there? Ed is not a stable man. He had a botched operation for a head injury during World War I and has a metal plate patching up his skull. And to top it off, he's a mean drunk," Marietta warned.

Since both Gay and Marietta scoffed whenever she mentioned that the bridge wasn't safe to drive over, or even walk across, Marcy disregarded Marietta's warning and they moved the next day. Marcy hated to leave her kitchen window where, on clear cold mornings, she could watch the few cars move along the road across the river toward the schoolhouse or county dump. She also enjoyed the line of sunshine that crawled slowly down the mountains, touching first the smoke from the breakfast fires in the little town, then the brightly painted gas pumps, the one painted house, the brown fields, and finally, the river.

But the sunshine never reached the cabin. It took a week for a sheet to dry. And when it rained, the water rushed down the mountain through the door, or cascaded under the house and down the rocks to the river 200 feet below. It was so wet that much of what they'd hauled over from Camp Desperation and stored in one of the sheds was nearly ruined.

They followed Ernie's truck filled with their frayed cartons up a steep road and pulled to a stop in front of a solid looking, steep-roofed house. No house sealed up in wet weather is very pleasant to smell, but this one stunk. The old man had closed it up without benefit of broom or mop. Underneath the dust and grime, however, lay solid two-inch thick floors, insulated walls, a bedroom and an attic sleeping room for the boys, a fine kitchen with a beautiful wood range, and a living room with a big wood heating stove. The house was unfinished inside, but the windows opened, the doors closed, and a little room on the back porch housed a flush toilet, a wood fired water heater and a stall shower. All they had to do was put in the plumbing.

Marcy opened the door to the old man's bedroom and immediately stepped back, her hand covering her nose and mouth. Glancing around in disgust, she spotted human feces on the floor and bedding. "Oh, Virgil, we can't sleep in there. It's filthy and it stinks!"

"I'll scrub the whole room with bleach," Virgil offered, opening the window. He then pulled out the soiled bedding and proceeded to scour the bed and floor.

In the kitchen, the beautiful blue enameled wood cook stove trimmed with chrome scrolls was twice as big as Marcy's little stove and even had water-heating coils attached to the back with a water storage tank behind. After Virgil finished in the bedroom, he and the boys drove back over the bridge to fetch the rest of their belongings. While they were gone, Marcy got a bucket of hot soapy water with plenty of bleach and scoured the rest of the house. When she finished cleaning, she put fresh sheets on the bed. The stench was gone, the whole house was clean and she was happy they wouldn't have to cross that bridge ever again.

Within a week, the boys and Virgil put in the bathroom plumbing, which was easy to install since, like most houses where there is a scarcity of flat land, the rear of the house stood six feet off the ground on pillars. There was no covering over this section, however, and since it was already December, every frigid breeze blew across the new pipes. Each morning before breakfast, Virgil had to thaw the frozen pipes under the house with a blowtorch or Marcy would have had to clamber down the steep, ice-covered hill to the creek for water to cook and wash dishes. But the cold weather brought Marcy and the boys something that they would never have again – their first white Christmas.

Snow came a week before Christmas and the family ventured into the woods on a frosty morning to find a tree. A fog had come upriver during the night and left inch-long frost crystals on the trees and bushes. The sun glittered on frozen puddles and streams, and icicles hung in giant corrugated columns from the flume that carried water to the schoolhouse. It was difficult to find a tree that wasn't too beautiful to cut, but they searched until the boys' toes were nearly frostbitten. They finally found a damaged tree to cut and hauled it back to the house.

They decorated the tree with hand-blown Christmas bulbs brought from Czechoslovakia by Marcy's mother, including Marcy's childhood favorite, a yellow duck with orange feet. They also strung garlands of wild rosehips and popcorn and finished with tinsel. With a pointed knife, Marcy poked a small hole in the tops and bottoms of raw eggs and blew out the white and yolk. After washing out the inside of the shells, they painted on Santa faces and then pasted on cotton beards, mustaches and hair. Marcy sewed a little red hat with a cotton ball on the end for each Santa and they hung the ornaments on the tree with bent paper clips.

With each armload of wood carried in for the blue enamel stove, Virgil sniffed appreciatively at the aroma of Marcy's fresh cookies and pies. The kids gathered black and white ruffled moss from nearby oaks to put on the stove to perfume the room. Every trip to the post office with the sled brought surprises in big packages to be pulled up the icy drive and put under the tree. For a week, they enjoyed the kind of weather that happens most often in remembrance. There wasn't a single thing missing and the perfection of an idealized White Christmas seemed about to materialize.

It snowed again on Christmas Eve. In addition to the light fluffy snow, they also had some real goose down and a rain of a few tears before midnight, for when Marcy came home from the store with Christmas dinner in Mr. Holland's Jeep chained up on all four wheels, Dick set a cage with two geese on the snow at Virgil's feet. "What are these for? I thought we were going to eat turkey! I don't care for goose dead or alive," Virgil declared.

"Ask the Missus," Mr. Holland said with a smile that turned into a snuffed giggle.

"Couldn't you get a turkey?" Virgil asked.

"Sure. Nice one. Well, good luck." Dick started his Jeep and slid all the way down the driveway to the road.

"What'd Dick mean by 'good luck'? And what are those two geese, Marcy?" Virgil asked when he came in the house.

"We're going to dress them. I met some folks at the store and offered to do that in exchange for the goose down. It sure will be nice in comforters at the Flat next winter! You know how nice those feather beds are!" Marcy exclaimed. "You go out and butcher them while I stuff this turkey. Then, when the kids are in bed, we can dry pick them and save all the down."

"Don't you have to dip them in boiling water?" Virgil asked.

"No, that ruins the down," Marcy replied. "Remember those two I did for Ray that time? It was real easy. Now don't worry, just keep the feathers clean."

Virgil took the geese to the woodshed and did his work. By the time they got ready to pluck them, the geese were so frozen stiff that he broke one wing trying to get them through the door. "Careful! Don't break the skin," Marcy cautioned.

As soon as Virgil laid one goose on the newspapers spread on the table, Marcy grabbed a handful of feathers. She pulled gently, then harder. Then harder. Virgil half expected her to throw it on the floor and put her foot on it to hold it down. Instead, she grinned weakly at Virgil. "Here, I'll show you how," Virgil said and grabbed a pinch of feathers. Skin and all came loose. "What's wrong? I thought they were easy," he complained.

"The ones I did for Ray were easy, and Mama said that they used to pick down off live geese in Czechoslovakia."

They worked out how to get the feathers loose, one at a time. By one o'clock in the morning, they had one goose plucked clean. "I don't care if goose down is a thousand dollars a pound, we dip this other one in hot water," Virgil yawned. "I can't even open my hands."

"Ok," Marcy agreed. "But I don't think it will work."

They heated water in a big tub and dipped the goose but found that boiling-hot feathers were even harder to pull out. The water wouldn't penetrate and it took hours of repeated heating and dipping before they had a plucked goose with a few patches of partially cooked skin.

After plucking the geese, Marcy spread the down to dry on baking sheets that she put in the warm oven. Virgil and Marcy placed the boys' presents under the tree, including a big Flexible Flyer sled. Marcy asked Virgil to fill the stockings with candy and goodies while she made the dough for kolachi, a traditional Czech pastry that her mother used to make every Christmas. Earlier in the week, she'd bought a bag of tangerines that the boys had been eating for days. Virgil put candy in the bottom of each stocking and then filled them to the top with tangerines.

In the early morning, Virgil and Marcy heard the boys creeping down the stairs to see what Santa had left. When Virgil and Marcy got out of bed, all the boys were snickering. "Look! Santa stole our own tangerines to fill our stockings!"

"Hmm," Virgil grinned as he lit the blue stove.

Marcy put a kettle of water on to boil and the boys opened their presents under the tree. For breakfast, Marcy served kolachi and steaming mugs of hot chocolate. It was a quiet time, not like the noisy Christmases they'd spent with relatives in southern California. They were glad that coffee had replaced beer and whiskey, and that this Christmas morning was celebrated with love, not hangovers.

Later that morning when they delivered the geese, they apologized for breaking the skin. "Oh, that's all right. We're going to skin them anyway."

"You mean we were so careful for no reason?" Marcy grumbled on the way home. "If we'd known they were going to skin the geese anyway, it wouldn't have taken half the night to pluck them!"

A couple days after Christmas, a big package containing three small toboggans arrived for the boys from Ray and Sue. In a note she'd enclosed in the package, Sue wrote they'd had another son and named him David. The big Flexible Flyer sled didn't work too well on the fluffy snow but the toboggans worked fine.

They had several hard freezes after that. The morning Virgil discovered the Ford had frozen and broke her block, the toilet stool, washbasin and shower were standing away from the walls and off the floor on columns of ice. But compared to the Hixson's place, they had bettered their sunshine quota by two hours; the sun came up over the mountain at eleven and set again at one.

Ernie told Virgil he could put liquid steel in the engine block crack to seal it. The next day, Virgil walked down to the Holland's store and bought some. It worked well so the following morning he planned to move the car down to the cleared road by the school. As he turned the Ford around, transmission fluid sprayed all over the snow, staining it blood red, and Marcy thought he'd run over one of the dogs. He drove off slipping and sliding down to the schoolhouse.

When another storm came, the road filled with snow and became impassable. The boys and their friends gleefully packed it down to make a toboggan run. The snow stayed a long time and they slid their toboggans every day with Hucky running after them.

Around the beginning of February, the snow-eating winds came creeping up their driveway and started melting the boys' toboggan run. The air held a promise of spring when a letter arrived from Ed. He was coming back to Denny but said not to worry about moving out; he'd be staying with friends. It was only fair to replenish his firewood supply so they all went into the forest on the weekend to cut wood. Virgil also paid Doug McGimski to bring another cord. "I'll have it stacked in after you move out," Doug promised.

One morning in mid-February, a truck with bare root fruit saplings sticking out the back crunched through the last vestige of the boys' toboggan track and rolled to a stop on the narrow driveway. Ed stepped out of the truck, followed by Doug McGimski. "We don't want to intrude, but Doug and I want to plant some roses out for the Missus," Ed called to Marcy, walking through a mud puddle with his heavy rubber boots as he headed for the house. "I have to find that shovel," he muttered and cocked his head to one side like a listening rooster as he came through the door.

"I expect you'll find it in the tool shed," Marcy said, dismayed at the blobs of mud he'd tracked across the floor.

Ed ignored her and roamed through the house. After he'd thoroughly examined the downstairs, he headed up the stairs, leaving a trail of mud there, too. When he finally came back downstairs, Marcy followed him outside. Doug had unloaded all the trees and roses and was just reaching in the truck bed to get two shovels. Marcy glared at Ed but he didn't seem to notice.

After they planted the roses and some spindly plum trees, Ed cocked his head again in that peculiar manner. "When will Virgil be home?" he asked.

"About four o'clock," Marcy answered.

"So, when will you be moving out?" he continued.

"Was it to be June or earlier?" Marcy asked. "School will be out in June and that's when we planned to move, just like we agreed."

The next two days while Virgil and the boys were at school, Ed came over and stomped into the house with his muddy boots, checking to see if his things were still there. When he finished with the house, he'd look in the woodshed. "You better fill it up before you move," he warned, wagging his head back and forth.

"Virgil already paid Doug to add another cord after we leave."

"It looks like a lot of sticks in there. Not good wood," he snarled.

"Did you hear me? Doug is going to get more. And Virgil fixed all your plumbing when it froze up this winter. He even fixed that sink by the hallway that was broken before we came."

Ed's wife came with him the next day. "You sure have kept the house clean and fixed it up real nice," she told Marcy. "Ed wants me to move back here but he's an alcoholic, and a mean drunk, to boot!" she confided. "He's anxious to get back to his bottle but I won't live with him unless he stays sober. The sorry fact is he's never sober when he stays in Denny."

When Ernie delivered the mail to the school the next morning, he told Virgil that they'd better move back across the river. "When that guy drinks, he's cuckoo, and right now he's telling everyone that he wants to move back into his house. I never would have suggested his place had I known he was coming back so early. I must also warn you that without provocation, he hit his best drinking buddy with a bottle and almost killed him. That poor miner is still wondering what he said to make Ed that mad." Ernie shook his head. "Virg, some of these old boys don't like anyone who carries a college handle on them."

"Well, some of the college trained minds I've encountered, I don't particularly like either," Virgil answered.

Ernie laughed heartily but then sobered. "One time I heard shooting in the bushes. When I drove up, I saw Ed had his rifle and he told me that two people in a car had threatened him. I looked to where he was pointing and there was nothing there. I really would watch him. I think that tin plate in his head is squeezing his brain."

The following Monday morning, just after Marcy had washed all the clothes and hung them on the line, Ed showed up and decided to burn his dump, which filled a long miner's ditch and hadn't been burned in years. The wet garbage sent up billows of smoke that penetrated the clothes and the house.

Virgil usually walked the mile home from school, but that evening, he could have won a medal for the uphill sprint. The house was hidden in dense clouds of black and greasy-yellow smoke, and the front porch was filled with the cardboard boxes he knew so well. "Where's the fire?" Virgil yelled when he saw Marcy come out the door with another box.

"There's no fire. He's trying to burn that hundred-year-old, waterlogged trash pile. He could have told me what he intended to do and I wouldn't have washed this week. He even burned up my compost heap!" Marcy sobbed. "I think the old coot is trying to smoke us out. Well, I've had it! He's ruined my wash, ruined the floors and ruined my days. If you still have the key to the shack across the river, we'll move out."

By dark that same evening, they had many of their badly worn boxes back across the river and Marcy cooked supper on the butane stove

Ernie had fixed that she hadn't gotten to use before. "It may leak when it rains and it might fall off the cliff, but I have my beautiful view and no one can walk through this house because it's got only one door," Marcy said. "You can just dump the rest of my pans and the bed clothes in a pile by the bridge," Marcy told Virgil. "I'll backpack them over tomorrow when you and the boys are in school."

The next morning as Gay walked her dogs, she saw Marcy loading her pack. "Are you still afraid of that bridge?" Gay grinned.

"Darn right I am! Look at that big crack!" Marcy pointed toward the middle of the bridge.

Although Marcy didn't want to live across that bridge again, she was more afraid of Ed, and before the end of the week, they were settled back into the Hixson cabin, bridge and all.

Playing in the snow

14 – Springtime in Denny

"Virg, let's take the boys and go to the Flat this weekend," Marcy suggested before school on their second morning back in the Hixson cabin.

"Well, it's still pretty early but I suppose the snow might be melted off enough by now that we could try to make it in," Virgil agreed.

On Saturday morning, they got up early and headed for the North Fork. The few patches of snow they encountered didn't stop them but when they circled around a bend in the road, they came to a halt. It had seemed years since their move to Denny, but hardly long enough for a 50-foot tree to grow where the road had been. There was no sign of the road. Grass, trees and shrubs grew as if there had never been a road at all. No cracks or fissures were visible as they got out and walked on over the new ridge.

They explored for a quarter mile and finally came to a spot where the road began again. From this side, they could see far up and down the mountain. The whole ridge had slid gently down about 200 feet, carrying the road, trees and shrubs toward the river at the bottom. "Marcy, can we make it if we have to pack all the way into the Flat from here?" Virgil asked. "Suppose they just leave the road as it is?"

"Sure we can!" the boys declared in unison.

"Sure we can," Marcy seconded.

They doubted the road would be rebuilt. After a depressing trip back to Denny, the resident ranger there assured them that it would reopen…eventually.

The early March springlike weather was irresistible so Marcy decided to do some exploring with Hucky while Virgil and the boys were in school. Ernie had mentioned a mine above their place called the Birdie M and Marcy set off to find it. She hiked a little way up the road and saw bear tracks in the mud. Hucky took off barking, so she decided to wait until the weekend when Virgil and the boys could be with her.

On the weekend, they all hiked up to the Birdie M. A two-story building tacked over with hand-hewn shakes sat in a meadow surrounded by the usual apple trees just starting to bloom. It was a nice place, but when they sat under the trees, a forlorn feeling came across Virgil and Marcy. "Someone had a good thing going here at one time. I wonder why it's abandoned now," Marcy mused.

"I don't know, but it does have a sad feeling," Virgil agreed.

When they later met Bill Meadows, an 81-year-old miner who had built the house, he explained the history of the place. As a young man, he had built the house for his young bride and they lived there happily for a year, until his in-laws came to visit. Her parents chastised them both so much that the girl got discouraged and left. Brokenhearted, Bill moved out and built a smaller cabin on the other side of the river, remaining a bachelor the rest of his life.

Marcy had heard about two other old bachelor miners who both lived on a flat along the river and knew a lot about mining. She had time on her hands so decided to go visit them.

Zack, in his 80s, was born in Norway and ended up in America by way of a sailor's job. The sea and he didn't agree and he moved deep into the mountains where he would never have to suffer seasickness or even see the sea again. Zack owned no car and religiously walked the two miles to the store, packing all his groceries in a World War I infantryman pack. The one thing he kept from his seaman days was a shipshape neatness to his cabin.

As Marcy visited with Zack, they heard a knock at the door. He got up, eyes twinkling. He opened the door and there stood Joel, Kelly and a little girl. "Hello!" he said. "Come in."

Once the kids assembled, Zack straightened the black stocking cap on his crew cut head, stooped his large frame down and addressed Joel. "Do you want a do...?"

"Dog biscuit!"

Zack straightened and took a honey can from a neatly arranged shelf and a box of graham crackers from a cupboard. He selected a spoon from a drawer and scooped a mixture of honey and wheat germ onto a graham cracker. Joel happily accepted the treat.

"Say thank you," Marcy instructed.

"Thank you, Zack," Joel said between bites.

Zack turned to Kelly. "And you want?"

"Monkey biscuit."

Zack went through the same steps but this time he cut a slice of banana and placed it on the wheat germ. Lastly, he turned to the girl, the oldest of the trio. "And you want a Gorilla biscuit," he stated, not leaving the hanging question as he had with the younger kids.

"Yuck! No!" she laughed. "Monkey biscuit."

Zack made another monkey biscuit and handed it to her. The children thanked Zack and ran out the door. "How about you, Marcy? Monkey biscuit?"

Marcy shook her head. "No thanks, Zack."

"Gorilla biscuit?"

Again, she turned him down. Zack smiled and proceeded to make a monkey biscuit but added a slice of onion and sharp cheddar cheese to the top. "Gorilla biscuit," he grinned, sitting down and taking a bite.

A paper bag sat on the table with a length of parachute cord tied to it. "What's that?" Marcy asked.

"A little bag I hang up in the trees for the kids to figure out how to get down."

He finished the Gorilla biscuit. "I hear you have a claim you want to mine. I've been mining for over 40 years and have seen most of the miners work the river," he told Marcy. "But I stuck to the high banks and was the only one that ever had any money. You tell your husband the high banks are the best places to mine." He got up and went to an alphabetically arranged bookshelf that included titles such as the Mining Engineer's Handbook and selected a midsized volume. "This is a good book for people starting out," Zack said, handing it to her. "Have your husband read this."

"Thank you," Marcy said and rose to her feet.

Zack accompanied her to the front steps. Some 30 yards away stood a shack with a swaybacked roof, a large collection of old rusting mining equipment in the back and a beautiful rose garden in the front. "Who lives there?" Marcy asked.

"Tom. Tom Murphy," Zack said.

"The roses are beautiful. Where are your roses, Zack?"

The earth tone tweed of Zack's sweater swelled with indignity. "Humph," he grunted and reached inside the door, lifted out a pitcher of water and poured it around a single, giant purple thistle growing next to the door.

Marcy turned away and smiled. She had apparently touched on a point of contention between the two.

"If you don't get torn to shreds by those *rose* bushes, you ought to stop by and meet Tom," Zack said.

Marcy thanked Zack for his time and advice and then strolled over and knocked at the other cabin. A small, elderly man answered the door and his heavy eyebrows rose in surprise. He invited Marcy in after she introduced herself. Unlike Zack's neat house, Tom's place had little trails in the dust-covered floors leading to all the pertinent places in the small single-room cabin.

One chair was all the seating available and Tom held it for Marcy to sit down, then he took a seat on the rumpled bed. Marcy glanced up worriedly at the sagging rafters. "What do you do when there's a heavy snow?" she asked.

"I hire someone to shovel it off," Tom explained softly, smiling at her concern.

"Do you mine?" Marcy asked. "My husband and I bought a mine over on the North Fork."

"I used to. Used to a lot, but I had a bad heart attack. Now I raise roses."

"Oh, I saw your roses! You even have a Sterling rose out there!"

Tom's shy demeanor gave way to excitement. "You know roses?"

"Some. I'm an avid gardener."

"Do you want to see my roses?" Tom asked, getting up from the bed.

"Sure. Please show me."

For the next half hour, Tom showed Marcy each and every rose, explaining their development and history.

From farther up the flat, Hanging Rock's husband, Luke, saw Marcy and came down to join the duo. "I heard Virgil's looking for another rig and have a Willys Jeep station wagon I'll sell him for $500," Luke said.

When Marcy told Virgil about the Jeep after school, he found Luke right way and bought it on the spot.

It seemed strange to be so homesick for a place they barely knew after only six months away, but homesick they all were. So much so that after school and on weekends, they started exploring trails, thinking they might be able to hike the 17 miles over Limestone Ridge to the North Fork.

Just above Denny, Beartooth Mountain forms part of a ridge that ties into Limestone Ridge. A steep Jeep road led to the Beartooth Mine, which had supplied the ore for the milling operation at the Hixson place. So this was a route they decided to explore.

Past the Birdie M, the road climbed steeply through a heavy fir forest, ending at the wreckage that was the Beartooth Mine. Broken down sheds and rusting machinery lay about near the partly caved in mine portal. "Let's go in the tunnel!" Joel exclaimed.

"Oh no, we don't!" Virgil ordered. "Stay away from that portal."

The boys had to content themselves exploring the machinery on the surface while Virgil and Marcy scouted around for a route to the Limestone Ridge summit.

"Look at this!" Joel cried to his brothers. A heavy-built weathered wooden box that had been padlocked closed at one time disgorged a cascade of brown sticks across the grass of the early spring, some crushed and bleached from a number of years exposed to the elements. Others were frosty with white crystals forming on the paper exterior. Joel walked onto the cascade and peered into the darkness of the wooden box. "There are thousands of them in here!"

"That's dynamite!" Kelly said.

"Really? I wonder if Meester Horn will let us take some home." Joel said.

Gaines stood to the side, looking uncertain about the discovery as Joel went off to find Mr. Virgil Horn.

"I don't think so," Gaines called after him.

Joel came back excitedly leading Virgil and Marcy. "Here it is!" he exclaimed. "Can we take some home?"

"NO! Stay the hell away from that!" Virgil ordered.

Unwilling to admit defeat, Joel tried once more. "Just *one*?"

"I said no and I mean no."

Joel's shoulders sagged in defeat and he ran off to find something else of interest.

Shortly, Kelly found something he couldn't live without, brightly colored dynamite wire strung about and in discarded little balls around the entire mining area. He eagerly started gathering it up. "Can he have that?" Gaines asked Virgil uncertainly.

Virgil looked at the discarded wire. "I don't see why not."

That was all Gaines needed to hear and he started helping Kelly gather the wire. They had quite a bundle and Kelly was wrapping the last section of wire up between his thumb and left elbow. The end of the wire slid down the cut of the road bank and attached to the end was a corroded copper cylinder the size of a pencil stub.

"Yikes! That's a blasting cap!" he yelled, jerking the coil of wire from his forearm and tossing it away.

"You have enough," Virgil said, suddenly wary of the safety practices of the long ago powder monkey.

The snowcapped crest of Limestone Ridge was still miles away beyond a twisted, complicated maze of green ridges. "We'll never get to the North Fork from here," Virgil announced. "It's time to head back."

They'd left the Jeep station wagon at the bottom of the badly eroded mountain road leading to the Beartooth Mine. On the way down the steepest section high above the Birdie M, Marcy slipped and fell on the loose shale. She sat up grimacing and holding her ankle. After several moments, she got up and tried to hobble on using a stick Gaines had found for her. Virgil could see that walking was painful and wanted to spare her the agony.

"Sit down and stay put," Virgil instructed. "Kelly, you stay here with Ma. Gaines and Joel, you both come with me to get the car."

"I hope he can make it," Marcy told Kelly.

"It's not that far. I think it will crawl up this old road," Kelly assured her.

Sitting incapacitated on a mountain called Beartooth got Marcy thinking about the name and suddenly she got up and started hobbling down the road. Kelly tried to stop her. "Ma! Stay there! You're going to hurt your ankle worse!"

Marcy grimaced. "Are you kidding? I'm not staying here like a wounded animal for a bear or cougar to finish off!"

The roar of an engine and the popping sound of spinning tires came up the road. A flash of green and tan showed through the trees and the Jeep appeared, backing up the hill. "Why is he backing up?" Marcy exclaimed.

"He'd never be able to turn around on this road," Kelly stated.

"I told you to stay put!" Virgil snapped after he stopped the Jeep station wagon and got out. "You've undoubtedly forgotten the trouble your mom went through after she walked on her sprained ankle." But when he saw the tears in Marcy's eyes, he gently eased her into the Jeep.

Their exploring was finished but Marcy could never sit still, even with an ankle four times its normal size and nowhere near a natural color, unless the natural color is that of a half-ripe eggplant. Virgil made a cold frame from salvaged windows and Marcy hobbled or crawled to make flowerbeds and tend to her plants in the makeshift greenhouse.

As spring arrived, little green shoots came up between the rocks all around the cabin. Marcy crawled through these to care for her plants and soon her injured leg turned red and swelled more and more. When the blisters formed, they knew the cabin sat in a huge patch of poison oak. After seven days, the rash should have healed somewhat but had turned an uglier red instead. She soaked it and swabbed her irritated skin with alcohol but it just got worse. She didn't say much about it during the week while Virgil taught school, but by Friday her leg was so swollen and painful that she told Virgil she'd better go to the doctor. So when school got out, they went to the emergency room at Trinity Hospital in Weaverville.

"Is this poison oak?" Dr. Polka asked.

"It started out looking just like it and then it got infected," Marcy explained.

"Well, it's a good thing you came in today because much longer and you would have lost your leg," he said as he treated the infection.

Two week later, Virgil left Marcy sitting on a chair with her ankle propped up and headed for the post office, taking the boys and their school buddy, Chayne, with him. "Stay in the Jeep, boys," Virgil said when he got out to check the mail.

Kelly fiddled with the rectangular 47.5-volt battery he'd gotten for Christmas from Uncle Dick. He'd inserted two sections of dynamite wire into the terminals and was threatening to zap Chayne who was teasing him relentlessly about Lorie Bryant, a girl at school. Angry voices outside the station wagon drew their attention and the boys saw Virgil, Ed and Doug McGimski in a tight cluster.

"You burned all my wood," Ed snarled at Virgil, his head jerking and strands of pure white hair flying. "You owe me 50 bucks!"

"I did not, Ed," Virgil said calmly, but a tinge of red showed above his collar.

"You did too!"

"Hold on, guys," Doug said, attempting to be the peacemaker. "I think there's a big misunderstanding here."

"I paid Doug here 50 bucks to cut another cord of wood for you," Virgil explained.

"Bullshit! That woodshed is half-empty. You're a liar!" Ed roared.

"Hold on. Hold on! HOLD ON!" Doug said, holding up his hands. "That's just it. I've already hauled three loads and I'm going to haul four more."

"He is a liar!" Ed burst out, completely ignoring Doug's explanation. "You'd better God damned well get me that 50 bucks!" His eyes bulged and his head jerked madly.

By this time, the red had crept up from Virgil's neck and his face was awash with color. Without taking his eyes off Ed, he unbuttoned the cuffs of his school dress shirt and slowly began to roll up his sleeves. The boys stared intently out the car window, mesmerized by the unfolding drama.

"What if he jumps your dad?" Chayne whispered.

"We're getting in it!" Gaines stated.

"Well, I'm with you," Chayne declared. "We need a plan. Each of us will go for one of Ed's arms and legs. Whose side do you think Doug will join?"

"Mr. Horn's," Gaines said.

Kelly busily stripped the insulation back on the wires sticking out of his battery. "I'm hooking this up to the metal plate in that SOB's head!" he fumed.

"Yeah! That crazy bastard needs some more shock treatments!" Chayne exclaimed.

Virgil's sleeves were now rolled above his elbows. "Ed, don't call me a liar again."

Doug stepped between the two men and faced Virgil. He shook his head slightly and then very subtly nodded toward the Jeep. Then Doug turned and placed his hand on Ed's chest. "I'll take care of this, Ed."

Virgil took the hint, climbed in the station wagon and drove away, leaving Doug talking earnestly with Ed.

"You were going to punch him, weren't you, Meester Horn?" Joel said.

"It wasn't the farthest thing from my mind," Virgil admitted with a grin.

Once they got home, the boys couldn't wait to tell Marcy about the near-scuffle. "Ma! Virg and old Ed almost got into a fistfight in front of the store!" Gaines gasped. "Ed accused Virg of not filling his woodshed. Virg asked him if Doug had brought any wood for it. Ed started hollering and swearing at Virg, calling him a liar. Virg really got mad and started rolling up his sleeves. We were all going to pounce on Ed if he laid a hand on our dad!"

"Kelly had the battery Uncle Dick gave him and was going to hook it to the metal plate on Ed's head!" Joel interrupted. "Doug McGimski told Ed that he hadn't got all the wood in yet but would do it right away. So that stopped the fight."

~~~~~

With more and more new leaves forming, Marcy had to have her hands in the dirt. By the end of April, she could walk on her ankle a bit and was more than ready to get down to the Flat and spade up spots for the plants she'd started, and Virgil was anxious to see what the winter had done to the equipment under their makeshift covers. "Virg, my ankle is much better. I think if I wrap it tight, I can walk down to the Flat this weekend. We need to get out of here."

"Are you sure?" Virgil asked. "Maybe someone has run a bulldozer over the slide. We can leave about three o'clock Saturday morning and then we won't be so late coming back if we can't get in."

They got to the slide a little after sunrise. A slight fog hung softly above where the road had been. More of the mountain had slid down and uncovered a spring that gushed out on the soft red mud. Marcy got out and looked at the slide. "Help me lace this boot tighter. I'm walking on in," she said.

"But it's over six miles," Virgil protested. "You can't walk that far on that ankle."

"I can and I will," Marcy insisted. "I'm not going to let these plants die. Let's hike!" she whooped and they all laughed and sang 'We are the happy wanderers.'

Last fall's crop of pinecones and needles littered the road. Although Virgil had implicitly believed the vehement charges against man ruining the environment, in that long six-mile walk to the Flat, one winter had done a fine job of obliterating all human tracks in the wilderness.

At the upper garden, the shelter Virgil had made from aluminum irrigation pipes and a discarded swimming pool cover had collapsed from the weight of the snow. Virgil's well-built white antique toolbox was full of water and rusty tools, while the kitchen stove under the oak had been pushed over and the garden hoses stored in the oven had been pulled out, bitten into sections about three feet long and scattered around the upper garden area.

The Flat was in better shape. The boards nailed over the windows were still on but the lock had been shot off the door, which was full of lead slugs, and their *No Trespassing* sign was plastered with broken eggs. "Someone came in after those guys last fall," Marcy said.

"Do you suppose those guys came back after we left and wrecked the place?" Virgil asked as he apprehensively opened the shack door.

Whoever had been around had contented themselves with spiteful, petty vandalism and nothing inside had been bothered. Marcy got a folding chair, sat down and gave a sigh of relaxation she'd been holding back all winter. "Home," she sighed.

Marcy got her plants into the ground at the upper garden. As always, the stay ended too soon but summer wasn't far off and when they got back to Denny, they felt refreshed.

Outhouse at the Flat

Boys' little shop at the Flat

15 - North Fork's Second Summer

"Summer at last!" Gaines shouted with the enthusiasm exhibited by most 10-year-olds once the school year finally ends. "Now we can go home to the Flat!"

They'd heard the slide had been bulldozed and Hobo Gulch Road was clear, so Virgil and Gaines decided to move some of the equipment and household goods to the Blue Ridge trailhead. It was two miles further to the Flat from Blue Ridge but Shotgun's new trail didn't have the steep hogback. They picked up the equipment that Virgil had stored at Ernie's place when they moved back to the Hixson's and headed for Blue Ridge with their sleeping bags, planning to sleep there. The next morning they drove back to Denny. For two days, Virgil and Gaines hauled equipment and household goods from Hixson's place to the Blue Ridge trailhead.

On a trip back to Denny, they met a packer doing some trips there who told Virgil that he'd move their things down on three mules for $80. Feeling that they'd imposed on Marvin enough, Virgil agreed and told the new packer to bring down just the heaviest things and they'd pack down the lighter items themselves.

A few days after school ended the whole family left Denny, got to Camp Desperation, which they renamed Desperation Point, and hiked down to the Flat. They pulled all the boards off the cabin windows and opened the door to air it out, deeply inhaling the sweet scent of azaleas and other wildflowers that grew abundantly around the Flat. It was good to be home!

The next day, Virgil went to town to get groceries, taking Gaines and Kelly with him. On the way back up Hobo Gulch Road, a loud bang erupted from the rear of the Jeep. Virgil pulled over in a wide spot just past Blue Bottle Spring, a little spring where someone had left a blue plastic Clorox bottle to use as a funnel, and Kelly and Gaines were out of the Jeep before it came to a complete stop. "There's oil leaking from the rear end!" Kelly cried.

Virgil set the emergency brake and got out. Peering at the oil leak it was obvious to Virgil that an internal component had been shoved out through the housing. Virgil opened the rear lift gate and got out a hammer. "What are you going to do?" Gaines asked.

"I'm going to pound that sheet metal back in and stop the oil leak. Otherwise, we're going to lose all the gear oil," Virgil explained. After moments of pounding, Virgil said, "I think I got it stopped."

"What came loose in there?" Kelly asked.

"It was a bolt, most likely, from the ring gear housing," Virgil told him.

"Will it still work?"

"We're going to find out. Get in."

The Jeep moved forward but an ominous rhythmic groaning came from the rear end. "Oh...I don't like the sound of that!" Kelly said, his eyes big.

"I don't either. The only thing we can do for now is engage the front wheel drive and disconnect the rear driveshaft. We're going to have to get another rear differential or a new vehicle," Virgil said as he crawled under the Jeep with his ever-present wrenches.

While Virgil was gone to town, the packer and three mules showed up at the Flat. Only two mules were loaded and the packer rode the third. He unloaded two small gasoline engines, a few pillows, sheets and other light items from the two mules. "Where's the rest?" Marcy asked.

"Dropped a heavy box over the side of the trail and sure as hell wasn't going down to get it," he growled.

"Eighty dollars for this tiny load?" Marcy cried.

"Yeah, but it would've been bigger if I hadn't dropped that box," he mumbled as he jumped back on his mule and rode off up Shotgun's trail with his pack string.

Virgil got home from town a short while later. He pulled out his pipe and slowly lit it while he surveyed the small load. After hearing what the packer had said, his eyes narrowed into two blue slits. "So, he said that, huh? Well, I'm going after him," Virgil said softly, rubbing the back of his neck.

"Virg, that's a four-mile hike and you just got back from town. Wait until he comes back," Marcy pleaded.

"No! I don't want him bringing any more down." Without another word, Virgil took off up the trail. In no time at all, he was back.

"Wow! That was fast! What happened?" Marcy asked.

"I just told him not to come back. I'll wait until Marvin's free before I jump in and hire a cheat like that again. The mules are costing us so much we would have been better off hiring a helicopter for our heavy stuff."

One of the first things they did that summer was disassemble the cook stove at the upper garden, slide it to the Flat on a stone boat and reassemble it in the summer kitchen area next to the heavy table under the cedar, fir and oak trees. Virgil and the boys also brought the redwood table and benches down from the upper garden and Virgil built a little table for Marcy's Coleman stove. At first, Marcy had some trouble learning how to operate the wood cook stove but finally managed to bake a lemon meringue pie successfully. After that, she spent time making homemade noodles and lasagna from semolina flour.

To keep perishables cool in the summer heat, Virgil made a swamp cooler. The swamp cooler consisted of a box made from old wooden fruit crates covered with burlap and chicken wire, with a door on the front side. A section of garden hose fed an aluminum trough with holes drilled in it to allow the water to drip down over the burlap. On legs made from wooden poles, the cooler sat about four feet off the ground in the shade where it could catch any available breeze and it kept their food cool but not cold.

They also replaced Butt Cutter. Using salvaged split rail fence boards and wire from Dan Raymond's cattle operation, they built an outhouse between four saplings growing in an approximate square. With no door, the outhouse had a beautiful view of the river.

One morning Virgil watched Marcy haul buckets of water from the river to do dishes. "I think I'll try to get water up here for your dishes and flowers," he said and set off to survey the river. Shortly, he returned to the kitchen area and poured himself another cup of coffee. "I found a place where I think a wooden platform can be built. Now I just need to find an empty one-pound coffee can to use to dig holes for my poles."

Marcy handed him a coffee can and he headed toward the river. "Wait for me!" Marcy shouted, reaching for another empty coffee can. "I'll help you scoop out the sand."

The cans were just the right size to scoop sand and dirt out from between the big rocks. Virgil handed her a bucket. "Put the sand in here and we'll pan it out later to see if it has gold."

Virgil peeled two poles and they put them solidly into the holes they'd dug. Afterwards, Marcy brought two gold pans down so they could check the sand. "Look at the gold!" Marcy yelled as she panned down to the black sand.

"Come look at mine," Virgil answered, admiring the gleam of fine gold in his pan. "This will be a good place to start mining when I get the sluice boxes done."

"Virg, if you don't need me anymore, I think I'll go back to the kitchen and make some gooseberry syrup."

"That's fine. I'm going up to the orchard site to check on some bigger logs for reinforcement."

Awhile later, Marcy heard Virgil shouting and looked up from her boiling syrup. "Look out! Look out!" Virgil yelled.

Virgil had tied a big log behind their small walk-behind, brakeless, two-wheeled David Bradley tractor without realizing the grade down to the kitchen area was so steep. The aftermarket jury-rigged clutch used a lever to tilt the engine forward and apply tension against the drive belt, which worked fine on flat land but proved uncontrollable on a slope.

Unfortunately, that wasn't the only modification on the tractor. Instead of having the engine kill button on the handlebars, it was located on the front of the engine and was impossible for the driver to reach. On the steep downgrade, the weight of the engine sitting in the front of the tractor caused the engine to tilt forward and engage the belt friction clutch and no amount of lever pulling would disengage it.

Tethered to the tractor by a chain, the log pitched and rolled as Virgil jumped back and forth across the whipping log while he fought to steer the tractor. He swooped towards Marcy, raking everything in his path with the big log. "Gaines! Gaines! Shut her off! Shut her off!" Virgil yelled but was moving too fast for Gaines to push the kill button located on the front of the engine.

Marcy grabbed the lit Coleman stove with her syrup in hand and ran just as he reached the kitchen area, shearing everything in his path. The big log bumped the table legs, causing all Marcy's jars to roll off, and the Coleman stove table went over with her wooden spoon and jelly-testing cup. Gaines came running but didn't get there before Virgil crashed into a huge boulder by the river and stopped. Virgil walked up to the kitchen and retrieved his beret from the sand. "Sorry about that, Ma. Do you need some help?"

"Why did you drag it through the kitchen? Why didn't you stop?" Marcy shrieked, still holding the lit Colman stove with the boiling syrup.

"I couldn't stop. The clutch wouldn't disengage," he explained.

"Well, you gave me a good scare," she gasped.

It took a day or two to repair the damage but by the end of the week, Virgil had a pier, a piston pump and a gasoline engine ready to start pumping. Virgil had read about the incompressibility of water in books but it was a real forceful demonstration when the engine started and the water reached the pump. Something had to give and that something was the bolts that held the engine down. The engine jumped up in the air and fell to the pier, still running, and started over the edge into the river before Virgil could shut it off. "See? I teach my boys by actual demonstration," he told Marcy. "They'll know how incompressible water is now. Won't you, boys?"

"Yes, Mr. Horn," they answered in their best schoolroom voices, but their grins gave them away.

"Maybe it's a good thing I have to start summer school tomorrow to study for my teaching credential," Virgil said. "It'll keep me out of trouble 'til we go back to school this fall."

A huge whitened ponderosa pine leaned over the apple orchard. Virgil knew the dead giant was a danger and made plans early one morning to fell it. Gaines and Kelly helped by cutting an escape path through the tangled hazel brush. The trunk of this monster was blackened and nearly half eaten away by a long ago fire. What remained was tough and heavily resinous. Virgil didn't think he could swing its fall away from the orchard so considered the orchard a calculated casualty.

The chainsaw malfunctioned repeatedly and it took hours to cut through the trunk. Marcy and Joel watched the towering tree from the outdoor kitchen, but the hazel brush and a stand of sapling firs obscured the bottom of the trunk where Virgil sweated over the cursed saw. Virgil had never cut a standing snag of this size and Marcy worried the top would break away as it started to move and would fall on him, a "widow maker" as Shotgun had called it in a logging story some months back. The sound of the saw cutting out and sputtering intermittently through the hours only added to her fears.

Sometime in the late morning, the saw stopped once again. From behind the brush and small firs rang out the sound of a steel maul driving home steel wedges. Tissy and Hucky raised a ruckus. The top began to move. The trunk swung through the air and disappeared into the trees in a billowing cloud of dust. The crash reverberated around the canyon walls as Joel and Marcy ran toward the drifting dust cloud. "Are you all right?" Marcy screamed with each half-dozen steps.

"Of course. Quit screaming," Virgil hollered from within the dust cloud.

When they reached the site, Gaines and Kelly stood triumphantly on the giant trunk as Virgil smoked his pipe nearby, looking somewhat shaken but happy. "Virg missed the orchard! It only took out a couple branches," Kelly crowed.

Gaines spoke more calmly. "Virg had a terrible time with the chainsaw not running right. We hope the saw will hold together long enough for Virg and me to mill out enough lumber from this tree to make a shed for a jewelry shop and the gas generator. We also want to mill that deadfall down by the kitchen area."

For the next couple of weeks with Gaines on the helper handle on the Alaskan chainsaw mill, Virgil cut studs, rafters and roofing boards for a small jewelry shop. In a little hollow below the old apple orchard up next to the steep bank left by a long ago mining operation, Virgil leveled a spot and set a 10-by-10 foot square pattern of flat stones for a shop foundation.

In this square area, Virgil and Kelly reassembled the Hobart World War II generator and got it running. With the electric power to run his old skill saw, Virgil dimensioned the new lumber and started erecting the shop, which even included an attic space for storage. On the outside, Virgil covered the studs with tarpaper to create walls and covered the three window openings with clear plastic. Virgil stood back and admired the little shed, the first one on the Flat. "This will have to do for this year. Next year I'll cut siding and get glass windows for it."

The rest of the summer passed like a surreal dream for Marcy. The fear she felt when it took Virgil so long to cut down the big snag combined with the stress of the past winter in Denny created growing anxiety. "I don't want to go back to Denny, Virg," she sobbed. "I want to stay here. I'm scared of that bridge and that horrid old man, Ed. I'm tired of all the petty gossip and bickering there!"

Hoping to distract and comfort her, Gaines frequently rubbed her feet and tried to show her the wind blowing through the cherry trees, but she hardly noticed and her tension and nerves lingered. In the evenings, after working in the little jewelry shop, Virgil read to Marcy and the boys. When the waning days of summer finally passed and the hum of September came, Marcy heard acorns falling and listened to birds rustling in the dry grass. She finally snapped out of her lethargy and was ready to go back to Denny.

Although taken a few years later, this picture shows the shop pretty much as it looked the summer of 1968.

Virgil and boys assembling the Hobart power plant

Tissy and Hucky

*Virgil, Hucky and Tissy in front of the
David Bradley tractor at the summer kitchen area.*

16 - Denny Again

A wonderful surprise greeted them when they returned to Denny. A new mobile home sat next to the schoolhouse that the district principal had convinced the school board to buy. Now they wouldn't have to drive across the precarious bridge and they were on the sunny side of the mountain. Shrouded in a hanging fog, Hixson's cabin stood dark and foreboding across the river.

The fully furnished trailer had a large kitchen, a living room, two bedrooms and a bathroom with a flush toilet. Two full-sized beds for the boys filled one bedroom and the other bedroom had a bed for Virgil and Marcy. After touring their brand new home, Marcy felt funny about bringing her old blackened cast iron kettles and pans into the sparkling new kitchen.

That school year, Virgil had all new students that came from families traveling with a logging operation from West Virginia, and with the new school year came new state mandates. A new program for rural schools mandated that first through eighth grade schools offer a kindergarten/preschool section for children as young as three years old but funding wasn't available for an extra teacher. The mothers were thrilled to bring their three year olds for Virgil to babysit even though some cried for their mothers throughout the day. Virgil asked Marcy to read to them, which she did frequently.

One evening, two local men who usually warmed the log across from the store came to visit and Virgil casually mentioned he didn't think kids that young should be in school. The next morning, the mothers stormed the schoolhouse and insisted that he keep their kids at school.

It was like a three-ring circus having the little kids in with the older ones. The little ones tired during the school day and needed naps, and Virgil learned to change diapers on some of the smaller ones, as well. Out of desperation, he cut flames out of cardboard, painted them red and yellow and tacked them on a chair that he called the Hot Seat. "From now on, any student, young or old, who won't behave has to sit in the Hot Seat," he declared. The kids were terrified of it and Marcy speculated they probably thought it was the electric chair.

On Halloween morning, Virgil got up early to go unplug the school's leaf-filled waterline and Hucky and Tissy went with him. Virgil had his back turned when the logging company's crummy came roaring down the road and Hucky leaped to attack it. The faithful little dog was struck. Although it wasn't his fault, the driver was very sorry but nothing could be done for Hucky. Virgil brought the little broken body home and they were all grief stricken. Gaines, who had named him Huckleberry, cried for the first time since he was a baby.

It was a somber Halloween. Gaines put on his costume but he was a cheerless clown. Marcy dressed Kelly as an Indian with war paint and black wool hair. Joel said he wanted to be a Toilet Paper Man. "Why?" Virgil asked.

"Like Kevin was in southern California," Joel answered.

So Virgil made a mask that looked like a toilet paper roll and painted eyes on it with two little Johnny mops for eyebrows and Marcy fashioned a coat from a white sheet. Joel wore the costume but he was angry. "I wanted to be a mummy with toilet paper wrapped around me, not a poop man!" Joel later explained.

Looking out the kitchen window after Virgil and the boys left for school the next morning, Marcy saw Ed standing in the road staring down at the schoolhouse. Marcy remembered Ernie's warning about Ed and it brought shivers down her spine to see him watch the school. Every day he came and stared. "I don't know what he might do," Marcy worried.

"I'll keep an eye on him," Virgil promised.

"Well, I will, too."

On a cold day with a dusting of snow on the ground, they drove to see Shotgun at the Dailey Ranch where he was wintering again. When they arrived, Shotgun was standing by his 1954 Willys Jeep Overland pickup and Virgil told him the story of the loose bolt being thrown from the rear differential on the Jeep station wagon. "Hmmm," Shotgun said, scratching his chin. "I'm trying to sell this truck. It has a dusted out V8 but the rest is sound. You could drop the engine from your Jeep into this one and have a good vehicle."

Virgil and the boys spent a good part of the morning going over the pickup, until Virgil finally agreed to buy the Jeep. When the deal was made, Shotgun walked them around the ranch and showed off his cattle. A rock-lined aqueduct carried water to the ranch and Shotgun explained that the man who owned the ranch had been a strong believer in hard work. His sons hauled most of the rocks and if he found any of them shirking, he would dump them in the cold river.

They sampled all the apples, some of which grew on trees nearly 70 years old from seeds and grafting stock brought over from Germany. The red and green apples were good but the best of all were the white ones. The Alaskan apple was white on the outside and pink on the inside with superb texture and juice. Shotgun let them pick three boxes of Alaskan apples. When they got home, they carefully wrapped each apple in newspaper to preserve freshness while in cold storage under the trailer. As Joel reached for a second apple, Marcy stopped him. "No. We're only going to eat one apple a day each," Marcy told them. "These are special treats so we want them to last."

For the next few days, the boys each helped themselves to an apple. Then one morning Joel happily went outside to get his daily apple but immediately ran back in, close to tears. "Something ate every apple!" he wailed.

"No way!" Gaines exclaimed as they all leaped up from the breakfast table and crowded out the front door.

Scattered all over the front yard were newspaper wrappers mixed with bits and pieces of white and pink apple and drooling drips of applesauce slobber. "Oh my God!" Marcy gasped as her hands flew to her mouth.

"Rudy's horses," Virgil stated.

"I'm going to shoot them!" Gaines cried.

"Can't," Virgil said. "It's open range so it's our responsibility to have kept the apples away from the horses."

"I hate them horses!" Joel sobbed and slammed the door on his way back into the trailer.

Virgil parked both Jeeps under a large overhanging madrone branch and he and the boys set to work exchanging the engines. All went well until they were lowering the Kaiser Super Hurricane flathead straight six into the new Jeep pickup. The engine mounts had been changed to accommodate the non-standard V8 and needed to be cut out and re-welded in the right position. Now what?

When Ernie showed up, Virgil asked about a solution. Ernie leaned his belly on the fender of the Jeep pickup and examined the mounts. "You're gonna need an acetylene torch and a portable arc welder.

Frank Smart is a mechanic working with the J. R. Stanley logging outfit. I'll talk to him and see if he'll stop by and do it for you."

The next evening, Frank showed up and agreed to do the work. Over the next few days, after working all day at the logging operation tearing one of the engines down on a huge TC12 Euclid dozer, Frank would do what work he could on the engine mounts before dark. When he finished the job, Frank would only accept $10 total for the hours he spent working on the mounts.

When the engine swap was completed, they also swapped the overdrive out of the old Jeep station wagon, but it created a problem in that the rear driveshaft from neither vehicle fit. Like the Jeep station wagon, they'd have to use front wheel drive only until they could get to a machine shop and resize the driveline. But once again they had a running vehicle.

One day after Joel and Kelly were out of school, an official government truck with a Bureau of Reclamation emblem on the door drove past the school and down the road toward the bridge that led to the Hixson cabin. The boys followed the truck to see if it would fall through the bridge before they could alert the driver to the danger. They found the truck parked just short of the bridge and two men opening up the little shed just over the bank from the road. Kelly had been curious about the contents of this shed and led Joel down near the men. "Don't cross that bridge," Joel advised.

"Don't worry. I'm not getting on, under or near that bridge!" one of the men laughed.

Peering into the small building, the boys saw it was full of water flow and temperature recording instruments powered by a number of different batteries. The men removed the batteries from the building and replaced them with new batteries from the back of the truck. "Can I have the old batteries?" Kelly asked one of the men.

"I don't care but it's not my call. We'll have to ask Bob. He's the boss," he said. "Hey, Bob! Can the kid have the old batteries?"

Bob thought a moment. "You can give him the seven and a half volt batteries and the number six batteries, but not the 90-volt battery."

"Why not the 90-volt?" Kelly asked, looking wistfully at the two-foot tall battery.

"Because it's not like your toy car battery or a flashlight battery. This one can shock you bad," Bob explained.

"No it can't," Kelly replied. "The internal impedance is too high and it can't deliver but a few milliamps."

The men exchanged surprised glances and Bob laughed. "Give the kid the battery!"

"Let's go get that old wooden wagon from the dump that Gaines was using to haul the milk jars from the Holland's," Kelly said.

They returned with the wagon and struggled to load all the batteries. It was a lot of weight for two little boys to move, slipping and sliding on the decomposed granite, but they fought the wagon to the top of the hill behind the school and then to the front yard of the trailer. "Man, a 90-volt battery! That's twice as powerful as your 47-and-a-half-volt battery," Joel commented, impressed.

Kelly intently studied the terminal of the battery, which was an internal socket type. "How do I get power out of that?" he muttered. Running over to a pile of discarded lumber left over from the trailer support construction, Kelly pulled a pair of needle nosed pliers from his pocket and proceeded to work a nail out of a piece of two-by-four. With the nail in hand, he headed back to the battery.

Joel's eyes widened when he realized Kelly's intent, remembering the story Marcy told about the horrors when Kelly had stuck a bobby pin into a house socket at age two. Although nothing had happened to Kelly, Marcy had summoned Grandpa Padilla to avert potential electrocution. "That's 90 volts!" Joel cried. "That's only a little less than the plugs in the house!"

"It won't shock me because I'm only sticking the nail in one terminal at a time. There's too much resistance to complete a circuit," Kelly reassured Joel.

But there was a lot less resistance than Kelly thought and one poke with the nail was all it took to prove it. Kelly let out a mighty yelp, jumped back and sat down hard. As Kelly stared reproachfully at the battery, Joel teased him about his earlier confidence. Kelly finally got up, made a wide berth around the 90-volt battery and retrieved one of the seven-and-a-half-volt batteries, then sat down cross-legged on the ground and started attaching dynamite wire to the terminals. They heard the school door open and Gaines approached them in his school clothes. "Where did you get all these batteries?" Gaines asked.

"Kelly begged them off those guys working on the water measuring station," Joel told him. "That big one is 90 volts and it shocked Kelly."

"No," Gaines said skeptically.

"Yeah! He was sticking a nail in the terminal!" Joel insisted.

"Couldn't have." Gaines saw the nail and picked it up.

Kelly spoke up. "It did."

"The resistance is too high. It caaaaannnt.....!" Gaines screamed, flying back on his butt.

"I told you!" Joel laughed.

What neither boy knew at that time was that the cardboard bottom of the battery had soaked up water from the concrete shed floor, which made quite a low resistance circuit through their bodies.

Gaines got up and looked at Kelly connecting a number of batteries together. "What are you doing?"

"I'm going to hook it up to the headlight I got from the old Ford," Kelly said.

"Hey, why don't we put a headlight on the wagon?" Gaines suggested.

Kelly scrambled up from his cross-legged position and ran to where one of the empty wooden apple crates sat tipped over under the trailer. He carried it back tossing out a few remaining crumpled newspaper wrappings. "What are you going to do with that?" Gaines asked.

Kelly was silent as he turned the crate upside down and placed it on the wagon. "I see," Gaines said and started helping him. Joel stood around and tried to be a part of the project but besides fetching a few things, he was too young to be of much help. But soon the wagon was fully wired with a control panel with indicator lights screwed into the side of the crate and the old Ford's headlight pointing from the front. A two-setting switch retrieved from the dump switched on the lights.

That night in the pitch dark, they took their contraption up on the main road above the school and pulled the wagonload of batteries back and forth over an eighth-mile stretch. When they saw headlights coming down the one-lane road, they'd run to a wide spot and turn on the wagon lights, and then as soon as the car passed, they'd turn the lights back off. Some drivers screeched to a halt after they passed, but to save batteries, the boys didn't turn the wagon lights back on again. The next day, tales of strange lights began circulating around the log.

The boys named their wagon Nightlight and had great fun for about two weeks until Mr. Holland saw them one evening. "You boys need to stop playing with that wagon on the road after dark. You might cause an accident," he said.

Every Friday, the principal sent a film with Ernie for Virgil to show in class. One morning, Virgil asked Ernie if he could pick up a film about mining. The next Friday, Ernie arrived with an old film about a miner from their district and he and Marcy decided to watch it, too.

The miner in the film introduced himself as Amos Decker and they realized he was a friend of Red Barnes. He was young and handsome with the roughness of a working miner. Ernie commented that he was a true miner from the looks of his callused hands. Amos demonstrated how to pan for gold, and every pan contained fine gold and small nuggets. "Man, that guy sure knows how to find gold!" Ernie said.

"We'll have to look him up or ask Red where he lives," Virgil said. "He can give us some pointers."

After seeing the film, Virgil and Marcy were very anxious to start their own mining operations at the Flat.

Christmas was two weeks away and they had the tree up and decorated in anticipation of an early celebration with Fran and Ivan. Snow fell like fine grain, sticking in their hair, eyebrows and lashes, and later turning into flakes as big as silver dollars. It was early in the season for so much snow and they worried that it would get too deep for Fran and Ivan to come as planned. To their delight, Fran and Ivan finally arrived with their car filled with presents from relatives down south.

"We had to stop several times to shovel out," Ivan said. "She said I was silly to bring the shovel but was darn happy I did when we got stuck," he continued, pointing to Fran.

"I had no idea that it was going to snow!" Fran protested.

During their short visit, Fran and Ivan filled them in on all the news from back home. They also told Virgil that his mom was happy he was teaching school and finally using his education instead of living down in 'that hole'.

After Fran and Ivan left, the Christmas tree shed its needles at an ever-increasing rate in the hot trailer and Marcy decided to take it down early beings they'd already celebrated Christmas. The boys helped Marcy take the tree down and then they threw it into the dump.

A few days later, Marcy ran into the forest ranger's wife, Helen, at the store while waiting for the mail. "Yesterday I was at the dump and it isn't even Christmas yet but someone has thrown out their Christmas tree!" Helen exclaimed. "Who do you suppose would do a thing like that?"

"I did," Marcy laughed.

Helen looked at her curiously. "Well, that tree was shedding all over the place so we threw it out," Marcy explained.

One early January evening Shotgun came over for dinner. "I'm going to butcher a steer this weekend. Are you guys interested in buying half?" he asked.

"You bet! Gaines and I will be over to help you Saturday," Virgil said.

When Gaines came home after helping Shotgun and Virgil butcher the steer, he showed Marcy his shirt. "This is my cow-belly-juice shirt, Ma."

"What do you mean?"

"When Shotgun stuck the knife in the cow's belly, the juice squirted all over my shirt," Gaines replied.

"Oh Gaines! Go take a bath!"

"Ok, Ma. But don't throw it away. I'm proud of that shirt!" Gaines replied.

They went back to pick up the meat the next morning and Shotgun led them to a shed made of galvanized sheet metal. In the snow, coyote tracks circled the shed. Shotgun opened the door to reveal two steer halves hanging on hooks. "I took the chainsaw and cut right down the spinal cord," Shotgun grinned.

"I guess that works," Virgil said as he and Shotgun carried one side to the Jeep.

On the way back to the trailer, they stopped for some groceries and a drunken miner they knew stumbled out of the store. They planned to drop off the steer's head at the dump on the way home and it was lying in the truck bed with the side of beef. "What do you think of this buck, Charlie?" Marcy laughed.

"My gosh," Charlie slurred, shaking his head. "That's the biggest buck I ever saw."

They made pastrami out of a good portion of the beef. Virgil made a wire screen to put above the gas heater in the trailer and Marcy jerked some beef to take to the Flat. Marcy also dried ripe persimmons that Shotgun had given her, which turned out to be sweet, chewy and delicious.

With their Christmas money, the boys bought a small welder to run from regular house current that they'd seen in a J.C. Whitney catalog and thought would be great fun. As part of the geography class, Virgil had them track how it was probably coming across the country from Michigan. This built great anticipation and when the Buzz Box arc welder arrived, Virgil plugged it in to the school's outlet and began a class on welding although he'd never welded before.

The Buzz Box had a short, however, and not only did it not work, the shorted windings in the transformer blew the regulator on the 10-kilowatt propane generator that powered the schoolhouse. The next day Virgil conducted school in the dark while Ernie Neill worked to fix the problem. They sent the Buzz Box back for a replacement, which arrived with the particleboard housing cracked, but at least it worked.

By late January that second year in Denny, the snow was piled deep on all the mountains and deeper in the shadowed valleys. All the families with schoolchildren had moved out to warmer places before Christmas but were expected back in the spring. For long, dreary months, the school doors opened and Gaines, Kelly and Joel came in, did their work and left at the end of the day.

Time and conscience dragged on into a late sodden spring and by the time the oyster mushrooms had bloomed and gone on their logs, the judges had bloomed on their log, as well. From the man who was on his side, Virgil heard that everyone was afraid the school would open in the fall just for them. It was bad enough the school district had bought a mobile home to house the teacher and his family, but to pay a teacher to teach only his own three kids was too much.

They needn't have worried. Virgil and Marcy had been away from their Flat too long, so when the time for signing contracts came around, Virgil declined. Since he was now a credentialed teacher, he could legally teach the boys at home with no cost to the taxpayers and no hassle over transportation either. Also, in reading the California Education Code, he'd discovered that anyone living more than a mile from the nearest publicly travelled road was exempt from compulsory school attendance.

Early in the spring, Tissy had another litter. One of the puppies was bigger than the rest and shoved all the others out of the way. Tissy never liked the aggressive pup much but they decided they needed a big dog for protection after losing Hucky. Marcy named him Bully.

*Christmas 1968 - Gaines holding the pop-gun
that later became a form for the concrete
intake of the water power penstock.*

*Joel and the new Flexible Flyer sled,
which was a favorite over the years and
was extremely useful hauling wood during
times when the North Fork froze over.*

17 - Easter Bunny Trail

Bully was a strong two-month-old puppy when Easter vacation came. As there were no other parents to consult, Virgil had prudently shaved one week off Christmas vacation and added it to Easter. They were going to the Flat expecting to get in a big garden in preparation for their first winter there.

Denny still had snow and Marcy worried that they'd have to walk the whole way in. She also worried that the frozen snow wouldn't hold their weight. Gaines declared he'd show her that walking on the snow crust wouldn't be a problem. He ran up on a big mound of snow and hollered for them to watch as he stamped his feet a couple times. Suddenly, the crust broke and he vanished. Slowly a red face appeared, followed by a wet, snow-covered boy. The mound was a huge snow-covered manzanita bush.

Kelly and Joel teased Gaines and Virgil chuckled as he got out the chainsaw. Marcy packed all the backpacks with bedclothes and food. She even had several dozen boiled eggs and coloring for the Easter egg hunt. Even though Gaines was two weeks shy of eleven, Kelly nine and Joel seven, they still liked to hunt eggs.

When the town folks heard they were going to the Flat, they shook their heads in disbelief. But the whole family squeezed into the cab of the Jeep pickup with baby Bully on Kelly's lap and Tissy in the chicken cage in back and took off for the North Fork. When they passed Helena and came to the Hobo Gulch turnoff, the road was clear. As they drove higher, small drifts of snow appeared in the protected draws and gradually became deeper and longer. Virgil had to stop and put the chains on the front tires of the Jeep after coming to a rather deep drift.

With every snowdrift Virgil drove the Jeep through, they cheered. Passing the section of the road that had slid in the winter before, the snow drifts vanished. "Hey, Mr. Horn, how come the snow is getting less now?" Kelly asked.

"I think this is one long section of south-facing road," Virgil replied.

The road made a long sweeping left turn to the north and then to the west. Ahead of them lay a long section of mostly bare, steep mountainside on which the road cut a narrow shelf. It faced directly north and a solid mass of snow covered the road. Farther ahead, they could see that snow slides had completely buried a section of the road. "That's all she wrote," Virgil stated, parking the Jeep to the side of the road. "We walk from here."

Gaines opened the cage for Tissy and she jumped out and baby Bully charged after her. They all hoisted their packs and at 10 o'clock in the morning on the last day of March, they started trudging up the snow-filled road with their heavy loads.

The snow had melted little on this side of the mountain and as they went up, it got deeper. The snow was frozen along this section of north exposed road but as they passed it, the sun appeared over the shielding ridge and weakened the crust. The first mile or two was fairly easy but as the sun came through the trees and warmed the air, Virgil and Marcy started breaking through. Exacerbated by the massive loads on their backs, their legs plunged through to their hips in some places.

Eventually even Gaines started breaking through. It was grueling work and they still had five miles to walk. "If it was completely soft, it wouldn't be so bad," Marcy gasped, taking a break. "It's when you get almost all your weight on the crust and then it gives way that makes it so exhausting."

By noon, they'd gone halfway and Bully was still jumping in and out of the deep tracks they left in the snow. The younger boys, who had gone ahead so jauntily, began breaking through the crust too. Their boots were constantly full of water and their feet began to burn. They could climb the road for a hundred feet, then rest, another hundred feet, then rest. "Don't worry, the west side will be free of snow," Virgil kept saying.

Virgil had found a stick by then and was pushing himself along. When Marcy fell through, she couldn't lift her feet out of the hole until Gaines threw off his pack and dug the granular snow away from her boots. Joel's face was twisted but he wouldn't cry and Kelly slogged along in silence. By two o'clock, they had reached the *Road Ends* sign and could only go 50 feet before resting. "Only a half mile to the top," Virgil panted. "It'll be easier on the other side."

Still able to walk atop the crust most of the time, Kelly and Joel moved slowly ahead. Walking up the Hazley road, Joel and Kelly were barely visible and Marcy started worrying about bears. She shouted for them to stop and wait. When she caught up, she found Joel curled under a drifted-over dogwood scrub, sobbing. "Now you stopped my momentum and I can't go any further!" he wailed.

"Joel, we're almost to Desperation Point," Marcy consoled. "Can you make it? We'll stop and get warm and eat," she urged as Joel nodded with tear-streaked cheeks and struggled to his feet. "I didn't want you too far ahead in case there are bears," she added.

They made it to the top at four o'clock. The sun was about an hour above the mountains to the west and the snowfields gleamed gold in the sunshine, blue in the shadows. Bunches of yellow-green trees stood separately on each side of the snow. They were surprised to see a section of dry ground at Desperation Point, where one edge was free of snow. They helped each other take off their packs and Marcy unpacked the big goose down quilt and laid it on the ground. Kelly and Gaines snapped dry branches off the trees and found some dry pinecones. Virgil found flat stones and retrieved some mesh wire he had up in a tree and soon had a fire going. They changed into dry socks and hung the wet ones on sticks all around the fire.

Out of Marcy's pack came a bag of tea, dry milk and sugar. She filled her little coffeepot with snow and soon they all had hot tea in beer cans left lying around by the hunters the previous fall. Marcy handed out sandwiches made from her hearty homemade buns filled with thick pastrami. For dessert, they had chocolate chip cookies. Joel fell asleep on the quilt and after a while, Kelly and Gaines joined him.

"Should we try to go down tonight or just stay here?" Marcy asked. "The boys have their feather beds."

"I think we'd freeze this high up. Besides, I'm sure the trail will be free of snow lower down. See how much is off this side?" Virgil answered.

After resting a while, the boys jumped up with the miraculous recuperation of youth. "Well, we'd better get going," Marcy said. "Joel, can you make it on down?"

"Sure I can," Joel smiled brightly, his previous misery forgotten.

"There'll be dry pants in the cabin but these dry socks will help until we get there," Marcy said.

It was all they could do to bend to pick up their packs but with grunts, groans and moans, they skirted what snowdrifts they could and started down the mountain. The only indication of the trail anywhere along the side of the mountain was an occasional outcrop of rock or a familiar tree, and on the shady sides, the snow was beginning to freeze again. Where the sun had shone the longest, they fell through to their waists. And on the frozen slopes, they dug their toes in and sidled across holding onto branches, their knees braced against the slope.

Below Clutch Tree, a great tangle of branches from a toppled live oak mostly blocked the way. It took five minutes to fight through this and Bully just gave up. He slid into a pocket under a branch and sat up, looked at the bank of snow in front of him and hung his head, refusing to heed the family's calls of encouragement. He stayed under Bully's Tree until Marcy finally went back, picked him up and added him to her load. This lasted a couple hundred yards until she passed him to Joel.

Because of his greedy eating habits, the puppy was chunky. Bully was too tired to put any effort into staying atop Joel's knapsack and let himself sag far off to one side. Joel was soon staggering sideways with the unbalanced load. "Ma! I can't carry him! He keeps sagging off one side."

Marcy stopped and lifted Bully off Joel's pack. "Can you carry him awhile?" she asked Virgil.

"Put him on top of my pack," Virgil sighed.

Bully rode there for a short while until he let himself slide off the side, rolling down the length of the chainsaw bar protruding from the pack before falling in a heap on the snow. "Come on Bully, Bully!" Gaines called.

Bully stood up and followed after Gaines, apparently deciding that they'd kill him with kindness if he didn't make it under his own power. By this time, Marcy could go no further with her heavy load. Virgil stashed the chainsaw, gas and oil behind a big tree, and split Marcy's load and took half, adding it to the tools and rifle he carried. "Marcy, for Pete's sake, how much are you carrying? This is almost as much as I was carrying!"

The sun had gone down and heavy clouds were piling up in the west. If it snowed now and turned cold, Virgil doubted they could get out in time to finish the school year. A purple haze settled in the gulches, making it difficult to distinguish objects like trees or rocks that they were beginning to find hard to avoid.

By the time they passed Wind Dance Lookout, it was dark. Below Wind Dance Lookout lay deep unbroken drifts and the dropping temperature formed a crust that supported them all. Partway down Marcy suddenly broke the crust and fell through to her hips in the snow. Exhausted, she struggled to get the leverage to free her legs. "I can't pull my legs out! I'm going to freeze to death!" she sobbed. Seeing his mother crying put Gaines in a panic and he frantically dug the hard corn snow away from her legs with his bare fingers until she managed to climb free.

Virgil had been breaking the path most of the day and was so tired that he had to drag his right foot behind him. Marcy, being close to her home now, forged ahead with new energy. At the drip line of each evergreen tree, the snow stopped and they slid four or five feet to bare ground and then crawled back up on the snow on the other side. When they came to the normally dry gulch below Cathedral Way, they could hear water roaring between steep banks of snow. A full moon began to break through a layer of altocumulus clouds and in some of the lighter moments, they found their way across where the water wasn't too deep to be waded. With their boots still full of water, Marcy, Kelly and Joel headed for home while Gaines and Virgil floundered along behind.

Gaines was lagging, worn out from taking his pack off and on all day to dig Marcy free, and when Virgil looked behind him, Gaines was no longer in sight as a dark spot on the snow. Virgil kept looking and listening for Gaines until he shifted his weight and fell down the steep bank of snow under a cedar tree. Virgil was still trying to get enough energy to crawl out and go back for Gaines when Marcy returned. "Give me the keys to the cabin," Marcy said as she helped Virgil remove his pack.

"Gaines is back there somewhere; I got to go get him."

"Don't you know where you are?" she asked.

"Sure! Stuck in a hole around the cedar by the apple trees," Virgil answered.

"If you strain your eyes a little, you can see the cabin. That's the kitchen cedar tree you're under," she said.

In that moment of relief, Virgil searched through every pocket for the keys, fearing that he had left them in the Jeep. He finally found them in the jacket he had draped over his pack and handed them to Marcy. Then Virgil went back and found Gaines just as he crawled up out of another hole at the next tree back. At the cabin, Marcy opened the door and Joel and Kelly dropped their packs on the floor while she lit the Coleman lantern. Shortly they had a fire going in the stove with the dry wood that Marcy had piled in the cabin in the fall but they were soon outside again with smoke pouring out the door.

In the light of the lantern, they saw the snow had piled so high on the cabin roof that it was one long drift from the ridgepole to the ground. Virgil got his prospector's pick to use for an ice axe, crawled up the snow and dug down to the flattened pipe, pulling it out so the smoke could escape through the hole in the snow. They all shed their wet clothes, which Marcy hung to dry on nails behind the stove. The boys climbed up into their bunks exhausted and soon they were all warm and dry in their beds.

"Know what day tomorrow is?" Virgil asked.

"No. What?" Marcy answered weakly.

"April Fool's," Virgil answered and drifted to sleep.

April dawned on snow banks so high that the lower limbs of the oaks were still caught in them. In the 120 feet from the cabin to the cedar trees that formed the roof of the summer kitchen, two separate drifts blocked the path. Though only three feet high, the way they felt, the drifts were insurmountable when they wanted to get to the kitchen stove, so they used the cabin heater to cook on for a few days.

The garden spots to be planted averaged three feet of snow and there was over eight feet piled between the shop and the cut bank behind it. The shed roof had warmed enough to allow the collected snow to slide off and turn to ice, and like the movement of a glacier, the frozen snow had pushed the rear wall, 600-pound generator, supplies and all over against the front wall. The attic storage space had collapsed and dumped box after box of wool rug rags into mud and ice mixed with nuts, bolts and screws. The roof sagged in the middle like a broken down pack mule and ice water trickled through a tray of jeweler's files under the bench. Virgil didn't bother to pick up the files but turned around and went back to the cabin.

For two days, they mostly sat in the sun, Marcy just able enough to cook a little food and her men barely able to supply the firewood. It took them the better part of a week to recover, slowed somewhat by the fact that they had to shovel pathways through the snow. But the warm sun melted the snow and their lethargy and soon they were shoveling snow off the garden spots so they'd be dry enough to plant in before they had to go back and finish the school year.

Easter morning the boys colored the eggs and Marcy hid them in tree branches and tufts of grass poking out of the snow. The spots of bare ground grew larger as they watched them and the day after Easter, Virgil and Gaines decided they could go see if Red was all right, since the postmistress had told them he hadn't been out to get his mail since the first of December. "Since we're going that far, if it isn't too bad, we'll go on into the machine shop and fix the driveline for the Jeep. With four-wheel drive, the way the snow's melting, we ought to be able to get quite a bit farther up the mountain," Virgil said.

"Take the flashlights from the car; you might need them. And don't buy anything you have to carry," Marcy cautioned.

"You don't need to worry about that...at all!" Virgil replied, slipping into his harness.

"Are you worried about Red?" Virgil asked Gaines when they were almost to Red's nest.

"Not really," Gaines replied. "But it's an awful long time since December when he picked up his mail."

"He's lived here 40 years, no need to worry now," Virgil assured him, but hurried on thinking they should have already found tracks in the remaining snow or other signs of Red.

When they got to Red's boar's nest, they found no recent tracks, no smoke from the chimney, no answer to their call. "He must have gone south for the winter," Virgil suggested.

Isn't today April 7th?" Gaines asked, peering in through the window.

"Yes. Why?"

"His calendar is on the right day then," Gaines said and the corners of his mouth relaxed.

But when they checked his mine tunnel and found a full can of snoose on the ground near where a section of roof had caved in, Virgil began to feel anxious again. He looked about apprehensively for a few minutes while Gaines looked farther up the trail. "Here's a track!" Gaines called. "It's going up."

At a place where the drift had been too wide to step over and too long to go around, they found one boot track, and when they reached the place where they'd cached a gallon jug of milk the week before, Red had written *Killroy wuz here*.

With their naïve fears for the old timer dispelled, they were able to pay attention to the condition of the road. "We can make it here" and "We'll have to shovel there" were frequent comments and by the time they reached the Jeep, they were certain they could drive all the way to the *Road Ends* sign once they had power to all four wheels.

"Good thing we didn't leave the chainsaw," Virgil said when he opened the Jeep door. The glove compartment hung open and the few remaining contents lay scattered on the floor mat where his toolbox had been. They couldn't believe that anyone would steal from an old Jeep parked on a wilderness road, thinking that anyone with a grain of sense would realize the necessity of having tools. But after searching the nearby brush and ditches, thinking that maybe Red had hidden them for safety, they were forced to admit that someone had.

The drive to town was quiet with both lost in thought.

"I'm not mad," Gaines finally said. "I'm just sad that people don't want to work for what they get."

Before they were able to install the rear driveshaft in the Jeep, they had to buy new tools to do it with, and when Virgil had to crawl from under the Jeep to go buy yet another wrench, his language and temperament were far from philosophical. It took more time to finish the job and when they got back to the snowline on the way home, the sun was already behind the mountains and the slush was beginning to freeze.

With the confidence born of the 'go anywhere' advertising claims of four-wheel drive vehicles, they gained speed and attacked the ice. For about a mile, they slipped and roared up the mountain. At one exceptionally shady spot that the sun only reaches for a few days in June and July, the snow was of just the right depth and texture to hold up the underbody of the Jeep while the four wheels spun uselessly. "It's no use trying anymore," Virgil declared.

They shoveled out from underneath the truck, pitching the snow over the 800-foot drop next to where the Jeep was stuck near the edge of the road. "Watch my wheels now. I'll back up to the last clear spot and then we'll hurry home," Virgil said, but in trying to keep the back wheels from sliding over the cliff, he had edged the front wheels toward it.

"Stop!" Gaines yelled just as the left front wheel dropped over the edge.

Virgil was stopped and he was scared. On the way down that morning, they'd noticed large cracks where the edges of the road were about to slide off into the canyon, and with this part covered with snow, Virgil had no idea of how close to a slide he was.

It's a good thing that twilight lingers long after the sun drops behind the mountains. As the outlines of the forest faded like sleep-dimmed plans, they found a solid root in the cut-bank and with chains, hand winch, shovels and vector mechanics, they rescued the Jeep and were on their way home while the snow splotched road was still visible. "Good thing the guy left us our log chains and winch," Gaines remarked.

"Sure is," Virgil agreed. "Our only chance of help would have been him coming back to take them and the broken screwdriver he missed the first time."

With very light packs and a crisp evening, they made good time up the road. And with new batteries in their flashlights, they weren't worried as the stars came out. But they weren't halfway down the trail when the lights became so dim that they rested and talked until the batteries built up enough charge for them to go on. They wouldn't last long and it was about 10 o'clock that night when Tissy wiggled up to Gaines. "I'm so glad to see you. It makes me feel like I'm already home," Gaines said, patting Tissy's head.

"We'll have new candle bugs built by the time school's out and we're really home," Virgil vowed.

Marcy had fresh English muffins she'd made in her Dutch oven on Hot Rock waiting for them when they returned. "Red's okay," Virgil told her as she handed him a muffin. "We saw that his calendar was marked yesterday and saw his tracks so we knew he'd walked out."

"Virg almost drove the Jeep over the edge of the north side," Gaines said. "He was backing it up when the snow started slipping. I was outside and yelled that his wheels were slipping over the side."

Marcy turned pale.

"But Ma, he was really mad because someone stole all the Jeep tools and all our rifle shells," he hurriedly explained when he saw her face and Virgil's glare.

"We saw the tracks of a motorcycle, also Winston cigarette butts all around the Jeep," Virgil explained. "Anyway, we did manage to drive the Jeep a little further up the road."

The snow melted rapidly as each day passed. By the day before they were to return to Denny, a small section at one end of the Flat was clear of snow, and Virgil and Marcy dug a square and planted peas.

In the wee morning hours on their last day at the Flat, Marcy awakened to Tissy growling. Tissy always charged out barking but this time she stayed close and just growled. From way off, Marcy heard a deep, masculine groan. "Virg," she whispered. "That's Bigfoot!"

This was only a few years after the famous Willow Creek video of Bigfoot was shot and tracks were found at Bluff Creek, making it very much a topic of conversation in the area at that time. "What's wrong with Tissy? Why isn't she barking?" Marcy fretted.

"She's just lazy," Virgil answered. "We have the 30-30."

"That book I was reading said someone shot a Bigfoot with a 30-30 and it didn't even faze it."

The next morning when they had to hike up to the Jeep with only one dog and a pup to warn and protect them, Marcy didn't have to coax the boys to hurry; none of them were about to meet Bigfoot on the trail.

Back in Denny, it rained for several days. They were on their way to Eureka to get supplies and buy the boys new boots. On the road out of Denny, several large boulders had fallen from a high bluff and Virgil stopped to roll them off. One boulder was so large it took all of them to heave it over the side so that they could drive by.

Suddenly, Marcy got a terrible fear. Almost out of control, she screamed at them to hurry. Virgil looked at her calmly but got behind the wheel and the rest of the family jumped in the Jeep. On returning, the county road crew was maneuvering a Jeep-sized boulder over the side. It had fallen off the cliff at the exact location where they had stopped earlier.

Several times over the years, Marcy had the same fear warning her that something bad was going to happen, almost like a warning from a higher force. In another instance, she made everyone run past a section of the trail by an old snag and when they came back, the snag was lying across the trail.

School dragged toward the end of the term and in tying up all the loose ends in Denny, they went back across the river to get the rest of the stuff that they still had stored at the Hixson place. Virgil had the Jeep loaded, including the 350-pound case of glass, when he thought to stop on the approach and examine the bridge. There were two-inch cracks in the dirt at each end of the bridge so he didn't breathe as he eased the truck across, fearing that the extra movement might cause it to collapse.

Virgil wouldn't drive back across for the final load, and while the ranger put up a *Danger!* sign, the boys rolled large boulders into the road to keep cars away from the bridge. Despite the huge rocks and the sign, one man refused to believe that the bridge wasn't safe and cleared the road enough to get to the bridge. He got angry when Virgil tried to stop him but the last time Virgil saw him, he was trying to get someone to pull his truck off the bridge. All four wheels had gone through.

Another loose end was the Pelton water wheel that Virgil had bought. They had to have cheaper power on the Flat than the gasoline generator and the first plan that Virgil had would have taken 10 years and an act of Congress to complete. He was working on the next best thing when he bought the wheel from Hanging Rock and Luke but by the time they got it out from Luke's claim, an eight-mile round trip on a wilderness trail, he was wishing he'd gone ahead with the first plan.

Since it had lain in the brush for 40 years, the wheel and shaft were rusted solidly together and it was necessary to try to get it out as a single unit. Virgil built a stretcher-like contrivance of two-by-fours and on the Saturday before Memorial Day, he and Marcy left the boys at home and started at sunup to get to the end of the road and hike nearly four miles back into the wilderness.

The road truly ends at a Forest Service corral but with the Jeep, they could save one-eighth mile of hard climbing on the trip back by driving on down to the mule bridge. The trail from the mule bridge to the Pelton wheel ran up the East Fork of the New River, following the normal pattern for a river trail in that it went up over one cliff to drop down on the far side, in repeating cycles. It wasn't bad on the way in, as they rested on the down side. Still, it seemed like ages before they finally got there. "Why are we always going where mules won't go?" Marcy asked.

Virgil knew what she meant. He had tried to hire packers to haul the wheel out but when they found out where the thing was located, they were suddenly busy somewhere else. So by nine that morning, Virgil and Marcy had retrieved the wheel and were the mules themselves. And by 10 a.m. they were sweating like mules, as well, so Virgil took off his shirt and sweater and draped them over the wheel.

Counting the weight of the stretcher, they were carrying close to 140 pounds. They strained to lift it and at first could carry it 50 paces before resting. By the time they got back over the hills and hollows to the mule bridge in the afternoon, they were going five paces, then resting. As they neared the mule bridge, a frantic voice called down from the trail above them. "Wait! Wait! We'll help!" yelled a middle-aged woman as she ran down toward the bridge. "My husband is backing the camper down. Is he hurt badly?"

"I'm not hurt," Virgil hollered back to her. "Do I look that beat?" he asked Marcy.

"Maybe she means me," Marcy speculated as they went another three paces and set the wheel down.

The woman ran up to them and jerked the shirt and sweater off the water wheel. "Oh! I thought it was an accident! I hope my husband can get back up that horrible road. I would have sworn someone was dead," she said and turned dejectedly to go tell her husband the news.

With their stretcher-case water wheel lashed on to the Jeep, and after a final tremulous backpack trip across the bridge to the Hixson place for a roll of hog wire, they decided to make a late trip into the Flat. As tired as they were, they thought they'd better go because a newspaper columnist had advised his readers to go poke around in old miner's cabins in the area over the Memorial Day weekend. The campgrounds were already overflowing, one cabin had already burned in the night, and the din of beer tops popping above the roar of motorcycles in front of the store made them uneasy about the safety of their cabin.

But this time there were no trucks or campers at Desperation Point and after unloading the wheel, which Marcy emphatically refused to carry further on that day or any other, they went on down the trail to see how their garden grew. At the Drinking Tree, where they could see out over their valley to the high peaks through the trees, Marcy looked all around as if she had awakened and found a dream come true. "This time next week, we'll be home for good," she sighed.

Denny bridge - August 1969

18 - Home for Good

June that year started out to be a beautiful month, with its cool mornings and warm days. Few apples graced the recovering trees and their gardens were little better than a promise but they were home for good. Virgil began whistling once more, pleased to see Marcy smiling so much. "Ah, finally we can continue our adventure," Marcy sighed.

The peas they'd planted on their Easter walk-in were about three feet high and the vines were loaded with pods that were supposed to be picked all at the same time. The squirrels knew this, of course, and regularly tested the pods for the optimum harvest time. But Marcy was watching as closely as the squirrels and it was a pretty even race until the family left the Flat for part of a day.

After enjoying their solitude at the Flat for two weeks, they decided it was time to check the mail and get more groceries. At the post office, Marcy received a letter from Gay with pictures of the bridge minus all the logs but one. Her letter explained the bridge had collapsed four days after they left and that some miners had picnicked under it just the day before.

When they got back down to the pea patch that evening, there wasn't a single mature pea in the whole patch. Tissy declared war on the squirrels but their burrows were under piles of river boulders left over from the mining operations of the Gold Rush so she couldn't dig them out. The pea patch was located in one of the mined out areas they were reclaiming so it was easy for the squirrels to keep watch on each vegetable they planted there.

As the beets got to table size, they were harvested for them and when the carrots got finger size, they were saved from the trouble of digging them up. The squirrels kept the lettuce from getting too big by vigilant nibbling, or made it into salad with the ripening tomatoes left atop boulders with the seeds eaten out. But when the squirrels cut Virgil's single tiny immature cantaloupe from the vine through the chicken wire cage he'd built around it, he declared war on them, too. He spent hot afternoons hiding behind rocks and bushes to the amusement of the blue jays, who deserted picking the ripening apples for the fun of pointing out his hiding places to the squirrels. With the help of the jays, all but one of the squirrels evaded him, and even though they ate that squirrel so as not to waste, Virgil's war died out.

As soon as Red saw the Jeep parked on top, he came to visit. "Virg, there's a strange green truck up on top. Looks like some animal control officer. Has a big cage behind it," Red said.

"That's our Willys Jeep and the cage was for the dogs," Virgil explained. "It's the same cage we used to haul the chickens up from down south."

Red sat down, took the cup of coffee Marcy offered and scanned the Flat with restless eyes. "When are you going to cut all this beeeautiful scenery down?" he asked, pointing to some small oaks and pines. "You'd better get your firewood for this winter. You can't eat just looking at all this beeeautiful scenery, you know."

"Do you know a miner named Amos Decker?" Virgil interrupted, referring to the local miner in the school film.

"Oh yes, old Amos. He's one of those types that if you ask him a question he tells you an answer whether he knows it or not. He lives at Barney Gulch and was the town's ladies' man. Heh. They loved him so much he had to beat them off with a stick," Red sneered. "What a guy! Next time we're in town, I'll introduce you. He'll be in the local bar." Red grew thoughtful and grinned. "What a slick master he is. Can sell a claim over and over by packing his fingernails and home-rolled cigarettes with gold dust. When he takes samples of dirt for the prospective buyers, he lets the ashes fall in the gold pan from his cigarette, and then he swishes his hand around so the gold falls out of his fingernails, too. Heh."

Virgil and Marcy glanced uncertainly at one another, both recalling the movie depiction of Amos as a great miner who knew how to find gold.

"But what I'm trying to tell you, about twenty years ago," Red continued, "I was coming back from town and bypassed my regular trail. I fell into a fissure and decided it was a good place to settle for the night. When I awoke the next morning, I saw all kinds of red crystals stuck in the banks that looked to be a poor grade of garnet. I pried some out and later showed them to another miner who I knew carried some brains in his dome. He confirmed they were garnets and I concluded there might be more valuable ones in with them. I'm trying to pull that old, faded picture out of my memory because I wasn't interested in gems at that time. If I can figure out where I saw it, you could use them in jewelry making."

Back in Denny, Shotgun had told them about a place in Eureka where they could buy 100-pound sacks of fishmeal, bone meal and animal tankage for $4 apiece and they hauled down 100 pounds of each to spread on the upper garden.

They plowed three beds with the gas-powered tractor and planted red potatoes, turnips, corn and radishes. Then they used a gasoline engine driving a pump to suck water out of the reservoir to water the garden. Kelly usually volunteered to water because he loved the white turnips and radishes fresh out of the ground and would head up the trail to the gardens with a saltshaker in his hand.

Everything grew lush and green. When they harvested the red potatoes in late summer, they got close to a thousand pounds and stored them in a big box Virgil had made with a blanket over the top. Bully decided to use it as a bed, which was fine as he kept the potatoes from freezing.

Toward the end of June during their third summer at the Flat, Virgil hugged Marcy and then whispered in her ear. "Will you be my little mule again and help me haul down the sections of two-inch black plastic pipe?"

They'd bought six 100-foot coils of pipe for the power system and water for the Flat. The torture rack Virgil devised for them to haul down the plastic pipe was made of five-foot lengths of thin walled steel pipe that slipped one into the other, which were tied on each side of the eight-foot diameter coils of plastic pipe. He fastened a soft strap around the two steel pipe ends sticking out and the strap went under the arms and over the shoulders of the person in back. The one in front stooped, placing the pipes on his or her shoulders as the person in back squatted and put the straps in place.

Virgil and Marcy took off to the top of the mountain with this contraption. After Virgil secured a big roll of pipe on the rack, they lifted it to their shoulders and bumped off down the trail. When they came to a flat section, the one in front bent over to keep it level and they successfully made three trips like this. All went well until the fourth load when Virgil tied the roll too high on the steel pipes and it grabbed him around the neck, Judo fashion, flinging him over the edge. Fortunately, the side wasn't vertical and was made of small rocks so he only got a minor bump on his head, but Marcy refused to help him with the other rolls, thinking she was somehow responsible for the mishap.

Feeling sorry for himself, Virgil rigged a cross-like affair out of steel pipes on his pack frame, and since the weight of a single roll wasn't too much for him by this time, he went up trail to get one. On the way down the trail, Virgil was congratulating himself on his brilliance, wit, ingenuity and every other flattering adjective he could think of when he came to a brushy section and his wide load started catching, first on one side, then the other. He ducked, pirouetted, sidled and slid, his great, black wings waving on each side like the mating dance of some awkward bird. He'd forgotten all his congratulatory phrases and had remembered the ones feeling sorry for himself when the top of the roll hit a projecting tree and he flew off the trail to nest in some brush.

Later, Virgil used every sweet word he knew on Marcy to get her to agree to help him finish bringing the pipe and water wheel down but she knew when she'd had enough and when they were up top, she either walked around the rolls of pipe and the wheel or gave them a secret kick. Much to Virgil's relief, they got a letter from Cecil and Diane saying that Cecil was taking a week off from work to come and help them with the waterpower project. "How soon will they get here?" Virgil asked Marcy as she read the letter.

"Ten days. Can you get your intake put in by then?"

Virgil had been mumbling for some months about a well-designed pipe intake for the water system called for by the Encyclopedia Britannica. Being familiar with a planishing and peening hammer in silver and goldsmithing, he hammered out an aluminum form using the formula in the encyclopedia and a toy air gun for a model. He was later glad that every waterwheel expert he talked to told him what he intended couldn't be done because he took extra care to make each part of their hydraulic system as efficient as possible.

A yard of concrete is a small thing when a transit-mix truck backs up to your forms and pours them full, but a cubic foot is a large undertaking when the cement comes down two miles of trail on your back and the sand comes by the same means from a river 500 feet below. When the cement had set, the forms were taken off, the clay tamped around the intake, the reservoir was watertight again and they were ready to start laying the plastic pipe to the lower flat.

Once Cecil and Diane arrived with their two boys, Cecil and Virgil hauled down the last of the pipe and the cast iron Pelton wheel. Bringing the Pelton wheel down was made easier by the vast difference in height; Cecil was six-foot-seven and Virgil just five-foot-eight. With Cecil carrying the front end and Virgil the rear, it was like carrying it level all the way down.

In the two years that the rolled up plastic pipe had been stored in a tin shed, it underwent a curing process in the summer's heat and the winter's cold. Some advertisers of plastics say that they have some with a memory. Their pipe not only had a memory, but a mind of its own, too, and it had made up its mind that it was going to stay coiled up as it remembered.

Although the only truly flat spot was the surface of the reservoir, they tried to change its mind by stretching it out on the ground as flat as they could, then piling rocks on it. Neither the weather nor the pipe cooperated, for it got cold and cloudy, and at night the pipe crawled out from under the rocks and coiled back up. "Virg," Cecil said after the third time this happened, "I've just got a few days. I can't stay here and argue with that pipe all summer. Suppose we could build a fire and heat it?"

"I'm afraid of building a fire big enough to heat a whole coil, but we might take a blow torch and heat small sections at a time," Virgil said. "Kelly, go get us the blow torch."

With five sons between the two of them, they had a lot of boy help on this job. Cecil and Virgil could barely make a move before it was anticipated and one of the five jumped to do it for them. When Kelly returned with the torch and with Keith carrying an extra can of gas, they tried heating the pipe enough to uncoil it, but when the pipe got hot enough to lose its memory, it also lost its will to live and collapsed.

"Only one thing left to do," Cecil said when another section had assumed the shape of a flat ribbon. "Hook it into the reservoir and let the weight of the water straighten it out."

"Sounds good to me. Let's give it a try," Virgil agreed. "Bring me that plastic reducer, Gaines, and we'll get started."

"I'll put the fitting on," Cecil volunteered.

"Come on, boys, let's drag this section of pipe over," Virgil said, and like Laocoon and his sons in ancient Troy, they fought the serpent over to where Cecil was just giving the fitting its final tap.

"One more whack ought to do it," Cecil said, but one solid blow later, it shattered. "Well, I fear that exceeded its design parameters," he smiled ruefully. But the smile quickly faded when he saw the stricken look on Virgil's face. "That was the last and only one on the Flat, wasn't it?" Cecil asked.

Virgil nodded slowly and sat down to think and smoke his pipe.

"I'll go get some parts," Cecil offered. "I could be back by evening."

"It's 120 miles to the coast and that's where you'd find them. Boys, bring up some boards, sand and cement. We'll fix it like a regular penstock," Virgil said. "While you're gone, I'll dig the hole for the form."

While the boys made several trips with knapsacks part full of sand and cement, Virgil dug a hole a foot square and a foot deep in the ground around the broken fitting and soon had a form built. By lunchtime, they had another cubic foot of concrete poured. "I'll bet some of the engineers at work would really enjoy working on this...the bill of materials being what you invent out of what little you've got," Cecil said.

The next morning, their cement block had set enough to hold water. "It would be a good idea to bury this pipe as it uncoils," Cecil suggested.

"I know it would, but if we're going to get this laid while you're here, we don't have time," Virgil replied.

They fastened their first roll of pipe to the penstock device, Cecil holding it upright on one side, Virgil on the other. Gaines had gone up to turn the water into the dam, which was filling quickly. As it filled with water, a shudder ran through the pipe and it began uncoiling slowly. Inch by inch, the pipe relinquished its memories and straightened out, much like the little paper toys of a New Year's party that go bra-a-a-ack when they're blown through hard enough to straighten them out.

But there wasn't enough pressure or the coil still had some things to think about, for as it reached the last 10 feet, it refused to uncoil further, the end sticking up in the air with the rags of their temporary plug fluttering in the wind like pennants at a gas station. They pushed the pipe down, only to have a section in the middle raise up. When the boys held the middle down and Cecil and Virgil pushed on the end, the plug blew out with a loud bang of trapped air, and drenched Cecil and Virgil with the downpour from the two-inch pipe. But it had worked, for before it had a chance to change its mind, they jumped on it and tied it to cedar stakes driven securely into the ground.

They repeated this process until the last section was laid. By evening, they connected 100 feet of two-inch rubber hose to the last piece of plastic pipe, capped it off, and five wet and muddy boys followed by equally wet and muddy fathers went down to the outdoor kitchen for dinner.

The next morning, Diane told Marcy she wanted to see a friend who had moved to a farm near Etna in neighboring Siskiyou County. "Come on, Marcy. Let the kids and the husbands fend for themselves," she said.

Cecil, Virgil and the boys were going to let the water into the pipe and Marcy wanted to see if it would work, but she agreed to go with Diane and changed out of her jeans into a skirt. Diane looked down at Marcy's legs and screamed. "You're not going to town with your legs looking so filthy are you?"

"I just took a bath," Marcy said. "I can't wash it off. I have blotchy spots from sitting by the little stove cooking," she replied as she changed back into a pair of pants.

After the women left, while the men arranged for pressure and flow tests on the pipeline, they built a big pot of 'one-of soup'...one of anything they could find. The boys took turns keeping the fire going while Cecil and Virgil directed the search for substitute gadgets for the test. Kelly came up with an old oil pressure gauge from a car in the Denny dump. Gaines came up with a wash boiler that he'd measured for capacity. Joel came in with a little fish for the soup. Keith came up with a downspout. Cecil had the watch with the second hand and Virgil had the pencils and paper. They detailed Kurt to watch the fire under the soup while the engineers straggled off with their junk for the test.

"This will tell the tale," Cecil said. "I just wish I had time to help you finish putting the wheel together, but we have to leave tomorrow. I'd like to stay for the big squirt."

The rubber hose stretched out in the sun like a giant, black sausage. The pressure had been building all night, and as the sun warmed it, the hose grew bigger and bigger, until it was twice the size of the plastic pipe on one end and the clamped-on fitting on the other. "Careful, it might blow," Virgil warned, as Cecil straddled the end of the hose to lift it to a better position to work on.

"The cap's sliding out!" one of the boys shouted. Cecil started to shove the hose aside, but the full force of the water hit him in the stomach, knocking him backward, where he sat until the reservoir emptied its thousands of gallons of cold water in his lap. As he struggled up, he said, "I guess I got to see the big squirt after all."

When the women got up the trail to the car that morning, Marcy remembered seeing a sign in Junction City that offered free Muscovy ducks. "Let's stop and get a couple on the way back," Marcy said as she put the wire cage in the back of Diane's station wagon.

When they finally found the friend's ranch near Etna, it was a bare desolate place, with pigs, sheep, horses and a number of other usual farmyard animals and fowl. As Diane's friend, Martha, showed them around, Marcy felt something rub against her ankle. She looked down and saw a tiny black and white striped kitten staring up at her, pleading. Marcy picked him up and he snuggled against her. "Here, take this one. He's stronger," Martha said, handing Marcy a wild one that scratched her arm. "They're all great snake killers."

"I'll take this one," Marcy said, patting the little guy and tucking him under her blouse. She knew the boys, and especially Kelly, would love it.

A short while later, they said their good-byes and Diane swung the station wagon onto the road. With the little kitten snug under Marcy's shirt, they stopped and picked up two Muscovy ducks, a male and a female. It was dark when they hiked down to the Flat. "I'm glad you're back," Virgil greeted Marcy. "I've been popping corn all evening. I thought they'd never fill up."

"Did you get the water in the pipe?"

"Yes, we did, and you have water to the kitchen now," Virgil affirmed. "Cecil was straddling the pipe when the coupling broke and the whole reservoir emptied in his lap. He was just telling us that he wished he could be here for the big squirt when it broke," Virgil continued. "I rigged up another coupling out of exhaust pipe clamps and steel pipe."

Marcy laughed. "I have to find Kelly to give him this," she said, pulling the kitten from under her shirt. "I also have two ducks in the chicken pen on top."

Virgil reached out to pet the kitten and suddenly drew back. "Take a good look at that cat. It looks like it has ringworm," Virgil declared.

Afraid of catching ringworm, Marcy dropped the poor little thing. She showed the kitten to Kelly but cautioned the boys not to touch him until they could check him out in the morning.

Marcella cooking

19 - Cats, Generators and Livestock

After saying goodbye to Cecil, Diane and their boys the next morning, they discovered that the kitten was indeed covered with ringworm and mange. "That cat is scraggly," Virgil said. "Look at his tail; he doesn't have any hair on it." His tone softened. "But he does have clear eyes and seems to have a great big spirit."

"I wonder if he'll eat a fish," Gaines said and grabbed his fishing pole.

He was back shortly with a small rainbow trout flapping in his hand. He tossed it on the ground by the kitten where it continued flapping wildly. "Why didn't you kill it?" Marcy asked. "He'll never be able to eat it alive like that."

She was wrong. The kitten attacked the flapping fish as though he had no ailments at all. Seizing the trout by the head, the kitten started devouring it. As the still flapping tail was about to disappear down his little gullet, the kitten's eyes bulged and up came the trout whole, only showing a few tiny teeth marks.

Without hesitation, the kitten set to work chewing his meal better. In his young life, he hadn't figured out that he couldn't chew food with his front incisors but in a few seconds, he had the trout over to the side of his mouth and was crunching loudly. In less than 30 seconds, they stared in amazement at the little kitten sniffing around the sand for any scraps he'd missed. "He wants another one!" Joel cried.

Gaines picked up his fishing pole from where he'd dropped it and started for the river. On his short little legs, the kitten followed. The rest of the group followed in amazement, watching the kitten tumble over river boulders, scamper through the black willow and gingerly pick his way through the thorns of the berry bushes along the river, watching Gaines and the fishing pole the whole while.

Using a number one silver panther Martin spinner, Gaines cast out into the riffles. Slowly, he reeled the spinner in. The tip of the pole bent and Gaines jerked back hard. Another wildly flapping rainbow trout flashed in a silver arc through the air. The line and the spinner ended up tangled in a willow bush but the trout continued into a berry patch. The kitten's eyes watched the path of the fish and he leaped into the brambles. They couldn't see the kitten but heard a wild rustling and shortly he emerged with the sand-covered trout flapping from the side of his mouth. Thirty seconds later, this fish too was gone, sand and all, and the kitten proceeded to again sniff for any pieces he might have missed.

"Don't catch him any more fish or he'll get sick," Marcy told Gaines. "He's a gluttonous little thing."

Over the days, with more fish, lizards, a soapy bath and a bag balm rub, the kitten became reasonably respectable looking. He felt pretty big, too, for his favorite food became rattlesnake. After chopping off the head, they gave him every snake they killed around the camp. Even as a baby, he fussed and fumed by the dogs' food until they moved away. Kelly named him Nosey but Virgil called him Tom and that's the name that stuck.

Virgil's ridiculed pipe organ blower, which had been sitting neglected ever since Marvin had gotten it down to the Flat, was to become the cover for the water wheel. Since the water wheel was the Pelton type, it worked on high pressure and low volume. In theory, the stream of water hits a ring of double cups or buckets on the rim of the wheel and the energy of the water transfers to the wheel and the water drops to the ground to run off, but theory and practice are two different things.

After measuring and re-measuring, they found that the Pelton wheel would just fit inside the blower case, so they set about converting the case to a splash shield to keep the theoretically 'dead' water from coming to life and ruining the generator. All they had to do was cut a hole for the nozzle and cut the bottom out of the steel case. Virgil soon gave up with a hand drill and hacksaw and the boys suggested he try their Buzz Box welding outfit to cut the steel. "It should cut this stuff," Virgil agreed. "Let's try it. Get the battery for the gasoline generator and we'll have it cut in no time."

Due to the four-gallon per hour fuel consumption and the distance to the nearest gas pump, the Hobart generator had only been started a couple times since all the parts had been collected in one place and assembled. Since they knew each piece intimately, they weren't too upset when it refused to start. Joel checked the gas lines, Gaines the carburetor and Kelly the fuel pump, while Virgil checked the magneto, but there was not a cough or putt when they tried it again.

Virgil removed the spark plugs and primed the engine, and was looking down the upright exhaust pipe when one of the boys pushed the starter button and got a cough. A blob of something splashed on his face, filling his eyes. When he could see again, there were little pieces of dirty spaghetti in his mustache. "Did you guys hide spaghetti in this exhaust pipe?" Virgil accused, knowing that the boys liked to take long spaghetti from the larder and toast it on the stove for a snack.

"No," the boys all assured him, and since their word was 24-karat, he began to take the engine apart.

Close examination revealed that rats or mice had plugged the exhaust pipe with spaghetti and popcorn scavenged from the food stores in the shop attic. When they got the manifold off, it was filled with soggy spaghetti, and as they pried the engine head off, they found the valves and cylinders were covered with a mixture of gluten, gasoline and mouse nest. "Kelly, I'll be glad when that cat of yours gets big enough to catch mice. Maybe he can keep them out of carburetors and exhaust pipes," Virgil said.

With help from the boys, Virgil worked on it for a day, snagging out the spaghetti and corn with a curved wire. When they finally got it cleaned and filled with gas, Virgil called Marcy. "We're going to start it. Would you like to see it run, Ma?"

Marcy took her little electric radio and went up to the shop to watch. Gaines kept pressing the start button but the generator only turned over laboriously and refused to fire. Kelly decided the cylinders needed to be primed with gas but all the gas on the Flat was in the generator's tank. Looking around, nine-year-old Kelly found the only piece of tubing on the Flat, a three-foot length of copper, and proceeded to siphon gas from the tank. What he hadn't counted on was that a squirrel had gnawed the insulation away from the positive battery cable. When the tubing made contact with the cable, it arced and ignited the fuel vapors coming out from the tank's filler spout. "Run!" Marcy screamed. "It's going to blow!" And they thundered off like a herd of water buffalo. From a distance, they stared at the flame dancing on the filler spout and waited for the cataclysmic explosion that was sure to follow.

When the area had not turned into a giant fireball after a few seconds, Virgil recalled training he'd had in the Navy when he and three seamen advanced into a flaming tank of burning oil. Virgil was at the hose nozzle and the instructor warned him to keep the nozzle on the fog setting. Otherwise, the flame would not be pushed out ahead of them and would circle around them instead. Nearby was a faucet and hose on the newly installed pipe system. With this turned on full, Virgil advanced and directed a fine fog of water on the flame, putting it out.

After some more work, the generator started but ran roughly. Suddenly, huge white fluffy popcorn shot from the exhaust and the engine began running smoothly. Disappointingly, the welder wouldn't work so Virgil had to cut the steel by drilling hundreds of holes with the electric drill. Marcy finally plugged in her radio and turned it on. They hadn't listened to a radio for more than two years and were unprepared for the negative news that blasted their ears. But one news story caught all their interest. Apollo 11 was sitting on the launch pad, going through the final countdown for the first moon shot. "We have to hear this!" Marcy exclaimed.

"Well, we don't have the gas to run the generator just to hear the radio," Virgil said.

"There's the little portable seven-transistor radio that Uncle Doug left," Kelly said. "It runs off batteries."

That night as they lay in their beds in the dark cabin, Marcy held the little radio over her head so the whole family could hear the weak signal. They tuned in off and on during the following week until one afternoon they heard what millions of people around the world saw on television: Neil Armstrong stepping onto the surface of the Sea of Tranquility. But in the days that followed, the news returned to wars, riots and murder, and Marcy put the radio away and vowed never to turn it on again.

The next project was burying the pipe for the water system so that the sun wouldn't rot it, but it was with some distress that they set to this task because they'd been enjoying the heated water. The pipe made its way down the hillside through a mixture of oak forest and dry open rocky slopes. By the late afternoon, the sun had heated the water in the black pipe and they'd been using it to shower.

When they turned it on, the static water in the pipe moved down through the showerhead. Blocked from the sun's rays in the deep oak forest, however, the heated water in the pipe was not a uniform temperature. But the joy of a hot shower outweighed the discomfort from the sudden rush of chilled water that periodically poured over them.

In Denny, Virgil had traded parts from the old Jeep station wagon to Ernie for a one-bearing generator to replace one they had that would no longer run. Although the replacement generator needed a shaft extension and the front bearing mounted on it for use with waterpower, it saved Virgil from having to carry the original one back up trail for conversion, which he couldn't have done anyway since the armature alone weighed 85 pounds.

They made a trip to Weaverville to drop it off at Karl Riker's machine shop and on the way back, they stopped at a little spring that flowed from a pipe coming from a dark heavy fir forest on the east side of Oregon Mountain. A pickup truck pulled in just ahead of them. "What's that in there?" Marcy asked as they pulled up.

Virgil and the boys looked at the back of the truck.

"It's a pig!" she cried. "A pretty little pig!"

As the boys joined their mother in the clamor about the pig, Virgil eased the clutch out, wanting to get away before he got caught up in something he'd sworn against. "Wait, Virg! I haven't gotten a drink," Marcy said.

"Are you really that thirsty? I'll get you a nice, cool soft drink at the next store," he promised.

A man with bright happy eyes, a huge dirty bandage on one hand and the most beat-up hat Virgil had ever seen walked back from the spring to the truck with a jug of water. A boy and a girl, along with the pig, awaited him there. When he heard the noise from their Jeep, he touched the brim of his hat and grinned. "Is that pig for sale?" Marcy asked.

"I'm not buying a pig," Virgil protested.

"Now, Virg, relax. I just want to look at him," Marcy reassured him, getting out of the Jeep.

"Ok. I'll get the water. Joel, hand me a jug," Virgil said.

As he returned to the Jeep with the water, he saw Marcy reaching through the boards of the rack, scratching a black and white pig's ears. "How much do you want for him?" she asked the man.

"Depends," the man answered.

"I'm not carrying a ton of pig feed down that trail!" Virgil declared.

"They don't eat that much, do they?" Marcy asked. "I can feed him scraps."

"We don't have scraps. We eat every scrap. We don't need a pig. I don't want a pig and…"

"Let 'em eat acorns," the smiling man interrupted before Virgil got too wound up. "Mine fatten up on dropped fruit."

"We got no fruit. We got no acorns," Virgil replied. "Every bit of food that pig would eat would have to go down two miles of trail on my back. I don't want a pig," Virgil repeated.

Virgil looked at the pig and noticed that he'd eaten half a sack of rolled barley since he'd been in the truck, which Virgil knew hadn't been too long. "Look at all that barley he's bought for that pig," Virgil pointed out to Marcy. He then turned to the grinning boy and girl quietly sitting on top of the barley sacks. "You kids don't want to sell your pet pig, now do you?" he asked.

"Don't make no difference to us," the boy answered. "We got a hundred at home."

"No, that there boar hog I just bought. Was going to improve my stock, but if you folks want him, I'll sell him for what he cost me, twenty-three cents a pound," the man said, taking his hat off, twisting it around three times and jamming it back on his head.

The boys were out of the Jeep by then, insisting that they'd gladly help carry barley, corn or anything else, if they got the pig. "Think of the pork chops," Marcy said, trying to appeal to Virgil's appetite to clinch the argument.

"Think of the butchering," he said, hoping the picture would change her mind. "By the way, Mister, what happened to your hand?"

"Hog bit me," he answered.

"See!" Virgil said, as if that precluded him ever buying a pig.

"But you wouldn't want the boys to go hungry this winter, would you?" Marcy gently scratched the pig's ears. Defeated, Virgil reached for his money and bought a twenty-dollar pig.

Three days later, they were up trail getting hog wire and barley when both dogs ran out from under the Jeep, hair raised and woofing. They stood stiff-legged at the edge, looking over the trail, growling. They'd never seen the dogs act this way except when they smelled a bear, and their reluctance to jump over the edge for a chase made them all think that a bear was coming up to see what food was to be found.

Suddenly, over the hump, a black animal came hurtling straight toward them. While they all jumped behind the Jeep, the pig sailed between the surprised dogs and laid down in the deep shade under the truck. With a deep sigh, he went to sleep. This is what Virgil had feared when he agreed to buy the pig. He knew that pigs can become so personable that it becomes necessary to sell rather than butcher them, and here their new pig had quite dramatically declared himself one of the family.

Without comment, Virgil unloaded his pack and put on the roll of hog wire. After talking the pig into letting him tie a rope on his hind leg, Virgil followed him down the trail. The pig kept stopping to lift one foot off the ground, then the other, to let them cool. Virgil followed his example and they did a little dance all the way to the Drinking Tree where Virgil let him lay down in the wet leaves below the spring to cool off. The rest of the family had become impatient with the dancing and had gone on down to the Flat. While the pig snuffled, snorted and rolled, Virgil puffed his favorite and only pipe, his spare one having fallen in a hole during the squirrel war. The wet leaves provided the only safe place on the trail to smoke in summer.

Virgil had his idea of how long a pig should rest but the pig had a different one, so with quite a bit of pulling and urging and some confusing help from Tissy, the pig looked Virgil over contemptuously, shrugged a pig shrug, and with a disgusted snort, started home. He trotted ahead without much prodding until they came through a tunnel of shade into The Oven. The pig took one look through the heat waves and as if he had seen all the devils in a pig's hell, he jerked the rope from his leg, ran over the side of the trail, circled a scrubby tree, and ran back up the trail with Tissy barking in close pursuit. Virgil threw off the hog wire, dropped his pipe and set off after the two.

When Virgil found him, the pig was sound asleep in the muck below the Drinking Tree. Virgil got quietly on his hands and knees, snuck up on the unsuspecting pig and grabbed his hind leg. The pig must have resented sneaks, for when Virgil was tying the rope to his leg, he grabbed the skin of Virgil's arm in his little white teeth and wouldn't let go until Tissy sank her little white teeth into his ear. Virgil grabbed a big stick and chanted a nursery rhyme back down to The Oven. "Stick, stick, beat pig."

When Virgil got back to his pack, he tied the rope to a scrubby tree. He wrestled the roll of hog wire onto his back and was looking for his pipe when the pig bolted up trail again, knocking the wire roll and Virgil's pack over his head as he fell to his knees. The scrubby tree jerked loose from the rocks but caught in the brush before the pig got a good start. Virgil put the nursery rhyme into practice the rest of the way home, where he dumped the pig over the fence into his temporary pen. "All right, Lucifer," Virgil said, as the 90-pound pig hit the mud. "You know where you can go."

Virgil resolved he'd have nothing more to do with Lucifer until it was time to butcher. Having been raised on a farm, when Marcy looked at a pig, she saw food so it didn't bother her to feed him and think of pork chops. Lucifer forgave Tissy for biting his ear and they became bosom buddies. Tissy went with Marcy when she fed Lucifer and the dog and pig would play together. Lucifer chased Tissy around the pen and then at the end of the game, they would kiss each other. Lucifer was very intelligent. He moved all the rocks in his pen to one side and Marcy let the water run in it to make a mud puddle. He burrowed in the mud until only his snout stuck out, blowing bubbles.

One evening at dusk while Virgil and Marcy read by lantern light in the cabin, the boys decided it would be a good game to tie a rope to the oak tree by the outdoor kitchen and play Piggy. They took turns tying their ankles with rope, pretending to be Lucifer. The game was in full swing when a loud guttural groan reverberated in the canyon from the ridge between the Flat and Rock of Gibraltar. With frightened gasps, Gaines and Kelly raced into the cabin and slammed the door shut. "What's wrong?" Marcy asked, startled by the dramatic entry.

"Panther!" Gaines gasped. "Something just roared from the ridge toward Rock of Gibraltar!"

"Where's Joel?" Marcy screamed.

"He's still tied up by the ankle under the tree," Gaines cried and ran out where Joel was hanging upside down by his ankle by the piggy rope. Gaines frantically untied the rope. Once loose, Joel fell to the ground and raced Gaines to the shack. The dogs, always ready to bark at bear, deer and other animals, were quiet.

"What did it sound like?" Marcy asked.

"Like-like, that s-sound you-you heard Easter," Joel answered through chattering teeth.

"It was loud!" Kelly said.

Joel crawled into his bunk and drew the covers over his head.

"Is the gun loaded, Virg?" Marcy asked.

"I'll check, but I think you guys are getting too excited. I'm sure it was just a cougar passing through and he's long gone by now," Virgil said, getting up from his reading chair and retrieving the 30-30 Marlin from the wall at the head of the bed.

He worked the lever action to confirm it was loaded, flipping a cartridge out on the bed. Joel peered out from under his covers. "Those bullets look awfully small for Bigfoot," he whispered.

"There's no Bigfoot," Virgil scoffed, pressing the expelled cartridge back into the magazine.

"That's a huge cartridge," Gaines said.

"One hundred and seventy grains of lead," Kelly added.

Remembering the book Marcy had mentioned at Easter about a 30-30 not touching Bigfoot, Joel wasn't convinced. His gaze turned to the Z-frame door, in particular the sliding bolt latch Virgil had made entirely from wood, and for the first time it looked flimsy to him.

An hour later, Virgil announced it was time for bed and reached up and turned off the gas on the Coleman lantern. The light faded from a brilliant white in the twin mantles to faint orange orbs that lasted near half a minute before going pitch black with a faint pop. There was no moon and complete darkness enveloped the cabin. But nobody slept for quite a while, listening in the darkness for any sound out of the ordinary. Finally, one by one, they all drifted off into troubled sleep.

In the wee hours of the morning, Joel woke from a fretful sleep to a deep growling from the front porch. In soundless terror, he listened until the growling quit. His heart pounded heavy in his ears but after a few minutes when the growling did not return, the tempo of the thudding in his ears slowed.

Suddenly, a heavy rattle shook the door as something appeared to be trying to rip it open. Between the fast tempo of thuds in his ears, Joel could hear the door latch bolt hammering in its wooden socket. The shaking subsided but then the growling returned, deep and angry.

Suddenly the door shook violently again, then silence.

Deep growl.

This cycle went on for nearly an hour, leaving Joel in a sweating terror. Finally, after a deep growl, there was a snarl and a yelp and Joel relaxed. The noise was only Tissy sleeping with her back to the door, alternately scratching ticks and growling at Bully, who was trying to encroach on her space.

Bully

Joel washing in the summer kitchen

*Organ blower shrouded pelton wheel
and the Hobart generator*

20 - Settling in at the Flat

Later that summer, they built the foundation for the water wheel and the generator, which was a major job. For two days, Virgil and Marcy went up trail and hauled down cement. The boys spent those two days hauling sand. It was so hot that they mixed and poured the concrete at night so it didn't set too quickly to trowel.

Once Virgil finished pouring the foundation, they had to wait for the concrete to set. When the cement was good and hardened, they placed the big cast iron wheel next to the generator and wired down a fire nozzle, pointed at one of the cast iron cups. "After all these years, I get to try out my pipe organ cover to see if it'll keep the water out of the electrical system," Virgil said.

Kelly and Joel ran up to the stream to let the water in from the reservoir.

"Cecil should be here to see the big squirt," Gaines said.

They were so anxious to see if the water pressure would turn the wheel that they didn't wait to bolt it down, but turned the valve slowly. When the water from the reservoir came down the pipe, the big old rusty wheel inside the pipe organ blower started revolving. The concave sides of the cover amplified the hiss of the water as it hit the buckets and the 'thup, thup, thup' as the cups began interrupting the jet increased in frequency until it made a low background sound, more felt than heard. It turned the generator faster and the pipe organ cover worked great keeping the water from spraying all over. "It works! It works!" Marcy and the boys shouted.

"Well, how about that?" Virgil grinned as if he'd been absolutely certain all the time, and then he reached down to turn the valve on full.

There was no load to hold the wheel back and the only thing that anchored the mounting was a black plastic pipe fastened to the nozzle. The background sound became audible, the hiss became a roar and a heavy thumping came from the shaking concrete foundation while the wheel, cover and pipe jumped up and down threatening to break the cement platform.

With the wheel mounted solidly and the generator put together, they still lacked a pulley of the right size to hook the two together. Virgil had ordered it several weeks before and started to feel like they must still be dependent on mule trains for freight delivery to the county seat. But the boys, who had worked hard, were determined to find out if the generator worked. They'd been wrapping strings around the shaft and by pulling, turned the armature enough to feel a tingle if they held both wires in their hands. "We're sure it's going to work," they insisted.

"We'll have to wait 'til the pulley comes," Virgil said. "Then we'll see if we wasted our time and money."

It is of little use to argue with boys whom you have taught that the truth is what they have observed for themselves, for it was just a short while before they came back to where Virgil was splitting shingles. "We saw a spark. Come on! We'll show you!" they insisted.

"Yeah, yeah," Virgil said but followed them.

The boys had a long nylon cord wound around the shaft. While one of them held the wires, another ran down the slope with the end of the string, spinning the armature fast enough that when the wires were touched, blue sparks flew. "That's good thinking," Virgil said.

The pulley finally came and power flowed through new wire that ran to their temporary shed that, like most temporary things on the Flat, had become a permanent shop. The machines for making jewelry worked, the lights burned, a power saw whined as they cut a board, and they realized they no longer had to grind their wheat by hand in the morning before they ate their pancakes.

The whole-wheat flour they used contained no preservatives and by the time they were using the last of a 100-pound sack, the weevils were using it as much as they were. They had found and been able to buy an old hand-powered gristmill so started buying wheat and grinding flour as they used it since they could wash the weevils out of whole grain.

Every morning before Marcy heated the griddle, they'd take turns at the handle and by the time the flour was ready, they were all awake and ready to start the day. But time spent in milling is time lost on other things that had to be done. So with a motor from an air conditioner, pulleys from a clothes dryer, and odds and ends from the dump, they converted the 'good old days' to present time and hooked the mill up to their new power supply.

A large bear started making his presence known and they wondered if he might be the cub Hucky had chased just below Mattress Point two summers before. They never saw the bear but when they measured his bite on a plastic bucket, they got an idea how big he was.

A bear or cattle goad is an electric gadget that gives a bear a nasty shock when he's doing something you don't want him to do, or encourages him to do something you do want him to do, like get away. But their bear goad was the opposite. After seeing what he could do with a plastic bucket or gasoline tin, they were goaded into carrying bigger loads of food supplies down the trail than they felt like and making more trips than they thought they were able.

They started building up their winter supplies and brought back several hundred pounds of grain, honey, sugar and pig pellets each time they went to town even though what they couldn't carry down immediately was in danger of being eaten. What they couldn't carry down, they left closed in the cab of the Jeep or stored in galvanized trash barrels chained to posts of the old mill frame with the chain to the post looped through the handles and up over the lid.

The bear caved in the cab of the Jeep and ripped out the ventilator on the hood before he found out how to open the door and eat 50 of the 100 pounds of sugar and all of the pig pellets. He left much irrefutable evidence of his upset stomach but that didn't discourage him and he visited the cans at the old mill the next night. By sitting on the lids of the cans, he was able to bend them up enough that the chains loosened and the cans of grain tipped over. Though still sick, he ate all the loose corn, wheat and chicken scratch, and dragged what was in sacks over the hill toward his home. On the next trip to town, Virgil mentioned that a bear had caved in the cab roof. Shortly after the arrival of hunting season, the bear was gone from their canyon.

For several days, Marcy stayed chained to her stove canning a bumper crop of string beans. She'd just finished canning the last batch and was letting the steam out of her pressure cooker. Bully lay in the sand with all four legs up, letting the sun warm his belly. When the steam died down, Marcy could still hear a hissing. She looked around trying to find the sound and glanced down at Bully. Coiled right next to him was a huge timber rattler, ready to strike. "Get the gun!" she yelled at Virgil.

About that time, Gaines grabbed Bully by the scruff of the neck and jerked him away from the snake. Virgil came running with the gun while everyone screamed excitedly. Still dazed from sleep, the dog never saw the snake but was waking up fast and not liking what appeared to be a summary canine execution. Then Virgil fired the rifle right next to Bully as he struggled to get away from Gaines, his eyes bulging. Bully broke free and ran for the cabin, disappearing under it in a cloud of dust. From then on, Bully was deathly afraid of the rifle and all they had to say was "get the gun" and he would run, tail between his legs, for the hole under the house.

Virgil threw the dead snake to Tom. Still lively even with its head cut off, it kept knocking Tom off his feet. He couldn't hold it still enough to eat but wouldn't let go. With his hind legs spinning in the loose sand, he dragged the snake into the almost empty dog food bag. The top of the bag was rolled down to allow the dogs to eat on their own and the stiff paper edges held the snake while Tom ate until he could hardly walk. But the dogs nearly starved themselves to death over the next month. Whenever they approached the food bag, they'd smell the snake and leap back in terror.

Tom turned out to be a fierce hunter and a sneak thief. Every night, he climbed on the cooler and stole food. Virgil hammered chicken wire around it but he ripped that off with claws and teeth. Bully and Tissy tried to kill Tom once but he gave them some nasty scratches and bites before he climbed a tree. His only injury was a damaged meow box that from that point on emitted the most hideous yowls. "He passed the test," Marcy told Kelly. "I'm sure he'll survive the wilderness."

Tom found he could squeeze into piles of rocks left by past miners and searched out ground squirrel nests to eat the babies. They could hear the ruckus way down in the rocks when he fought with a mother squirrel. He came out of one encounter with part of his lip bitten away and on another occasion had an eyelid bitten off. Seeing him sleeping with his exposed eye open was creepy, especially when Marcy passed her hand over it and he didn't respond.

They loved to sit under the cedar trees at the outdoor kitchen area in the evenings, watching the bats fly low. Tom watched them swoop down. "You'll never catch those, Tom," Virgil told him. "They're too fast for you." Just as Virgil finished, Tom leaped into the air and snagged one. "Whoops! You sure did, you quick sneak," Virgil laughed.

One time Tom was gone for a week. Kelly searched and searched for him and finally decided something had eaten him. But after a few more days, Tom appeared, a big rotten spot on his chest with two puncture wounds where a rattler had gotten him. The ordeal changed Tom's personality. Prior to the snakebite, he would only tolerate the family and at the first sight of a stranger, he would vanish for about three days. After the snakebite, he turned into an affectionate cat to all. Although he had avoided people in the past, he became friendly to everyone and the whole family missed the extreme independent nature he'd had in his early years.

On winter nights, Tom entertained them. He stayed outdoors during the day but was allowed in the cabin in the evenings until the family went to bed. He loved popcorn with a passion and came yowling for some each time he smelled it. Kelly would stick buttered kernels on each of his claws and they'd watch as he held his paw up, daintily biting off each kernel, one by one.

Kelly carried Tom around with him most of the time. "How come Kelly gets a cat and I don't?" Joel asked.

"The next time we go to the Garedos, we'll get a kitten from them," Marcy promised him.

Holding to her word, they stopped at the Garedos the next time they went to town. When they got out of the Jeep, they smelled a strong odor of burning corn. Al and Alvereta's daughter, Sara, was running the fruit stand and smelled it, too. "I'm burning my tamale pie!" she hollered back at them as she raced toward the house.

Virgil stooped behind the Jeep and chuckled. "Those darn mice have stuffed the tailpipe full of cracked corn and it's burning."

"It sure smelled like my pie," Sara said after Marcy told her about the corn in the tailpipe. "Why didn't you bring Red?" she asked, looking wistfully into the Jeep.

"He didn't need anything from town," Marcy grinned, suspecting that Sara was sweet on Red. "We're looking for a kitten. Do you have any?"

"You want a kitten?" Sara led them to the back porch and scooped one up that shared her golden hair color. "I call him Goldilocks."

"We'll call him Goldie," Virgil stated.

"He won't eat anything but this," she said, handing Marcy some canned milk and a box of expensive cat food.

Joel patted his cat and carried him out to the Jeep.

"He'd better get used to rattlesnakes and dog food because I'm not going to spend good money on feeding him canned milk," Marcy told Virgil after they left. "We can't even afford canned milk for ourselves."

He turned out to be a coward but how could he help that after starting out in life with a name like Goldilocks? Gaines took an instant dislike to him after Goldie snuck in the shack and pooped on his bunk.

Rain was beginning to become frequent now and after school hours, Virgil and the boys worked on a woodshed addition to the cabin. The thought of their soggy wood supply in Denny pushed them until dark every evening to get the poles, split more shakes and mill the boards so their wood supply would be dry. As each day passed, Virgil learned more about time schedules in the wilderness. Although he had planned to have a least the shell of a house up by then, the sill logs were waiting at the river's edge until he could devise a way safer than the walking tractor to get them across the Flat to the new building site, since they had abandoned their original building site at the upper garden.

One raw morning they were eating breakfast under their hastily stretched awning, the leaky one, moving their plates from one spot to another to avoid drips while drops of rain splattered on the griddle. Marcy was trying to cook wearing one of the boys' bright yellow rain hats while water ran across the sloping ground and formed puddles of mud underfoot. Virgil pulled out his pipe, filled and lit it. Thoughtfully he puffed, remembering the drifts of snow under the cedar tree where the camp kitchen now sat and thinking about how the canvas wouldn't hold any snow. Then the days of rain and subfreezing temperatures they'd experienced in Denny drifted through his mind. "Do you think you could use the wood shed for a kitchen this winter?" Virgil asked.

"If the stove will fit and me, too, I think I could manage a lot better than out here on snow shoes," Marcy answered. "If you could build some shelves to store my summer's work on I'd be real happy," she continued, pointing her pancake turner at the boxes of vegetables and fruits in jars being soaked by splattering rain.

By the time the soaked boxes started collapsing, Virgil had the shelves built in the woodshed, and instead of shakes, had clear plastic windows. They managed to condense the summer kitchen's 500 square feet down to 56 square feet. They put the wood cook stove in the middle with a chair in front for Marcy and the redwood bench against one wall for the boys. Virgil sat on a cut tree stump on the other side of the stove, sharing his spot with Tom. Marcy cut a round of red carpet to keep down the slivers on Virgil's stump and with everyone sitting in the new kitchen, it was extremely snug but warm and dry and Marcy loved it! With the stove burning, the kitchen stayed nice and cozy but they knew the heat would be unbearable once the weather warmed and they'd have to move the stove and kitchen back out under the cedar trees each summer.

In the fall, as soon as breakfast was over, the boys got ready for school and with their books under their arms, came to the table under the trees. The mumble of memorizing multiplication tables mingled with the fading summer's song in the river. Fraction tables and spelling lists fluttered in the autumn breezes and when they started scraping frost from the table before breakfast, they knew they'd soon have to move inside.

The shack was still dark and a lantern hanging from a wire in the rafters didn't light enough space for the schoolwork of three boys. "Marcy, we have to have lights to the cabin. Do you suppose we can spend any more money on wire?" Virgil asked.

"How much would it cost? I don't mind if we can have a little money left for an emergency," she answered.

After counting cash and pacing distance, they discovered that the cost of the wire would leave them with just $19 to last until they could make and sell some jewelry. "We can't do it," Virgil said. "And at the rate the gas for the lantern is going, that won't last either."

"We'll work something out," Marcy assured, and they did.

They were looking through the ruins of the flume tender's cabin one Saturday when the boys brought Virgil a piece of junk to identify.

"Why, that's a magneto from an old crank telephone," Virgil said. "Red keeps talking about using telephone wire to fix everything. Let's see if we can find some more."

Not many yards down the river, the boys began seeing insulators tied to trees. For those that weren't broken, the boys climbed the trees, unwired them and brought them along. They soon found some with the wire still in them and by evening of the next day had enough wire down across the river to reach the cabin from the generator. For arithmetic in school, they figured ohms, voltages and amperages for their wire, but with the most generous of tables in their electricity books, they were in doubt of getting enough power to run their Christmas lights.

"Well, all your other authorities on this whole power project have been wrong. Let's put up the wire and if it doesn't work, I'll have a good long clothesline," Marcy suggested. But she never got to hang so much as a sock on the line. When they finished setting freshly peeled poles with their cross arms and insulators across the Flat and wired the cabin, their 250 watts of light streamed out of the newly installed picture window across the Flat where the late fall winds were beginning to blow the rain-spattered leaves toward the gray-black river.

The power plant put out a total of 600 watts and they were grateful to get away from the expense of the Coleman lamp and be able to read by electric light. There wasn't enough water flowing down the creek to keep up with the outflow to the Pelton turbine but the storage over the day provided three hours of light in the evening.

They called one of the spots where they crossed the river Emerald Pool because of its beautiful green color. A huge log had come down the river in the 1964 flood and wedged itself over the pool and they used it as a bridge to cross over the river to get firewood when the water was too cold to wade. Virgil wanted to do something that would be easier for all of them and decided to bolt together an iron cable car. He put the cart on a black polyethylene rope spanning the river in front of the summer kitchen area and the boys could load on wood. A smaller tether rope pulled it back and forth across the polyethylene rope.

The boys soon discovered that they could ride the cart over on the three-eighths-inch rope, saving them the trouble of going all the way to Emerald Pool. The only problem was the slow stretch of the rope; they could only get across if they moved fast. "Why don't you come across the rope like we did, Virg? Then you don't have to walk all the way to Emerald Pool," Gaines yelled from across the river.

"I'll give it a try," Virgil yelled back as he got on the cart and started to pull himself across with the tether rope. It snagged on a boulder, stopping him right in the middle of the river. He yanked on the rope and every time he did, the nylon rope stretched down in the river dipping his hind end in the cold water. The more he struggled to get it loose, the more the rope bounced up and down dipping him in, a little deeper each time. Knowing how much Virgil abhorred cold water, they weren't surprised when he started cursing. When the tether rope finally jumped free of the boulder, he pulled himself back across the river and saw everyone laughing. He told them to get the wood themselves and headed for the shack to dry out.

Ray heard the story and showed up with 300 feet of three-eighths-inch steel cable on his next visit. The flat spot across the river where they cut wood was about 20 feet higher than the kitchen area, with most of the elevation gain coming in a near vertical rock face on the far side of the river. The river had cut a steep set of rapids through the boulder-covered rock bar between the kitchen cedar and the far flat. Virgil and the boys decided to attach the cable to the kitchen cedar tree and stretch it across the river to use to haul across heavier loads of firewood and logs for a log cabin. A large fir that had been dead a long time leaned heavily over where the cable would span the river canyon so Virgil decided to cut it down before stringing the cable.

As he cut into the trunk of this snag with the Remington chainsaw, the saw bar suddenly buried itself into a hollow void at the core of the tree. Instead of wood chips, a mixture of punk wood and foul smelling ants, known in the area as piss ants, poured out. As the snag fell and struck the ground it broke open, strewing the nasty little creatures all around. "Watch out!" Gaines yelled. "Here they come!" Avoiding the ants, they carefully tied the cable around a stout fir that was behind the fir snag. As dusk fell, the cable-stringing project was completed.

That night in the cabin, the boys were doing schoolwork while Virgil and Marcy read. Suddenly, Gaines yelled and slapped at his leg. "A piss ant bit me! One of them must have been on me when we came across the river."

Kelly sat cross-legged on the floor with his schoolwork on his lap, as was his habit. "Ouch! One got me!" he said, scrambling to his feet and dumping his schoolwork on the floor. "There's a whole trail of them coming under the door!" he exclaimed, looking at the floor in amazement.

The next morning they went to investigate and saw a solid line of ants marching across the 300 feet of cable and then another 100 feet to the cabin. The undulating line of ants seemed to march to a chant, 'A home for a home, an eye for an eye!' Kelly discovered that tapping the cable sent a sharp wave across the wire rope, knocking every last marching column off into the rocks and river below. This turned into a war game with the boys and a few days later the ants conceded defeat and stayed on their side of the river.

❦

As the boys studied, Marcy picked the patch of Indian Dent corn and shucked the dry kernels off the cobs. By rubbing two cobs together, the corn came off fairly easy. She shucked out 100 pounds and it lasted almost three years in tightly closed cans.

The row of pumpkin seeds they had planted in spring gave them pumpkins big and small. They had plenty of pumpkins for canning and for Jack-O' Lanterns. When Halloween came, the boys picked out the big pumpkins to carve. Marcy told them to use their imaginations and make costumes from scraps. Although Virgil had a prejudice against Halloween when the boys were very young, he nevertheless made them masks out of papier-mâché, some of which were works of art. "Come and trick us at the shack when it gets dark," Marcy laughed.

Gathering all their materials together, the boys went to a huge boulder they'd found that was gouged out like a cave and dressed themselves up as brown goblins in costumes made from gunnysacks. They called the rock the Elves' House.

Marcy decorated the shed with corn stalks and put candles inside their Jack-O' Lanterns to light the entrance to the door. Inside the shack was dark. Marcy made a black peaked hat, put some black lines around her eyes and blacked out one front tooth. With black yarn hair, she looked spooky. "Trick or Treat!" the boys yelled.

Marcy lowered her voice. "Come in, come in, my pretties," she cackled, and for a second, they were tempted to run.

❦

The nights were beginning to freeze and the wind blew leaves across the Flat like so many colored kites. The time had come to butcher Lucifer. Virgil got a 35-gallon trashcan of water and lit the fire under it. He looked glum but tried not to show it to the boys. Marcy almost called off the butchering but instead told the boys the same words her mother had told her. "Pigs are food. Look at all the ham and bacon we'll have."

What Marcy didn't tell them was that when it was time for the butchering, Mama, who seldom drank, would steal away to her room with a pint bottle of whiskey. Marcy couldn't stand to see Lucifer shot either, so she hid in the shack. All her talk about bacon and ham evaporated and she quietly wept for the pig.

Tissy went with Virgil, and when the shot rang out and the pig lay kicking in the mud, Tissy stared in disbelief. She looked up at Virgil with such unbelieving eyes that a wave of sadness came over him. After that, Tissy wouldn't come near him for a month.

After the tragic moment was over, Gaines helped Virgil dip Lucifer and scrape him after they hauled him out of the boiling water. Marcy still couldn't confront it until they had him gutted and cut into pieces to make into bacon and ham. Marcy felt better about the whole thing when she saw how eagerly the boys cut into their first pork chops but Virgil felt the loss of the pig and Tissy's love greatly. He never was a hunter type but he knew when it came to killing, it had to be his job until the boys grew up.

Thanksgiving came, the first they would celebrate at the Flat. Doug always joined them for Thanksgiving dinner and this year was no exception. He brought a turkey with most of the trimmings and they invited Red to join them as well. As her side dishes bubbled merrily on the wood cook stove, Marcy pulled the turkey from the oven and set the roasting pan lid on Virgil's stump while she basted the almost-done bird. The lavish dinner included mashed potatoes, gravy, yams, cranberries, their own canned corn and beans, fresh homemade bread, and apple pies made with apples from the orchard.

They planned to eat outside since it was a warm sunny day so Marcy dug out her lace tablecloth and filled jars with late-blooming flowers to place upon the table. She asked Virgil to get the turkey and he placed the steaming pan on the edge of the table while Doug and the boys helped Marcy carry out all the side dishes. They sat down as Virgil sharpened the knife with an Arkansas stone, and with forks poised, they eagerly watched as Virgil lifted the lid. There, lying on top of the turkey was Virgil and Tom's dirty old red rug, which had stuck to the inside of the lid when Marcy laid it on the stump. She was horrified but everyone else exploded with laughter. Virgil removed the rug and carefully peeled away the cat hair covered skin before carving the turkey.

They all dished up their plates and Marcy put Red's food through the grinder, as he still hadn't bought his 'Killer Teeth' as he called them. After dinner, Red got a faraway look in his eyes. "You know, Pantywaist, that was the first holiday dinner I've had since I left home as a young man."

It rained for many days and the river started rising. Virgil and Marcy stayed up watching it during the night. When Red came the next morning, they asked if he was scared the river would flood him out again. "We stayed up almost all night watching it," Marcy told him.

"What you watching it for? No one's gonna steal it," he grunted.

Storage became an expanding problem. It began raining constantly, and if it wasn't raining, it was sloppy snow. The water dripped from the eaves onto the tops of the trashcans full of rice, wheat and beans placed against the side of the house. "Marcy, we'd better check those cans. Condensation is liable to ruin the supplies," Virgil said.

"Ok. You saw off this ham hock while I put a batch of beans to soak," Marcy replied. "Then we'll check."

In addition to pork chops, Lucifer had become bacon and ham by this time and when Virgil remembered how Lucifer had bit him, he could bite him back and enjoy it.

When they tried to lift the can of beans to take it to the kitchen out of the rain, they couldn't budge it. While Virgil held a raincoat over the can, Marcy lifted the lid. "Virg, did you put that other sack of beans in here, too? This can is full to the brim."

"No, didn't you? I'll go check. Should be under the kids' bunks," Virgil said as he went in the shack. "It's still there," he said as he came back out to hold the raincoat again.

"I'll scoop out enough to fill the bean box in the cook shack, and then we can move it," Marcy said.

She took several scoops and poured the beans into a steel box that held about 30 pounds. They didn't ping when they hit the bottom, but sort of thudded. The next scoop of beans was wrinkled and when the bean box was full, Virgil worked his arm down through the beans still in the can. "No wonder we couldn't move it. The bottom's full of water," Virgil said and tipped the can to pour out several gallons of brown liquid that joined the stream already making its way through the cook shack door to turn the dirt floor to mud.

"We'd better not throw them out. Maybe I can dry them in the oven if I take the wood out," Marcy said.

When they dragged the can into the cook shack, it filled the space between the stove and the door. It wouldn't go through the small space between the stove and the storage shelves so it sat in the doorway, while the stove settled slowly in the mud, breaking the seal where the stovepipe went through the roof. More brown water ran down into the warming ovens where the salt had been stored to keep it dry.

In the steamy warmth of the cook shack, the beans swelled more rapidly. Every cookie sheet, bread pan and pot had beans in it, one stacked on top of another. Virgil inspected the lid and found a pinhole leak left from when he had repaired the bear damage. While he was gone to the shop to solder it, Marcy burned her hand on a dry pan of beans, dropped it and in trying to catch it, hit another pan, and like the walls of Jericho, they all came tumbling down. "Thank goodness the rice is in plastic bags," Marcy said as she started shoveling beans and mud into a bucket for her compost pile.

Red showed up one Sunday and announced he was leaving for the winter to stay in Corning. He left singing, 'I'll see you when the roses bloom again.' They didn't expect him until spring but he walked in on them several weeks later to show off a new eight-transistor battery powered radio. "I turn my eight tramp sisters on and they keep me company all night."

"We thought you were still in Corning," Marcy said. "When did you get home?"

"About a week ago. It was costing too much to stay out," Red explained. "When I opened my shack, I found a ringtail cat living in it. I enjoy watching him when he comes in at night. I stayed perfectly still the first night and he hopped up on my chest and stared right into my eyes. He's been coming every evening. I put food on my chest and he hops up and eats it. Now he eats out of my hand like a house cat. They make fine pets," he said, drinking a glass of carrot juice Marcy had made from carrots she'd stored in clean, wet sand.

"Pantywaist, this juice tastes just like orange juice," he muttered, licking the orange rim from his mustache. "I'll have to watch my strawberries come spring or that ringtail will eat them up. Heh, talking about strawberries," Red continued, "last year I picked a few and threw them in my mouth and chomped them down before I realized I'd swallowed something else with them. I could feel whatever it was hopping around in my stomach. Soooooo, I put a teaspoon of DDT in a glass of water and drank it and the hopping stopped."

"Oh no! You could've killed yourself taking that!" Marcy gasped.

"Let me tell you something. DDT has saved my life many times, just as saltpeter has. It was a time I'll never forget when I shot a buck and ate the whole liver because it tasted so good. The next day I paid for it because I couldn't urinate. Plugged kidneys, I guess. I was in misery for two days and knew I had to do something quick before I got urine poisoning. I put two heaping tablespoons of saltpeter in a glass of water and drank it. That unplugged me for sure! I almost filled a gallon jug before I finished. I put that jug on my window sill and after it settled, I noticed it was half filled with debris like sand."

Little snow fell that year and winter passed quickly. Scarlet fritillaries, Virgil's favorite wildflower, bloomed early that spring. From April to June the apple trees, wild azaleas, mock oranges and poison oak filled the canyon with heady and wonderful scents.

After a terrific lightning and thunderstorm one night, the dogs started barking. Marcy ran outside ringing her cowbell, screeching and yelling. She saw a black shape that didn't back away from her or the dogs so she ran back into the shack. The next morning, they found hog tracks.

Another night, the barking dogs again brought Marcy out with her cowbell. She heard the laughing cackle that the dogs were freaking over and a hyena came to mind. As she was not in Africa, it became a very frightening unknown and she retreated into the cabin and crawled back in bed. The boys all three lay in their bunks, eyes round as saucers. "Oh Virg, what is that?" she trembled and snuggled next to him.

"Why don't you go out with your cowbell again and find out?" he chuckled.

"Are you serious?" she asked.

They never did find out what it was.

Virgil wanted to scout out a way to route the trail lower so it wouldn't be such a steep walk up and down Cathedral Way so they decided to go to Rocky Point, the bluff area that formed the buttress for Wind Dance Lookout. As they walked below Wind Dance Lookout, Bully took off chasing some animal, as usual. He was on the upper side and dislodged a huge boulder that was only staying up by a prayer. It came crashing down, creating an ever-expanding rockslide that barely missed Joel.

They made their way around the steep broken area until gigantic boulders and talus debris impeded their movement, so they took refuge on a little ledge. They could look far up and see the rim of Wind Dance Lookout. They were breathing hard in the heated air flowing upslope when the stench of rotting carrion assailed their noses. Gaines and Joel worked their way out to a pinnacle and observed the mountainside below. "There it is," Gaines said.

"What is it?" Marcy called.

"Looks like a dead deer."

Virgil, Kelly and Marcy made their way to where Gaines and Joel stood. Below was the disfigured twisted doe, her head bent back over her body at an unnatural angle and her sunken eyes fixed on the femur piercing her stomach. Blackened with dried blood, the bone seemed poised to strike the doe's head. Either in a panic from a mountain lion or in a moment of carelessness, she had fallen from the rim of Wind Dance Lookout. They all stared sadly at the unfortunate doe and Marcy announced they were leaving before one of them fell.

"Well, we aren't going to make a trail this way," Virgil decided and they left the area a lot more carefully than they came, keeping Bully on a close leash. After that, they watched cautiously where he went, keeping their eyes focused up above them when he chased anything on their uphill side.

The peace and happiness of living at the Flat had settled in on them and Marcy thought that the bliss would last forever. One day while Virgil and Red were in town, a forest ranger came down. The dogs didn't see him until he was right next to Marcy and then they started barking. He introduced himself and said he should have been down two years ago but didn't get around to it. "What I want to know is, are you going to do any mining?"

Flustered, Marcy smoothed down her hair before answering. "Yes," she said.

"Well, I hope you do because if you don't, you're squatting on the National Forest and you'll have to move out."

"Well, sir, if we don't mine, we can't stay because our mail-order jewelry business would flop," Marcy explained. "We don't have any other income."

"It looks like you're doing more building than you are mining," he observed, eyeing the shack.

"That was an old broken down tool shed that we patched a little to cut down the wind blowing through the cracks in the winter," Marcy said with an edge to her voice. "You know, Virg was teaching school in Denny for two years and it takes time to get settled in and get all the mining equipment ready."

He stared at the shack. "You mean that building was here already?"

"Yes. We just fixed it up a little." Marcy walked over and opened the door. The ranger peered in and saw that, although neat, it was obviously an old shack.

"We have our jewelry equipment set up and some of our jewelry. Would you like to see it?"

Marcy showed him the jewelry shop and he seemed impressed when he saw all of the equipment. "Is Red mining?" the ranger asked.

"Yes. He's looking for gems and has a tunnel started," Marcy replied.

When Red came the next Sunday, Marcy told him about the forest ranger. "Did he ever get to your place?" she asked.

Red's eyebrows shot up. "So that's who sabotaged my tunnel! It was all caved in when I came back from town. Those forest monkeys want to glorify the old mining days and the only way they can do it is to get rid of the present day miners. An elite group wants to build mountain cabins they can rent when the city gets too much for them, like they do in Russia."

"Honestly, Ma, I'm getting nervous and want to start our mining operations," Virgil said. "I've got to make sluice boxes before winter."

Bedframe and pulley cable car for hauling wood

Virgil splitting wood

Marcella in her summer kitchen

Kelly and Joel inside the shack

21 - Characters of the Canyons

"I need to go to town," Red announced one day while visiting at the Flat.

"Ok," Virgil replied. "We need a few things from town, too. How's tomorrow sound?"

The next day, they all loaded into the Jeep and headed for Weaverville. When they got to town, Red wanted out at the Diggins, a bar on Main Street. "You can pick me up when you're done shopping," Red said.

At the end of the day, Virgil pulled up to the curb about halfway between the Diggins and the hardware store. Marcy waited in the Jeep while Virgil and the boys went into Morris Hardware. Suddenly, she saw Red stumble from the bar and look around wildly. Before she could get out and wave him over, he started yelling. "Virgil Horn! Virgil Horn!" Red bellowed, looking up and down the street.

Marcy ran over and grabbed his arm. "The Jeep's right over here, Red," she said as she led him up the sidewalk.

Heading west on Highway 299, Red sang and slapped his knees and leaned heavily against Marcy, like a sack of grain. Somewhere Red had found a lizard and tied it on his hat, and while Red flailed his arms about, the poor little creature ran around the rim looking for a way to escape. Marcy hated to sit in the middle because she always got a headache from the gas fumes coming through cracks in the floorboard of the Jeep. Between Red's antics and the gas fumes, it promised to be a long trip home.

Earlier that year, they'd seen a fully-made bed set up next to a tent in a little gully over the bank on Hobo Gulch Road. Up on the road above the tent, three boys rode bicycles and the oldest of the three had several firearms crisscrossed on his chest. They seemed friendly enough, however, and smiled and waved as Virgil drove slowly past.

On their way to town that morning, the tent in the gully was gone but the postmistress told Marcy the family had moved to a trailer along East Fork Road, which Virgil had noticed on the way out. Now desperate to get a break from the gas, alcohol and body fumes, Marcy asked Virgil to stop and meet the trailer dwellers.

In the hard-packed dirt in front of the trailer, a Ford Galaxy sedan lay on its side. A cable ran from the frame of the Galaxy to the winch on the front of an old Dodge Power Wagon. On the ground below the underside of the Galaxy sat a toolbox with the majority of its contents scattered on the ground. Virgil surveyed the scene and shook his head as he rolled to a stop.

Four people sat around a table under a large fir tree in front of the trailer. A big man wearing a plaid logger's shirt with the sleeves ripped away stood up and walked toward the Jeep. A few hairs stuck straight up from his balding head and the hair around his ears was wet. A dripping neoprene wet suit hung from a line stretched between two trees and Virgil surmised that the man had been dredging in the river.

Virgil introduced himself and then Marcy, Red and the boys. Extending a large hand with only two fingers and a thumb, the big man warmly shook hands with each in turn. "I'm Otis Trull," he said and then waved his two-fingered hand toward the other three people around the table. "And this is my wife, Bambi, and Rusty and Sharon Bolt. Have a seat, but watch the dog crap."

An odd assortment of lawn chairs and modern steel-framed kitchen chairs stood empty. A big shaggy dog on a cable run lunged at them but came up short and expressed his displeasure at the short chain by barking noisily. Bambi, a petite woman with bright blue eyes and blond hair, turned swiftly and proved that her small size did not restrict her lungs. "Sam! Shut the hell up before I come over there and kick you in the nuts!" she screamed.

Sam shut up and padded through the dust into his house, where he glowered out darkly, and Bambi turned back to Marcy with a friendly smile. "Why didn't you ever stop to see us when we lived on Hobo Gulch? We used to watch you drive by."

"We thought you guys lived up there to get away from people," Marcy explained.

"Hell, I get 10 or 20 people stopping by every day. Always glad to have a few more."

Otis sat down heavily and then roared toward the trailer. "CINDY! Get that coffeepot out here before I beat you with a wet noodle!"

A pretty blond teenager opened the door and started down the steps carrying a huge coffeepot. There was a loud commotion behind her and three younger boys, a black lab and a white husky mix burst from the trailer and banged down the steps, nearly knocking her off her feet. "Brock, Mike, Jerry! I'm going to kill you little bastards!" Cindy screamed, her vocal heredity clearly established.

Bambi proudly introduced all of her children, extolling their attributes as she did so. The youngest, Jerry, was near the age of Joel. Thin, blue-eyed and dark-haired, Jerry energetically lobbied for Cindy to pour him a cup of coffee after she finished pouring Marcy and Virgil's cups and refilled others around the table. "Gimme some!"

"Not a chance, Little Bungy!"

Judging by the blazing eyes and the flailing fists whaling into his sister, Jerry did not approve of her nickname for him. Cindy just laughed at him and his punches. "Run along, Little Bungy."

Brock grinned broadly at the antics, revealing a huge silver tooth. "Want to see a bear hide my friend got?" he asked excitedly.

The boys agreed and they all set off to a small wooden shed nearby, except for Jerry, who was occupied with punching his sister. "Take Bungy with you, Brock," Cindy called out.

"Come on, Little Bungy!" Brock called.

Jerry laid into Brock who took it for a while but soon asserted his size and dominance and threw Jerry to the ground and warned him not to get up. Jerry muttered a name under his breath and then rolled away to avoid the kick he knew was coming. "Keep rolling, Bungy," Brock said, kicking at Jerry again.

Jerry kept rolling, right over a huge pile of dog manure. "You just rolled over a pile of dog crap!" Brock exclaimed. Disbelievingly, Jerry grabbed a handful of the sticky brown goo clinging to the back of his shoulder and whipped his hand around for a sniff test. With confirmation bringing him to his feet in a rage, he came at Brock swinging. Laughing, Brock held his foot up to ward off the brown-smeared brother.

"Rusty and Sharon here live up on the East Branch of the East Fork, just over the ridge from where you all live," Bambi explained for the quiet couple.

Although neither had a chance to talk much, Rusty enthusiastically invited Virgil and Marcy to visit him and Sharon.

Virgil nodded toward the dripping wetsuit. "Were you dredging?" he asked.

"Yeah." Otis' eyes sparkled. "Just got out. Blew a damned hose."

"Are you getting any gold?" Marcy asked.

"Bambi! Get the gold pan," Otis ordered. Bambi went into the trailer but left the door ajar. Bending over a well-worn couch, she pulled a gold pan from under it and returned to the table. Otis took it from her and pushed the gold pan in front of Marcy and Virgil. A layer of small gold nuggets covered the bottom of the pan. "How do you like that?" he asked.

"You got all of those here?" Marcy asked in amazement.

Otis pulled a small pill bottle from the front pocket of his plaid shirt and handed it to her. Small nuggets covered the bottom of the bottle and one large round nugget rolled around on top of them. Marcy's eyes grew big as she gaped at the size. "Like that, don't you?" Otis roared. "One half ounce right there," he declared and launched into the tale of finding it. Eventually he asked, "Are you having any trouble from the Forest Service?"

"No, we haven't," Virgil answered.

The squad of boys walked past in the general direction of the river. "Stay away from that river!" Otis yelled at them.

Otis was a former logger and like most people in Trinity County, he loved to gab about his adventures. "When I quit logging, I got a temporary job on the county road crew," he stated. "My boss asked me if I could detonate dynamite. Heck, I never touched dynamite in my life but told him I could. He told me to blow up a big boulder that was in the road and I figured that the best way to do it was to put the charge under the boulder. All that did was blow a big hole under it that it fell into."

Bambi sighed deeply. Obviously tired of listening to the same old stories, she decided to tell a few of her own. "Marcy, yesterday I heard one of my chickens squawking out in the hen house. I ran out and saw a big eagle making off with one of my best laying hens. She was so heavy that the eagle couldn't lift off. I grabbed my broom and whacked it and sent it crashing against the trailer. It lost a few feathers but dropped the hen."

After pouring them another cup of coffee, she continued. "When we were living on the Hobo Road, the kids came running in and told me they saw three naked people in the woods. I couldn't believe my eyes! Sure enough, two women and one man were standing there stark naked. I grabbed my shotgun and fired over their heads. You never saw such startled faces; they scattered as fast as the shot. I guess they were playing 'nature lovers' in the wilderness and didn't think anyone was around," she chuckled.

"Do you see a lot of rattlesnakes around your place?" Virgil asked Otis.

"There are a few but I think the chickens and dogs keep them away," Otis replied, reminded of another story. "When I was on the road crew, a bulldozer operator was pushing a stump over. One of the roots tore loose and flung a ball into the cat skinner's lap. It was a ball of rattlesnakes just coming out of hibernation. He leaped out of the cat and saw that they were starting to unravel so he dumped diesel oil on them and lit a match. Just then, some young college-type fire officer was driving by and cited him for starting an illegal fire."

The stories continued long into the evening and it was late that night before they said their goodbyes, climbed into the Jeep and headed back to the Flat.

～~✦~✦

Creatures of the woods, which included the insect world, tended to seek shelter and a board and batten constructed cabin gives little barrier to their invasion. Marcy awoke one night and saw Kelly sitting straight up in his top bunk bed, flashlight pointing at the wall, his fist beating the cardboard covered ceiling above his head. "What's wrong, Kelly?"

"I heard something scratching under the cardboard so I peeled it back and found one of those striped fat-belly bugs lying on his back waving his arms at me. I squashed him under the cardboard."

"Ugh! That's a Child of the Earth," Marcy surmised.

Marcy had just gotten back to sleep again when she awoke with something crawling on her cheek. She brushed it away but it squashed, giving off a nauseating rotten odor. Marcy jumped up and grabbed Kelly's light.

"What's going on?" Virgil asked, waking up.

"Some awful, and I mean awful, smelling bug squashed on my face," Marcy said as she scrubbed her face with tissue.

"Go back to sleep," Virgil grumbled.

Marcy wiped her face one last time, turned the pillow over and was almost asleep again when Virgil leaped up. "Did you hear that? I just threw something across the room. It was so big it cracked when it hit the wall."

"So? Go back to sleep," Marcy said but she felt creepy-crawly the rest of the night.

Early the next morning, Virgil wanted her to look at his mustache. "What is that on it?" he asked.

"Spider webs!" Marcy screeched. She grabbed the fly swatter and searched the room. On the windowsill above their bed, Marcy saw a mound of white powder. Looking up from the mound, she saw the biggest gray spider she'd ever seen. The size of a quarter with its belly bulging, the spider stared down at Marcy and wrapped herself around her egg sack. "Virgil!" Marcy called. "That's what crawled on you," she said, showing him the spider.

"She's not doing any harm." Virgil reasoned. "Besides, she'll eat the other bugs so let's leave her alone."

"If I feel her crawling on my side, I'll throw her on you again," Marcy declared.

They called her Shelob from Tolkien's Lord of the Rings. As Marcy cleaned the cabin a couple weeks later, she pulled back the sheets and saw a knobby looking Shelob crawling across the bed. Marcy swept her to the floor with a fly swatter and hundreds of the knobs fell off, scurrying in every direction, the tiny baby spiders dislodged from where she'd carried them on her back. "That's it!" Marcy said. "We're going to get some spider spray!"

"Why don't you use some of the mosquito spray?" Virgil suggested.

Taking his advice, she sprayed all around the shack and after that, they weren't troubled with spiders.

Red was still keeping his promise to come see them every Sunday, plus some. When he finished preaching, he'd reminisce about the past. Marcy and Virgil found his tales interesting and he was pretty good at not repeating the same stories.

One Sunday he told them about the mule driver who brought a 400-pound brass water wheel down to run the sawmill at Baxter Gulch. "It was to be used to cut the lumber downriver for the flume. The driver put hooks on stout branches hanging over the trail. When he brought the mule down, using the hook, he'd remove the wheel from her back so she could rest." Red stopped to open his snoose can. "They cut a lot of lumber with that wheel. They even gave Dan Raymond the lumber for your shack to store tools in." He put a pinch of chewing tobacco into his mouth. "The Raymonds lived in a cabin across the river before it burned down."

"I saw where Dan had built a nice corral for his mules," Virgil said. "The gate was ingenious. He'd carved a hole in a big tree stump and put a sharpened pole into the hole to act as a pivot when you opened the gate."

"Yes, old Dan was pretty clever," Red said while rubbing the stubble on his chin, his gaze continually darting about, as usual. "I saw him trap quail in one of his homemade cages. He'd reach inside of the cage very gently and let the skinny birds loose, and keep the fat ones for lunch. He gentled them so much they eventually became tame like chickens." Red sat thinking awhile. "If you ever go to see the saw mill, you'll pass a pond close to my place," Red continued. "A fellow by the name of Strawberry Jones used to live there. The cabin is gone now but Strawberry Jones' pond is still there and every spring you can hear the frogs croaking. If a bear hears them, good-bye frogs! He'll make a meal out of them every time," he chuckled. "Heck I was tempted to make a meal out of them a time or two myself. I remember times in my life when it was hard pickings. I found that I could seine minnows with a screen and cook them. And the wild grass seeds had almost too many stickers to eat but I ate them anyway after pounding them to a pulp. Pantywaist, if you ever get in a position like that, remember what I'm telling you."

"What about the digger pine nuts?" Marcy asked. "They're good to eat."

"Yeah, if you can beat the squirrels to them. Remember the Digger Pine Indians are extinct now because they depended on them. Even the inner bark of the sugar pine has sweet juice if you peel it in the spring," Red declared. "I got pretty hungry before I got my pension," he continued. "I took half a jar of instant coffee, mixed it with enough water to drink the slurry before I went to see the doctor to see if I would be eligible for the pension. My heart was racing just as I thought it would and I got the pension and now they even give me Social Security. The good life's with me now and I can save a lot of money if I stay in the canyon all winter," he boasted.

Most people thought Red was finding a lot of gold when he came out and did expensive shopping after saving his checks all winter. He encouraged the idea by telling everyone that he buried his gold in the garden. But Red confided that 'his gold' was really the contents of his outhouse.

⌦⌫⌦

Red showed up mid-week, eyes wild, and begged Virgil for some of his pipe tobacco. "I ran out of snoose," he explained.

Virgil gave him half his pipe tobacco. With a shaking hand, he stuffed a big wad in his mouth and then told them about a plant that looked like kinnikinnick. "I made a cigarette out of it with toilet paper but afterward I thought it was some kind of dope because it made me feel like I was going crazy."

"We're going to town tomorrow, Red, and we'll get you some Copenhagen," Virgil assured him.

The next morning, Red stomped down the trail again and dumped his pack down. "I brought you a present, Pantywaist," he grinned.

Marcy thought he'd brought her another fish but when he reached in his pack, he pulled out a dead ringtail cat. "What happened to your pet cat?" Marcy said incredulously.

"It ate my cheese and I shot it."

With sad faces, Joel and Kelly reached over to pet the dead animal. "Don't you have lids for your larder cans?" Marcy asked.

"Yeah, but I forgot to put them on."

Marcy wondered what kind of man kills a pet that he'd tamed himself. Tom came in, grabbed the dead ringtail and dragged it off. Later, they found him lying under a tree, his belly huge. He was howling and passing gas so badly they thought he was going to die. He'd eaten the whole ringtail, hair and all.

Red knew he'd touched a nerve with Marcy and it seemed pure spite when he came over the following Sunday with a beautiful lynx he'd shot. Marcy was furious. "Why are you killing animals just for fun?" she yelled.

Red glared. "Well, Marcy, it wasn't just for fun. I brought it for you to cook," he said sarcastically. "You're always saying it's fair game if you eat it."

After Red left, Tom came in to sniff the lynx. "Here's something you can get sick on," Marcy snapped at him. But Tom just licked her face and let out a sorrowful meow. Marcy was surprised and asked Virgil why Tom would eat the ringtail but seem totally distraught over the lynx.

"A ringtail isn't really a cat, it's a coon," Virgil explained.

About a month later, Marcy was on her knees cleaning up her lower garden, her face and legs streaked with dirt, when the dogs announced company. They heard the mountaineer call and knew it was Red. The boys no longer came when they heard Red's call. Virgil frowned and continued pounding nails and Marcy kept on shoveling. Down the trail came 'Lord Red' himself, clean silver hair gleaming in the sun. Dressed in a new pair of Levis and a clean shirt, he carried a shiny new handsaw. Virgil looked up. "Well, hello stranger."

Red walked straight, with dignity, and his fingernails were trimmed and clean. During his usual two-hour visit, he spoke like an Oxford graduate and a cultured gentleman. Marcy invited him to join them for dinner. In response, his normal "Nope, just et" was replaced with "Why thank you, lady. I believe I will." At the table, his manners were suitable to a formal state dinner. He then picked up his saw, flexed it and held it vertically between his knees. As he tapped and flexed the saw, beautiful music filled the air. "You see, Marcella, I can be a gentleman *if* I want to be," Red said proudly when he stood to leave. He walked away with a carefree wave of his hand as Marcy gaped in disbelief.

Virgil shook his head. "I would think he was just putting on an act but he had to have been exposed to that culture somewhere. The old devil's been hiding something from us."

After that, his visits were back to the usual, dirty old Red, yelling at them. "I'm trying to tell you, it's all written down. And it will be a robot world. Religion will be smashed into shards on the altar of discontent before 'His' coming."

"Do you want to go crevicing for gold before someone else comes down?" Marcy asked Virgil and the boys early one morning, just as the sun's long golden fingers crept down into their canyon. "It seems like we haven't had any time to mine like we want to."

The boys loved to hike and crevice for gold in the cracks of boulders. With their packs loaded with gold pans, crevicing tools, wire brushes and a lunch, they headed upriver but the dogs started barking and they stopped in their tracks. "Darn! Who do you suppose that is?" Marcy groaned.

A tall young man with a copper beard and long copper hair, wrapped in a serape greeted them. He extended his hand and introduced himself as Dale Pendell. "George Jorstad sent me to see you folks. I have a gold mine close to his claim and I do some mining."

They'd heard of George but hadn't met him yet. Virgil offered Dale a seat, figuring Dale was a miner and they'd have things in common. Dale gratefully sat and told them he was on the lookout for Indian rock art. "I'm putting together a series of stories about people I meet in the wilderness. It's not started yet but will be called *The Gold Dust Wilderness*."

Marcy stoked the fire and heated water for coffee. She'd just baked a batch of rolls she'd intended to take on their outing and offered one to Dale while pushing wild blackberry jam towards him. "You saved my life, Marcy. Thank you," Dale said as he dug into the jam. Then he pulled out a label and told them he was the inventor of a health drink made from birch bark called Osceola Cola. "It's sorta like birch beer but contains no alcohol," he explained. Dale downed the last of his coffee. "George Jorstad said you make jewelry."

Virgil perked up at the prospect of a customer.

"Any chance you could make me a knife?" Dale asked.

"Sure, I could do that," Virgil nodded.

"Great! I'd love if you'd make me one that has magic in it," Dale continued. "Can I trade one of my books for it when I'm finished?"

Virgil thought for a few seconds. "Yes, I can do that," he grinned.

Marcy could tell Virgil was excited about the knife project and decided Dale's book was a good trade even though they needed money. Dale had wandered over several states gathering information and sketches on Indian rock art and wanted some included on the handle of the knife. He took out his sketches and discussed the knife design with Virgil.

As they talked afterward, Virgil mentioned Red's experience smoking a plant he thought was some sort of kinnikinnick. Dale was interested in plants with a 'kick' and wanted to know what the plant looked like, so Virgil told him what ridge Red had pointed out. "The way Red acted, I'd be pretty darn careful before smoking it," Virgil warned.

"I want to go meet Red anyway," Dale said. "I'll be back in a few weeks and will remember your advice on the weed."

Virgil worked on the knife for several days, following Dale's unusual and intricate designs. It turned out to be a wonderful piece of art – a truly magical knife. Some months later, Dale returned with one of his books, a lovely hand bound volume of silkscreened petroglyph sketches. Dale loved the knife Virgil had made and they were all pleased with the exchange. "Could I use some of your petroglyph designs for jewelry?" Marcy asked. "I'm making silver pieces along with our gold."

"Sure, they're authentic, use all you want. Share the wealth, you know," Dale replied. "I'm interested in writing a series of poems and short stories and thought you could help me by telling me more about Red. He's so unique and blends in with the woods and animals. Even the paper wasps fly in and out of his shack at will. He's in perfect harmony with nature," Dale observed. "What a wonderful person to write about."

"You must be kidding," Marcy scoffed.

Dale looked puzzled. "What do you mean?"

"He killed his pet ringtail cat and a beautiful lynx. He also told me about putting DDT in the mud where the mud daubers were getting material for their nests. He said he watched them as they gathered the mud and when the poison started reacting, they rubbed their heads before they toppled over."

Dale gaped at Marcy in horror. "Did he really do that?"

"He isn't some benign old man living peacefully in the woods," Marcy said.

Virgil looked at Marcy. "What mirth must burst from idols when they fall and break?" he quoted.

"Yes, Virg, I had Red on a pedestal as The Grand Old Mountain Man," Marcy admitted. Dale exchanged glances with Marcy and she felt that he, too, had made an idol out of Red. Sometime later, Dale sent them two small pamphlets containing a series of his poems.

Another winter approached and Virgil watched as Marcy beat on the pipe of the kitchen stove and rattled the grates under the firebox trying to get more heat under the pancake griddle. The front pancakes were coming off the griddle pale and white. "I'll have to build a woodshed this year," Virgil stated as he stared at the firebox filled with damp wood.

Virgil and Gaines scouted about looking for dead trees. Using the Granberg mill, they sawed boards for a week before they had enough for the woodshed roof. Joel and Kelly peeled poles for the frame. When they finally finished the roof boards, they nailed them on the pole rafters and covered them with tarpaper. Marcy hauled the rounded slabs left over from cutting the logs into boards and hammered them on the pole frame to enclose the walls on three sides. The finished woodshed resembled a log cabin. "Now, all we have to do is fill it with wood," Gaines said.

Getting firewood to the Flat was a long job, as they had only manual labor to haul every cord. Sometimes they backpacked wood from a quarter mile away and consequently, they never got their wood in until the winter rains had already started. A mix of snow and rain was falling when a shortage of dry wood forced Virgil and Gaines across the river to cut more. The slushy, soggy snow penetrated all their clothing. After hours in this weather, they came into the shack, both in a moderate stage of hypothermia. Shivering, they stripped off their wet clothing while Marcy poured them hot drinks but it was some time before they finally got warm.

Gaines packing branches to the woodshed

Filling the woodshed

Woodshed with siding

22 - Winter Snows and Earthquakes

Their second Christmas at the Flat crept slowly upon them. Since the shack was so small, they looked for a perfect small, fluffy tree to put on a little table in front of the window. They found one growing by itself on the side of the mountain and just one string of lights and a scant amount of Christmas decorations covered the whole tree.

A few days before Christmas, Marcy awoke to a hushed silence enveloping the shack. When daylight came, two feet of powder snow greeted them. Wasting no time, the boys raced out with their toboggans and packed it for a run, and were still sliding down the path that evening with lighted torches of rich pine marking their runway.

They all made Christmas presents for each other. Virgil made a little end table for Marcy. Kelly and Joel made Gaines a wooden-handled knife with a Tiger's Eye stone on the tip. Gaines made Joel and Kelly some miniature mining tools. They all made Marcy a copper mobile.

Virgil doubted Marcy's sewing abilities after seeing what she'd done to a pair of wool pants Ray had given her. She'd initially cut them down to make a pair of warm pants for Gaines but they were too small for him, yet too big for Kelly. She cut them down again and the resulting pants were too small for Kelly. Well, she still had Joel. She cut the pants down again and all would have been fine except the zipper reached from the waistband in the front halfway to the waistband in the back. The fly was so huge Joel refused to wear them.

Marcy wanted to prove to Virgil she could sew and decided to make him a pair of wool gloves. She tore apart old gloves to use as a pattern and used new wool scraps. When the gloves were finished, she was surprised and pleased how well they turned out. On Christmas Eve, Virgil stared at the gloves in disbelief and tried them on immediately. Over the years, Virgil gave Marcy the best compliment possible; he wore them all the time.

Virgil killed two roosters they'd bought in Redding earlier that year. Marcy stuffed them with wild oyster mushrooms, garlic, onion, celery and breadcrumbs, also roasting some Jerusalem artichokes on the side of the chickens. She baked the usual pumpkin and apple pies, cookies and homemade bread. She still had tomatoes ripening on the windowsill so she sliced them with onions and sprinkled them with garlic, vinegar and oil. Marcy also opened their own home canned corn and beans, which she sprinkled with dried sweet basil and garlic.

After Christmas dinner, everyone snuggled in their beds reading new books they'd gotten from relatives back in Sylmar. Marcy stepped outside after dark and looked at the little shed nearly buried in snow. The Christmas lights glowed through the square window and reflected off the little snow-covered fir tree outside their door, giving the illusion that it too was lighted. The isolation was complete and all was quiet; even the river sounded hushed. Peace flowed through Marcy and she chuckled, thinking that the complication of buying Christmas gifts was minimal on the Flat.

Early in January as the sun melted the snow in the daytime but it froze hard at night, Virgil thought they could walk out to town. The post office was a 10-mile hike but they were all eager to check the mail for late Christmas presents and cards.

At four in the morning, they loaded up with backpacks and candle bugs. The snow crunched like sugared corn flakes under their boots. Marcy was on a steep hill trying to balance by hanging onto a dead branch when the branch broke, sending her flying downhill to land on her face in a snow covered fissure. "Hey Ma! Are you okay?" Virgil yelled.

"Surprisingly, yes." she answered, climbing back to where the rest of the family stood holding their lighted candle bugs.

"Me Tarzan, you Jane. Glass Mountain slippery," Virgil teased when he saw she wasn't hurt.

When dawn came, the frosty green conifers stood in the silent winter morning against faint pink strands of cirrus stretching across a turquoise sky. When they reached the Montgomery's place a half mile from the base of Hobo Gulch Road on East Fork Road, Dave Montgomery gave them a ride to Trinity Oaks. With rosy cheeks and noses and their snow-dusted caps, they arrived at the restaurant that also housed the post office. John, the owner, had a fire going in the fireplace and was delighted to see them. "A late Merry Christmas to you!" John greeted. "I see you still have a lot of snow up at your place."

John took them to a corner where all their presents and cards waited and brought them steaming cups of hot chocolate. They invited him to join them and share the cookies Marcy's mother always sent at Christmas. A large, round faced, jolly looking man sat at another table. Overhearing their conversation, he got up and strolled toward them. "Hi," he said jovially. "I'm Emery Beattie. You must be the Horns I've been hearing about. I live at the Enterprise Mine near the end of the East Fork Road. Probably your closest neighbor, besides old Red Barnes."

Virgil knew of the Enterprise Mine, the largest hard rock mine in the North Fork drainage. Its main shafts and mine portals were at the base of Backbone Ridge below where the slide across the Hobo Gulch Road had stopped them a few years before. Since World War II, the Enterprise had pretty much lain idle. "Are you going to start production on the mine again?" Virgil asked Emery.

"Sure am," he said. "Had a little setback the other day, though. My brother was up on the East Fork Road with the backhoe clearing out a slide. Seems he weren't paying much attention when he was backing up and he backed the hoe over the bank."

"How's your brother? Is he ok?" Virgil asked.

"He's fine but had to leap off before it went over," Emery went on, whistling and using his large hands to convey the severity of the fall. "Now the hoe, he went down 300 feet to the East Fork crik. No trees, nothing."

Kelly stared in horror. "What happened to the backhoe?"

Mr. Beattie beamed a wide smile down at Kelly. "He hit the boulders so hard in the crik bed that he broke into nothing more than a pile of broken iron. Had to take the D8 into the crik to get the pieces out."

Mr. Beattie entertained them with more stories about his orchards near Sebastopol and his recent move to the Enterprise. When they'd rested and felt they should head for home, they reluctantly started packing their goodies into their backpacks. John graciously drove them as far as he could before the snow and icy road stopped him. Well after dark, they staggered down to the Flat, unloaded their packs and started the fire.

January, with its sunny days and freezing nights, made the snow hard enough to walk on and they remembered Red Cockroff's maple syrup making instructions. Virgil got his hand drill and told them each to bring coffee cans to catch the sap. Kelly proceeded to cut a garden hose into four-inch pieces. "We'll use these as spigots," he explained.

After drilling into the maple trees, Virgil pounded a piece of hose into each hole. They tapped small nails into the trees above the spigots and hung the coffee cans with wire bails. They checked the cans periodically and as the sun got higher, the sap dripped faster.

The next morning they checked the cans first thing. The sap had stopped at night but commenced again when the sun came out. Standing by a huge maple down in the streambed, Virgil yelled for Marcy and pointed at lumps on the tree. "Look at this. Dan Raymond must have made syrup here, too. Here are parts of grown-over nails and the crushed ends of wooden spigots," he said.

At the upper garden close to the stream where the maples grew, Virgil placed a grill over a bonfire. Once they'd collected five gallons of sap, Gaines would pour it into a flat pan Virgil had welded for that purpose. Kelly got the idea to split a long hose in half to use as a trough. He ringed it all around the maple trees and the sap ran into it, then into a bucket at the end, saving them from going to each tree. They got almost a quart of syrup from every five gallons of sap, which Virgil read was better than the maple trees in Vermont. The next morning they had real maple syrup with their pancakes.

Marcy had the urge to hear the news late one night in early February. They still had the little radio and her resolve not to listen gave way. She turned it on and between bursts of static, heard there was some sort of catastrophic event in southern California. Piece by piece, bits of the story came through but any time an announcer started to say what had happened, the radio signal faded into static background noise. They knew there'd been riots and antiwar protests going on so Virgil surmised it must be a huge riot.

As they strained to hear the news, they soon realized Highway 210 was closed. Interstate 5 was closed. Sepulveda Boulevard was closed. Nervous reports about the condition of Van Norman Dam came through the static. A report came through about a collapsed wing at the Olive View Hospital, a construction project their friend, Dick Peterson, had worked on. "Hell! It has to be an earthquake," Virgil concluded.

As more and more reports came in, they found not only was it an earthquake but the epicenter was right on Sylmar. Completely isolated, no one could get through to the area, or call in or out. They worried about the safety of relatives and friends. As Uncle Gary was a ham radio operator, they thought perhaps they could get the Jeep out and contact a local ham in Weaverville. If the telephones were out, Gary would be on the emergency channel, if he wasn't hurt or dead. Vern Ryan, the owner of Ryan's Store in Weaverville, had told them earlier about Lyle Taylor, one of the first ham operators in Trinity County. Lyle might be able to contact Gary.

The weather was clear the next morning and the snow had hardened enough to walk up trail. But when they reached the Jeep parked at the mill site, it was still sitting in two feet of snow. The snow packs at the lower elevations in Trinity County's mountains become drifted not by wind but the melting and freezing between winter storms. South and west facing slopes, which receive the weak winter sun more than north and east facing slopes, melt down at a greater rate. The greater the number of sunny spells between snowstorms, the greater the disparity between the slopes. The weather patterns that winter had brought this phenomenon out stronger than any, except their last winter in Denny.

The hard corn snow had built into piles around the Jeep's doors where it had slid from the cab. Virgil tried to open the door but it stopped, grinding with a gritty sound against the coarse snow. They'd brought all three of their shovels from home, one flat blade and two pointed ones. One of the pointed shovels had lost half its handle to some earlier over-strenuous project and Virgil used this one to excavate the snow so he could open the door. Inside a smell of dankness, old motor oil, stale gasoline and some kind of urine made Virgil wrinkle his nose. "Whew! That stinks!" His next words were mixed with expletives. "Some rat, squirrel or mouse has chewed a hole in the rubber gear shifter boots."

On the 1954 Willys Jeep pickup, the bench seat hinges up so a person can access two storage areas beneath. It was there they found the source of the urine smell, in a huge rats nest made from stuffing torn from the seat. Kelly had the hood open and was hooking up the battery terminals, which Virgil kept disconnected to avoid a slow drain that would discharge the battery over the long periods between town trips. Virgil climbed behind the wheel and grimaced. "What's wrong?" Marcy asked.

"That damned rat has totally chewed all the padding out of my side of the seat. The metal springs are grinding against my bony butt!"

As Virgil pressed in the clutch, the pedal screeched loudly against the sheet metal flooring and Marcy covered her ears. "What is that?" she yelped.

Virgil bent down and peered at the floorboard. "That rat has chewed the rubber grommets out from around the brake and clutch pedals trying to get in." He set his jaw. "Oh well." Putting the key in the ignition, Virgil called out to Kelly and Gaines who were both bent over the open hood examining the six-cylinder flathead super hurricane Kaiser engine. "Are you clear? I'm going to see if this heap will start."

"Not yet! I'm still filling the radiator with water," Gaines yelled back. While Virgil was shoveling snow away from the door, Gaines had gone the hundred yards up the road to the little spring that had kept them supplied with water during their first days at Camp Desperation and had brought back a five-gallon bucket. After the block froze on the old Ford station wagon in Denny, Virgil always drained the radiator after each winter town trip. Antifreeze was a luxury they could not afford. Gaines finished and capped the radiator. "All clear!"

The key turned and clicked in the ignition, but that was the only sound. "The battery's dead," Kelly said.

Virgil climbed out of the cab and got a half-inch wrench from under the seat. He walked through the snow to the side of the engine compartment and took the battery terminals loose. From his pocket, he took out the pocketknife he carried everywhere and began scrapping the battery terminals and the terminal connectors with the blade. He had reconnected the terminals and was tightening the bolts with the wrench when a rat crawled up the bell housing onto the head block. Virgil had obviously been thinking premeditated revenge, for the extremely rare killer side of him emerged and he cracked the rat over the head with the wrench. Somewhat addled in its motions, the rat jumped off the engine and made a run for the woods. Tissy, who hated anything smaller than herself that moved, snarled viciously and lunged for it. Bully leaped back in horror from the four-legged creature scampering across the snow. The rat never made it 10 feet and Tissy spent the next 20 minutes gnashing it with her teeth, even after it was long dead.

"Are we ready?" Virgil called settling behind the steering wheel again.

"All clear!" Gaines called back.

This time the engine turned over in its normal sluggish manner but did not fire. The battery sounded very tired. Starting the Jeep had always been a major operation and the cold weather and long period of inactivity made it even more of a problem. Some years later Kelly realized that even though the Jeep had a six-volt system, the engine they'd put in it from the first Jeep had a 12-volt starter motor. When they eventually converted the Jeep to a 12-volt system, it started without a problem.

Kelly had gotten the other door open and was digging around behind the seat. "Hold on, Virg. Don't run the battery down." He found a piece of tubing behind the seat and an old candle bug in the pickup bed. Putting the tube down the gas filler port he sucked on the tube until he got a siphon going and a mouthful of gas that he violently spat out. For his efforts, he had about half a cup of gas in the bottom of the candle bug. Ahead of the game, Gaines had pulled off the air filter and Kelly poured a few teaspoons of the gas down the throat of the carburetor. "Now try it, Virg."

The flathead roared over a few seconds, then violently belched an orange fireball out of the carburetor throat and died. Gaines and Kelly leaped back from the open hood. "The timing's too advanced," Kelly decided and started adjusting the distributor. "Now try it." This time it started up strongly and smoothly and they all cheered.

While Virgil, Gaines and Kelly started the pickup, Joel and Marcy shoveled snow out from in front of the tires so they could get the one pair of chains on the front. After the chains were on, the job of just turning the Jeep around was a long one. But after about a 10-point turn, Virgil had the Jeep heading up the mill road. They all jumped into the Jeep but Virgil stopped them. "I don't want anyone in here going up the mill road."

The boys and Marcy got out, immediately apprehensive, for now they knew Virgil wasn't confident of getting the Jeep up the mill road without sliding it over the steep hillside. Virgil started, leaving them to follow. Between snow banks, he accelerated way beyond any speed he had driven the road before. The mill road had weathered away, so at spots was no wider than a foot beyond the width of the Jeep's tires. At other sections, the trees thinned out and revealed the North Fork 1,100 feet below.

With this knowledge in mind, the boys and Marcy ran behind, breathing hard. They watched the sliding and lurching green of the Jeep blend into the trees and vanish around the corner by the spring. Now with only the unnaturally loud roaring of the Jeep reverberating off the spur ridges to inform them of Virgil's progress, they stopped and listened. Suddenly, the sound rose to a violent scream punctuated with loud bangs, then total silence. The boys and Marcy stood frozen in a circle staring at each other's horror-stricken faces. Kelly broke the circle at a dead run up the road and the rest of them followed. Marcy almost never ran but the adrenaline poured through her veins and she postholed through the snow behind her sons.

The tracks of the Jeep were twisted and tortured, at places veering within inches of the edge. With great relief, they came upon the Jeep halfway up the steepest grade, still on the road. Virgil was still in the cab but had the door open, sending out clouds of smoke as he puffed his pipe. The snow around the tires was stained ocher with clay and dirt and clouds of steam billowed from under the hood. "She's high centered," he informed them. "We have to dig out from under her."

Kelly cautiously opened the hood expecting to see the radiator torn out but happily found that the steam was only snow vaporizing off the exhaust manifold. Digging the snow out from under the Jeep proved to be a frustrating job. Once they dug to near the center of the vehicle, getting the clods of snow out became a real pain. Eventually the Jeep settled and Virgil was able to back down the hill 100 feet. Joel set to work digging the snow from the road and Gaines and Marcy joined him with the remaining shovels.

It took them hours of digging to clear the snow from that steep, 250-foot long section. Exhausted, they stopped and Virgil climbed behind the steering wheel. He roared up the hill past them and they followed behind, their hearts in their throats. Virgil made it to the double-back corner at Desperation Point where the snowfield was not much more than 50 feet long but was nearly four feet deep of dense packed snow. The boys attacked the drift with renewed vigor as this was the last snowfield of the uphill climb, but by the time Virgil churned through the remnant of this drift, dusk was approaching. They would not make it to town this day and ahead lay the long walk back to the Flat. Tomorrow they would try again.

Turning the radio on again that night, they calmed down when they heard there were few fatalities from the earthquake. The next day, they went back up and spent all morning fighting their way through the drifts on Hazley Road. Finally, they reached Hobo Gulch Road and Virgil let the rest of the family ride with him. The snow had melted clear on a good portion of this road but in the protected draws, the snow still drifted deep. As they came to these drifts, the boys were out with the shovels before the Jeep had stopped. If the drifts appeared shallow enough not to high center the Jeep, Virgil would gun it and they'd charge sliding and spinning through the drift. Before long, it became almost fun. They got the Jeep out on the county road at 2:30 that afternoon. When they finally located Lyle, the ham operator, he didn't think he could contact Gary because he didn't know Gary's call sign but assured them he would try.

Getting updated information by KFI and KFWB AM broadcast radio eased their worries, as there were no reported fatalities near any of their relatives or friends' homes. The snow had melted considerably and they went back to town after hearing the phones were back online in Sylmar. They were relieved to hear that all their friends and relatives were fine. A few weeks later, they got a letter from Virgil's sister, Leta, telling them that the man who'd rented their old adobe house got restless and left the house a few minutes before the quake struck. It saved his life because the adobe, with all its big beams, bricks and memories, had collapsed into rubble. Marcy was thankful they'd decided to move to Trinity County early.

23 - Dental Work and Soft Drinks

On a cold wet morning, the fire was weeping along in the stove Virgil had stoked with oak wood. They'd mined earlier and were just coming back to the shack. Marcy wanted to try making bark baskets and had left redbud bark simmering on the stove in the shed. "Smells just like a wickiup in here," Virgil said.

Marcy enjoyed the earthy incense as she started work on her first basket. Suddenly a back molar started aching. Knowing they couldn't get to the dentist, she tied a string around the offending tooth and told Virgil to pull. A short attempt later, Marcy held up her hand to stop him. "Stop! I'll do it myself! You're jerking my jaw out!" she squealed.

Marcy tugged the string back and forth all day loosening the root of the tooth considerably, but the pain was too great to make the final pull so she gave up for the day and tried to untie the string. For an hour, she worked at the string dangling from the corner of her mouth. Finally, in tears of pain and frustration, she found Virgil working in the jewelry shop. "I can't get it out," she sobbed. "And I can't sleep with this hanging out of my mouth!"

"I'll get it out," Virgil said calmly but despite his best efforts, the wet swollen knots wouldn't come loose.

"What am I going to do?" Marcy cried, rising panic in her voice.

"Hold your horses," Virgil said and located a razor blade knife. "Hold still. I'm going to cut it out."

"Don't cut me!" she shrieked.

"I won't! Just hold real still," Virgil instructed. Carefully, thread by thread, Virgil cut through the string.

As it fell away, Marcy sighed in relief. "I'm never doing that again," she declared.

For the next two weeks, she worked at the tooth in the evenings sitting on her bed in the cabin and it loosened a little more each night. One evening as Virgil read in his chair at the foot of the bed and the boys sat around the floor doing schoolwork, Marcy let out a triumphant cry. "There the SOB is!" she said as she threw the molar on the bed.

Infection spread to her front tooth but this time she drew some money from savings and went to the dentist, hoping he could save it. The dentist diagnosed gum disease and told her the tooth would have to come out. Virgil asked the dentist to save her tooth after he pulled it so he could make her a false one but when they got home, Virgil realized the tooth was too discolored to use. He searched around the shop looking for a piece of plastic that would match her other teeth but everything he found was either too white or too yellow. He finally found a section of 30,000-year-old mammoth tusk given to them years earlier by an old friend. It was the right color after he cut, ground and polished it on the lapidary unit and with determination and ingenuity, he shaped and made her a plastic and silver bridge and it was almost impossible to tell that the new tooth was false.

Virgil finished the tooth just before they went to town. On the way, they stopped at the Trull's and Bambi handed Marcy a cup of coffee. Marcy showed Bambi her new tooth. "I definitely wouldn't have guessed it was false," Bambi laughed.

Sharon and Rusty were there, as well. Rusty invited them to come see their place and Virgil promised they would the following week.

Later that day at the market, Marcy ran into several friends and noticed their eyes focused on her tooth when they talked to her. She ran her tongue across it and the new tooth felt funny. Marcy gave Virgil a big smile. "Does my tooth still look okay?"

His eyes widened and a grin spread across his face. "What's wrong?" she asked and hastily took out her mirror. The tooth now looked like a fang and was the color of coffee. Bambi's coffee had stained the tooth and caused it to swell. When they got home, Virgil replaced the mammoth tusk with a piece cut from a plastic radio knob and that tooth lasted several years with just an occasional repair.

They worked extra hard that week to get caught up so they could go see Rusty and Sharon. The road to the Bolt's place forked down on the right from Hobo Gulch Road just before Hazley Road turned up to the left. They dropped steeply through a number of switchbacks until they came to a dilapidated bridge with a barricade and a *Tired Bridge* sign. "Shall we try it?" Virgil asked.

"It looks better than the one at Denny and not nearly so high," Marcy observed, so Virgil moved the barricade and drove across. The road ended at a large open-walled shed. From there, they followed a well-used footpath for three-quarters of a mile up the sharp ravine of the East Branch of the East Fork until they came to an A-frame house with plastic windows.

A metronome-like clanking came from farther up the stream and they followed the sound. They found Sharon and Rusty watering a small garden perched on a rocky bench 50 feet above the East Branch. "What's that noise?" Kelly asked before anyone had even had a chance to say hello.

Rusty smiled. "That's a hydraulic ram pump. Do you want to see it?"

Kelly's chin bobbed enthusiastically and Rusty lead Virgil and the boys down a trail that was nothing more than a series of slide chutes to the river. The ram pump was a heavy cast iron device with a large bulbous protrusion rising from the top. A four-inch pipe terminating at the pump ran up the river to a small catch basin of water formed by stacked river rocks. A clanging plate of steel rhythmically and sharply terminated a large fountain of water rising from the pump.

"Works on the water hammer principle," Rusty said. "That steel plate shutting off the fountain of water is creating enough pressure to lift a smaller amount of water up to 90 feet in the air. That's what we're watering our garden with."

"What's the bulb on top?" Kelly asked.

"That's the air chamber. It smoothes the outflow water so it don't come out in spurts."

"Hydraulic ram, hydraulic ram," Kelly kept muttering.

"You drove over the bridge?" Sharon asked in horror when Virgil mentioned where they'd parked.

"I thought you just put that sign on the bridge to discourage people from crossing and stealing your stuff. I saw tires tracks after the bridge," Virgil said.

"Oh no! That sign is telling the truth. I have a little cut down car I run back and forth on this side of the creek," Rusty explained.

"Well that bridge looks a lot better than the bridge we had to cross in Denny and it didn't fall down until right after we left," Virgil said.

Rusty raised his red eyebrows. "Right *after* you left?"

"Well, about a year after we quit driving across it."

"Lucky," Rusty said.

The Bolt's A-frame cabin was cozy and smelled of the elderberry wine brewing on the benches inside. Sharon went down to the creek and came back with coke bottles filled with cold, delicious homemade root beer. "I haven't tasted homemade root beer since my dad made it when I was a kid," Marcy said. "Sure brings back memories of him. When he opened a bottle, a geyser spewed out leaving my sisters and me only a fourth of a glass each. How come yours aren't doing that?"

"You have to keep it cool after it's fermented," Sharon explained. She wrinkled her nose as she told Marcy of the time they went to Red's cabin to see if he would let them float downriver from his place to look for nuggets. "You wouldn't believe what he tried to feed us! He had some beans rotting on his stove. He threw soda in them and told us they would sweeten up and be all right."

Marcy smiled, remembering the rotten fish he'd given her.

When they were ready to leave, Rusty and Sharon followed them out to make sure they made it across the bridge. Everyone except Virgil got out of the Jeep at the bridge but it just creaked slightly as he crossed and there wasn't that throat-tightening fear brought on by the Hixson Bridge.

The next morning Marcy was enthused about making some carbonated drinks like Sharon's root beer. She didn't have root beer extract so she decided to try berry juice instead. "Do you think it will work, Virg?" she asked as he worked in the shop.

"That'll be fine," he answered.

Marcy suspected he wasn't listening but continued anyway. "Virg, she told me to keep it cold after it barely fermented. Should I add a tiny bit of yeast and put it someplace warm to get it started?"

Virgil nodded as he concentrated on how to extract microscopic gold out of black sand using cyanide.

When Marcy finished the concoction, she poured it into gallon-sized glass vinegar jugs. Seeing that Virgil was gone, she crawled up to the attic of the shop and stored the filled jugs in their little storage area.

The weather was very hot and Virgil was still working in the shop on his project a few weeks later. He'd made a jar that contained a motorized paddle to stir a slurry of black sand mixed with gold dust in a cyanide solution where the cyanide dissolved the fine gold. As it was turning, he worked on some silver and opal martini olive picks.

Suddenly, there was an explosion overhead. Virgil started at the first explosion, nearly sticking an engraving tool into his hand. Behind and above him, Virgil had built a shelf for his chemicals, which included nitric acid, sulfuric acid, hydrochloric acid and potassium cyanide. This shelf of toxic and potentially explosive compounds was the first thing that crossed his mind. Before he had a chance to start moving, a deluge of hot liquid poured down over his head and back. With his hands over his head to protect his face and eyes, Virgil ran from the shop.

Outside in the sun Virgil stared in anguish at what appeared to be blood and knew that he not only was drenched in powerful acids, but that the bottles had cut him to ribbons, as well. But then he tasted the blood running down his face and into his mouth. *Blood is not sweet*, he thought. Marcy heard the explosion and came running and saw the red berry juice covering his hair, face and mustache. Unlike Virgil, she knew at first sight exactly what the red liquid was. Virgil shook the juice out of his beret with an extreme look of disgust as he touched the sticky liquid while Marcy failed in an attempt to suppress laughter. "What the hell is this stuff?" he growled, now both mad and disgusted at the loss of dignity and the nasty sticky liquid.

"It's a carbonated blackberry drink I put in the attic to ferment. I'm sorry," she apologized with a chuckle.

Virgil still wasn't finding the humor in the situation as he cautiously climbed up to investigate the stiflingly-hot attic, where all the gallon jars had shattered but the Coke bottles she'd filled were intact. "What does it look like up there?" Marcy giggled.

"Take a look for yourself," Virgil said as he handed down a wooden shingle peppered with large shards of glass. "The glass is embedded all over the place and much of it has gone through the tarpaper."

Marcy quit laughing. "Gosh Virg, that was close."

"For God's sake, warn me next time."

"But Virg, I told you I was going to store them there."

"Grab that heavy wooden crate down there, with the pulleys in it. Dump out the pulleys and I'll hand these Coke bottles down to you." Carefully, as if he was handling nitroglycerin, Virgil handed the bottles down.

"Well, obviously they're done fermenting," Marcy laughed. "I think I'll put these in the river to cool, then open one and see if the boys like it," she said once the last bottle was in the box.

"Well, I'll just stay here and clean the sticky shit off my tools," Virgil replied, climbing down from the attic.

After several hours, Marcy retrieved one bottle from the cool river and called boys to the kitchen area. She got three glasses and placed one in front of each boy. With a bottle cap remover, she ceremoniously lifted the cap off the coke bottle. What came out was no ordinary champagne fountain but a supercharged high-pressure blast that carried a full 70 feet away. All that remained in her hand was an empty bottle. The boys stared with a mixture of disappointment and fascination at what they'd just witnessed. As they stared at their empty glasses, the look of disappointment deepened.

"Kelly, go down by Washing Rock," Marcy instructed. "There's a crate of bottles down there. Get another one. That bottle was probably a fluke."

It wasn't. There was a tiny drop in the bottom of the second bottle, though, and Marcy took a sip. "Should I get another one?" Kelly asked, getting set to make another run to the river.

"No! It's wine! The sugar in the drink has turned to alcohol," she said and the disappointed boys left the kitchen.

Red showed up the next day and Marcy told him the story about the drink. "Get me one, Pantywaist. I'll show you how to do it," he said. He slowly lifted one edge of the cap and sucked at it when the liquid started to seep out. As the pressure dropped he would lift the cap a little higher and suck on it some more. "Pantywaist, I'm an old hand with home-brew," he grinned and drank the whole bottle without losing a drop.

Virgil handed Red a rough rock that had a point of gold at the end and didn't look like it had rolled around in the river. "How about this? Marcy found it downriver on the bank."

Eyes riveted, Red reached for the rock. "Yeah, it's fine if you could find the vein," he said as he dismissively tossed the rock aside.

They didn't think any more about it until they wanted to show the rock to someone else. They searched where Red had tossed it but never found the rock again.

After Red left, Marcy started thinking about a party they'd had when living in the adobe house. Marcy had asked if anyone knew anything about water witching and a friend, Jim, said he did. So Virgil asked Jim to find the cesspool so they could get it pumped out. Jim got a couple clothes hangers and bent them to fit into two beer bottles. He gave one to Marcy and kept the other. The trick was to hold the bottle just so and the wire would spin around and point to where the water was. With both wires spinning, they found the water lines and goose pond but not the cesspool. Then Marcy's witch started spinning and pointed at Jim. "I know why! I'm full of beer!" he laughed.

If the water witch could find water for her, Marcy wondered if it could find gold. She went into the shack and got a wire clothes hanger. Instead of putting it into a bottle, she bent it into an L shape and held the short end. She asked it to point to gold. The wire spun around like it was alive and kept pointing to the river. Marcy walked toward the river and it spun around a couple times and pointed down into a shallow part washing over some bedrock.

Marcy had learned from Bambi to fan the sand with her hand to float the lighter sand away, leaving the heavier black sand and gold lying on bedrock. Marcy kept fanning until all the sand was gone and the bedrock exposed. The sun was just right and glittered on her first nugget lying on the exposed bedrock. Goose bumps popped up all over and she almost got scared of the witch but after that, she was out in the river witching all the time. She always found gold but never a nugget as big as her first one.

Marcy missed having a bathroom and the luxury of a bath every night. The only way to get a hot bath was to spend hours heating water on the wood stove. Because of the trouble, baths were limited to once a week. There had to be a way to save time and the heavy lifting in order to get a bath and Marcy was determined to find it.

Marcy spied the 35-gallon galvanized metal garbage can Virgil had used to scald the pig and decided it would make a good tub. She dragged it down to the sand bar, set it up on rocks over a fire pit and filled it with water from the river. There was plenty of driftwood lying around so she gathered an armload, piled it under the garbage can and lit the wood. The flames curled up from the bottom and it didn't take long for the water to heat up. She placed an orange crate next to the tub to use as a step and hung a towel on a convenient willow branch nearby. What a glorious hot bath it was as she hunkered down in it!

She was singing and soaping when the bottom of the can started getting too hot. She didn't realize the fire was still blazing; in her mind's plan, she thought the wood would burn down and stop heating the water. But the flames continued to heat the thin metal that formed the floor of her tub. When her soles started burning, she grabbed the top edges of the garbage can and lifted her feet up off the bottom. Soon the muscles in her arms started shaking and failing. Slowly she settled back into the can, pulling both knees up as she did to keep her feet from getting burned again.

Now she was wedged in, unable to get her feet down even if she wanted to and her arms were too weak to pull herself out of the can. All the while, the fire that was supposed to have burned down kept popping and crackling, adding even more heat to the water. This was not a good position to be in, either for a person's modesty, dignity or physical wellbeing. For a number of minutes she struggled to extract herself with her modesty and dignity intact, but as the water started to simmer, physical wellbeing won out. "Heeeeelp!" she shrieked. "Heeeeeeelllp!"

Her shrieks brought Virgil at a dead run. "What's wrong?" he shouted.

"I'm stuck and the water's boiling me!" she cried.

Virgil assessed the situation for a second and then heaved and pulled on her soap-slickened arms, attempting to free her, but he couldn't get a grip. "Hurry! I'm boiling alive!" she shrieked again, now in a major panic because a quick rescue was obviously not going to happen.

Virgil looked at the bucket she'd used to fill the garbage can and contemplated dousing the fire but ruled against it, for a scalding cloud of steam would surely result. The boys were way up on the mountain building miniature roads for their toys so he couldn't call them in time, so he did the only thing he could and just tipped the can over. In a gush of soapy water, Marcy popped from the garbage can like a cork and landed on her face in the sand. Covered in wet sand, she scrambled to her feet, grabbed the towel and stomped to the river to rinse off. When she came out of the water, she saw Virgil grinning as he talked to the boys. They'd heard the shrieks and had come running and she overheard some jokes about needing a few potatoes and carrots.

Joel, Gaines and Kelly - 1971

24 - Adventurers, Younger and Older

They got a letter from Doug saying he planned to ride a bicycle up from San Jose in early June and had been getting his legs in shape by riding it all over town. "Virg, that's a 300-mile trip up here. Those flatlands in San Jose are not like the Trinities. I don't see how he can make it," Marcy worried.

"He's getting close to 40 and thinks he has to prove something to himself," Virgil grinned. "Remember, I moved here at that age."

Doug was supposed to arrive within three or four days so Marcy cleaned out the winter kitchen and put in a cot for him. They began to worry when he didn't show up and Virgil decided they'd go look for him if he didn't come on the fifth day.

In the late afternoon, Doug limped down the trail with a full beard and a backpack loaded with groceries. His face was drawn and he collapsed on a chair. "Why didn't you come to look for me?" he gasped.

"Thought you wanted to complete your whole journey and didn't want to interfere with your adventure," Virgil answered.

"Well, I'm not going to ride the blasted thing back. I had to drag it up the Hobo Road because it was too rocky and steep to peddle."

"How are you going to get home?" Marcy asked.

"The friend I borrowed the bike from will pick me up if I call her."

After a week, Doug finally felt like he could walk straight again. He went with them to snipe for gold and helped with the gardens. Virgil asked if he wanted to try his hand making jewelry and he made a silver ring for himself. Marcy had canned lots of blackberries so she made Trinity Tarts, one of Doug's favorites. "Marcy, if you set yourself up a table in San Jose and sold these, you could make a fortune," Doug told her.

After two weeks, Doug had become so much a part of them and the Flat that they were sad when he felt it was time to go back to San Jose. He asked Virgil to drive him to a phone booth to call his friend to come pick him up. The Flat felt sad and empty after Doug left but they knew he'd be back.

In the 70s, the Flower Children were invading the woods and they often saw newcomers sitting on the banks of Hobo Gulch Road reading books. Virgil speculated good-naturedly that the books were probably by Henry Thoreau, the author of choice for many of the young people at that time.

"Look at them sitting by the road! What's wrong with them? Can't they go further into the woods? With all this traffic, it'd be hard to experience nature like Thoreau did," Marcy laughed.

"Don't forget the bears and cougars, Ma. Thoreau was forced out of his town when he started a forest fire. That's why he lived at Walden Pond. I guess he did learn something there, though," Virgil said.

One day, a young man and a pretty blond girl came down to the Flat looking for rattlesnakes. He wore a snakeskin headband over his scraggly light brown hair and had rattlesnake fangs on a leather cord around his neck. He was collecting the snakes to sell for anti-venom serum.

"Where are you from?" Marcy asked the young girl.

"I came from Wisconsin and just met Al yesterday on the Hobo Road," she said, gesturing toward the young man.

"Aren't you scared to just pick up with anyone like that?" Marcy said, eyeing the wiggling snakes in his sack. "If you were my daughter, I wouldn't let you do that."

Her eyes filled with tears. "It's an adventure, that's all," she said and Marcy couldn't fault her for that.

Coming home from one of their weekly trips into town, they rounded a bend on Hobo Gulch Road and nearly ran over a tall man wearing a black beret. He'd stopped at Blue Bottle Springs and heard them coming, so he stood in the road hoping to flag them down. When Virgil stopped, he asked if he could get a ride to Hobo Gulch Campground. Virgil explained they were turning off in two miles but that he was welcome to ride up to there. "I'm camping at Hobo Gulch," he said as he jumped in the back of the Jeep with Kelly and Joel.

He said he was Ted Carter but they later learned his given name was Eugene, though sometimes when he did something that might get him in trouble, he went by the aliases Finwing Klutz, Dr. Phinster P. Phinch, Dr. Fruiti P. Fly or Phinias T. Hogg. Ted was a botanist and an electronic engineer who came to the area to collect wildflowers for his graduate thesis on the flora and fauna of the Trinity Alps. He also told them he had a friend he visited with a claim at the upper North Fork. "Do you know George Jorstad?" Ted asked.

"No. We've heard of him but haven't met him yet."

Ted hiked all over the mountains looking for wildflowers and they'd come across him on Hobo Gulch Road picking up all the beer cans littering the ditches and hanging them on the trees and bushes by the road. "Swine'o American'os," he'd declare, using a Latin name like he did for plants. "Now they can see how their cans look at eye level."

Every day as he gathered plants, he'd stick more cans on the trees, infuriating all who saw them, especially the Forest Service employees who had to remove them. When Finwing as he now called himself saw his cans were being removed, he doubled his efforts and climbed to the very top of the trees to stick the cans on the highest branches. Some were so dangerously placed they wondered why he didn't fall over the cliff. Of course, this didn't set right with the rangers who had to climb or snag them off, so they patrolled the road trying to catch the culprit.

They never did.

Red wanted to go to town again and Virgil wondered if it was really important. They knew he was thinking about drinking but that was none of their business so Virgil told him he'd be at the top at nine o'clock. The rest of the family decided to go, too. Arriving in town, Red ran into a grizzled old man stumbling out of the Diggins. "I want to present you to Amos Decker, our well known ladies man," said Red.

Amos was the miner in the film they'd seen in Denny but Marcy couldn't believe he was the same man. With tobacco juice running down both sides of his mouth and his hair hanging like greasy ropes, he looked at her with drunken eyes and grabbed her hand as if he were still the handsome lad of yesteryear. *So this is Romeo*, Marcy thought.

Beings that Amos was the man from the mining film, the talk turned to the current mining projects. After some discussion, Amos walked over to thirteen-year-old Gaines and slapped him on the shoulder. "Young man, you look like a person in need of a pump."

Gaines looked at Amos in surprise. He'd been working on a two-inch gold dredge and a pump was the one component he lacked. "Do you want to sell one, Mr. Decker?" Gaines asked.

"Hell no. Go ahead and take it," Amos said. "I'll never use it."

On the way home, they stopped by Amos' place on Barney Gulch to get the pump. The pump weighed about 70 pounds, so with Kelly's help, Gaines took it apart and between them, they lugged the cast iron monster down to the Flat. The five-horsepower Briggs and Stratton engine had seen lots of hours and some time in its past had suffered a catastrophic rod failure that had broken out one whole side of the crankcase. It had been patched with a makeshift cover of fiberglass and resin but for a free gift, it was all right.

The next week Gaines needed another part to finish the dredge so Virgil drove him to town and they ran into Amos again. "Why haven't you paid me for the pump?" Amos demanded. "I need cash in a big hurry!" he yelled.

"You told me I could have it for nothing!" Gaines gasped.

"Hell no, I didn't," Amos insisted, his hands shaking.

Gaines was so mad that over the next two days, he packed all the pieces of the pump back up the trail. Virgil drove him to Amos' again and they dumped it in front of his shack.

"He was in desperate need of doodle juice," Red explained when he heard about it. "You should've bought him a gallon and he would've left you alone," he told Gaines.

"Yeah, 'til the next time, and the next time, and we would've been paying for that pump until the liquor store dried out," Virgil shot back.

Virgil laid heavy tarpaper down on the floor of the shack and nailed it flat. Then he put down square vinyl tiles. With antique wooden hand rabbet planes he brought from Sylmar, Virgil made window frames for two of the big plate glass panes they were saving for the new house. He expanded the old window openings and installed the new windows. Once the glass was in, Marcy used her treadle sewing machine to make curtains, creating a cozy look and feel inside the shack. Using poles the boys had cut across the river, Virgil built a little porch out the front of the cabin, taking his time to make it artistic.

Virgil wanted to shingle the roof and outside walls of the cabin and Kelly had found an old froe buried in the dump that they could use to make shakes and shingles. Virgil searched for dead or dying cedar trees but most were rotten in the center. He cut down one good cedar on a hillside where the wind caught it but it was so twisted the shakes looked like propellers. Finally, after looking all over, Virgil and Gaines found one that was growing on the level. He sawed it into two-foot sections, which they took turns splitting into shingles with Kelly's salvaged froe. Before long, they had a pile big enough to complete the job.

With the new shingles, the shack now smelled like sweet cedar inside and out. The tan shingles nailed on the old black shack matched with those on the porch and made it look like a new building. Marcy couldn't believe that the ugly duckling had turned into a swan. Even Red was impressed. "It looks so pretty, why don't you put it inside so it won't get dirty?" he said.

For the first time, Marcy felt civilized in the shack. All their freshly washed blankets and sheets smelled of sun and wind. The down quilts had been soaking in the sun all morning and smelled sweet and fresh. Marcy closed her eyes thinking what a nice place this was to live in!

Shack with porch & Marcella's flower gardens

Shack with new shakes and porch

25 - High Country

Several bald, craggy peaks, called Thurston Peaks, crowned Limestone Ridge. They'd always wanted to hike up to the 7,500-foot high peaks so one hunting season on a beautiful Indian summer type day, Virgil and Marcy decided it was time for the trip. Loading up their feather ticks and food, they left at daybreak. With no sign of a trail, they just followed the crown of a spur ridge up. Marcy always thought their trail was steep but not compared to the trek they made that day! The higher they went, the more dwarfed and twisted the trees became and along the ridgelines, the wind-combed trees distorted into exotic shapes.

It was a glorious sight to see the autumn leaves in translucent pastel colors as the sun shone through them. They climbed a spur ridge that tapered into a higher ridge covered with dense huckleberry oak brush. On this north-facing spur ridge, years of heavy snowdrifts had flattened the brush into down slope facing lines of barricades in what seemed to be a design to keep intruders away. The brush was 10 to 12 feet high and once in the thicket, they could see nothing but snarled branches. "Are we going in the right direction?" Marcy asked Virgil.

"I can't really tell but we just have to keep moving up and eventually we'll reach the top of this ridge," he replied.

Soon their bleeding brush-scratched arms forced them to put on coats for protection even though the heavy exertion was breaking a sweat on all of them. In a little pocket of red firs, they came upon a tiny spring seeping from the mountain. The tracks of wild game had churned the lower part of the seep to sticky mud but at the head was a clear little pool. "I'm weak from hunger," Joel complained, staggering in last. "Can we eat something now?"

Gaines and Kelly stayed silent but looked hopefully towards their mother. "I don't know," Marcy said. "What do you think, Virg? Should we wait until we get to the top?"

Virgil looked at the boys. "I say we eat one sandwich now. We can drink water here and not have to use what we're hauling."

Everyone dug eagerly into their packs and got out a heavy brown bread sandwich. After finishing the meal, they each carefully took a drink of water, so as not to disturb the muck on the bottom of the pool. "I'm ready now!" Joel said, enthusiastically hoisting his pack back on.

In mid-afternoon, they finally reached the crest of the higher ridge and the brush thinned out somewhat. Heading west toward the sun, they followed this ridge ever higher. Joel's renewed vigor soon faded and he lagged once again. Virgil stayed behind Joel, encouraging him on. At nine years old, Joel didn't complain much but when he did, it was about being hungry.

The cones were dropping from the red fir, breaking into scattered piles of light tan platelets. Joel stooped and retrieved a fir nut from the pile of a broken cone and cracked it with his teeth. The shell wasn't very hard and crumbled easy, almost too easy. "Is that green like a pistachio?" Virgil inquired, seeing the nut between Joel's teeth.

The look on Joel's face went from eager anticipation to disgusted horror. "Yuuuck! It's a deer turd!" he cried, choking out green chunks. "Water!" he gasped, spitting violently.

"Just spit it out. We have to conserve the water," Virgil said. "We're going to be away from water for two days."

Joel continued to gag and spit for the next 300 yards up the ridge. Finally, they entered a dense little forest of white fir with a relatively level floor but beyond that the ridge rose again into brush and weathered rock outcroppings. Marcy, Gaines and Kelly were already climbing. "You better hurry up, Joel," Virgil urged knowing that the outcropping was just the top of Limestone Ridge and still several miles south of the Thurston Peaks.

Joel plodded, head down, one step ahead of the other. Upon reaching the crest of the pinnacle, he stared in wonder at the land bathed in a late afternoon light, falling away on three sides. A warm pleasant breeze rising on the afternoon-heated western slopes cooled the sweat on their faces. "There's the Twin Sisters!" Gaines said, pointing south at the twin peaks rising from the spine of Limestone Ridge below them.

"There's Desperation Point," Kelly observed, pointing down and to the east.

"Oh my gosh! Backbone Ridge is tiny!" Joel gasped, staring in amazement at the long, low timbered ridge, stretching from the valley of the Trinity River, north to the Backbone Ridge lookout, which showed up as a tiny cube in an ocher colored scar upon the pinnacle of the highest peak of the ridge. Excitedly, the boys each rushed to be the first to identify landmarks. "Look at the Little Thurston!" Joel cried, pointing to the tan and umber peak rising from the ridge north of them. "It doesn't even look the same from here. Let's go climb it!"

They made their way north along the ridge, skirting rock outcroppings and navigating through highly stunted patches of huckleberry oak. About 200 yards north of where they'd summited, the ridge dropped 1,000 feet to a smooth looking saddle. Marcy looked down the long broken slope and paled. *I can't do this. I can't do this!* she thought. *There's too much open space. Just exposed air. I'm getting height fright!* She took a deep breath. *My body feels like it's pulling me over the cliff.* Virgil looked over at Marcy. "What's wrong?" he asked.

"It's too much space or something. I can't take it." Marcy groaned, her legs starting to tremble. "I'll never be able to climb them!"

"Take it easy," Virgil soothed. For a few minutes, he tried to calm her enough to try but soon realized it was not a smart plan so late in the afternoon. "Okay, we'll go back to that little forest just before we reached the top and camp there overnight," he said. "In the morning we'll try again and see if you're feeling better about it then."

Marcy nodded, her teeth chattering.

They found a particularly sheltered spot among the stand of white fir and made their beds. Marcy laid a long bed of feather ticks for the boys while she and Virgil shared a wool blanket. She was a little bit concerned because she had to scrape aside bear dung from every spot. Also, although warm down at the Flat when they left, the wind here had a chill. Up at the base of the ridgeline rock pinnacle was a little flat spot of bare ground. Virgil built a fire ring and lit a hot little fire with dead branches the boys gathered.

Marcy took out her aluminum pot and filled it with water, putting it next to the fire on a flat rock to heat. Then she unpacked a bag full of sandwiches and passed them around. Soon there was hot water for Virgil's tea. She'd brought up a pan, butter, salt, popcorn and a large paper bag. Over the hot little fire, she popped the corn and placed it in the paper bag with melted butter and salt. They took the bag to the rocks on top of the ridge and watched something they hadn't seen in years, a beautiful red sun setting into the coastal mountains to the west. They passed the popcorn bag around as they watched.

Most of the water they'd hauled up was in a plastic gallon vegetable oil bottle and most of this disappeared after they consumed the salty popcorn. Virgil shook the jug. "This won't get us through tomorrow," he said ominously. "We'll have to start back in the morning."

The boys looked at each other in horror. "And not even try to climb the Thurstons?" Gaines said.

"We'll die of thirst without water," Virgil explained.

"I'll go down to that spring right now and get more," Gaines declared.

"Now? It's almost dark!" Marcy said.

"I can be down there and back in 20 minutes," Gaines reasoned.

Virgil was skeptical. "That has to be 1,000 vertical feet below us."

"How are you going to find that little tiny spring in all that brush in the near dark? Did you see all the bear dung?" Marcy said, shaking her head.

"I can find it and I can run most of the way down, and I am not scared of bears," Gaines insisted, even more determined now because of all the challenges placed before him.

Virgil was silent for a short time. "He'll be 14 next spring. Let him go," he finally said.

"Be careful," Marcy fretted.

"I will," he replied as he grabbed the water jug and his hatchet and set off down the mountain at a run.

The chill wind picked up, waving the brush and the white fir tops. The dark purple shadows in the canyons crept up over them and the last pink to the western horizon faded to dark violet. "Where's Gaines?" Marcy worried. "You're going to have to go find him, Virg!"

A snap of dry brush and a voice came from the gloom of the forest. "No, he's not." Gaines walked into camp with a full water jug, tired but happy with himself for saving the next day's climbing mission.

Exhausted after the strenuous day, everyone went to bed. Later, Marcy woke up freezing. Then Virgil awoke and was so cold that Marcy could hear his teeth rattling. The wind moaned softly through the dark trees and they tucked the blankets tighter around themselves, snuggling together for warmth.

Nearby, Gaines woke up and whispered to Kelly and Joel. "Are you guys awake?"

"Yep, and freezing!"

"Let's go light the fire," Gaines said.

There was a sudden rustling in the dark. Then three shadowy figures climbed through the brush to the fire ring where a few dark crimson coals still gleamed in the ashes. "Kelly, where's your flashlight?" Joel said. "I can't see to pile up the tinder."

"Here," Kelly said, switching on a long silver metal rechargeable flashlight he'd made from discarded nickel-cadmium battery cells he'd revived.

Soon Joel had a little flame dancing and Gaines threw down a large armload of dead dry brush. Shortly, the little flame grew through the extra fuel and danced higher, sending columns of sparks into the wind. "I wonder what time it is," Kelly said.

Gaines looked up at the brilliant constellations. "There's Orion," he said. "With Orion in that position to the horizon at this time of the year, it has to be about one a.m."

Far away, they could see the lights of Junction City and a glowing in the sky above Weaverville and Redding. They caught several glimpses of headlights from cars passing through a few sections of Highway 299. Occasionally, far away on dark ridges, headlights flared briefly as deer hunters on logging roads navigated the twisting spurs and draws and forests.

Several hours passed and the thin crescent of a waning, orange moon crept over the dark silhouette of Sawtooth Mountain. Joel propped his feet on a boulder near the fire. "You're going to burn your socks," Kelly warned.

"Naw, they won't," Joel said.

With his feet warmed by the fire, sleep overcame Joel. He awoke a while later to Gaines kicking his feet off the boulder. "Hey idiot, you're burning your socks off!"

Kelly switched on his light and Joel examined the holes in his socks. "I guess I got them too hot," he said sleepily.

"It's a wonder you didn't burn your feet off," Kelly laughed.

When the faint red glow of dawn finally appeared, they rejoiced. "How did you guys sleep?" Marcy asked, walking with Virgil into the fire area. "How long have you been up?"

"Terrible," Kelly answered. "Joel's feet got so cold he stuck them in the fire and burned holes in his socks."

"We've been up since about one," Gaines said.

"Shoot! We should have gotten up, Virg. All that time we were freezing, they had a fire going. Well, help me get some more wood on the fire and I'll make something hot to drink," Marcy said.

As the sun came over the peaks, they hurriedly took just water and headed out. When they got to the overlook above the saddle, Virgil found a pathway down through the brush that allowed Marcy to suppress her fears. Climbing out of the saddle, the brush became thicker and Marcy recognized a shrub that looked like Oregon bay. The leaves looked just like commercial bay leaf so she pinched one off and inhaled deeply. Immediately it felt like someone had stuck a sharp knife in her head. The pain was awful. She'd read the Indians had used bay for headaches and started wondering if it was a bay bush at all as she stumbled around and lost her bearings. Virgil looked back. "What's up, Ma?"

"Oh, Virg, guys, stay away from those plants; they almost killed me!" Marcy warned, and the headache stayed with her for nearly an hour.

At the very foot of the peaks, they'd climbed high enough to see a thin line of the Pacific Ocean over nearly 100 miles of ridges. "You guys go on. I'll wait for you here," Marcy said, feeling nauseous as she stared at the narrow rocky ridgeline going up to the Thurstons. Although Marcy thought the bay leaf caused her misery, they later surmised it was probably altitude sickness taking its toll.

"I'll stay with you, Ma," Virgil said, and they retreated to a cool grove of red fir to wait.

The boys climbed the Little Thurston and when they returned, the long decent back to the Flat began. Shortly, Kelly, Gaines and Marcy doubled over with terrible cramps. As many animals had used the spring where they drank, they wondered if they'd caught a bug from drinking the water and named the spot Belly Ache Spring.

Twin Sisters viewed from camp

26 - Crops and Frost

In early January 1972, the temperature had been below freezing for about a week. From the old gravel bench on top of a long, 25-foot high, near-vertical section of the river's far bank, water that had seeped out over the week had frozen into translucent milky-colored sheets of ice. As Joel, Kelly and Marcy came out of the cabin door, they saw movement across the river. A big cinnamon bear stared at them, uncertain as to whether he should cross. Marcy stood transfixed; this was the closest she'd seen a bear.

Finally making up his mind, the bear lumbered across the river swinging his head from side to side. Kelly, not quite 12 years old, stared at Marcy, waiting for her to do something. When he saw that she wasn't, he ran into the shack and brought out the rifle, which he cocked and had ready to fire if the bear came closer. Asleep on the porch, Bully awoke and sighted the bear. With a deep growl, he charged after the bear, leaping into the icy cold river and sending curtains of water into the air. The bear turned and fled toward the frozen bank as Gaines and Virgil came around the corner of the shed to watch.

Not counting on the ice, the bear leaped hard up the bank and skidded, then slid back down with Bully closing in. They feared Bully was heading for a fight that he couldn't hope to win, especially tangling with a bear that appeared to be cornered. But they'd underestimated that bear's ice climbing abilities for he finally clawed and skittered his way up and ran into the woods. Bully tried to climb the ice after the bear but soon gave up. Bully came home with his tongue hanging out, dripping saliva. Marcy gave him an extra serving of food and told him what a good dog he was.

July was very hot in the summer of 1972. While they took a break from work and cooled off one afternoon under the kitchen cedars, two people emerged from where the trail came down near the hydroelectric generator and walked towards them. "Who could that be?" Virgil wondered, looking disgustedly at Tissy and Bully sleeping under the table.

The face of the person in the lead came into view and revealed a hot, sweating Ray. "How do you expect to get any work done, sitting under the trees in the shade?" he laughed. The dogs exploded from their deep slumber into a fury of barking, charging out trying to look ferocious. "Great watchdogs. Good thing I wasn't a bear."

"Hey Ray, how you doing?" they greeted.

"Great!" Ray said and waved an upturned hand behind him toward a young man with shoulder length blond hair. "This is Jeff, the son of a good friend of mine who has a large cattle ranch down south." Ray dropped his bulging backpack, took a handkerchief from his pocket, mopped his face and went on. "I got to get a drink of your good water and jump in the river, and then we have to go up trail and get two piglets." He put the handkerchief back in his pocket.

"Oh no, not more pigs. I can't go through that again!" Marcy said as she filled two glasses with cool water from the hose they kept running next to the kitchen area and handed them to Ray and Jeff.

"Come on, Jeff, I'll show you the swimming hole," Ray yelled after draining his glass.

When they were gone, Virgil shook his head. "That's Ray."

"He said he had two pigs on top?" Marcy asked, never certain about taking what Ray said at face value.

"Yes, he did. Just what we need is more pigs," Virgil said, thinking about the slaughtering again.

Ray and Jeff returned looking refreshed. "Ready to go get your pigs?" he asked.

"We can't go up in this heat!" Marcy exclaimed.

"Got to. Pigs can't take heat and might die on top," Ray said, so they all soaked their clothes with water from the hose and Marcy got her big straw hat.

When they got up top, the piglets were in a cutoff 55-gallon drum in the back of Ray's black pickup. They were the same age but of uneven size, one about 15 pounds and the other about 25. "How do we get them down?" Marcy asked Ray. "They're not as big as Lucifer was when he walked down."

"In wet gunny sacks tied on your backpacks!" Ray wetted a sack with water from a five-gallon jug. "Here Marcy, hold this sack open." From the 55-gallon drum, Ray lifted a loudly squealing piglet by the ears and dropped it kicking into the sack. With a piece of red, white and blue plastic rope, he tied the sack shut.

Joel gasped at the shrill squealing. "You ripped his ears out!" he stammered.

Having grown up around livestock, Jeff reassured Joel that it just scared the piglets and didn't hurt them. Joel looked skeptical, though, as Ray repeated the process with the second piglet. Virgil tied the squirming, undulating gunnysacks to two backpacks and Joel and Marcy volunteered to haul them down.

"You two go ahead and get them into Lucifer's old pen, and give them lots of water," Ray directed. "Virg and the rest of us are going to haul down cracked corn I have here."

"I have chickens in Lucifer's old pen," Marcy said.

"Doesn't matter. They won't bother the chickens."

The piglets lay quiet in their sacks until Joel and Marcy put on the backpacks, then the squealing started again. Joel and Marcy couldn't believe that piglets could squeal so loud. Despite the deafening noise, they started down the trail.

After a while, the piglets quit squealing but Marcy's started struggling. They soon discovered that trying to keep piglets in sacks tied to backpacks had to be the hardest loading job there was. A bulging section of the sack began sagging out one side of the pack frame, throwing Marcy off balance. Marcy's back muscles knotted up on the strained side and she reached back to push the sack of pig back into the center of the pack frame. This worked only marginally but started the shrill squealing again. In sympathetic solidarity, Joel's pig started squealing too. Marcy's pig continued struggling and soon drooped out the opposite side of her pack. "This squealing is going to bring a bear," Joel stated.

This thought had already crossed her mind and now confirmed by Joel, made Marcy madder at the situation. She reached around to the squealing pig snout drooping out the side of the pack and gave it a hard shove. It was well over 100 degrees in the shade but on the bare rocky hillsides, great waves of convective heat well above the shade temperature assaulted them. Red faced, sticky with sweat and with a number of back muscles knotted in pain, Marcy fumed. Here she was, stupidly letting Ray talk her into going down in the heat after she'd vowed never to do it again after the heat exhaustion their first summer.

The pigs were quiet but Marcy's sagged out the downhill side of the pack and she didn't want to touch him for fear he'd start the squealing again. Finally, the pain in her twisted back forced her to reach behind and push the rounded bulge back to the center of the pack frame. But that bulge was the pig's hind end, she found, for a dark tea-colored stream poured out over her hand and down her arm, and the chorus of squealing renewed except this time Marcy was in the chorus herself.

When they finally made it down the trail and turned the piglets loose in the chicken pen, they observed the social interaction between swine and fowl. The chickens all had different personalities, exaggerated by the fact that they had a mix of standard and banty chickens. The standard chickens often got bored with sitting on eggs and left before they hatched. The banties made much better brooding hens but with their nervous excitable nature, if they became too agitated, they'd kill their own or another's brood.

Gaines had a chicken he'd named Big Egg, a standard white chicken that consistently laid an egg every other day. Her calm disposition made her their favorite and she was unperturbed by the new additions to the pen. The banties grouped up, squawking and fidgeting nervously, but the piglets were too tired and hot to pay them any mind and lay panting in a damp corner of the pen. When the rest of the guys showed up later that afternoon with the cracked corn and urea Ray had brought, the piglets were up and ready to eat and Joel and Marcy were thankful they'd survived the trip with no lasting effects.

After Ray and Jeff left the next day, Marcy filled an empty coffee can with urea and headed for the garden. She'd given up on being able to make enough compost for an all-organic garden and had some peppers yellowing from lack of nitrogen. She spread the translucent pellets of urea around the plants and watered them liberally.

The next morning Marcy checked the peppers to see if they'd changed color. They had. They were black and dead. Having gardened for years, Marcy knew you could burn plants with too much fertilizer but using all-organic methods as she had in the past, it was harder to burn plants. Highly distressed, she checked the label on the sack and found it was 40-percent soluble nitrogen. No wonder her poor peppers had passed into the next world!

The pigs grew rapidly and as they grew, they ate more. The summer's harvest came and Marcy canned, and as the canning work dwindled, the amount of food scraps dwindled. Soon they had to make a trip to town to stock up on a couple months' supply of cracked corn and oats for the growing pigs.

On the way back to the Flat, they stopped to see the Trulls. Bambi took Marcy aside. "Rusty and Sharon split up," she confided.

"No! Not them!" Marcy exclaimed.

Marcy was saddened. She'd gotten used to their far-out neighbors and enjoyed knowing they were kindred souls, even though they didn't see them often.

After leaving the Trull's, they met Rusty driving out of his claim and stopped to talk. Rusty's eyes were sunken and he looked sad. "Sharon and I have split up," he said.

"We heard that," Virgil replied.

"Virg, I've got a demon on my back and have decided to give my life to Jesus. Sharon can't abide by that so she packed up and left. I heard once that only a few people could live by themselves in the wilderness without losing some of their sanity. I guess I was one that couldn't hack it," he sighed.

"Is there anything I can do to help?" Virgil offered. "Sometimes it helps to talk to someone."

"No, Virg, Jesus has already helped me and I'm sure he'll be there for all my needs."

They returned to the Flat and tried to put the sadness of Rusty and Sharon's failed marriage out of their minds.

The last thing to harvest that year was a patch of sorghum they'd planted to make molasses, but first Virgil had to build a sorghum mill. With limited parts and raw materials available on the Flat, the only thing he could find for a frame and drive assembly was the Roto-Hoe tiller, the same one he'd attempted to make into his mule to haul equipment down the trail years before. So off came the digging tines and in their place Virgil, Gaines and Kelly built a double steel roller assembly.

The sorghum looked a lot like corn stalks but without ears. They stripped off the leaves for the pigs and stacked up the canes to run through the steel rollers where the juice would run down and collect in their trusty old 35-gallon galvanized tub. It became apparent with the first few canes that the drive roller needed to also mechanically drive the secondary roller as the canes tended to stop part way through while the drive roller spun uselessly. So it was back to the workshop to redesign the mill.

A day and a half later with the modifications done, the canes were crushed and squeezed nicely, at least until the roller spring Virgil had forged snapped. It was another delay of about a day while Virgil forged a new stronger spring. Finally, the mill was running at full capacity and the 35-gallon tub filled with the lime-green juice of the sorghum canes. When it was full, they carefully lifted the tub onto a makeshift fireplace and lit a fire to start the long process of boiling it into syrup.

During the extremely long process, they'd built much anticipation to try this fantastic sorghum molasses. Gaines tried it first and grimaced. "It tastes like iron!" he said, his face contorted in disgust.

Sure enough, the acids in the cane juice had etched enough iron from the rollers to give the molasses a distinct taste, and not a good one. It was a big letdown but after standing around for a while discussing what went wrong, they decided to try it again. After the second taste, with no expectations of wonderful new syrup, they agreed it was marginally palatable.

So the last of the harvest was over and with it the first and last crop of sorghum in their canyon. The Roto-Hoe went on to participate in many more projects, most of which had nothing to do with tilling a garden.

A cold pounding rain drove them indoors near the first of December. As the boys did their schoolwork, the raindrops grew larger. "It's turning to snow!" Joel suddenly exclaimed. The raindrops soon turned to great half-dollar sized flakes making them the first snow of the season. All afternoon it dumped snow, building up to about four inches before tapering off at dusk.

The next morning was clear and cold and the wet snow of the day before had frozen hard and crunchy. Virgil had come down with the flu and rested in bed that day so the boys made the most of the new snow and packed a sled track. The morning of the next day brought very cold, heavy overcast skies. The white frost that had collected on the dark green Douglas firs and Jeffrey pines clung frozen all day. Feeling better, Virgil went into the woodshed and realized that at the rate they were burning wood with the cold weather, they needed to gather more.

The family split into two groups. Virgil and Gaines went across the river to cut wood while Kelly, Joel and Marcy stayed on the house side to receive the wood as they sent it across on the cable car. The 100-yard span seemed like a long way, made more so by the attempts to yell across over the sound of the river breaking its way through the boulders. Instructions were often misconstrued and only through disgusted gestures from the sender did the receiver learn the communication had been misread. In the end, they resorted to writing notes and sending them back and forth on the cable car, and at lunchtime, Marcy packaged up a meal and sent it over to Virgil and Gaines.

The three on the house side of the river took turns unloading the cable car, loading the sled, sliding it to the woodshed and stacking up the wood. As long as they kept active, they stayed warm. As the work moved into the later afternoon, a veil of whiteness drifted ever so slowly down from the higher ridges to the lower ones. Virgil signaled they were shutting the operation down on the far side and he and Gaines started back to the house. By the time they'd returned home, the veil had reached the Flat and revealed itself to be tiny light snowflakes drifting to the earth, resembling miniature tufts of down. "I hope it snows 10 feet!" Joel happily exclaimed.

"I don't," Virgil said, warming his hands over the stove in the cabin.

As darkness closed over the canyon, it snowed ever harder. Virgil had placed the summer kitchen table out near the cook shack for Thanksgiving dinner and it stood there now in the circle of light escaping through the big picture window, providing a nice gauge of how much snow had fallen. The boys had a hard time concentrating on their schoolwork because they kept checking to see how deep the snow had built up on the table.

Eighteen inches of new snow rested upon the table as dawn broke. Pink tinged billowing cumulus clouds floated in front of the deepest blue sky. The day was brilliantly sunny but the temperature never got above freezing and heavy cloaks of snow clung to the trees.

About mid-morning, a horrible squawking came from the pig and chicken pen bringing the whole family running to see what was getting the chickens. The largest pig had Big Egg pinned against the chicken wire, savagely trying to eat her. Virgil beat the pig off and Big Egg limped bravely away. "That's it. I'm butchering today," Virgil declared.

Marcy suspected Virgil was using his present anger to make the job of killing the pigs easier.

"Are you going to kill them both now?" Joel asked.

"Yes," Virgil answered. "I don't want the second pig lying around for hours thinking about what happened to her friend. We need the food but never treat the animals with disrespect."

It was soon done and they were both hanging in the tree. With the help of the boys, Virgil had one of the pigs dressed and scraped by dark. The second would have to wait until morning. But by morning the air was biting cold, leaving both pig carcasses frozen solid. Virgil tried without success to dress the second pig. Ice had formed over the swimming hole and crystals of ice were building up from the boulders of the rapids. Though it was clear and sunny, nothing warmed up.

That night the warmth of the cabin rapidly escaped through the walls and they kept the fire roaring in the little stove. When Virgil went out to light the fire in the cook shack the next morning, he came back inside to wait for the cook shack to heat. "It's 20 below zero out there," he announced, standing near the roaring stove.

"Beings the thermometer broke last winter, how do you know?" Gaines asked.

"You can tell by the way the snow squeals when you walk on it. The louder it squeals, the colder it is. When I was a boy in Iowa it got to 35 below and back then it only squealed a little more than it does now," Virgil explained.

The ice crystals forming on the boulders in the rapids had built up enough overnight that there were now ice dams, creating pools of deep green water where none existed before. The sheet of ice over the swimming hole was thicker and the boys set out to heave rocks on it to break it for fun. Virgil and Marcy both gave them dire warnings not to go out on the ice. They came back a short time later and said it was thick enough to walk on because they'd thrown 50-pound boulders off the cliff above the swimming hole and the ice didn't break. "Can we walk on it?" Joel asked excitedly.

"No," Virgil said.

"Come on and at least check it out," Joel begged, so Virgil accompanied the boys to the swimming hole and after much testing, agreed to let them walk on it. They played for hours on the first ice rink they'd seen at the Flat.

The extreme cold continued day after day and the roaring fires they kept burning rapidly ate away the wood they'd stacked in the woodshed. They were going to need more wood. The rapids under the cable had changed into a set of terraced pools four feet higher than the normal river level. This presented a problem as the cable sagged lower than this when the loaded cable car crossed it. But with the ice, a rare opportunity became apparent.

Earlier floods had deposited large, three-foot diameter logs of Douglas fir on the rock bar along the lower opposite bank of the river. Walking across the swimming hole, Virgil carried the chainsaw and began cutting bolts of wood from the logs, mindful of imbedded rocks and sand forced into the logs on their violent trip down the river. They hauled whole bolts with the sled, across the swimming hole and up to the woodshed and soon had several cords of wood.

One day they awoke to find the brilliant blue skies replaced with a heavy overcast. Again, Joel was excited by the prospect of more snow, and by afternoon was rewarded with big white fluffy flakes. In the morning, however, he was disappointed to see that only a couple inches of white stuff had fallen. Suddenly, a high-pitched, hissing rattle came from the roof. The white stuff turned out to be sleet packing the dry powder snow down to a wet 12 inches. Over the day, the sleet gave way to a heavy rain, which by the next morning had brought the river up. Before their eyes was a rare northern type breakup. The river was high and muddy, choked with great sheets of ice a foot and a half thick and piles of ice jammed up on the banks.

Joel and Marcy put on their raingear and walked to the swimming hole, which was piled up with large broken ice floes. While they watched, the whole mass started to move on the swift current below. Rapidly it gathered momentum toward the rapids under the rope. Washing Rock, a huge oval boulder anchored at the threshold of the rapids, was now a rolling mound of water with the monstrous pack of ice racing straight for it. Striking the submerged boulder, the ice pack exploded with a thunder-like rumble, breaking into a mud stained mass of crushed ice that then streamed on down the river.

With the warmer temperatures, the pigs thawed and Virgil dressed the second pig, figuring it wouldn't be any good. But when he swabbed the chest cavity with vinegar, they were pleased to find that there were no harmful effects from the delay in dressing it out.

Snowy rock bar

North Fork frozen to a depth of 12 inches

Swimming hole frozen over

27 - Sawmills, Waterwheels and Paranoia

Virgil slumped on the two sill logs he and the boys had just spent a week getting across the river and up to the flat area where they planned to build the log cabin. It was a gut-wrenching, equipment-busting quarter-mile haul, every bit of it human powered, and he was exhausted. They had long ago discarded the idea of using the Granberg Alaskan chainsaw mill attachment to cut lumber for a bigger cabin and jewelry shop. The mill was slow, wasted wood and produced crude lumber, and they had a fume issue with the chainsaw.

"We have to build a sawmill," Virgil said. "Each one of these logs weighs nearly a half-ton and my hernia isn't going to last for the number of logs we have to haul to build a cabin. The only trouble is we need an engine for a sawmill."

"Will the tractor engine work?" Gaines asked.

"No. It's only a seven-horsepower Wisconsin and wouldn't have the power to drive a saw blade big enough to cut boards. I'd use that 24-inch circular blade Ernie Neal gave me," Virgil replied.

"What if we use the Hercules from the gas powered generator?" Kelly suggested. "It's four cylinders."

"We need that to weld and we'll need welding to build this thing," Virgil replied.

"We can do all the welding first and then rob the engine," Gaines suggested.

Virgil puffed on his pipe and thought on this. "Let's go up to the shop and look at that old 1923 Audel's carpentry book. There's a picture of a sawmill in there."

Virgil held the book while the boys gathered around and studied the picture.

"There's all those bed frames at the old dam tender's cabin we could straighten on the forge for the track and carriage," Gaines said.

"Let's go get them!" At barely 11 years of age, Joel didn't fully understand the mechanical concepts but did understand building a big fire for the forge and cranking the handle on the air blower. "I want to get the forge going!"

"Ok Pyro, you and Gaines go get the frames and see what we've got," Virgil said. "Kelly and I will work on making a grinding setup to change the teeth on Ernie's blade from crosscut to a rip saw."

A couple hours later, Gaines and Joel had dragged over a pile of blackened twisted bed frames. Joel immediately began piling thick pieces of fir bark on the forge and soon had a roaring inferno. Gaines held a twisted frame in the forge. "Slow down!" Gaines barked as a shower of sparks blew from the flames onto his bare arms and down the back of his neck, singeing his hair. "You don't have to crank the blower so hard!"

Joel slowed his furious cranking on the cast iron 1901 forge blower and the flame settled to a steady low roar. Gaines withdrew an orange glowing section of angle iron and hammered it on a one-foot section of railroad track they were using as an anvil. Bit by bit, he straightened the bends and twists from the pieces.

"How do these look, Virg?" Gaines asked.

Virgil looked over the stack of angle iron and pulled out four eight-foot pieces. "We'll use these for the tracks. There's still some bends but you'll never get those little ones out and these are the straightest."

Gaines looked concerned. "I can hammer on them some more… Ouch! Joel quit cranking that blower! You're blowing sparks on me!"

"Don't worry about the bends," Virgil said. "A little bit of slop isn't going to hurt." Virgil looked at the few pieces of junk lying around the shop area. "We need a heavy frame for the log carriage."

Kelly sat cross-legged in the dust wiring a cord onto an electric motor in his lap. "Hey, what about the old Hobart generator frame up top?"

"That's 150 pounds. We'll never backpack it down," Gaines said.

Virgil thought about it. "We could drag it down with ropes."

"I'll go now," Gaines offered.

"No. Wait until morning when it's cool," Virgil said.

They worked steady on the sawmill over the next several weeks. Virgil built a base for the track, engine and blade assembly using some logs they'd planned to use on the log cabin and he set the frame up on a level gravel bar below the kitchen area. He then spent days drilling and filing two sections of angle iron to act as a crude rack for a rack and pinion head block drive on the log carriage.

The weeks passed and the sawmill took shape. Finally, Virgil announced it was time to do a test run. Virgil and Gaines lifted a dry, nine-inch diameter, six-foot long fir log onto the carriage and secured it with the small pick-shaped log dogs. Gaines picked up the hand crank he'd forged from three-quarter-inch rod and cranked several times on the Hercules engine while Kelly manually held the butterfly choke. The engine fired on one cylinder, belched out black smoke, then roared to life. At 1,800 revolutions per minute, the 24-inch saw blade made a vicious hiss. Everyone waited breathlessly to see if anything would fly apart. One mistake with this machine would cut a person in half in less than a second.

Finally satisfied that nothing was going to fly apart, Virgil stooped over and pushed the carriage toward the hissing blade. The newly shaped and filed teeth cut into the dry wood with a loud scream, spewing out a cloud of sawdust. A quarter of the way through the log, Marcy suddenly screamed for him to stop. Virgil leaped back from the carriage and Gaines killed the engine. "What?" Virgil yelled as the engine and blade noise died.

"I heard a noise!"

"What noise?"

"I don't know… it just sounded strange."

Virgil backed the carriage and log away from the blade. Gaines and Kelly crowded around the blade and mandrel, examining all the moving parts for looseness or damage. Finding nothing out of the ordinary, Gaines cranked the engine up again and once again, Virgil pushed the carriage forward. As the blade neared the end of the cut, Kelly stepped forward and held onto the fresh-cut slab of wood. Once it fell free, Kelly moved it out of the way. Then Gaines cut the engine ignition and everyone moved forward to look at the cut face on the log. "Look how smooth the cut is!" Joel exclaimed.

"That didn't take long at all to cut," Gaines marveled.

Virgil puffed his pipe and smiled broadly, his beret covered with sawdust. "We need to flip the log face down now," he said.

Gaines scrambled to get a hammer to knock the log dogs out of the wood so they could roll it face down. The second cut went even faster than the first. They rolled the log once more and cut the third side square to form a cant.

"Now we start slabbing off boards," Virgil said and turned the hand crank to advance the cant a board's thickness past the blade. The first smooth, pale yellow board fell into Kelly's hands, and then another and another, until a total of five boards were neatly stacked next to the sawmill. They were all elated! The jewelry shop and a larger house were on the way.

They loaded on a fresh green log. This time, the sawmill cut fine for about halfway and then the engine lugged down. Virgil strained against the carriage and suddenly smoke came from the blade. Virgil backed the carriage out and Gaines cut the engine. Kelly ran up and touched the blade, then jerked his hand away. "The blade is dished and hotter than heck in the center."

"It looks like it's going to need a little adjustment," Virgil said cheerily. "The blade probably isn't aligned with the track." Indeed, it was off by a thirty-second of an inch. "It has to be accurate to one one-hundred-twenty-eighth," Virgil said, reading the Audel's book. "And it has to have one one-hundred-twenty-eighth lead out on the cut to compensate for the pressure against the front of the blade." Virgil carefully aligned the saw.

"Blade looks like it's flopping when it's running," Gaines said after the engine noise died away. "And it's cutting crooked."

"The blade has to have tension," Virgil recalled from past reading. "It has to be slightly dished when it isn't running. Then when it's up to speed, the rim stretches and it runs true."

"How do you get it to dish?" Joel asked.

"You pound on the mid-section and stretch the metal," Virgil said, removing the blade.

That worked for one board then it started cutting wedges again. "One-eighth cut in," Gaines stated, measuring the two ends of the last board.

There was now quite a stack of wedge shaped and wavy boards. "Probably needs aligning again," Virgil said.

It didn't.

"I think the way you're pushing on the carriage is throwing a tweak in the alignment," Gaines observed. "If we both push the carriage, it should straighten the tweak out."

But the sawmill produced another wedge. All talk at dinner that night was of the sawmill and ways to get it to cut straight. "I think the carriage can't be pushed by hand like that without tweaking the cart," Kelly said.

"What about a hand crank cable and winch pull through?" Gaines suggested.

Virgil nodded.

They spent the next day building a hand crank winch out of junk from around the Flat and parts they'd found in the river from the old mining days. With Gaines cranking, the first two boards had less than a sixteenth-inch taper in eight feet. "I think we've solved it," Virgil said as he and Gaines strained to lift another green log onto the carriage.

As the blade whined through the log, Joel shook his head as the engine lugged down again. Gaines frowned as Kelly tossed the slab with fresh burn marks onto the waste pile. Gaines started cranking the carriage back. The blade had deflected enough through the prior cut that it now tried to cut a new line but the forces acting on the carriage were upwards instead of down. Nothing restrained this force and the carriage suddenly rose off its tracks, heading for a catastrophic derailment when the extra load on the engine stalled it.

They stared at one another wordlessly, realizing how close they'd come to disaster. Finally, Virgil broke the silence. "I have to remember to back up the head blocks next time. That blade looks like it's still slapping," Virgil said. "I'm going to hone the mandrel collars with 600-grit grinding compound and get them flat."

A few straight boards then more wedges. A day of adjustments and modifications soon became weeks. They did dozens of blade re-tensioning, collar grindings, track alignments, bearing adjustments and engine speed adjustments. Then they built a saw guide and experimented with Babbitt metal, wood and fiberglass material for the guide bearing surfaces. Sometimes the sawmill cut a few straight boards, raising their hopes that the cure had been found, only to resort back to wedge cuts again.

"The book keeps saying that each tooth has to cut exactly the right amount of wood and I don't think I can pull the log through smooth enough. We need an electric motor and gear box to pull it through," Gaines said, disgusted at the latest wedge cut.

"But summer's been so dry we don't have any water in the reservoir to run the generator," Virgil pointed out. Then he pulled out his pipe and stared at the river flowing around the smooth shape of Washing Rock in a set of rapids just 50 feet away. "We could harness the water there with a paddlewheel and move the generator down here for the summer."

Virgil set to work and spent days shaping the spokes for an eight-foot wheel from some of the boards they'd cut on the new sawmill. With an artist's touch, he striped the spokes and even edged the paddles with red paint. He made the hub of laminated wood mounted to an old car axle. From junk, Virgil and Kelly made some ugly but functional pillow block bearings.

The stumps of two trees killed by a past flood served as anchor pillars for two horizontal fir poles. On top of these poles, they nailed down a platform made of wedge-shaped boards. With some of the straightest boards, Virgil constructed a trough-shaped raceway and the boys and Marcy installed it in the river, stacked up a rock diversion dam to channel the river into the raceway and then placed a board across the raceway entrance to stop the flow of water so they could install the paddlewheel. "Here comes the water!" Kelly yelled as he pulled away the dam board.

The large wheel started turning in the hot summer sun, dripping sparkling drops of water on them. The red highlighting paint reflected in the clear green rippling water. "That's beautiful!" Marcy exclaimed, staring at the wheel.

"Kelly, go get the RPM counter," Virgil said and on bare feet at a dead run, Kelly set out for the shop to get the handheld counter.

"We need a watch to time it."

"I'll get my pocket watch," Gaines replied, heading for the cabin.

Still running and now breathing hard, Kelly returned with the RPM counter. As Gaines timed a minute, Kelly counted.

"Start!" Gaines barked.

"One, two, three…ten, eleven…"

"Mark!"

"Eleven RPMs," Kelly announced.

Virgil pulled a matchbook cover and a pencil stub from his front pocket and started doing long division. "That means we have to gear it up 164 to one."

"That's a lot!" Gaines said.

"It is, but let's see what we can arrange," Virgil said, and he and the boys set off for the shop while Marcy returned to work on the garden and start dinner.

Two days later, they had a series of gears and pulleys mounted on the platform. "Should we get the generator now?" Gaines asked.

"We need to test it first," Kelly said, sliding off the platform into the whitewater that spilled over the rock dam and pulling the board out from in front of the raceway.

Slowly, the wheel started turning as the head built. They could hear the groaning of the straining wood as the two-inch deck planks bent under the torque of the turning axle. Suddenly, a loud popping drowned out the groaning as the first set of gears started skipping teeth. "Shut it off! Shut it off! We're stripping gears!" Gaines yelled.

Kelly jumped to set the dam board back in place, slipped on the slick boulders and went down in the water. On his belly, he reached out and jammed the board in place, stopping the wheel. "Are you hurt?" Marcy called.

"I'm all right," he muttered, limping back up to the platform with blood running down his wet, bare leg from a gash in his knee. "What was slipping?" he asked.

"The main gear drive," Virgil answered. "The wood is flexing. Let's try and tighten it up."

It didn't work. Nothing worked to gear it up. The wheel seemed to have infinite torque as they could never stall it and it sheered multiple keys and sheer pins trying to convert the torque to speed. But in the end, they had to give up. They did attach the wheat and corn grinder to the wheel, however, and it ground hundreds of pounds of flour and cornmeal over the summer before the drought broke and 10 inches of rain in three days brought a freshet that destroyed the whole platform. The only thing they were able to save was the wheel itself, all else became flotsam and jetsam.

Stopping at the Trull's on the way home from town, they learned a man with two daughters, a son and a young male friend had filed a claim four miles below them at Black's Flat, the same area where Red Cockroff had once filed a claim. "They're living in a tent," Bambi said. "I hope they don't freeze to death if they don't get their log cabin done by winter."

"Hey, did you guys hear about the shooting at Denny?" Otis interrupted. "I can't tell you if it's true or not, but I'm inclined to think it's the truth. A bunch of hippies moved in there; some were mining and others weren't. The Forest Service decided to give them all mineral tests. Well, the hippies heard the tests were rigged, so decided to put the examiners to a test. One was to hide behind a rock and shoot into the air to distract the rangers during the mineral exam while another dumped an ounce of gold into the sluice box. But the bullet ricocheted when it hit a rock and a chip struck one of the mineral examiners in the neck. All hell broke loose but the guy holding the gold threw it in the sluice box unnoticed. You can imagine the tension building on both sides. Then when the sluice box was cleaned out, there wasn't a trace of gold in it. So that started a big fight. After that, the Forest Service called in the Big Guns to monitor the exams."

"The Big Guns?" Marcy asked.

"Federal marshals," Otis replied. "It's almost like the Old West," he chuckled.

Will we be next? Marcy wondered. She looked at Virgil but his eyes refused to meet hers.

When they got home that night, a haze with a net of rainbows encircled the full moon and the night birds and bats had just started to fly. With a sigh, Marcy thought about all the hard work they'd done to find their freedom, dignity and contentment and the same thought kept going through her mind: *Will we lose it?* "Virg, I don't want to hear anything about what the Forest Service is doing to the miners any more. Something beautiful we have here is being snatched away. I never dreamed we'd be under such tension."

"I understand, Ma, but as long as we're mining and going by all the laws, I'm sure we don't have to worry," Virgil reassured her and the boys.

Two days later, Red Cockroff showed up, his old black stocking cap pulled down close to his eyebrows. "Have you heard about those people who filed on my claim?" he asked.

"I thought you'd lost it," Virgil replied.

"Heck no! And I'm going down there and tell those guys a thing or two."

They heard no more about it until a week later when they met up with Red at the Trull's. "I'm helping them build a cabin," Red explained. "I want to get them ready for winter and also decided to help them mine."

"There's a cute girl down there; that's why he's staying," Otis whispered.

"Well, that explains why he didn't tell them to get off his claim," Marcy chuckled.

Virgil was working in his makeshift jewelry shop on a custom gold wildflower pin for the Backbone Ridge lookout firewatch when Red Barnes showed up for his monthly haircut. Otis had driven him to the top because he'd had Virgil leave him at the Diggins the last time they were in town. He'd stayed away many days, bunking out at Amos Decker's place.

Red looked pale and peaked and his eyes were red. *A good hangover,* Marcy thought.

"I met a guy in the Diggins and took him over to Amos' place. We were drinking good old Christian Brothers brandy. I heard a thump and saw my friend fell off his chair dead! I never thought I had to worry about Christian Brothers brandy before, beings that they're Christians."

"Booze is booze and it'll do that to you," Virgil answered.

Red looked at Marcy and held his hand up to his hat. "Come on, Red. Sit right here." Marcy pointed to a chair. "I have electric clippers now," she continued. "They make a lot of noise but they cut ok."

Red sat on the chair Marcy offered and Virgil went back into the shop to work on the pin. Marcy started to cut his hair and joked with him, as usual. "Oops! I almost got your ear that time. Wow! There goes the other ear," she joked, the hair clippers howling.

But Red didn't laugh and started leaning to one side. "What's wrong? Sit up straight," Marcy said.

Instead, Red slumped over. Marcy bent to peer at him and saw his eyes rolled back, his heart pounding furiously. He started to fall out of the chair and Marcy screamed for Virgil. Virgil ran out of the shop and grabbed Red's shoulder to keep him from falling. "Gaines!" Virgil called. "Get that tarp and lay it out!"

When Gaines had the tarp spread on the ground, Virgil and Marcy eased Red down onto it. "Red… Red, can you hear me?" Virgil asked.

Red lay there for a while, as if asleep. When he finally opened his eyes, his skin looked young and smooth and his eyes were brilliant. "Oh, I had the most beautiful dream," he said. "Why did you wake me?"

"Are you all right, Red?" Virgil asked.

Red stared at Virgil a while and then frowned. His features changed to those of an old man again and he climbed to his feet. "I also dreamt you were trying to kill me with those clippers, Pantywaist."

"What's the matter with you, Red?" Virgil said softly.

Red glowered silently at Virgil, grabbed his backpack and started up the trail.

"Are you ok to hike, Red?" Virgil called after him.

"Fine," Red said, disappearing up the trail.

"He had a heart attack!" Marcy said. "His heart looked like it was going to jump right out of his chest. Do you think we ought to go after him to see if he makes it home all right?"

"Let's go down by the kitchen where we can see him walking up to Wind Dance Lookout," Virgil suggested. "If he makes it up there, he'll be all right."

They saw Red striding slowly up the open area below Wind Dance Lookout. His age hung heavy on his shoulders but it looked like he'd be all right. Marcy worried whether he had the strength to make it to his place. "He's tough, Ma, he'll make it," Virgil said.

The next day, Virgil hiked downriver to check on Red. "How was he?" Marcy asked when Virgil returned.

Virgil sat on a chair, his face pale. "He had a strange attitude but seemed ok."

"What's wrong with you now, Virg?"

"I'll just lie down for a little while. That's a long walk."

Red still came over to visit but wouldn't eat or drink anything and watched them all like a hawk. "My father once told me someone would poison me if I didn't quit drinking," Red said and stared hard at Marcy.

"What in the world is wrong with Red?" Marcy asked Virgil after Red left.

"I hate to tell you this, Ma, but lately every time I take him anywhere, he tells everyone he meets that I'm hiding out from the law and trying to kill him to take his claim away."

"My God, Virg, did you tell him you could sue him for slander?" Marcy gasped.

"No, I just stand there beside him as he tells the clerks and anyone else he can talk to. I feel like one of these days he'll trip himself up," Virgil said calmly.

"I'm going down to his place right now and tell him a thing or two!" Marcy declared.

"Stay away from him, Ma. He's not sane," Virgil insisted.

Marcy had a stubborn streak and didn't listen. She stormed up the trail and nearly stepped on a rattlesnake, but that didn't even slow her down. She gave the mountaineer call when she came in sight of his cabin and he came out. "Howdy, Pantywaist," he snorted.

"Why are you saying those bad things about Virg?" Marcy yelled.

"Well, he's trying to kill me to get this claim," Red growled.

"Kill you? Why, he doesn't even like to shoot a deer!" Marcy screamed.

"Because there ain't no deer," Red said.

"As for wanting your claim, you're nuts if you think we want your worthless claim! We're going to the sheriff tomorrow and have you arrested for slander!" she said and stomped away.

When Marcy returned, Virgil was furious. "Well, I got the ball rolling," she explained. "I told him we're going to the sheriff and will sue him for slander."

The next morning, they saw Red walking as they drove down Hobo Gulch Road. As Virgil pulled up abreast of him, Red turned toward them, his eyes wild. "We have an appointment with the sheriff, Virgil Horn!" Red bellowed and climbed into the bed of the pickup. He sat down with his back against the tailgate and stared at the boys, who sat with their backs against the cab.

"Virg, he might hurt the boys," Marcy agonized.

"I'm watching him, Ma. Settle down. I want him ranting like this to the sheriff."

As Virgil drove, the wind whipped Red's greasy, gray hair away from his face, emphasizing the insane stare in his eyes. The boys were all silent and Joel and Kelly turned their faces to look forward.

"We have an appointment with the sheriff," Red repeated.

The boys were still silent.

"Your dad is trying to kill me!" Red yelled into the wind.

"He is not! You're sick, Red. You need help!" Gaines yelled back.

Red looked at Gaines' handheld CB radio and his eyes narrowed. "You carried that radio with you the last time you came to see me. I know what you were trying to do!" Red shouted.

"I carry it everywhere. We love radios," Gaines said.

"I was working in my mine that day, getting ready to set a charge," Red said as though all the pieces were starting to fit together in his head. "You were trying to set the charge off and kill me."

"You're sick, Red. I was not!"

"The hell you weren't! You even had me bring over a blasting cap to test your plan!"

Suddenly, Gaines remembered when they first got the radios from Uncle Gary and Virgil asked Red to bring a cap and dynamite wire over to test whether the boys transmitting would set it off. Virgil knew the boys would be hiking around testing the radios and didn't want them inadvertently to set off charges Red might be setting. "Red!" Gaines yelled. "We did that test just to make sure we didn't accidentally set your dynamite off!"

"Why did you bring that radio to my place?" Red snarled. "You were trying to set it off."

"No, Red. You need help."

"You dad has all that cyanide to poison me."

"That's for leaching gold and you know it, Red!"

"You people want all the claims in the canyon, including mine."

Gaines turned away from Red. There was no point in arguing, it was just making Red more insane. Virgil pushed the Jeep faster than normal until they finally reached the courthouse. Marcy's knees shook so hard she could barely walk. Red jumped out of the Jeep. "Thanks for the buggy ride, folks," he said lightly and started toward the Diggins.

"Oh no, we have an appointment with the sheriff, Red," Virgil told him quietly but firmly. "You're coming with us to the sheriff to tell him what you've been spreading about me all over town."

Climbing the stairs to the upper floor of the courthouse, Red and Virgil approached the counter. A husky middle-aged man wearing an undersheriff's badge and a nametag of Laag stepped forward. "Can I help you gentlemen?" he asked. Then he recognized Red and gave him a friendly greeting. "How you doing, Red?"

For a moment, neither man spoke. "Go ahead, Red," Virgil prompted.

Red cleared his throat. There was nothing insane in his voice at all as he spoke about his beliefs that a man named Virgil Horn was conspiring to kill him. Red asked if radios could make his dynamite detonate prematurely when he was working his mine and the undersheriff's answer was in the affirmative. "Would you think it's normal for a man to have a large supply of potassium cyanide and sulfuric acid?" Red asked.

"I would say that's a little odd," Officer Laag agreed.

Calmly and logically Red continued to lay out his case that this man, Virgil Horn, was systematically poisoning him or trying to set off his dynamite while he was setting charges in his mine tunnel. With increasing anxiety at the extremely logical and reasonable case Red was laying out, Virgil pointed to himself. "I'm Virgil Horn."

Undersheriff Laag's eyebrows shot up. "Hey, Mike," Laag called to a younger deputy behind a desk. "Will you finish taking this report from Mr. Barnes, here? I need to question Mr. Horn."

Mike stepped up to the counter and Undersheriff Laag motioned Virgil to follow him into an office. He asked Virgil a few questions about the cyanide and radios. When Virgil finished explaining, Undersheriff Laag nodded his head. "I thought so. Red has a problem. I'm going to have Deputy Munson take him up to the hospital and get him a mental evaluation. In order to get him to go, I'm going to tell him that we're taking him to test his fingernails and hair for cyanide. To Red, you are officially in jail until we get him out of here."

"Thanks," Virgil said. "Red's been raving wildly all morning but the minute he walked in here, I would have bought that case against Virgil Horn myself."

They stopped at the post office and the postmistress looked worried. "Be careful of Red. He told me he had to do something and it was going to be bad."

Marcy was scared every time they went up trail and passed Red's turn off. He was a good shot and had told her once that if he heard something in the bushes, he just fired into them, not checking first to see what it was. For a short time, Marcy even felt she might want to move out of the canyon. After brooding about it awhile, Marcy got very angry. "No! Neither he nor anyone else is going to run us out of our home!" she declared.

"That's the spirit, Ma. Don't kowtow to anyone. I'm glad you came to that conclusion; I'm on the same track. We can handle anything the old fool throws at us." Virgil looked at the boys. "Everything will be all right, you wait and see," he said and rumpled Joel's hair.

The next time they went out, they told Undersheriff Laag what the postmistress had said and he told them Red's exam at the hospital revealed a recent stroke and hardening of the arteries, both of which affected his brain. He sent a deputy down to Red's place to confiscate his rifle and the sheriff ordered Red never to come near them and they were to stay away from him. Undersheriff Laag later told them

Red was always asking for his rifle back. "I told him it wasn't the right time of the moon yet and he seemed to accept that." He also told them Red wondered how he could survive down in the canyon without the Horns.

The last they heard of Red, he'd poured gasoline instead of kerosene in his wood stove while drunk and caught his cabin and himself on fire. He burned over 70 percent of his body and walked seven miles before someone picked him up and took him to the hospital where he later died. Sometime afterward, an old timer told them Red was a credited mining engineer from a wealthy family and his sister was a well-known pianist. *That accounts for his knowledge on minerals,* Marcy thought, sad it had all ended this way.

As Virgil and Marcy sat under a pine tree, a beautiful peaceful feeling came over them. The clouds turned sienna red and swirled in weird circles like giant waterspouts and they felt Red was finally at peace.

Construction of the waterwheel

Virgil sharpening the sawmill blade

The forge

28 - *Mineral Exams and High Water*

In the summer of 1973, they got a letter from the Bureau of Mines notifying them of an upcoming mandatory mineral examination required because all the North Fork of the Trinity would be included in a new wilderness area. Marcy slumped in the Jeep, and as always, Virgil tried to console her. "We have a good claim, Ma, and if they don't cheat, we should pass the exam."

The examining team flew in by helicopter in August. Terry Close and half his team came in the first group and the rest of the workers arrived about 20 minutes later. All business, they started setting up their sluice boxes immediately. For about a week, Terry's team worked hard digging test pits. The family watched anxiously as the examiners came close to finishing. At the conclusion of sampling all the excavations, Terry declared the claim could be mined profitably. The examiners were all smiles and Marcy cried with happiness when Terry announced they had a valid claim.

The dry summer of 1973 ended with rains starting in October and the wet weather continued with at least some rain or snow every day through January. The river had been up and down all fall and early winter but they hardly paid attention to it anymore except the boys who loved to explore the ever-changing gravel and rock bar formed by the high water.

That fall, Tissy delivered a litter of one, a little male that looked much like a grub worm with his naked, wrinkled white face. He had the same faded blue eyes as Tissy and they initially called him Grub Worm but soon shortened his name to Grubby.

Around the middle of January 1974, a heavy wet snow built up to about eight inches before the falling snow turned to rain. The rain lasted three days and most of the snow melted off, bringing the river up once again. The rain had stopped but an overcast of heavy clouds rode above the Flat on a southwest wind. Joel's rainfall record showed that a total of six inches of rain had fallen over the previous three days.

Taking advantage of the drier weather, they spent the day getting wood. The boys were disappointed that the river didn't recede that day and expose the new river bars. As they hauled the last load of firewood to the woodshed and stacked up a supply in the cabin, the rain started again and an hour later, the river was on the rise.

The boys stood on the riverbank near the racing water and watched as the muddy torrent ate away at a huge boulder bar on the far bank. The steady rumble of the rolling boulders could be felt as well as heard. The most exciting part was the sudden appearance of huge logs, colors ranging from dark umber to bright tans. The rocks had stripped the bark on these last logs, exposing the tan wood underneath. "Can you imagine swimming in that now?" Joel asked.

"You'd be dead in a minute," Gaines stated.

At the far south end of the Flat, the canyon narrowed back down to a high field of bedrock that checked the flow of the muddy water, forcing it to slide to the right in angry frothing protest. "If you fell in right here, I wonder if a strong swimmer could make the far bank before he got caught in that," Kelly mused.

"No! That water is going better than 25 five miles an hour!" Gaines said.

"Here comes a huge one!" Joel cried, excitedly pointing toward the swimming hole as a 150-foot long, six-foot diameter ponderosa pine log gushed into the thrashing waves that were now the summer swimming hole. After a fast entry into the swimming hole, the log seemed to pause as though making up its mind whether to follow a channel that had formed against the far bank on the island boulder bar or follow the normal summer channel in front of where they stood.

The summer channel won out and the log gathered speed. The root ball of the log was a full 20 feet across and as it passed over the deeply submerged Washing Rock, it struck with a deep thud, jarring the monster violently. "Here it comes!" Kelly called.

It raced past them grinding and rumbling against the submerged boulders of the riverbed. The rain was coming hard now and 50 feet behind them, the door opened to the cabin and Marcy stepped out onto the porch. "Guys," she called. "Get out of the rain."

The boys returned to the cabin talking excitedly about what the new river channels and bars would be like in the morning. Marcy stood at the window, looking at the raging river. "I just saw what looked like a stiff, bare human hand and arm raise out of the water!" Marcy exclaimed, looking appalled.

The boys stared at her in horror. This melded too closely with their earlier discussion about trying to swim the river. Had somebody upriver fallen in? "*Really?*" Gaines demanded.

"I don't think it was but for a second it looked like it. It probably was a stripped branch of a willow bush," she replied.

Darkness fell and they heard the rain pound the roof over the roar of the river. The boys had a hard time concentrating on their schoolwork and it was just as well because about eight that evening the incandescent light started dimming. "Power's going out," Kelly announced.

Everyone stopped what they were doing and stared at the light. "Yep," Gaines confirmed. "Can't be from lack of water!" he laughed. "The creek must be really roaring up there and I bet it tore out the intake."

As the light faded to yellow and then orange, Virgil got up and took a book of matches from his front pocket and lit a candle bug. "I'll go turn the valve off so it doesn't drag crap down the line," he said as he headed out the door.

The family fell asleep to the sound of rain on the roof. The first few times the river had come up in the early years, Virgil and Marcy had nervously gotten up every few hours to check the water level but they never got up to check anymore.

Marcy awoke around midnight and listened to the rain. The river was quieter and she sleepily turned over, drifting back to sleep. Suddenly she remembered something Red had told them. "As long as the river is roaring, it isn't so dangerous, but beware if it gets quiet," he'd warned.

She looked at the phosphorescent face of her Big Ben clock. Noting it was a quarter to one in the morning, she concentrated on the sound of the river again. The hushed river was no longer relaxing, but foreboding. Unable to go to sleep, she got up and put on a coat, lit her candle bug and stepped out on the porch. Tom, his fur glistening with drops of water, yowled loudly and she let him in the house.

Crystal water ran from the eves and splattered in a puddle in the pathway leading from the porch. She walked to the summer kitchen area and down to the gravel bar where the sawmill was located. At the edge of this bar, she came to a sudden stop. Right in front of her, muddy waves of debris-laden water slammed against the gravel only two inches from the top. The river was three feet higher than she'd ever seen it, which was a huge difference considering that the three additional feet of depth was spread across 300 feet of width and moving at a greatly increased speed. Apprehension overcame her.

Though a candle bug is great for casting a soft diffused light for walking, it's impossible to see beyond eight feet when using one, and in the streaming rain the visibility was even less. Marcy could only listen to what was going on beyond the cone of yellow light. Rumbles, hissing, sucking, splashing and surging, all in varying levels, met her ears.

Quickly she headed back to the cabin. Virgil was asleep and she gently shook his shoulder. "The river's real high, Virg," Marcy whispered so as not to awaken the boys.

"How high?"

"Two inches below the top of the first bank."

Virgil sat up in bed. The sawmill was on that bank. Marcy turned the candle bug toward the boys' bunk expecting to see them all sleeping. Three sets of eyes looked at her. Virgil got dressed and went out with Marcy. All three boys climbed out of their bunks, got dressed, as well, and went out to the sawmill.

Marcy stood at the edge of the gravel bar staring at dirty waves now crashing over the top of the bar. A wavy line of leaves, twigs, pine needles and other plant debris was being pushed back from the waves' advancing high mark. "Where's Virg?" Gaines asked.

"He went to get chains and the come-along," Marcy replied.

"I'm going to help him," Gaines said and Kelly went with him.

The bobbing yellow lights and the clinking of chains announced their return. "Put this chain around the oak tree, Kelly," Virgil directed in the darkness. "Gaines, help me get the chain secure around the Hercules on the sawmill. Ma, shine you candle bug over here."

For a while, there was only the clinking of chains, then Virgil's voice joined in. "Where's the come-along?"

"Here," Joel said, fetching it for him.

Virgil hooked the cable end of the come-along to the chain around the Hercules engine mounted to the sawmill. With fingers shaking from handling the chilled, dripping wet chain, Virgil manipulated the release lever on the hand winch until the cable played out with a chattering sound and he was able to connect the other hook of the come-along to the chain Kelly had secured around the oak tree. Quickly he ratcheted the come-along until the cable was taut. "That'll do for now," he said. "Let's go in and get dried off."

Inside the cabin, Virgil dragged the few live coals forward in the stove and stacked several pieces of wood on them. He blew on the coals until a flame burst out on the wood and then closed the stove door. The crackling of the fire gave off a measure of comfort.

Kelly took a candle from one of the candle bugs, dripped some hot wax on the little table below the front window and anchored the candle to it. Tom lay curled up on one of the beds, purring, and Kelly picked him up. In subdued tones, the only talk was of the current crisis. "Hey Virg," Kelly said after a while. "Why does the river get quieter as it gets higher?"

"I guess it's because the water is covering all the boulders so deeply that it no longer makes any noise."

"I wonder what the dogs think of this," Joel said.

"Tissy was on the porch when we went out," Gaines said. "She didn't go with us. I don't know where Grubby and Bully are but probably in the woodshed."

Kelly laughed. "They're probably wondering what us idiots are doing out in the rain in the middle of the night. They're not stupid."

"Listen to it rain now!" Marcy said.

For a while, the family listened in silence to the pounding of rain on the roof. Joel climbed onto his second-level bunk and peered out the window. "I can vaguely see the river now. Is it getting light?"

Marcy bent to look at the clock by her bed. "It's only four-thirty."

"Not getting light," Virgil said.

"Where's the moon?" Kelly asked.

"I think it's in the last quarter," Gaines replied.

"Must be a little moonlight filtering down through the clouds," Virgil said.

Joel continued to peer out the window. "I can barely see some logs floating by," he reported.

"Is it over that rock bar across the river?" Gaines asked.

Kelly had now also taken up a position in front of the window. "It looks like it," he replied.

The heavy pounding on the roof tapered away slightly. "The rain seems to have slowed up," Marcy observed.

"I probably ought to go check the sawmill," Gaines said, pulling on his boots.

Kelly scrambled to get his on as well. "I'm going too."

"Be careful," Marcy called after them.

They soon returned. "It's flowing around the sawmill now," Kelly announced dramatically.

"How's the tie down looking?" Virgil inquired.

"We checked it and it looks good."

"I hope we don't lose our sawmill," Marcy worried.

As the first true daylight filtered through the clouds, Virgil got up and put on his beret. "Well, come hell or high water, I have to go to the privy."

The rest of the family went out to check on the sawmill and found the main logs of the platform bobbing and jerking on a newly developed current that had formed where the gravel bar had been. Where the summer rock bar normally lay was now a solid mass of rushing, heaving chocolate water. Virgil joined them and started ratcheting the come-along, pulling the whole sawmill partly up the bank below the outdoor kitchen. "That's the best we can do for now," he sighed.

A low spot behind the cabin had filled with water pouring from a stream cascading from the lip of a pond in a depression left by an old mining operation behind the woodshed. Grubby showed up, soaked to the skin and the color of mud. "I think Grubby was sleeping under the cabin and got flooded out under there," Kelly said. Grubby's fur parted in a straight line from his nose to his soggy wet tail. His spirits were high, though, from surviving a near drowning in his young life and he raced around oblivious to the rain that was making him ever more bedraggled.

As the hours passed, the rain continued to intensify. The high waves curled around the oak tree by the outdoor kitchen and sucked the sand out from under it. Marcy's compost heap that she'd piled against the tree was gone. The restraining chain tied to the sawmill gnawed and chafed at the bark of the black oak, and willows fought the river currents, struggling and whipping up and down like live things.

Marcy had all her canned goods stored in the lean-to kitchen and was getting worried. With each increase in the rain's intensity came a matching increase in the level of the rushing river that was now sending muddy waves halfway up the bank below the kitchen area. Once the water reached the top of this bank, the cabin would be flooded. "I think we need to start thinking about moving our stuff to higher ground," Virgil finally said.

"We could set up Ray's large camping tent on that flat by the woodshed and we could move the beds in there," Marcy suggested and Virgil nodded slowly.

"Come on guys, let's go get it set up," Gaines said to his brothers.

"I'll start moving all the kitchen stuff into the woodshed," Marcy said.

"Leave the stove for last, just in case the rain stops," Virgil suggested.

It was raining so hard now that a quarter-inch of rain fell on the tent canvas just in the time the boys got it rolled out and were staking it down, driving even greater urgency to the task. In the back of their minds was the sudden wall of water that had come down the river and wiped out Red's place during the '64 flood. Using the wheelbarrow, they moved all Marcy's canning to the woodshed, along with the other kitchen supplies. Then in a hard coordinated effort, they set to work on the possessions in the cabin. As hard as they tried to hurry, the bedding still became damp in the short move to the tent. They moved Virgil and Marcy's mattress next, followed by the sewing machine, books and all other items in the house except the wood stove, which they held to move at the last minute.

The rain had let up a bit by about one in the afternoon so Virgil told the rest of the family to take a nap in the tent and he would monitor the river. Later, the sun shining through the tent awoke Marcy. Joel and Marcy were the only ones still in bed and they both jumped up and ran out. The river was down and they found Virgil sweeping out the bare shack. Gaines and Kelly were staring at the river, which had split into two massive channels. A flat bar sparkling silver with water was in front of the shack and a section of their lower garden had caved in. The change was so severe they felt like they were looking at a new river. There were tightly woven fences of roots, branches and other debris the river had twined around the standing willow bushes and the few remaining alders. The sky was a brilliant blue and drops of rain still clung to the leafless trees, blinking like fire opals in the sun. "I can't believe the change," Marcy said as they walked on the eroded banks.

"In 100 years one miner couldn't do this," Virgil said as they looked down at the exposed bedrock. Virgil leaned over and snatched at something. "How much will you pay me for this?" he said, and opening his hand, he showed them a gold nugget.

Marcy laughed. Bambi had told her the best part of a flood is the gold nuggets left exposed on the bedrock. The algae discoloration was gone, and the sand and rocks scrubbed clean. "Should we move back into the house tonight?" Marcy asked Virgil.

"We need to get some idea what the weather is going to do. I sure don't want to have everything moved back in only to have it start raining again tonight," Virgil said. "Do we have any radio that works around here?" he asked, looking at Kelly and Gaines.

"No, but we have that TV Uncle Doug brought. It's up in the shop," Kelly replied. "The signal is too weak here to get a picture but the audio comes in."

"If we can turn it on and see if we can get a weather report, it would let us know what way to jump," Virgil reasoned.

"We still don't have any power," Gaines remembered. "I'll go up and fix the intake."

Daylight was fading when Gaines returned but the incandescent light was getting brighter as the water poured back into the reservoir. Kelly had the TV on the bare floor of the cabin and was getting ready to switch it on. "Is the voltage high enough yet?" Gaines asked him.

Kelly looked at the light. "Should be."

The TV came on with a loud burst of white noise. Kelly quickly switched through the channels, each bringing white noise and a pure white snowy picture, except Channel 12 where a woman's voice came out clearly. "This is the only channel we can get," he announced.

"Leave it there," Virgil said. "They should break and give us an hourly update on the weather."

In the empty little cabin sporting only a stove, a bare light bulb hanging from a cord attached to the collar ties on the rafters and the little TV, the family sat on the floor and listened to a cooking show over the sound of a roaring river. They had no clue it was Julia Child demonstrating how to bake a non-soggy-bottom pizza and Virgil had no clue the public TV channel didn't have local news or weather on the hour. But after several hours, they figured that out. "I guess we'll sleep in the tent tonight," Virgil decided. "Tomorrow will give us a clue."

In the morning, the river was way down and had lost its muddy color. Only light misting rain showers fell. "We're moving back in today," Marcy said. "Everything in the tent is damp. The canned goods can stay up here; I don't want to trust them by the river again."

And they spent the day getting life on the Flat back to normal.

Flooding around Rock of Gibraltar

29 - Goats and a Geodesic Dome

Ray frequently talked about them at his hardware store but was always careful not to tell the exact location of the Flat. After listening to Ray's tales, one customer figured out where they lived.

Greg surprised them, showing up unannounced, and Marcy immediately felt uncomfortable around him. He was a strange fellow who said he intended to spend a couple weeks with them. They'd never met him before but during this hippie commune era, it wasn't uncommon for people to want to move in with them. They let him stay because they thought he was Ray's friend. "What happened to the goats Ray brought you?" Greg asked.

"We gave them back to Ray. It was a good thing, too, because we couldn't find a Billy to breed them," Marcy said.

The boys didn't feel comfortable around Greg either and decided to play a prank on him one night. After dark, they crept over by his tent and started howling and mimicking other wild animal sounds. Greg burst from the tent but went back in when he saw Marcy smiling.

After two weeks, Greg showed no signs of leaving. He expected to be fed but was never around for work and Marcy was tired of their guest. "Get rid of him, Virg, or I will," she declared.

Virgil finally told Greg that he was going to town to get groceries. "It's time for you to leave, Greg. We have a lot of work to do."

About two weeks after Greg left, Ray came down with a white Saanen goat. Despite crippled back legs, she didn't have trouble walking but did have a bad cough. "Greg told me you were in desperate need of a goat."

"That idiot!" Virgil protested. "We never told him that."

"Well, you've got one now. She's from good stock, only her legs are weak. Here, just give her this and her cough will get better," Ray said as he reached in his pack and pulled out a bottle of Geritol. "Her name's Fifty-Two, it's her number," Ray explained. "And here are her registration papers. Genuine Saanen."

Fifty-Two liked Marcy but hated the rest of the family. She followed Marcy all over the mountain, browsing on manzanita. They wanted to have her bred and Marcy heard about a family near Weaverville that had a Billy goat, so when Fifty-Two came in heat, they took her up the trail and tied her down in the back of the Jeep with the boys tasked with holding her. The boys didn't like this at all. They were starting to notice girls and didn't feel riding around in the back of an old Jeep pickup holding a goat down portrayed the right image to young ladies. But since the stupid goat would try to leap out while Virgil was driving, they had to endure it.

When they arrived at the goat farm, the young man there looked skeptically at Fifty-Two's crooked legs. "I hope she can have a kid with that deformed pelvic bone," he said.

They decided to try to breed her anyway and the young man told Marcy to come back in three days. When they returned to town, Marcy was anxious to see how her goat was doing and they picked her up first thing. Fifty-Two was fine, her belly round from greedily devouring two bales of alfalfa. They tied her down in the Jeep again and Virgil drove and parked in downtown Weaverville in front of Van Matre's, a dry goods store on Main Street. Marcy and Virgil went into the store to pick up a few items and talk to the owner.

It was noon and the normal parade of high school kids made their daily lunch pilgrimage to Ryan's Store and other downtown establishments. A group of girls approached on the sidewalk and the smell alerted them to the Jeep's presence before they even saw it. "Yuck! What's that disgusting smell?"

"Whatever it is, I'm *not* hungry anymore!"

A pretty blond doubled over with a false gag reflex. "I've never smelled anything that smells *that* bad!"

Then they passed the Jeep. "It's that Billy goat!"

With a look of pure revulsion, the girls turned to each other, whispering but still audible to the boys. "How can they stand to hold onto that *thing*?"

The blond nudged her brunette companion with her elbow. "Would you like a hug, honey?" she said in a contrived deep voice.

The blond got a hard shove for her question, nearly falling off the curb, and the whole group burst into hysterical giggling before disappearing into Ryan's Store. Several more groups passed with reactions similar to the first before Marcy and Virgil exited Van

Matre's. "Are you staying warm, Kelly?" Marcy laughed as Kelly held onto the goat.

A puppy or a pretty dog might be a chick-magnet but apparently, a crippled old mean-tempered nanny goat in the back of a Jeep is not. Beings they couldn't get a much worse image in the community than the Billy Goat Boys and there wasn't enough money to buy the insane bell bottom jeans popular then, which they wouldn't have worn anyhow, they developed a unique style all their own. Joel took to wearing a World War II Army Air Corps Class B wool jacket and a Union Calvary Officer's black hat and Kelly had a long brown wool coat with a brown acorn shaped stocking cap that made him appear like a Scottish elf. They each strapped knives to their belts and a homemade bandoleer of .22 rifle shells draped across Kelly's chest completed his outfit.

When they next stopped at Ryan's Store, Mickey, the clerk, looked at Joel and Kelly with their long coats and big hunting knives hanging from their belts. "Did you pick these guys up on the road?" the older man laughed.

"Oh, they wear them to stay warm in the back of the truck," Marcy replied, unaware of the real reason for the outlandish outfits. "I know they look like gypsies."

The next time they saw him, Mickey lifted a big box of clothes from behind the counter. "Thought the boys might be able to use some of these," he said. The box was full of clothes Mickey had worn as a young man in the 1920s. Kelly discarded the brown stocking cap for a bowler hat from the box, bringing his appearance to a cross between Poncho Villa and a character from Laurel and Hardy. The kids coming out of school still stared at them but they were the Billy Goat Boys no more.

❧

Fifty-Two had one kid they named Doug, after Uncle Doug, much to his consternation, because he was up for a visit when the baby goat was born. Fifty-Two hated her kid and butted him away when he wanted to suckle.

One morning Fifty-Two butted little Doug so hard there was an audible snap and he bleated in agony. She had partially broken off one of his baby horns. Doug retreated to the corner of the pen and hung his head, a steady stream of blood oozing from the gaping socket under the twisted horn.

After several hours, Marcy went to check on Doug and found him standing in the same spot, a pool of blood beneath his head. Fending off Fifty-Two as she lunged to butt her kid again, Marcy led him out of the pen and went to find Virgil who was working on the sawmill, now moved to a flat spot well above the river's flood plain. "Virg, Doug's going to bleed to death if we don't bandage his horn up," Marcy worried. "There was a big pool of blood under him."

Virgil pushed up the black jeweler's visor he was using to see to sharpen the sawmill blade and examined the broken horn. "I'm not going to get a good bandage on there," Virgil said as he reached out and gently tried to prop the horn back in its socket.

Doug let out a blood-curdling bleat and bolted, jerking the tether from Marcy's hand. "He's going to bleed to death!" Marcy cried as she went after him.

Virgil found part of an old sheet and tore it into strips for a bandage. "I'll try and be gentle, little guy," he said to the goat when Marcy led him back. Very gently, Virgil wrapped the bandage around Doug's head and was about to tie it off when he touched the broken horn.

"Blaaaaaaaaat!" Doug screamed and bolted again.

This time, however, Marcy was holding tight to the tether. Doug reached the end of the tether around his neck, at a dead run. He head jerked over his back and in a cloud of dust, his body back-flipped onto the ground.

Joel was standing nearby looking stricken. "He's going to break his neck!" Marcy screamed. "Joel, help me hold him!"

With two people holding him, Virgil was able to get the bandage tied. Still he kept bleeding. "Virgil, what are we going to do?" Marcy asked, now nearly in tears.

"I have to take off the broken horn because I can't get direct pressure to stop the bleeding with it on there."

Virgil got a pair of pruning shears and wiped them down with alcohol. Marcy stared at him with horror. "You're going to take it off with *that*?"

"It's all I have."

Marcy didn't like the mental image of taking the horn off with pruning shears. "What if I smear a heavy coat of Bag Balm over it?" she suggested.

Virgil didn't like the shearing idea either and readily agreed. The horn seeped a bit through the Bag Balm but then stopped bleeding.

From that point on, Marcy had to feed Doug with a bottle. Whether due to his traumatic childhood or the general nature of goats, he turned mean when he got older and would chase the boys and butt them. Of course, they hated him and Marcy would catch them wrestling him to the ground. When Gay Holland and a friend came down to visit, Marcy asked if they knew of anyone in Denny who wanted to buy a goat. Gay knew of a family that would be delighted to have him. Soon, the man who wanted Doug came down himself and trotted the little goat out.

Ray had left a roll of hemp rope at the Flat in 1969 and Marcy asked Virgil if he could hang a swing for her and the boys from the oak tree by the kitchen area. After Virgil hung the rope with a smooth stick tied with a clove hitch knot for the seat, Joel got on and tried to make it swing. Lighting his pipe, Virgil watched, noticing Joel wasn't working it very well. "Here, let me show you how it's done," Virgil said.

He stuck his pipe in his mouth, climbed on the seat and started pumping his legs until the swing climbed into the air. What he didn't know was that Kelly had constructed the swing's rigging with a rotten piece of pine as a spacer. Although adequate for Kelly's weight, it snapped under Virgil's weight just as he reached the highest point in his arc. Virgil crashed down in the sand, his pipe flying out of his mouth. Seeing he wasn't hurt, they all laughed. "Is that the way to swing?" Kelly grinned.

The swing game got its start that day but it was too tame for them. They moved it from the low branch and tied it in the top of a Jeffrey pine Joel had limbed and topped to give light and space to the apple orchard. The pine grew from a sharp little spur ridge left over from an old mining excavation.

What made this swing unique was that from the one rope leading down from the top of the topped tree, in a maypole like arrangement, the boys had fastened three loops. In a cluster, the boys would launch themselves off the spur ridge, and at the same time they were orbiting the tree, they'd spin around each other. If the launch timing wasn't carefully choreographed, the landing would be off and their legs would entwine, and they'd crash into the dust in a terrible tangle of arms and legs.

The base of the tree was the big worry for if they angled wrong on launch, the orbit would be too elliptical and take them out and slam them into the tree base and wrap them around it like three bongo balls. All of it was dependant on fractions-of-a-second timing. This didn't deter the boys and they kept at it until they had perfected many different styles of complex graceful orbits with beautiful landings.

When they'd demonstrate for visitors, they made it look so easy and graceful that their company always wanted to try. Most were dissuaded when asked about their health and life insurance or if they were averse to wheelchairs. During one demonstration, the boys got carried away and Gaines fell, landing on all fours, and injured his back. He was never as enthusiastic about swinging afterwards. Jeffrey pines are notorious for rotting within a couple years and a loud deep cracking from high on the pole shut that swing down.

They moved the swing to a fir tree above the swimming hole where it swung out 40 feet over the water. Neither Virgil nor Marcy ever tried it, but after drinking a few beers and a couple glasses of whiskey, Doug set his mind to try it much to the dismay of the boys. They tried every which way to discourage him, especially in his condition, but like most of the Horns he was extremely stubborn and prepared to fling himself off the bank.

If Doug fell off the rope, he'd go into the river and maybe not get too hurt. But if he missed the entrance angle, the boys calculated he'd slam into the tree so they set themselves up as sentries around the base of the fir. Cringing in horror they watched Doug drunkenly botch the takeoff and sail in a sharp parabola out over the swimming hole and then head straight back for the tree, arms outstretched. It took the concerted effort of all three boys to keep their uncle from bashing himself into a bloody pulp on the tree trunk. Mentally and emotionally, the boys were unprepared to deal with untrained visitors attempting to kill themselves so they never demonstrated the swing again.

Swing over the swimming hole

In the summer of 1973, Ray had brought up a cart with a hand-operated brake that he'd fabricated out of steel tubing and a dirt bike tire. At the time, Ray told Virgil he'd brought up a mule. Virgil was exasperated; he hated mules and donkeys, considering them more trouble than the weight they could haul. He was greatly relieved when Ray showed him the cart, though not for long.

Shortly after Ray left, Gaines and Virgil tried to haul a load down and the center of gravity was so high, it nearly knocked Virgil off the steepest part of the trail. In disgust, Virgil unloaded the cart and threw it down the mountainside. The boys retrieved it, modified the center of gravity and tried it again. It was a job pushing the cart up the trail but for heavy loads, it was far easier than backpacks.

In June 1974, Doug wrote telling the boys to bring the cart up trail on a specific date. When he arrived, he had a dismantled geodesic dome packed in a trailer behind his car. Made from one-inch by two-inch redwood, the triangular frames were four feet on each side. "I built this dome for a friend's small swimming pool which she didn't want any more, so I thought it'd make a neat kitchen," Doug explained.

When all the pieces were down at the Flat, the boys helped Doug assemble the dome. Doug had brought up a large roll of 6-mil translucent plastic sheeting, 10 rolls of duct tape, staples and a staple gun. The triangles bolted together into pentagons and hexagons using carriage bolts. These pentagons and hexagons then bolted together with triangles filling the spaces between to form a 15-foot diameter hemisphere.

Before they assembled the triangles, Doug instructed them to staple the plastic on the frames. Once they finished assembling the hemisphere, Virgil got his home-built wooden ladder and climbed to the top of the dome to seal all the joints with the duct tape. "It shouldn't leak rain at all," Doug said. "This is the way I had it set up over Gladys' pool."

"We'll use boards I cut with the sawmill to build the base," Virgil said.

The futuristic-looking dome with the network of silver duct tape made a strange sight on the Flat. "How do you put in a door?" Virgil asked.

"I'm not sure but if the opening's too big, it might weaken the structure," Doug cautioned.

Virgil and Gaines formed the foundation of the decagon shaped platform using stacked, interlaced river boulders. The sawmill was still mostly cutting tapered boards but with a lot of culling, they managed to get enough to lay a pine plank floor on a framework of two-by-six fir joists. With just enough wood left, they built a four-foot high cripple wall around the perimeter of the platform to set the dome on. The dome was actually stiff enough and lightweight enough for the five of them to lift it into place. They all stood back and examined the structure. "It looks like a space observatory," Gaines remarked. "I wish I had a 10-inch refractor telescope to put in it," he joked as he'd been talking about a 10-inch telescope for years.

Virgil looked at the doorway to the platform. "I'm going to have to take a couple triangles out of the structure in order to get the doorway through," he said between puffs on his pipe. "Then I'm going to create new triangles to build a dormer-like roofline."

Virgil not only built the doorway structure and a door, he also built a cabinet and installed a stainless steel sink. They moved the kitchen stove in, followed by the redwood table. Kelly set up a heating coil in the stove's firebox and Gaines built a platform for a 15-gallon hot water tank behind the stove. Then he plumbed hot and cold water lines to the sink, and found and installed an old faucet. Marcy lit a fire in the stove and a half hour later turned the sink faucet on as the rest of the family anxiously watched. "Oh my gosh! Hot water!" she crowed. "No more heating dishpans on the stove."

They sat at the redwood table and enjoyed the sunny view, but when the weather heated up, it was unbearably hot inside the dome until Virgil laid a tarp across the top. Marcy missed the breezy outdoor summer kitchen but as soon as the cool autumn came, they were glad to be in the dome again as it had so much space and the light was great. Virgil even held school in it.

On the way back from the mail one day, they found Ted Carter walking along Hobo Gulch Road. He told them he'd found a cabin he could stay in until the miner returned the next summer. When Ted lived at Hobo Gulch Campground, the Forest Service ranger had tried to run him out. Ted wouldn't budge and they even tried to ticket him but he just ignored them. When the cold weather came, Ted moved by his own accord into his friend's cabin.

Late that autumn, they stopped to see Ted. A grapevine grew over and around the posts and rails so they picked and ate grapes as they sat and visited on the tiny porch. Ted had tacked witty notes all over the walls inside the cabin. Beneath a big *Only You Can Prevent Forest Fires* Smokey the Bear sign nailed to the log walls next to the door was a sign in Finwing's block-style printing, *If God had wanted forest fires, he would have invented lightning.* And Ted's quirky style didn't stop with posted notes. In the bathroom, he had a cut out paper tongue hanging from a huge pink shell that looked like big lips.

It rained a lot that fall and early winter. Joel griped about the rain because he wanted snow so he could learn to ski. On the 28th of January, 1975, they awoke to snow drifting down adding to a few inches already on the ground. "Are you happy now? You got your snow," Marcy said as Joel came in for breakfast that morning.

Joel scowled. "No. I'm sure it'll turn to rain this afternoon just like it has all winter." He sat down and started buttering the pancakes Marcy served him. "This isn't real snow. It has to snow over a foot before it's a real storm."

Despite Joel's prediction, the snow did not turn to rain that afternoon but came down even harder and by nightfall, 24 inches had built up. As darkness fell, Joel smiled broadly. The next morning he was up almost as early as Marcy to see how much snow had fallen. Skiing over the deep snow, he took multiple measurements. "We've got 34 inches!" Joel announced as he kicked snow off his boots and came through the door of the dome. "It's still snowing but getting warmer and wetter. Most likely it's going to turn to rain," he added dourly.

Again, he was wrong. It kept snowing for another week though it didn't build up any deeper than 38 inches compressed into a heavy snow pack. At Desperation Point, 1,200 feet higher than the Flat, they knew the snow must be a lot deeper.

Joel enjoyed his time outdoors trying to ski, shoveling snow from the path between the cabin and the dome and clearing snow from the roofs. One of Marcy's big worries was one of them getting sick while so deeply snowed in so she sent Joel to rest and recuperate inside the cabin when he came down with a cold.

Two days later after Marcy finished shoveling snow off the woodshed roof, she stopped by the cabin to see how Joel was feeling. Joel's boots still sat in the entryway but the cabin was empty. "Oh man, this is great!" she fumed. "He has a cold and walked up to the dome through the snow with bare feet!" Marcy slammed the door and marched up the trail toward the dome. As she passed under the old outdoor kitchen cedars, she saw the boys standing together in the snow. She stopped in her tracks and lit into Joel for wading through the snow with bare feet while sick. "If you don't take care of yourself you'll end up catching pneumonia and we can't get you out to a doctor!" Marcy chastised.

Joel grinned stupidly and she lost her temper. Raising her voice even higher, she really yelled at him. Without warning, the whole load of snow draped high in the cedars let loose and pounded over her, blasting down her neck. As the veil of snow cleared, raucous laughter greeted Marcy. "You screamed so loud you knocked the snow out of that tree!" Joel said, holding up his left foot to reveal a different pair of boots.

Despite the dripping wet snow running down her neck, Marcy had to laugh, too.

⌇⌁⌁⌇

The weather alternated between light snowstorms and sunny weather through February. As Marcy washed dishes one morning, she heard Bully woof once loudly and tried to look out the smoky plastic covering the dome but could only see his dark silhouette lunging through the snowdrifts. She ran outside. Across the river near the swimming hole, a single doe struggled to escape in the deep snow. Until then, Marcy hadn't realized how powerful Bully was. In a matter of seconds, he crossed the frigid river and closed in on the doe.

Watching in horror as Bully attacked the doe, Marcy shrieked for him to come but he had bloodlust and paid her no mind. Marcy didn't know a deer could scream but as Bully tore into her neck, the doe screamed in terror and desperation. The commotion brought the boys out of the cabin. Gaines immediately grasped the situation and ran for the 30-30 rifle. He fired into the air and Bully, who had never gotten over his terrible fear of the rifle from the rattlesnake incident, turned and ran for the space under the cabin where he hid out the rest of the day.

Meanwhile the doe made her way slowly down the far riverbank. They watched as she tried to cross about a hundred yards downstream. Halfway across, the doe weakly fell in the water. For a few minutes, she struggled to get up and keep her head above the surface. Finally, they saw the fight for life go out of her and she raised her head for one last breath of winter air before succumbing to her fate. Her body caught in the shallow riffles, steaming slightly as her life's heat radiated for the last time in the cold air.

March brought a beautiful early spring and violets covered the Flat and scented the air. The snow melted fast and they started cleaning up the winter's mess around the Flat. During spring and summer the past couple years, Kelly and Joel had started sleeping in a makeshift loft in the woodshed. With much enthusiasm, they moved their beds to this summer sleeping area.

Marcy had tomatoes, peppers and cabbage plants started in trays in the dome and put a diluted mixture of fishmeal on them. When she came back inside a few minutes later, the dome was black with blue bottle flies. She couldn't believe it, as they'd never come in before when she used fishmeal but she always noticed that flies came inside just before a storm.

Fifty-two needed a new barn so they set to work leveling a spot at the edge of the woods. The boys hauled many loads of gravel for the floor and they planned to pour a concrete slab over this gravel.

After the first 10 days of March, the snow melted to the point that they made it to town. They bought mostly building supplies for the goat pen this first trip, including five sacks of cement they planned to haul down in the next couple of days. They planned to make another trip the next week to restock the larder.

With the final brush cleared around the goat pen, the boys stayed up late that night enjoying the mild evening air around the brushfire. To their amazement, it was dumping snow the next morning. Two feet fell by evening but Kelly and Joel insisted on sticking out their sleeping arrangement. Nightfall brought lighting and thunder ripping across the mountains accompanied by driving sleet mixed with rain.

Virgil was up first the next morning, which was Saint Patrick's Day. Marcy got up later and Joel woke up, too. Virgil had shoveled a narrow path up to the dome and had the stove lit and was drinking a cup of coffee when they walked in. Above the stove, one whole pentagonal section was inverted and sagged ominously. "The door ruined the integrity of the structure," Virgil explained.

"Virg! That's going to collapse!" Marcy cried in a panic.

"I don't think it will. I've been watching it," he answered.

Joel stared intently at the protruding pentagon. "No. I can see it moving."

Virgil shook his head but decided to humor them and left to find a board or something to prop it up. As Joel and Marcy watched, there was no doubt the structure was failing. They wanted to get out but to get to the door required walking under the bulge so they moved to one side.

Finally, the last fibers in the redwood broke and the roof came crashing in, followed by a huge mountain of snow that buried the stove and Marcy's seedlings. Virgil burst through the door, wild eyed, carrying a two-by-four prop, expecting to find them squashed. Marcy looked at Virgil across the mountain of snow, through the rain and sleet now pouring out of the heavy gray skies into her kitchen, and shook her head. Then she and Joel climbed over the mound of snow to get to the door. "I hope you have enough snow now, Joel," Marcy groaned.

Gaines and Kelly came out of the shack and helped shovel snow out of the dome and off the stove. Virgil tried to prop up the split end with a board but it leaked badly. All Marcy's tender plants were smashed but with more boards propping it up and a blue tarp Virgil and Gaines put over it, the dome became livable again.

A sunny spring day followed and Marcy hoped for a quick melt off of the snow as they were low on food. That night another winter storm slammed into their mountains, even worse than the one two days previous. In 24 hours, it dumped another 36 inches of snow. Four feet of snowpack now lay on the Flat. They knew the road would be closed and Marcy tried to figure out what to cook as the only supplies left were oil, dried milk, canned green beans and sugar.

Virgil and Gaines decided to go fishing to supplement the dwindling larder. The fishing was terrible but along the trail up the river, they found a deer that had died of a .22 caliber gunshot wound. This the dogs could use so they cleaned it and brought it back to hang up. Each dog got a big slice of meat each day and they were eating better than the humans were.

One afternoon Virgil took a butcher knife out to cut the dogs their daily portion. As he cut the meat away, he heard strange voices behind him. Turning, he saw Red Cockroff and another man wading through the snow toward him. "How you doing, Virg?" Red hollered.

Virgil stared at Red, then down at the bloody hunk of meat in his hand. *This looks bad*, he thought. Red took in the scene and guffawed loudly. "Got yourself some kitchen meat, eh?"

"Uh…actually no," Virgil stammered. "We found this deer." Virgil jerked his head toward the carcass hanging in a tree. "It…it was dead. She died…"

"She! She, huh? Nothing like spring doe." Red roared with laughter and the man with Red grinned widely, as well.

Virgil tried again. "Someone had shot her with a .22…"

".22, huh? Nice and quiet."

"Actually she was dead when we found her… We're just using her for dog meat," Virgil persisted.

"DOG meat! Is that what you call it now?" More roaring laughter.

Virgil grinned in defeat knowing he'd probably never convince Red otherwise. He tossed the piece to Tissy and Red stopped mid-guffaw and gaped after the retreating dog with her daily portion of fresh meat. "When I lived out in the woods I always had camp meat." Red shook his head. "You really don't have to throw your meat to the dog."

"It was just a little piece. How the hell did you get here through the snow?" Virgil asked. "Come on down and Marcy will make you some coffee."

"This is Paul," Red said. "We wondered how you folks were doing. We've been wading snow for three days. I could use that coffee."

Marcy was surprised to see Red. "How'd you make it through all this snow?"

"We had one hell of a time climbing up the canyon," Red replied.

"Could we make it out?" Marcy asked.

Red looked her up and down and roared with laughter. "No way could *you* make it! We didn't *even* try to come up the Hobo Gulch Road and over the high gap. We came all the way up the North Fork. The snow was *belly* deep on *me*!"

Marcy knew they were hungry but all she had was green beans and milk. "Would you like some?" Marcy asked but they refused.

After Red and Paul left, Marcy decided they should try to make it to town so they hiked up to the Jeep the next day. Thinking they wouldn't have more snow beings it was so late in the season, they'd parked the Jeep down by the old mill site instead of up at Desperation Point when they came back with the cement. Snow was piled up high on top of the Jeep and all around it so they went to work with shovels to dig it out. After they'd cleared away some of the snow, Virgil got in to see how far he could move the Jeep but when he turned the key, nothing happened. "Is the battery connected?" he yelled.

Gaines lifted the hood. "The battery is gone."

Virgil got out and slammed the door. "Someone stole the damn battery," he said, peering under the hood.

"I have that huge old Tractorline battery down at the Flat Otis gave me years ago," Gaines offered.

"The rats!" Kelly burst out. "They stole the set of chains Emery Beattie gave us for the rear tires!"

"They also took the tarp off the cement in the back and it's all wet," Joel observed.

Virgil was furious. "Well, the cement should be all right. The sacks still have the protective plastic coatings."

"Except someone shot them with birdshot."

"What?"

Joel had out his big knife digging lead beads from the now solid sacks.

"Let's go down and start up early tomorrow morning," Marcy suggested, having seen enough for the day.

Just as they got ready to leave, Ted Carter came down the mill road on snowshoes, carrying a backpack. He'd walked six miles to bring them food. "I was worried about you being stranded without food so here's some canned ham and bread," he said.

"Someone stole our battery!" Marcy blurted.

"And your chains and the clothes," he added dryly.

"How did you know?" Marcy asked.

"The sheriff told me. Two young brothers, one with a wife and kids, were going to Hobo Gulch Campground and got stranded on the way when their battery ran down. They took your battery and then got snowed in up there when the storm came. They had three small children in the car and one of the brothers decided to walk out and get help. He walked just past your turnoff before he suffered hypothermia and died. Not knowing where they were, family in Eureka got worried and phoned both the sheriff and the Forest Service.

"Undersheriff Laag had a funny feeling they were at Hobo Gulch Campground so he told the sheriff he was going to take the big Caterpillar out there. The sheriff didn't think it was a good idea but Ted packed some sandwiches and went anyway. When the Forest Service heard about it, they told him the big Cat would wreck the road and were going to cite him but he disregarded their threat. About 100 feet from the body, he had a strange intuition and got out of the Cat. The body was covered with snow but he walked over to it and found it. Then he got the Caterpillar to the campground and rescued the rest of the group. When he brought them to the sheriff's office, the kids admitted they'd stolen the Jeep's battery. 'Borrowed it' I believe were their words.'"

Speechless and bug-eyed, they all gaped at Ted. "So as soon as you can get out, stop by the sheriff's and he'll give you your battery," Ted added.

"Come on down and spend the night with us," Marcy suggested. "And here, have a sandwich. I bet you're exhausted," she said.

"No thanks. I want to get on home before it gets late."

They thanked Ted for his magnificent effort and then he made his way back up the snow-covered mill road.

The next morning, up trail they went again, Gaines with the 60-pound battery on his backpack. The snow had melted considerably so they didn't have too hard a job shoveling to get to Camp Desperation and then down Hazley Road, and the Caterpillar had cleared Hobo Gulch Road during the rescue. They went to the sheriff's office to retrieve their battery and Undersheriff Laag confirmed Ted's story. Also, he'd kindly charged their battery and topped off the fluids.

A couple months later, they received a note from the brother of the young man who had died. He thanked them for the use of the stuff from the Jeep and apologized for any problems it may have caused them. Whether he or his brother had shot the cement sacks full of holes remained unknown but if they had, they paid a far higher price for the deed than was necessary.

One-wheeled cart that Ray made

30 - A Kitchen and Vandalism

Marcy was watering her plants in the dome when a loud banging and thumping issued from under the floor. She went out, got down on her knees and peered into the dark space under the platform. She could vaguely see Tissy thrashing around fighting with something but couldn't see what she was attacking. Marcy called sharply for her but Tissy paid no mind.

Suddenly, Tissy started yipping and barking mixed with crying. In a panic, Marcy yelled for Virgil who was working on jewelry at the shop. Virgil heard the panic in her voice and came at a dead run. "Tissy's fighting with something under the dome! She's getting the worst of it!"

Virgil immediately crawled under the dome. Although it was too dusty to see what was going on, Marcy could hear Virgil calling and talking to his dog. A moment later, he came sliding back out dragging Tissy by her hind legs. The dog that had rarely left his side, even as he taught school in Denny, was thrashing about in mindless convulsions. He stroked and called to her quietly. After several minutes, her body quieted down and she regained recognition of him.

Virgil examined Tissy and found a lump that could only be a mammary tumor. Having heard her yipping, the boys showed up. Tissy staggered to her feet and slowly went in a circle to each and licked them. She did this repeatedly although it was totally out of her character to be friendly to anyone but Virgil. It was painfully obvious she was telling them all farewell and the boys all had tears in their eyes. She died later that afternoon.

Ray showed up with Patrick, a friend from down south. Ray seemed withdrawn and they asked what was wrong. "Sean's been diagnosed with muscular dystrophy," Ray said. "I had to get away up here and get my mind off it."

Virgil figured a long walk would be good for Ray and talked them all into going to see the pond and mill site Red Barnes had told them about. They thought the pond was a good three miles from the Flat and knew the mill site was even further. But never having been there before, they had no idea how far it really was.

After they passed Red's trail, they came to a dark, heavily wooded forest where great boulders with moss caps sank under thick layers of pine needles and leaves. A tiny sliver of sun slipped through the trees. Scattered about in the gloom were bleached-out animal bones, including various skulls. Into the gloom, a dark shape slipped away into the deeper shadows. "This must be Bone Forest," Joel whispered.

They didn't know what had dragged the bones there. A cougar or bear, perhaps? Or maybe it was Red's hunting ground? They didn't tarry long as the place had an eerie feel, as if something sinister lurked in every dark corner. As they continued on, they were all thinking about the dark shape they'd seen. To make matters worse, Virgil mentioned that the big heavy limbs leaning down over the trail would make great jumping off spots for a cougar. Marcy knew he was just saying that to get a rise out of Patrick who had been whining incessantly about how far it was. Instead, he got a rise out of all of them, and they glanced around nervously and went faster to get past this stretch of the trail.

They didn't realize it when they reached the pond. All they saw was a dank mosquito-filled swamp with water grass and cattails crowding its shallow depths. Exploring the deep woods around the swamp, they came upon a beautiful red fox curled up sleeping on the ground. On closer examination, they found it was dead but there was no apparent injury. Already somewhat spooked from the earlier events, Ray stared nervously at the dead animal and wondered whether their own bones would soon lie bleaching in these woods, left by whatever mysterious killer lurked in the forest. Studying a recently toppled tree, Joel uncovered the cause of the mysterious death. "That fox had its den in a hollow underneath the root ball of that tree," he explained. "When the tree fell, it crushed the fox in its sleep."

"That's it," Ray readily agreed with Joel's conclusion, relieved to have a logical reason for the death.

Virgil stared across the swamp. "I guess this *is* the pond," Virgil said, disappointed.

"Is this what we walked all that way to see?" Patrick complained.

Red had told them many times about the pond and they were all disappointed to find just a swamp instead. "Let's go see if we have better luck finding the mill," Gaines suggested.

"How far is that? Another five miles?" Patrick asked sarcastically

"It's about a mile past this swamp, according to Red," Marcy replied.

The trail switchbacked steeply to the river. At the river's edge stood a little weathered board and batten shed, unused and a bit dank inside but at one time in the depression years it had been someone's meager home. The river here was deep and swift, breaking over huge boulders into whitewater. They tried to figure a way to cross the river to see the old sawmill site that was supposed to be a quarter mile up the creek that poured into the North Fork on the opposite canyon wall. The risk of being swept away in the surging whitewater was too great so they settled for building a fire on a little rock bar in front of the shed. The only food they had brought along was a small slab of bacon, which Marcy cut into cubes that the group roasted on sticks over the fire. Ray had grown quiet which meant he had an idea working in his mind. Not long after, he informed Virgil he thought it would be easier to eliminate the switchbacks by climbing the ridge behind the little shed. Virgil shook his head and tried to explain how steep it would be. Ray hadn't lost any weight and wasn't agile on steep terrain. Virgil could see Ray was tired and knew he was trying to cut miles off the return trip, but he also knew Ray would never admit it.

Ray kept arguing the point and managed to convince the boys it was a good idea only because they welcomed the chance to explore. Finally, they decided Ray and the boys would take the shortcut while Patrick, Virgil and Marcy would use the switchbacks.

Virgil was right; it was steep and rocky with many talus slopes to fight. Ray fought his way up the canyon wall nearly falling and rolling several times. The boys were in good shape and it was a lark for them but they worried about Ray. His face was beet red and his blue shirt, soaked with perspiration, clung heavily to his back and chest. The boys worried he was a heart attack waiting to happen, and to make matters worse, Ray felt he had to make it to the main trail before the other group to prove his point. Ray and the boys did reach the trail first and Ray proudly proclaimed he was right, never admitting that the shortcut had nearly killed him.

Everyone was exhausted and famished on reaching the Flat and Marcy made a tamale pie. Marcy had once told Ray they'd eaten a ground squirrel so every time he came over, he'd question the meal. "What kind of meat are you serving me, Marcy?" Ray always asked.

"Skunk," she'd say with a laugh.

Famished from the excursion, this was the first time Ray didn't ask what kind of meat she was cooking. He was just too hungry.

Tossing another tapered fir plank on the waste pile as it came off the sawmill, Joel frowned. "What we need to do is just buy new steel and rebuild it without all this fire twisted stuff."

"That's fine but we don't have the money to do that," Virgil retorted. "We have to work with what we have."

They'd been cutting pretty much steady the whole month of May. After spending the winter in a somewhat decent kitchen housed in the dome, they knew they couldn't go backwards and the dome was not trusted after the heavy snow that winter. "But we're never going to get enough cut to get the whole house up," Joel persisted.

"I'm thinking about building the house in sections. I don't want Ma to have to go back to the cook shack this winter," Virgil said. "I think we can build the kitchen section this fall." He walked over to the stack of straight two-by-fours they'd accumulated and counted them. "We only need 24 more to finish the kitchen."

"Really?" Joel said, suddenly encouraged.

"Let's go across the river and cut some more cants," Gaines suggested.

"While you guys do that I think I'll stake out the foundation for the kitchen," Virgil said.

"What are you doing?" Marcy demanded when she saw Virgil driving stakes and running string.

"Thought we might start working on some kind of structure here," he said evasively.

"The house!"

"Well, at least a kitchen for now."

"I can't believe you're actually really starting the house. It's been so long!" Marcy stepped inside the string perimeter and looked at the ground. "I'd love a cellar to store my canning. Do you think it is possible to dig a cellar here?"

"We can give it a try. If we don't run into bedrock, it might work."

As the boys grew older and stronger, Virgil and Marcy's workload eased. The boys got shovels and started digging but the hard-packed dirt refused to yield. "This isn't going to work. I'm going to put that Roto-Hoe back together and use it," Virgil said, looking to Marcy for approval.

At the present time, the Roto-Hoe was torn apart and some of its parts were used to run Marcy's wheat grinder. "Steal from Paul to give to Jerry," Marcy groaned. "Oh well, if it gets me a cellar."

"It's rob Peter to pay Paul, Ma. I'll put it back together after we dig the cellar, if we can dig it," Virgil consoled her.

The hoe softened the dirt enough so they could shovel it out but it was filled with river boulders, which they stacked to be used later for mortared rock walls in the cellar and the foundation for the kitchen. Two weeks of hard manual labor later, they'd excavated the cellar pit and it was an exciting day when Virgil directed Gaines how to mix mortar for the rockwork. Virgil selected six or eight boulders from the saved stacks and dropped them down in the pit, then climbed down to arrange them along the south wall. "Okay, Gaines, hand me a shovelful of mortar."

Handing down the shovel filled with mortar was not an easy job but it worked. Virgil got to work setting the boulders and formed a nice little section of rock wall before Gaines announced that the first batch of mortar was gone. "Do you want me to mix some more?" Gaines asked.

Virgil shook his head. "I'm going to make a mortarboard. The shovel isn't working that well."

Virgil climbed out of the pit, cut a section of pine board and plugged in the jointer-planer Karl Riker, the local machinist, had given him a few years before. The planer, running at a geared up speed from a recycled vacuum cleaner motor Kelly had rigged up, was quite noisy. Virgil had to make two passes with the four-inch planer to smooth an eight-inch board. The first pass completed, Virgil flipped the board and pushed it most of the way through the high-speed rotor. Suddenly, the board kicked back and jerked Virgil's forefinger into the knives. Before the blood obscured the cuts, he saw it had flipped his fingernail over backwards and jammed it into the bone in his finger. "Oh, damn!" he said.

Marcy came running. Virgil's face was white and blood gushed from his finger. Gaines was helping to steady him and Marcy raced to Virgil's other side. They helped him to the cabin and stopped the bleeding but he was still extremely pale. "Get me some hot tea," Virgil said.

Marcy wrapped a blanket around Virgil and made him some tea. His color slowly came back as he recovered from the shock. Virgil looked at the white bandage on his finger. "I won't be able to mortar the rocks with this," he said dejectedly.

"I can do it," Gaines said.

So Gaines took over and proved to be a natural with cement work. Kelly and Joel washed and hauled the rocks and mixed the mortar for him, and Gaines laid the cellar walls. Every day, Marcy opened Virgil's bandage and smeared his finger with Bag Balm. Although it kept the finger from becoming infected, it seemed like a long time before he was able to pull the fingernail chips out of the wound. They completed most of the mortar and stonework by mid-summer, which was much longer than they'd planned. But no one project could get full attention when they were trying to keep everything else operating.

They met Emery Beattie on one trip into town. He'd just gotten back from Oregon with a half-ton truck loaded with cheap plywood. When Virgil told him how slow the kitchen was going, Emery offered to sell him plywood sheets for two bucks apiece. That suited Virgil fine as he wanted to lay them over the rough pine subfloor in the kitchen that he'd salvaged from the dome flooring.

The boys struggled bringing the plywood down to the Flat with the one-wheel cart. Although the cart was great for compact loads, hauling the large four-by-eight-foot sheets of plywood wasn't working. They finally built a similar cart that held the sheets vertical and made them easy to haul. As a side benefit, the new cart made hauling pipe down easy, as well. They called it their earwig cart, as it resembled one. They laid the plywood sheets over the salvaged pine boards. "The kitchen should be done by winter," Virgil told Marcy.

Years earlier, Marcy had envisioned a dream kitchen and scribbled a picture on how she wanted it to look. "It has to have a lot of windows, and I would love you to carve jaybirds on my kitchen cabinet doors," Marcy told Virgil.

After six years of moving her large wood cook stove to or from the outdoor kitchen area each fall and spring, Marcy figured they could set up a temporary kitchen in the woodshed that fall until the permanent kitchen was done. The boys were no longer small and it was way too crowded in the cook shack when the whole family gathered for meals, and the woodshed was only 10 feet from where the new kitchen was being built. The boys helped Marcy carry the redwood table and benches and placed them neatly in the woodshed. Marcy hammered some shelves up and they muscled the heavy cast iron cook stove up to the woodshed without dismantling it first.

Housing the kitchen in the woodshed didn't seem bad until Tom and Goldie found it. "Oh Virg, why didn't you remind me of Tom's bad habit of climbing on the table and stealing food?" Marcy grumbled.

"You should've stayed in the cook shack; the cats couldn't get in there," he answered.

Cooking in the woodshed that fall was an experience Marcy would never forget. The cats did their thing on the ground and then slept on the table. Every morning, Marcy had to shovel out cat shit and scour the redwood tabletop. Marcy put chicken wire around the front entrance but every morning when she came in, she found that both cats had still used her dirt floor as a litter box. Virgil tacked galvanized roofing around the shed to keep the cats out and also to make it warmer. "It looks like the barrios in Mexico City," he said, examining his handiwork.

It got so cold that Marcy found she could make the flaky Danish pastry that requires icy utensils and dough. Marcy tolerated it because her dream kitchen was turning out just the way she wanted it as little by little, the new kitchen began to form. Virgil and the boys worked to get the roof and sides on. Virgil was even making a bay window for her plants and the loft above would be big enough for a bedroom. The weather was good for building as a persistent high pressure blocked most of the Pacific storms. But what was good for the kitchen project was not a good sign for the next summer's water supply.

Fall was passing into winter and conditions were getting more and more unbearable in Marcy's barrio kitchen but her spirits were always buoyed by seeing the progress on her new kitchen. Everything seemed to move so slowly though, with all the processes necessary to get any extra lumber. The trees had to be felled across the river, limbed, cut into cants and skidded to the cable car landing. From there the boys sent them across the river in a long series of processes that would take a day in itself. The sawmill was still unpredictable and many cants were wasted when the mill cut unusable tapered wedge shaped lumber. And if enough were ruined, the whole process of getting more cants would be repeated.

Kelly and Virgil got set to go to town to get building paper but discovered the engine on the Jeep had frozen up. So work stopped on the house as they went up to work on the Jeep. Virgil studied the engine head as Joel leaned over it with a breaker bar and socket wrench. "Go ahead, and start pulling the head. I don't know how we're going to get a new head gasket here though," Virgil sighed.

Joel slowly started breaking the torque on the old rusty bolts. Only one stubborn bolt remained and Joel struggled to break it loose without breaking it. "It's coming… It's coming…"

The bolt came out but had broken off just down from the head. All the guys observed it in dismay. "Now what?" Marcy asked.

"Try and work the head off around that broken bolt and maybe we can get a pair of vise grips on it and twist it out," Virgil said.

The head came off and Kelly set to work with the vise grips. With a sharp 'tink' the bolt broke off in the head block. Gaines cursed. "Now we're in trouble."

"We're just going to have to figure a way to drill that out," Virgil said with an outward calm that failed to cover his inner perturbation.

The guys got together and set about making an action plan. Gaines would rebuild a 120-volt electric drill at the Flat and make it run on 12-volts DC so it would run on the Jeep battery while Kelly made a Briggs and Stratton engine-powered battery charger. Joel and Virgil would continue to work on the frozen engine.

They found the engine was frozen with a syrupy gum. By burning down a pan of gas from the tank, they found it had the same residue left on the bottom when all the gas burned away. From a can of gas not from the tank, they repeated the process and there was no residue. Someone had dumped sugar into the gas tank in a malicious little prank. Now, not only did they need a new head gasket, they also needed a fresh tank of gas. "Don't people realize how critical that Jeep is to us?" Marcy wondered.

"Either they're really vicious or just don't have a clue," Virgil replied.

"We need to convey to people that might be thinking about doing this how important this Jeep is to us," Marcy continued.

"I think I'll make a sign to put in the back window," Virgil said.

Virgil made up a little sign explaining the situation and asking people to please not mess with the Jeep. Marcy loved the sign as it was very poetic but the boys hated it because it was too syrupy. The boys were more in favor of electrocution by touching the gas cap, radioactive contamination upon opening the hood or various other ghastly consequences for sabotaging their Jeep.

While work progressed on the Jeep, Sharon, their former neighbor who had been married to Rusty Bolt, showed up with her new husband, Chuck. Seeing their predicament, Sharon and Chuck decided to go get new gas and a head gasket for the Jeep, which was greatly appreciated.

Gaines finished his drill and Kelly the battery charger. Now it all had to go up trail. The battery charger was heavy but with Kelly's help, Gaines got it to the top. Virgil had found that lacquer thinner cleaned the syrup off the cylinder walls and now all they needed was to get the broken bolt drilled out and the head reinstalled.

It was a slow job and soon the battery went dead. Kelly set up his charger and they waited in a warm sunny spot as it charged. After a while, Gaines went to disconnect the charger from the battery and got a lesson in the properties of hydrogen gas. A sharp explosion drowned out the sound of the charger's engine and left Gaines leaning over what was left of the battery, holding a tiger clamp in his hand, looking utterly stunned. He was unhurt but not the battery. The hydrogen gas generated by the charging process ignited when Gaines sparked the tiger clamp against the battery terminal.

So once again, they made a round trip down and up the trail to bring the old Tractorline battery up so they could work on the Jeep. After they completed the drilling, Virgil tapped the hole out. Once they replaced the head, the old engine started up. So at last they got back their transportation and could resume work on the kitchen.

They'd brought a case of used storefront windows from L.A. that Ray and Virgil salvaged when they replaced them with new ones on one of Ray's window jobs. Marvin's mule Bridget had brought the heavy case down years ago and Marcy gave her a bunch of apples for her effort. With hand planes, Virgil made all of the window sashes, which took him weeks. Gaines made stout stairs to go down into the cellar and Kelly put in the plumbing and electrical wiring. Joel helped Virgil put in the kitchen sink and yellow Formica countertop. When they began laying the floor tiles, Marcy decided it was time to dismantle her cook stove and clean it with lye water. The lye stripped the grease and it ran down in brown rivulets as she sprayed it with the hose. After she wiped it down with newspapers, the stove's original cast iron sheen showed through and she was proud to see it looking so new.

Instead of early fall, it was early January of 1976 before the new kitchen was ready and they were all happy when the time finally came to start moving in. The redwood table came first, followed by the benches. The stove was heavy but with coordinated effort, they finally placed it in its proper spot. They carried all the dishes and other essentials and placed them on the shelves Virgil had made. It was a great satisfaction for them all when they could slam the door shut to keep out the cats but it didn't last long. Tom was furious and climbed on the windowsills and howled at them. They paid him no heed so he started biting and scratching Virgil's hand-planed window frames. "Look what he's doing," Marcy told Virgil.

Virgil ran outside, grabbed Tom by the tail and flung him off. No sooner did he land on his feet then he leaped up on the windowsills again. They slapped him with rolled up newspapers and threw him off over and over but still he came. Finally, after being screamed at and whacked with countless newspaper rolls, he got the message and sat in the woodshed with a most angry look. "Well, I guess that stopped him," Kelly said, though it hurt him to see his cat in trouble.

Tom still tried to come in at night, biting more holes in the window frames, and Virgil was mad enough to shoot him. Marcy tacked chicken wire over the windows and they finally discouraged him from coming in. Tom took his anger out on poor Goldie so they made little boxes under opposite sides of the roof of the woodshed for the cats to sleep in.

The boys encouraged Virgil and Marcy to move their bedroom to the loft above the kitchen and they all loved the arrangement. Virgil and Marcy had their privacy at last and the boys had more space. When Virgil and Marcy awoke to Vivaldi's *Four Seasons* at full volume, not only did they think it was nice to hear, they also realized the boys finally had privacy to do what they wanted.

The cupboards under the sink still needed doors and Marcy wanted to catch Virgil before he got too involved in another project. "Sweetie, do you think you could start carving my kitchen panels by the sink?" she asked. "It's such a pretty day and I'll supply you with cookies and coffee."

She looked out the window a while later and saw him sitting by the back door carving jaybirds on the panels. All around him were real jays, flapping their wings and sneaking bites out of the dog food bowl. Marcy marveled at his live models staying so close to him as he carved their images in wood. When he finished, one panel had a jaybird sitting on a branch eating an apple while the other showed one with his wings spread as if ready for flight.

Cooking in her new kitchen on the wood stove that winter was wonderful, but in summer it was like shoveling coal into a locomotive. The kitchen reached 120 degrees and every guest who walked in walked out again because they couldn't stand the heat. They had so much company that year and Marcy had so much canning to do that she honestly knew how a roasting turkey must have felt.

During one of Gary and Emy's visits, Gary saw what she had to go through so he sent her a one-burner propane gas stove for Christmas. Eventually Marcy learned if she made the bread dough at night, it raised well enough that she could bake it in the wood stove early in the morning before it got hot. And her sister, Marie, sent Marcy a crock-pot she could use to cook stews and beans overnight so she didn't have to fire up the wood stove.

Marcella's 'half chick' kitchen

Grubby

31 - Sylmar

Their last chicken, Big Egg, disappeared. Big Egg had always been the favorite and they all felt bad when she came up missing. Of all the chickens, she never caused any trouble in the flock and was the only one that consistently laid eggs every other day, winter or summer. The rest of the flock had picked on her and Big Egg was the chicken the pigs tried to eat. Once a hawk grabbed her but Marcy ran out flapping her arms and yelling until he let her go, uninjured. Marcy wondered if Big Egg had finally met her fate with the hawk.

Several days after Big Egg's disappearance, Marcy walked up to the upper garden with Bully and saw him make a beeline to a spot under a redbud tree. Bully saw Marcy looking at him so he turned away and ignored her but started spinning around and acting guilty. Marcy went to the spot and found poor old Big Egg, all chewed up and dead.

"You rotten dog!" Marcy scolded. "Poor Big Egg. She got chased all her life until *you* finally killed her. You get meaner with age."

Bully had bitten one little boy already and they had to lock him in the shed whenever children came to visit but this was the first time he'd attacked a chicken. One morning a month later, he was gone. They searched for him all day and into the next. He never returned so must have met his fate as Big Egg had met hers. Not long after Bully's disappearance, though, Marcy missed him despite his increasingly nasty disposition.

❧━✦━☙

Over the years, Virgil, Gaines and Joel had grafted many apple saplings and several were now bearing abundant fruit. Harvesting was always fun and they stored the apples in the woodshed where they could keep watch over them. Marcy put out food for the cats on the woodshed roof and every morning it was gone so she assumed the cats were eating it. After a dusting of snow one night, Marcy went out in the early morning and found bear tracks. *So, that's who's been eating the food,* Marcy thought and decided not to leave out any more because it was attracting the bear to the woodshed where the apples were stored. But as soon as he found the easy food supply gone, the bear sniffed out the apples and had eaten one crate before they noticed. "Kelly!" Marcy called. "Put a hotwire around the woodshed to keep that bear out!"

Kelly ran a wire around the open front of the woodshed and charged it with electricity from a one of his transformers wired into an extension cord. The next morning, the woodshed was in shambles. It appeared the bear had gotten in unscathed and then got shocked trying to get out. He'd gone berserk and torn up the inside, throwing equipment outside the woodshed. Eventually he broke through the heavy log slab siding on the back wall. But that was not all. Marcy had left laundry hanging on the clothesline overnight and he'd selectively pulled only her clothes from the line and stomped them into the mud. "Uh oh!" Kelly said when they saw it. "That bear associated your smell with the cat food and is targeting you, Ma."

Kelly's theory seemed too close to the truth and Marcy felt hunted. Although they didn't see any sign of him again, about a month later Gaines was cutting wood up above the kitchen and discovered the bear's hideout at the base of a huge fir tree. The well-used bed had a clear view of the kitchen door and was littered with items scavenged from around the Flat, including some of Marcy's clothes. Gaines showed his discovery to Marcy. "That bear must have been lying here all day watching you come in and out of the kitchen, Ma."

Marcy paled. "Is he still staying around here?"

"Naw. He hasn't been around for weeks. He must have given up on eating you."

Through a letter from Virgil's sister, Meree, they found out that Virgil's mother was in Sylmar, visiting from Arkansas. She'd been to the doctor and her heart was failing. From a phone booth in Weaverville, Virgil called and Meree told him if he wanted to see his mother alive, he'd better come visit. They evaluated whether it was possible to make the trip and Virgil and the boys decided that after some work and a new set of retread tires, they could drive the Jeep down to southern California. Virgil phoned Meree and told her they'd be leaving on the coming Monday, which was three days away.

Back at the Flat, they laid out their plans. Marcy was to wash and pack a week's worth of clothing for each member of the family and cook a turkey for sandwiches. Virgil and the boys would go up and down the trail to work on the Jeep, which had a number of mechanical problems that had kept them from even making trips past Weaverville for fear of breaking down far from home. As this was their first trip back to Sylmar since they'd moved, there was quite a bit of excitement. Grubby was the only dog they had left and they'd take him along in the cage they'd brought the chickens up in from Sylmar. They didn't worry too much about the cats as both were good hunters, but Marcy set out extra food for them anyway and hoped that no other animals ate it.

Marcy had everything ready on her end by Sunday morning and when Virgil and the boys returned early that afternoon having done all they could for the Jeep, Kelly suggested they leave that evening. Both Gaines and Joel solidly endorsed this idea. After a while, Marcy was also convinced but Virgil held out for sticking to their original plan to leave the next morning. "If the old Jeep breaks down on that long road at night, it could be a real problem," Virgil pointed out.

"Heck, we can handle it," the boys said in unison.

"We have all the tools with us," Kelly reasoned.

"No. I don't think so. You just can't see that well to fix stuff at night," Virgil persisted.

"Oh, we'll see all right," Kelly said and took off at a dead run to the cabin. He was back in just a few moments, carrying a big bulky looking device. From a wet cell nickel-cadmium helicopter turbine battery, he'd built a monster flashlight using a motorcycle headlight for a bulb. Virgil grinned. Marcy could see he was wavering and she stepped in for the kill.

"At night, there won't be any rush hour traffic," Marcy said.

That did it. "All right, we'll go tonight," Virgil agreed and the boys exploded in activity packing the clothes and blankets onto pack frames.

It was dusk as they drove away from Desperation Point, the boys huddled in the back under blankets while Grubby sniffed the air from his cage against the tailgate. There was little risk of rain as very little rain had fallen all winter and the weather was warm and springlike at this time in March. At least they thought it was warm, until they stopped to fill up with gas in Weaverville. "Is it cold?" Marcy asked.

"It's not bad," Gaines said. But the faces of the boys under the florescent tube lights at the filling station were bluer than they should have been so Marcy decided they should rotate into the cab, with the exception of Virgil, their only driver.

Kelly and Marcy took the first turn in the back and it wasn't long until Marcy thought she would freeze. Her teeth chattered and she pounded on the window for Virgil to stop. "Virg, get that tarp out and cover us. It's terribly cold out here. And get Grubby out of the cage so he can warm us, too."

After an hour of navigating the intensely twisting highway east of Weaverville and passing the shimmering moonlit Whiskeytown reservoir, the lights of Redding appeared, spread out across the upper Sacramento Valley. South of Redding on Interstate 5, the Jeep's slowness became even more apparent as other cars rapidly passed them by. Virgil had no way to know what speed they were going because the speedometer on the Jeep had never worked. The Jeep had an overdrive from a Studebaker installed but plowing through drifts of snow had torn out the cabling. As they crept down the Sacramento Valley, a giant full moon hung over the blooming fruit orchards and tracked their progress.

At one o'clock in the morning, they reached the town of Woodland and Virgil pulled off the freeway to refuel. It took a bit of driving around before he found an open gas station where a teenage boy rubbed sleep from his eyes as he came out to fill up the Jeep. Kelly, Marcy and Grubby stuck their heads out from under the tarp. Grubby stared at this stranger in his normal fashion, with eyes wide open in pale blue orbs. After the groggy teenager started filling the tank, he glanced over the pickup bed and saw Grubby. With a start, his eyes flew open to match the dog's. "Holy cow! Look at that white eyed dog!" Leaning over he stared intently at Grubby. "Is he blind?"

"No," Gaines replied.

"Hey, Joe!" the teenager yelled over his shoulder. "Get out here and see this white eyed dog!"

Joe came out of the garage section of the gas station, banging and crashing over car parts. "You ain't just kidding. That is a white eyed dog. What kind is he?"

"Australian shepherd mix," Gaines said.

"Man, that's a beautiful dog!"

As they pulled away, the two adolescents continued to marvel over Grubby's eyes.

At two in the morning, the Sacramento interchange system was nearly devoid of other vehicles and Virgil made his way down Old Highway 99. "How come you don't take Interstate 5 all the way down?" Kelly wanted to know.

"Because Ray told me there's nothing for miles on five. If we get a breakdown, I don't want it to be out in the middle of nowhere."

A little out of Modesto, Virgil turned off the highway and bounced over a couple bumps onto a little orchard access road. Virgil parked under an almond tree in full bloom with large pink flowers. "I have to sleep a bit," he said. "I'm seeing double."

They all fell asleep almost immediately. What they hadn't realized, however, was that the bumps Virgil had crossed were railroad tracks. Soon, a huge freight train rumbled up the San Joaquin Valley, triggering the crossing arms, bells and lights at the tracks. They tried to sleep for a couple hours but a steady supply of trains from the industrial centers along the west coast put an end to that. Around five in the morning, Virgil gave up and headed for their destination.

A little past Bakersfield, Virgil yelled, "Take note! This is going to be a first!" Ahead, a decrepit, sluggish septic tank service truck belched poorly burned black diesel smoke into the noonday air. Foot by foot they gained ground on what was to be the first vehicle the Jeep had passed on the trip. As Virgil pulled up alongside, the young man behind the wheel glanced over and grinned at the sight of the old green Willys Jeep pickup chugging away for all it was worth. Blowing out an extra-large banner of black smoke, the truck driver took it to be a race and pulled ahead. And so ended the first and last chance the Jeep had to pass another vehicle.

The first mile climbing the Tehachapi Mountains went well and the air had warmed. Then, without warning, the engine cut out and the Jeep lurched violently. Over and over, the engine cut out and the Jeep lurched. "Oh my God!" Marcy cried as the 18-wheeler trucks swerved out of the truck lane to pass them.

Virgil pulled off onto the freeway shoulder in the shade of a steep cut bank and slowed to a stop. Kelly was out and running for the hood before the Jeep stopped rolling, with Gaines on his heels. Within seconds after the tires came to a halt, the hood was open and the diagnosis was underway. Kelly pushed and pulled different wires and tubes. Suddenly he jerked his hand away from the copper gas line that ran next to the exhaust manifold. "Vapor lock!" he announced.

"That gas line is routed too close to the manifold. It's overheating," Gaines said.

"Can we reroute it?" Joel asked.

"No. It's not long enough."

Virgil considered the problem. "Get a wet rag and wrap it around the line," he said. "I'll stop every 10 miles or so and we can re-wet it to keep it from catching on fire."

Hearing the plan scared Marcy. The word fire and the part about having to dodge trucks to stop every few miles put her close to tears. As a young girl growing up in San Fernando, she'd heard many stories about trucks losing their brakes and crashing into people on this section of road, known simply as The Grapevine in those days, and she hated this mountain with a passion.

As they approached Sylmar, Marcy told Virgil to stop somewhere so they could change clothes, wash the dog hair off their faces and comb their hair. "I don't want our relatives to think we've turned completely into hippies," she said.

Their first stop was to be Leta and Dick's house, Virgil's sister and brother-in-law, and they arrived at four in the afternoon, a full 23 hours after they'd left Desperation Point. Leta hurried out of the house to greet them. "Did you meet Ray?" she asked.

"No," Virgil replied. "Why?"

"Maree phoned him and told him you were coming. He said you'd never make it in that old heap, and left yesterday morning to pick you all up in his van."

Virgil shook his head. "That crazy Ray."

"You better call him and see if he's back."

When Virgil called, Ray was home and very tired. He'd reached Desperation Point the night before, just an hour after they'd left. Seeing the Jeep was gone, he turned right around and drove nonstop back to Sylmar.

Ray stopped by Maree's place the next day to see them. He seemed withdrawn but they attributed it to his long drive the days before. "Stop by before you head home," Ray said as he was leaving.

They had a good visit with all the relatives. Virgil's mom seemed in fine spirits and even wanted to ride in the Jeep to Fran and Ivan's place. Once they got there, however, she wasn't sure she ever wanted to ride in it again.

Anxious to see what their old place looked like after the earthquake, Leta drove them over to the adobe house. Sadness washed over them as they realized it was all truly gone. They walked around in the tall weeds that had taken over and found one of the kids' forgotten toys. After a while, the boys got antsy and didn't want to look anymore.

On their final night in the San Fernando Valley, Fran put together a party at her house and invited all the relatives and friends. John and Vicki showed up, along with two grown daughters and their families. John struggled to get out of his car. "Vicki! Help me get this slide projector out of the car," he puffed.

Along with the projector came a case of Coors. "What's the projector for?" Marcy asked.

"I have all the pictures I took at your place on slides. I'm going to do a slide show."

Virgil, Marcy and the boys were thrilled; they had virtually no pictures of those early years. Beer passed around to those who wanted it and the evening began. The boys had little experience with parties and felt awkward at first, but Fran noticed their discomfort and located several broken appliances that they readily set to work fixing.

John never moved very fast and this night he really took his time, slowly setting up the projector. Something wasn't working right and

John scratched his black beard, his technical diagnostic skills obviously impaired by the Coors. Immediately attracted to any technical problem, Kelly went to help him. After looking it over, Kelly flipped the power switch in the back of the projector and the screen lit up, prompting a cheer from the room. With exaggerated dignity, John picked up the remote control and settled deeply into an easy chair next to the projector. "The show is on folks!" John boomed.

The show started not at John's trip to their place but about twenty years before, covering all the parties and events that John had photographed over the years. Before each slide, John gave a long narrative on the circumstances around the upcoming image. Once the picture displayed on the screen, he held it there until all comments were over, which turned out to be longer and longer periods as the adult beverages loosened many tongues.

It was 11 p.m. by the time the slideshow finally moved to *The Trip to the Horn's* as John described it. To their dismay, they realized John and his family had travelled up the California coast, photographing everything along the way. Each slide was taking longer but the slow pace of the show built anticipation for the main feature. Having heard a lot about their place, many of the partygoers were anxious to see these pictures of 'paradise' or 'the hole' depending on whom they'd talked to.

The slides creeping ever slower, John moved up the Trinity River, finally coming to the white three-rail fences and red brick buildings of the old Helena ghost town. In slow motion, John reached out and fumbled behind the projector for the switch that had evaded him earlier and the screen went black. "That's all, folks!" he slurred and his head dropped to his chest in slumber. A chorus of disappointment arose from the crowd but John was not to be disturbed. *The Trip to the Horn's* was over.

They were ready to leave the following morning but made one last stop to see Ray and Sue. When they arrived, Ray took Virgil into their backyard to show him his garden and Marcy stayed to talk to Sue. Ray and Sue's boys, Sean, David and Kenny, were at school. Sue looked strained and Marcy asked how Sean was doing. "He's in a wheelchair now but he's doing real well in school," Sue said. "Ray got Seanie an electric wheelchair and he goes everywhere with it."

Sue talked on about Sean's condition and caring for him, the pain of seeing her oldest son wither away evident on her face and Marcy felt terrible for her friend. "David and Kenny are getting older now and must be a lot of help," Marcy said, trying to be as positive as she could.

Sue's face contorted, holding back speech. Suddenly, she blurted, "Kenny has it, too!" She broke down into deep heart-wrenching sobs.

"Oh no!" Marcy cried. "How's David?"

"David is clean," she sobbed. "He's such a help. I'd never be able to do everything without him."

Now Marcy understood why Ray was so subdued. They visited with Ray and Sue longer than they'd planned and it was the middle of the afternoon by the time they left Sylmar.

Riding in the Jeep was always an experience in sound, a cacophony of squeaks, thuds, grindings and rattles. Virgil and the boys listened with ears tuned to the various noises as they climbed up Interstate 5 toward the town of Gorman, at the crest of the Tehachapi Mountains. All sounds seemed to be in the normal range for the lines around Virgil's eyes had not deepened.

It was on the long downhill run to Bakersfield that Marcy noticed the lines deepening around Virgil's eyes and asked if something was wrong but he denied anything was bothering him. As Virgil stopped to make the passenger rotation, Marcy saw a quiet discussion amongst the boys but the only word she caught was 'shimmy'. Marcy could stand this no longer. "What's going on with this pickup?" she asked Joel once they'd settled in the back of Jeep.

"Oh, just a little shimmying feedback in the steering wheel," Joel replied, trying to sound unconcerned.

Marcy could feel the shaking. Of course it had to be on this darn mountain again that the steering is going out, she thought.

Despite the shimmy that became more pronounced with every mile, they made it down the mountain. Virgil took the off ramp at Mettler and pulled into a rundown garage. "I'm going to have the wheels rotated," Virgil stated as he got out of the Jeep.

Two guys came out and put the Jeep on the lift where they started poking around, nowhere near the wheel lugs. An older man, red-faced and reeking of alcohol, staggered from the office to join them. In the back of the Jeep, he spotted the aloe plant Ray had given Marcy. "Hey lady! That's an aloe plant. Did you know it's great for burns?" he slurred enthusiastically.

"Yes, I do know about aloe plants," Marcy replied.

Under the Jeep, one of the men shook a long rod as he talked to Virgil and Marcy wanted to hear what he was saying. But the herbalism expert moved closer and continued on about the merits of aloe as though she'd expressed no knowledge of the plant whatsoever. Marcy stepped away from the rancid smell of alcohol.

"Here's your problem!" the man shaking the long rod cried triumphantly. "Your pitman arm and drag link is worn out."

"Can you get the parts?" Virgil asked skeptically. "And how much will it cost?"

"I can have the parts here tomorrow and it wouldn't cost more than the three or four hundred dollars."

Four hundred dollars was all the money Virgil had in his pocket. "Can't wait that long," he said. "Just tighten them up."

Like a man who thought he had a great fish on his line, the pitman arm guy carried on about the horrible consequences of the drag link coming off. "It'll hold," Virgil said firmly.

Deflated, the man set about tightening the drag link, trying to salvage what he could of what would have been a lucrative job. After paying an inflated price for the advice and work, they headed north again, not discovering until a few months later that although the pitman arm and drag link were fine, the kingpin bearings were shot to the point that the left front wheel was ready to fall off.

In the dark evening hours, Joel and Marcy were still taking their turn in the frigid back. Marcy was dozing when an extra loud thumping awakened her. As she listened with trepidation and tried to force herself back to sleep, an explosion that sounded like the whole back end had blown off sent the Jeep swerving onto the shoulder of the freeway. Kelly was out of the cab lugging his flashlight contraption before the dust had cleared. "Tire blew."

"How's that possible? We just bought new tires!" Marcy wailed, nerves totally on edge.

Gaines crawled under the Jeep. "Hey, the rim split," he called. "The inner tube bulged out and was banging against the brake line. That's what the thumping was."

It was then that Joel discovered the jack would not lift the Jeep high enough to change a tire. Virgil kicked at the soft sand on the freeway shoulder. "Dig a hole under the tire."

The dust drifted through the beam of Kelly's light as the boys dug a deep hole under the tire so they could put on the spare. After they removed the jack, the tire sat deep in a soft sandpit. "Lock the hubs, Kelly," Virgil directed. "It's going to take four-wheel drive to get out of this hole."

The Jeep crawled effortlessly out of the hole. Despite the cramped, uncomfortable ride, they were pleased they had the Jeep or they would have been stuck. A full 24 hours after leaving Sylmar, they thankfully walked back down to the Flat.

Virgil's jaybird carvings for Marcella's kitchen

The Anderson family played a major role in the history and development of the Flat.

32 - Gold Nuggets

Most of the gold they'd mined was tiny nuggets and fine flakes and Joel noted this one day while he watched Virgil extract the fine gold from black sand. "Why don't we ever find any nuggets over a pennyweight? Not one of our nuggets has ever been over that. Miners on the East Fork are always finding bigger nuggets. I wonder if the lode deposits on the North Fork drainage just don't produce free gold in bigger pieces."

Virgil looked up from the black sand and peered out from under his jewelry visor. "I don't think that's it. The biggest nugget Otis Trull found was actually on the North Fork drainage. We just haven't found the right place for the big ones yet."

Joel sat in silence as he thought about this. Finally, he said, "I think I'll make a model of our section of the river and charge it with flour gold that will simulate nuggets on that small scale."

"That'd be interesting," Virgil said.

"Trouble is, the river channel isn't static and the historic channels are going to have as much of an effect, if not more, on the gold deposits as the current channel," Joel continued.

"That's going to be hard to figure. Awful random," Virgil commented.

"I guess I need to study the rock formations around here and try to figure how the different ones erode and influence the historic river channels," Joel decided.

This set off months of self-study in geology and hydraulic mechanics and Joel's historic model took form some time later after hours of painstakingly simulating the different rock formations with different kinds of clay. Then he spent days of simulating the river flows using a hose and valve, including hundreds of 10-year and scores of 100 and 1,000-year floods. To this, he added a couple of 10,000-year floods.

Though the simulated canyon never quite eroded to what the modern real-life channel resembled, it did show a pattern on where the heavy gold deposited and that was on the riverbank beyond the cedar trees that shaded the summer kitchen. Over the years, they'd mined sections of this area but the model inspired Joel to start mining there again.

He set up a little aluminum Keene sluice box in the edge of the river and set to work excavating the hard red cemented gravel laying over bedrock and washing it through the sluice box. A 700-pound blue green boulder, the kind that Virgil called a blue baby, soon halted his progress. The blue babies were extremely hard and tough and were unbreakable by any means they had on the Flat.

He searched out the old come-along, chains, steel pry bars and a handyman jack and set to work moving the boulder. Its shape was very close to that of an M&M and chains did not grip that shape well. But hours later, sore and tired, he'd moved the boulder enough so he could start excavating the gravel from under where it had lain. Load by load he carried buckets of gravel over the boulder and rugged bedrock down to the sluice box at the river's edge.

The sluice box entrance had about 12 inches of smooth aluminum bottom that gave way to riffles. As Joel dumped gravel into this section, it formed a tongue shaped patch of gravel that slowly washed away. Suddenly through the rippling water, a gleaming yellow object emerged from the tongue. Bright yellow rocks distorted underwater had fooled them many times, but as this object emerged, it left little doubt of its identity. Yellow rocks do not stay put in a rushing current of water; they roll away.

Joel's hand shot into the water and retrieved the nugget. It resembled the shape of a much smaller nugget they'd found some years earlier. This was without a doubt the biggest piece of gold they'd ever found and he rushed to show the rest of the family who were all busily pressing apples to make cider and apple cider vinegar. "Isn't it funny how nuggets tend to resemble each other?" Joel said casually, handing the nugget to Virgil.

Virgil rolled the nugget around in the palm of his hand. "They do, don't they?"

The rest of the family gathered around in excitement. "How big is that?" Marcy asked.

"I don't know but I want to find out if it's over one pennyweight," Joel said.

They followed Virgil to the shop and watched as he set up his handmade gold scales and weighed the nugget. "One pennyweight, 18 grains," Virgil announced.

"How many pennyweights in an ounce?" Marcy asked.

"There's 20 pennyweight in an ounce and 24 grains in a pennyweight," Kelly told her.

"Yes! That broke through the one pennyweight barrier!" Joel cried starting out the door. "I'm going to see if there's more!"

"Well, I guess we can go back to making vinegar," Gaines said sardonically.

Joel excavated the gravel revealing the shape of bedrock as a large bowl with one wall cut away. As he dumped the last of the gravel from this bowl into the sluice box, the tongue washed away and once again revealed gleaming yellow. This time the nugget was a round flattened disc over two times the size of the last one. Compared to all their others, this was huge.

Gaines bent over the apple press re-pressing a big tub of brown apple pulp while Virgil ground fresh apples in a large meat grinder. Trying real hard not to show his extreme excitement, Joel handed the nugget to Virgil. "I guess they aren't all the same shape."

Virgil stared at the nugget in the palm of his hand.

"I suppose he found another little piece of gold," Gaines said from the press 20 feet way.

"Just a little one," Virgil said and held it up between his thumb and forefinger for Gaines to see. Gaines stared in disbelief for a second and then ran over to see the nugget, which weighed in at five-pennyweight, three grains, just over a quarter ounce.

As Joel went back to his mine and the rest of the family went back to their tasks, Gaines grinned sheepishly. "I predict vinegar is going to be more valuable than gold some day," he muttered.

Over the years, over 80% of the coarse nuggets they mined came from this one area.

A couple months later, Ted Carter showed up. While they sat around the table visiting and Ted enjoyed a can of Pabst Blue Ribbon beer, Joel showed him the five-pennyweight nugget. Ted grinned and puffed on his pipe, then reached into pants pocket and pulled out $100 and tossed it in front of Joel. "Nope. Not for sale," Joel said.

Ted smirked, pulled another $50 from his pocket and tossed it in front of Joel. "Nope," Joel repeated, shaking his head.

Another $50 went on the pile. This was about five times the value of the gold nugget by weight. Joel just grinned and shook his head. Ted finally reached in his pocket and tossed his whole wad of cash on the table in front of Joel, a total of between $500 and $700. Again, Joel shook his head. Ted took a sip of his beer and grinned. "I guess not," he said.

Marcy loved to pan for gold and broke open a lot of rock cracks with a bar to pan the thin layer of sand wedged between, a practice called crevicing. After her near-sunstroke incident, she'd made herself a sun hat from dead iris leaves, which had faded into soft light and dark shades of brown. She was alone panning when something hit her hat. She saw a brown feather floating down in the river and looked up just in time to see a hawk circling over her head. As she shook her pan, the hat must have looked like a fat duck bobbing on the river.

She finished panning the gravel in her hand and then dumped it in the coffee can used to collect all the black sand. Gathering it up, she went to tell Virgil about the hawk. Working in the jewelry shop, he listened to her story with amusement. Marcy handed him the coffee can of black sand concentrates. "Can you get the gold out of this?" she asked.

Virgil nodded and took the can from her. "I've been thinking about making some gold items for Ray and Sue. They've done so much for us. Could I use your gold here to help out?" Marcy thought it was a great idea and readily agreed to give up her gold for the project.

When Virgil started a project, it often seemed to Marcy he wasn't really putting much effort into it. When he was finished, however, the complexity and beauty of the project always startled her. Only after he'd finished, could she see all the work he'd put into it.

Later that day she wasn't paying much attention to what Virgil was doing. Then she saw him hacking out a piece from a broken and burned two-man crosscut saw. "What are you making, Virg?" she asked.

"You wait until I finish it," he replied with a sly grin.

Days went by and she was extremely curious. Periodically she crept up to discover him drilling holes in three different colors of jade they'd brought with them from Sylmar. The jade was very hard and it took Virgil over a week to drill through the pieces with carborundum and a rock drill. Once he had the jade drilled, she could see he was making a dagger with a polished blade for Ray. The boys looked over his shoulder from time to time, fascinated with what he was doing. He stacked the jade pieces on the handle shank and ground them down into a smooth grip with the lapidary. The three different shades of jade faded one into another, creating a lovely effect.

Then Virgil carved a bighorn sheep's head from wax and cast it in silver on their hand forge, using the lost-wax casting method. As the finishing touch, he cast two curling horns in 18 karat gold and soldered them to the sheep's head. He screwed the sheep's head to the top of the multi-colored jade handle and laid it in a velvet-lined box. Marcy was awed. It looked so rich, like something found in a pirate's treasure chest. Virgil also made Sue a pair of gold nugget earrings.

Ray came to visit and saw the knife. "Virg, that's too much!" he exclaimed. "What'd you do that for?"

"I'm trying to let you know that I appreciate all the help you've given us."

"This place is like a resort," Ray answered. "It relaxes me so much and I'd have to pay hundreds of dollars if I were to go to one. That's why I give you things."

During the time that Virgil worked on Ray's knife, a couple men walked down the trail. With a pointed beard and round receding hairline, they recognized one of the men as Jerry Miller. He'd come down a few years before with an older man named Andy Anderson when they were dredging up on Rattlesnake Creek, a tributary of the North Fork, five miles above the end of Hobo Gulch Road. This time, Jerry arrived with a man in his thirties with shoulder length blond hair and glasses. "Hi, Jerry," they greeted.

"Hey. How's the Horns doing?" he replied brightly. "Remember Andy?"

"Yes," Virgil answered slowly. This was not Andy.

"This is his son, Gary Anderson."

"I was wondering how Andy had shed so many years," Virgil laughed.

Gary was solidly built and had steady blue eyes and a firm handshake. He shook hands all around. "My dad and I bought the Oklahoma City placer mining claim over on the East Fork," Gary said. "Jerry said you were a jeweler, Virg. I thought you might be able to clean up some of my gold nuggets."

"I sure can," Virgil said.

Gary took a plastic bottle of nuggets from his pack and handed them to Virgil. Then he drew a big canned ham and a couple dozen eggs from his pack and handed them to Marcy. "I thought you might like a ham and a few eggs."

"Thanks!" she said.

"I'll just put your nuggets in an acid bath and clean them up," Virgil said and headed into the jewelry shop.

"Works for me," Gary said and started talking to the boys about mining.

"Did you grow up mining?" Joel asked.

"No. I grew up around the farms of North Dakota. After joining the army and doing a tour in Vietnam with the 101st Airborne Division, I moved to Walnut Creek."

Virgil came out of the shop carrying a little glass dish full of Gary's nuggets in a fuming acid bath. "They turned green," Virgil said, looking out from under his large jeweler's visor. "I'll try a different acid."

"Thanks," Gary said lightly.

"Is this North Fork gold?"

"No. We dredged all summer up on the Rattlesnake. All we found was a one-quarter-ounce nugget. It was shaped just like a little rocket ship." Gary took off his glasses and wiped them down with a red handkerchief. "These are all the nuggets I mined on the Oklahoma City."

"What size dredge do you run?" Joel asked.

"I have a four-inch Keene. The one we ran up on the Rattlesnake was a homebuilt six-inch with a 10-horsepower Clinton engine. It was solid cast iron and the heaviest damned engine. I wouldn't mind having a light six-inch so I could start at one end of the claim and work all the way up the river on the East Fork."

With a perpetual grin as if everything was a jest, Jerry shook his head. "Gary is way too serious about dredging."

"Yeah. Unlike you and your test holes," Gary replied. "I'll come up from Walnut Creek and the river is pocked with all these little holes. Jerry, you'll never get a good test with the size holes you're digging."

Jerry just laughed.

Virgil came out of the shop with the glass dish again. "It turned red now."

"Well, I don't know anything about cleaning gold so I'll leave it up to you," Gary said.

"Placer gold often contains impurities that can change the color. I'll try another cleaner."

For the next few minutes the boys showed Gary and Jerry some of their projects.

"Hey, Gary. Your gold turned black this time," Virgil called.

"Well, I guess I don't care what color it is as long as the weight doesn't get lighter."

"Let me get some fresh acid and try that," Virgil said and the fresh acid cleaned the nuggets to a bright sheen. As they were leaving later that day, Gary promised to bring his wife down for a visit.

33 - Pranks and Drought

Trains they'd seen on the trip to Sylmar and a story about an old miner who thought he saw trains running up the East Fork were the catalyst for a project of the boys. The old miner, Knox Delaney, had a habit of drinking too much hard whiskey and began suffering delusions. As he told stories to a group of bemused listeners, suddenly and without warning, he'd visualize a train coming up the East Fork. In a horrible panic to save his drinking buddies, he'd abruptly start grabbing and pushing them to move. "Here comes another train!" Knox would yell. "For God's sake, move aside and let it pass!"

So the three boys got together to create the phantom train. Listening to amateur radio operators on short-wave radio, they became quite versed in the lingo. Sometimes a pulsating grinding signal would sweep across the amateurs, blanking out communications. It was the signal of the over-the-horizon low-frequency radar of NORAD. To the amateurs, it was nicknamed the Rigger Raggers and the strange noise closely matched that of a passing freight train.

Gaines found a long plastic funnel for filling an automatic transmission that, with much practice, could be blown in a close approximation of a train's main horn. Joel discovered that shaking a section of aluminum sheet roofing in a rhythmic manner created the sound effect of passing freight cars. They wanted to create the impression of a huge wreck at the end so cobbled various sound effects together to achieve a realistic simulation of a massive wreck.

Gaines recorded their masterpiece on a cassette deck and used an external jack to plug it into a large speaker with a built-in tube amplifier. Kelly retrieved his helicopter battery light. They hid the whole setup behind Ray's tent where guests usually slept and laid out an extension cord to power the amplifier. Then they awaited their first victim, who happened to be Sam. He was thin, about 40 years old, with long weedy blond hair and faded blue eyes that watered all the time. Due to the afternoon heat, everyone agreed Sam should spend the night and leave early the next morning.

Marcy played along with the boys and throughout the evening, she mysteriously mentioned that at eight o'clock, Rana would pay them a visit. Sam didn't know that Rana, which means frog in Spanish, was just a bat that had found a way into the unfinished structure and flew into the house precisely at eight o'clock every night. As the light faded and the hour approached, Sam furtively peered around, eyes widened and pupils dilated. "Hey, man, you're starting to freak me out here," he said nervously. "Who's Rana?"

"You wait, she'll be around shortly," Virgil joined in, talking about Rana as if she were some surreal ghost that floated in on the night air.

As they sat in the dark, Rana made her debut. "She's here!" Marcy announced.

Sam jumped out of his chair. He was relieved that Rana appeared to be nothing but an ordinary bat but was none too happy with this symbol of dark powers. Then, just before everyone went to bed, Marcy told Sam about the old gent who saw trains on the East Fork and even embellished the story. And so the mood was set as Sam nervously went to sleep in Ray's tent.

Quietly, Kelly took his flashlight contraption and Gaines grabbed the funnel for the horn, and they snuck up into the woods and waited for Joel to plug the recorder into the extension cord. Joel waited until he was sure Sam was asleep and then plugged it in. As the rumble of the train got louder, Kelly came closer to the tent with the light and Gaines blew on the funnel. They were right near the tent when Sam ran out shrieking. "GET THAT TRAIN THE HELL OUT OF HERE!" Joel unplugged the recorder and they all ran and hid in the woods.

The next morning, Sam walked up to the kitchen with one side of his jaw drooping. "Did I hear a train last night?" Sam asked solemnly, stroking his jaw.

Together they laughed and told him about the joke. "You scared the crap out of me! I spent half the night thinking about what I'd heard and finally figured you guys had set me up. That is until I went out this morning and could find no evidence of an audio system." Sam rolled his eyes and slurred on. "I was thinking I've played around with the occult but these people are way too weird. They can conjure these events into my mind telepathically."

As Sam talked, the slurred speech, the sagging half of his face and the definite non-uniformity of his pupils made them almost as scared as he had been. Had they given the poor guy a stroke? He told them his jaw really hurt so they advised him to go to the doctor. They saw Sam again two weeks later, looking fit and well and he explained what the doctor had diagnosed. "A gland in my neck had become badly infected and swollen. It was pressing against my carotid artery, cutting off the blood flow to my brain."

After that, the boys were cautious about playing their trick. They did try it on Vicki and John when they came back to visit but it backfired when John ran out of the tent cussing because they'd turned the light on just as he took the film out of his camera, exposing it all.

<hr />

For a year, one of the old wooden buildings in the ghost town of Helena housed the Helena Post Office after it was moved from Trinity Oaks, a little community a mile or so down the highway. The dilapidated building was almost ready to collapse from dry rot.

Across the street stood an abandoned rectangular structure of brick that had been the post office and general store many decades earlier. Having stood there since 1858, the brick building was one of the oldest structures in the county and had been partially restored with funds from the California Department of Parks and Recreation. A large concrete deck had been poured out front and 100-year-old locust trees heavily shaded the parking lot. Due to the poor condition of the rotting wooden structure, the U.S. Postal Service decided to rent the brick building for the post office.

Rumor had it the new postmistress was a nineteen-year-old girl, which was very unusual as most postmistresses were well into middle age. Virgil had lost some mail due to the incompetence of a previous postmistress so there was a bit of worry about what kind of service a teenager could supply.

The whole family was headed to town and Virgil decided to stop on the way to see if Bea Montgomery, an elderly widow without a car who ran the last hydraulic mine in the East Fork area, needed anything from the store. Bea was out on the porch of her charming home when Virgil pulled up. "Hi, Bea," Virgil called from the driver's window. "We're headed into town and thought you might need something."

Bea walked over to the Jeep. "Thanks but no. Emery took me to town a couple days ago," she said.

They visited a while, as Bea knew a lot about mining and the area. "Well, it's getting hot so we have to get going," Marcy finally said. "I guess there's a new postmistress who's only nineteen."

"I haven't seen her yet," Bea said.

Marcy laughed. "The boys are kind of anxious to see her."

Gaines and Joel glared at their mother while Kelly looked uncomfortable. Bea laughed dryly. "I hate to pop anybody's bubble but I read in the Trinity Journal that her name is *Mrs. Black.*"

Out in front of the new post office, a small blond boy on a tricycle raced wildly from one end of the concrete deck to the other. The high end of the slab was almost three feet off the ground and the tike raced at top speed toward this drop only to slam on the brakes at the last minute, stopping just inches from the edge. As they stepped up on the concrete slab, he pedaled over to them and looked up. "Hi!" he greeted with a broad grin.

They greeted him in return and went into the new post office. Inside was a freshly tiled, small lobby. The wall opposite the entry housed a series of combination post office boxes, a small postal window and a door to the room beyond. A face with incredibly blue eyes framed by long, straight, light brown hair parted in the middle appeared in the postal window. "Can I help you?" she asked. The window was somewhat low and she had to stoop to peer out, forcing her to tuck her hair behind her ears to keep it off her face.

Marcy asked a rather obvious question. "Are you the new postmistress?"

"Yes. I'm Crystal and I think you've already met my son, Sean, on the porch."

"How old is Sean?"

"He's nearly two."

"Almost two! He's incredibly advanced," Marcy observed.

Crystal looked out at the rest of the family in the small lobby. "Hi," she said brightly. The boys briefly greeted her back, somewhat intimidated by her cuteness. Virgil introduced the whole family and then asked if she could mail a jewelry package by registered mail, return receipt requested, addressee only, and insured for $500.

Crystal competently set to work on the task. As tongue-tied as the boys were, Crystal was not. She explained she was the daughter of Robert Jones, the owner of the local Lazy J Logging Company, and that she lived up at old Knox Delany's place and that she had to cross a footbridge to get to the house. She talked about how Sean was absolutely fearless on his tricycle.

Crystal finished with Virgil's package and Sean started banging on the door. He was too short to reach the knob and Crystal opened the door from the back room to let him in. She had long legs and the slim body of a teenage girl and certainly didn't look old enough to have an almost two-year-old son. The 120-year-old building was filled with youthful energy of the young mother and her son as she attempted to catch him running around the front room as they made their exit.

It was during trips to town that they met most of the local characters, usually at the post office. With his tricycle, Sean became a well-known greeter to the locals. Ed Tolin and his wife, Muriel, were an older couple that lived at the end of one of the twisty driveways that intersected East Fork Road. Seeing the Horns at the post office, Muriel invited them to stop by for a visit. It was too hot to go down the trail so Virgil thought this would be a good time to see their mine. Virgil followed the Tolins down the steep twisting, rutted driveway, bouncing the Jeep on large cobbles torn lose from the roadbed. "How does Ed get that VW bug up this road?" Virgil muttered through clenched teeth and the Jeep lurched skyward as the left rear tire leaped over a boulder he'd failed to miss.

Great piles of glistening obsidian, stacks of petrified wood, giant geodes, agate and many other rocks formed the backdrop of the immaculate setting of three buildings. Ed parked his cream colored VW in a garage building that also served as a woodshed and a workshop, and he and Muriel got out of the car. Virgil parked in front of the garage and stuck his head out the window. "I see some rock hounding going on here."

"We spend the winters in Quartzsite and scour the desert for rocks," Ed replied.

Ed had built a charming, steep gable-roofed house with the lower walls made of mortared stone of wide geographical origins. Tucked under a large live oak tree sat a gazebo-like screened-in kitchen for Muriel's summertime canning. Marcy complimented Muriel on how well built and neat everything was. Muriel looked at Marcy with eyes that slightly bulged from their sockets, giving the impression of an intense stare. "Ed made everything to last so when we're dead, our son or some other young people would have a beautiful home and we would have a legacy. But then when Ed worked for the Forest Service, the District Ranger forced him to sign a life tenancy document giving them authorization to burn or tear the place down after we die."

While Virgil and the boys went down to see Ed's mining operation, Marcy and Muriel settled into wicker yard chairs next to the summer kitchen in the shade of the big sprawling oak. A steep hillside rose behind the house, but instead of a dry baked rocky slope, an extensive, multi-level series of terraced beds displayed unique and wonderful flowers. "I love your flower beds," Marcy said.

Muriel looked at the network of beds. "I spent many years hauling river rocks up and mortaring them in place," she reflected.

"It looks just beautiful," Marcy said.

"Did you folks ever get to see the China Lady's house?" Muriel asked.

"No. Was it something special?"

Muriel stared off into space as if she were looking at the house. "Oh yes. It was the most unique house I've ever seen. It was built like a birdhouse and people came from all over just to look at it. I got a lot of flowers from her. She was Chinese and she was a dear."

Marcy was fascinated. "Is it still around?"

"Oh no. When she died, the Green Mariah came and burned it down."

"The Forest Service?"

Muriel nodded slowly and Marcy felt cheated that she'd never see it. "You know, Muriel, the Forest Service is destroying a lot of monuments. Someday all remnants of the mines and miners will be gone and future generations will miss a lot."

"Yes and this place will be gone, too, when we die. Ed built it so nice and took such pain with it." She stopped, close to tears. Muriel got up heavily from the wicker chair. "Do want to see inside?"

"Yes!"

Inside, expertly fit fir planks varnished to a beautiful honey-colored shine paneled the walls. Neatly arranged handmade shelves showed off many cut polished rocks and glittering half geodes. Her kitchen, like the rest of the house, was neat as a pin. "How about some nice cold lemonade?" Muriel asked.

"Thank you, that would be great," Marcy replied.

Down at the dredge, Ed showed Virgil and the boys some nuggets he'd found just that morning. "You know, Virg, I'm getting almost too old to go underwater dredging anymore. Old Tom Hockens was my age and suffered a heart attack when he was down in the river. It sort of scared me. He did survive but that was the last of his mining days."

When the sun started to sink behind the mountains, Marcy decided it was time to leave so they could get down the trail before darkness fell. They enjoyed getting to know the Tolins and promised to stop by again.

⤐⧫⤎

Fall came with cold dry weather forming ice along the riverbank. The chilly wind blew through the cracks around the kitchen windows but the woodstove kept the room warm and cheery. Marcy and the boys were making Christmas ornaments while Virgil carved a replica of their little shack on one face of a block of wood so they could print Christmas cards using the woodcut printing method. As they merrily prepared for Christmas, the Andersons showed up.

Just as he'd promised, Gary brought his wife and their two-year-old son down for a visit. With calm gray eyes and long beautiful light brown hair, Lonie reminded them of country singer, Crystal Gayle. Little Rocky had bright blue eyes and hair so blond it was nearly white. Interested in everything, he was on the move at all times. "Brrrr," Lonie shuddered in her down parka. "It's cold out there."

Marcy opened the stove and threw more wood into the crackling fire and Lonie appreciatively held her hands out toward the heat. Gary moved away from the stove and stripped off his heavy plaid shirt. Rocky worked his way around the kitchen, examining everything at his level.

When there was nothing of interest left at the level of a two-year-old, Marcy picked Rocky up and showed him the shelf of Virgil's woodcarvings. Spying the goat through the window, he pointed his little fingers. "That's Fifty-Two, my goat," Marcy said.

"Go see goat," he said, speaking for the first time since they'd arrived.

"No, Rocky," Lonie said, taking him from Marcy's arms. "It's cold out there. When you warm up, we'll take you to see the goat."

"Go see goat," Rocky repeated.

"You remember that two-and-a-half ounces of gold I had you clean last summer?" Gary asked Virgil.

"Go see goat," Rocky continued.

"Yes. What about it?" Virgil replied

"Someone walked off with it from my house," Gary said.

"Go see goat," Rocky insisted.

"*What*! Did someone break in?" Virgil asked.

"No," Gary said. "The last time I saw the gold was sometime before we had a party."

"Go see goat," Rocky kept on.

"Rocky, we'll see the goat later," Lonie said.

"Did you call the police?" Virgil asked.

"No," Gary said, shaking his head. "I'll deal with whoever took it myself, if I find them." His eyes narrowed. "That represented a lot of hours of dredging."

"Go see goat," Rocky persisted.

Gaines got up. "Do you want me to take Rocky to see the goat?"

"Sure," Lonie said and she carefully bundled Rocky up.

As Gaines and Rocky disappeared out the door, they once again heard, "Go see goat."

Gary laughed. "Gaines is going to get run ragged!"

Lonie and Marcy were busily frying bacon, eggs and potatoes that Gary and Lonie had brought down when Gaines hurried up the path in front of the kitchen window. Carrying Rocky, Gaines looked stressed. As they came in the kitchen door, Marcy noticed Rocky was wet from the waist down, with icicles hanging from his clothes. "Gaines! How come you let him wade in the river?" Marcy cried.

"I didn't! He wanted to see the river so I took him down along the bank," Gaines protested. "He pulled out of my hand and before I could do anything, he jumped into the river."

"It's ok," Lonie said. "I brought him another set of clothes."

Despite being soaked, Rocky wasn't even shivering. "Gary, please hold Rocky while I take off his wet pants," Lonie requested.

"He's a tough little Swedish boy," Virgil said. "You can handle it, can't you, Rocky?"

Gary held Rocky up toward Virgil. "You tell Virgil that you are a *Norwegian*, not a Svede."

"Norviegian," Rocky said. "Go see river!"

"No river," Gary said and Rocky began crying.

Marcy picked him up. "Look at that!" she said, pointing at things around the room to distract him until he quieted.

The winter of 1977-78 was unlike any fall or winter they'd yet experienced at the Flat, with virtually no rainfall or snow. What they did get was misty and insubstantial and the creek feeding the reservoir never rose enough that winter to power the main hydroelectric plant. Gaines and Kelly rewound a car alternator to 120 volts and built a small Pelton turbine to drive it. It only put out enough power to give them a few hours of reading light at night.

When spring came, Marcy planted the normal sized garden. The spring months passed with no rain. Summer approached and they knew no rain would fall then. The water coming into the reservoir had reduced to a trickle. Something had to be done or the gardens would dry out, so Virgil and the boys began looking at the river in front of the old kitchen area where the river split and one fork had a fair amount of drop. "It's time to build a new river paddlewheel and place it in this fork," Virgil decided.

Gaines designed a smaller wheel than the one Virgil had made in 1973. A smaller diameter would get more speed and not as much energy would be lost in gearing. Emery Beattie had given Virgil a little double-action piston water pump that Virgil hoped would pump water up to the gardens when driven by the new wheel.

By the middle of July, there wasn't even enough water for the kitchen and Marcy again had to haul river water in buckets to wash the dishes. This step backward was very disheartening. The gardens began to die as they couldn't haul enough water by hand to keep them damp. Now nothing else mattered but to get the river pump done.

The pump didn't work at first but Virgil and the boys kept working on it. As Marcy made the rounds of the gardens and saw how wilted they were, she made her way down to where Virgil and the boys were working. Virgil sat on a big boulder filling his pipe with tobacco, a smile spread across his face. Wearing shorts, the boys stood in the rushing tailrace of the paddlewheel talking excitedly. "Is it working?" Marcy asked.

"Take a look at that water squirting out of the little pipe," Gaines yelled over the rushing sound of the tailrace water and the rhythmic thumping of the wheel.

"Can I get a hose?" Marcy asked.

"Yes, but I have to make sure everything is running properly before pressurizing the system," Kelly answered, leaning over the spinning pulleys and belts driving the pump.

Marcy hurried around the Flat finding hoses and dragging them down to the river. Back at the river, the boys sprayed each other with the water coming out of the pump. "Can we hook it up now?" Marcy asked.

Kelly stopped spraying Gaines. He reached for Marcy's hose and screwed it onto the pipe from the pump. After a few moments, the paddlewheel slowed as the pressure built up. Suddenly, the pump started hammering and knocking loudly. Kelly scrambled barefooted over boulders, slipped and half fell into the tailrace before reaching the pump. "What's wrong?" Marcy yelled.

"Needs air," Kelly muttered, manipulating a little brass protrusion that resembled the valve stem on a tire.

Slowly the hammering subsided. Joel splashed out of the tailrace, grabbed a five-gallon bucket and headed for the end of the hose to check how much water it was pumping per minute. A steady stream squirted from the end of the hose. "Gaines, time me while I fill this bucket," Joel said.

Gaines reached in his pocket but his hand came out empty. "Hold on! I set it on a boulder before I started wading in the water," he explained as he ran to retrieve his watch.

While they waited for Gaines to return, Joel pressed his thumb against the end of the hose and sprayed the dry topsoil. A cloud of dust rose releasing the wonderful smell that comes with the first drops of rain on parched earth. Gaines returned and held up his watch. "Get ready, get set. Go!"

Joel placed the bucket under the stream of water. They all watched as the clear liquid swirled around in the filling bucket. The moment it reached the brim, Joel yelled, "Stop!"

"Forty-three seconds," Gaines announced. "That's about seven gallons a minute."

Virgil did some mental calculations. "That's over 10,000 gallons a day."

They went around the Flat gathering hoses so they could connect into the domestic water supply. When that was completed, Marcy ran into her kitchen and turned on the faucet. Clear cool water poured out; no more hauling buckets. With a little maintenance, the pump worked twenty-four hours a day for the rest of the season, until the fall rains finally arrived and broke the drought. Over the years, Virgil and the boys made several waterwheels, progressing from a smaller wider wooden wheel to steel turbines, and various versions of this water pumping system evolved to cope with dry years.

Crystal & Sean - the new postmistress and her son

34 - George Jorstad and Amateur Radio

Late one morning, George Jorstad and Emery Beattie walked in to see Virgil about getting some jewelry made. George was a small man and appeared even smaller next to Emery's bulk, but within that small frame was a lot of energy, especially for a man in his late seventies. George spent each summer on Pfeiffer Flat about 15 miles upriver from them in a cabin he and his new bride had built in 1937. His mother-in law came to visit and bewailed so loudly about her daughter's living conditions that George's wife, Adzie, left just a few years after they'd built the cabin. George seemed to have a bitter spot for his ex-mother-in-law, even after all those years.

"Her, with a college degree, too!" Jorstad spat out, mimicking the long-ago mother-in-law. "She showed up with one little chicken one time," Jorstad said, rubbing his white beard. "At *least* Adzie will have eggs!" he went on, quoting the mother-in-law again, and then looked around appraisingly. "Your place looks like the Hanging Gardens of Babylon, but my goodness, what a snake heaven," George said as he gingerly stepped along Marcy's winding paths between flowers and vegetables. "It reminds me of a wild English garden, too."

"It's wild, all right," Marcy told him. "Most of the time, my flowers come up despite me. I don't have time to thin them out."

George was well educated and despite his years and miles far from civilization, he'd formed strong opinions on nearly all subjects. In this, Virgil found a kindred spirit. In fact, George and Virgil resembled one another and Marcy figured their ancestors probably came from the same tribe. Soon George was deep into the jewelry project idea. From his back pocket, George took a large glass aspirin bottle full of water and half filled with well-burnished gold nuggets. Virgil looked at the bottle and the vintage of the cap. "You've had the bottle a while, haven't you, George?"

"It's been in my back pocket since the early fifties," George said with pride. "I have two purposes with this. First, I'm tired of selling my gold for scrap value and second, I want to commemorate the mines and miners from Trinity County. Can you make medallions out of my gold?"

"Yes," Virgil answered.

"I have a number of ideas to start with, though I want to see how they sell before making the whole line. These need to have character, tool marks, and show handmade qualities." George looked fierce. "I don't want them to look perfect *machine* made!"

"That isn't a problem," Virgil assured him.

"Good!" George said happily. "There was Long-tunnel Johnson who was obsessed about digging a tunnel. His wife got disgusted and left him. He dug in his tunnel for years and finally died in it. There are several others I want also, but the first one I want made is the Jorstad Placer. At first I wanted them to be a full ounce, but I don't have that much gold on hand and that would make the price too high. A half ounce and the size of a quarter is what I think will work. Maybe some of them can be dime sized."

"I can't make them exact weight with lost wax casting, the method I use," Virgil informed him.

"That's all right, close is all I need. I want my donkey on one side and *North Fork of the Trinity River, California* printed in capital letters around the circumference. The obverse side should have a picture of my cabin in the center with *The open and unkempt Jorstad Digging, 1937* printed in capital letters around the circumference."

"I can do that," Virgil told him.

So began a line of commemorative medallions commissioned by George Jorstad. Each new commission came with a long typewritten letter, musing and thoughtful, with several hand-drawn sketches placed in gaps in the typing. Different wording was suggested and discarded. The typing was light at times, and at other times dark and bold, almost splattered as he pounded the keys. Then in the middle of the letter, the color would change to red. By the end of a long letter, his thoughts came together and he presented the final version.

One by one the letters came, each with a little over a half ounce of nuggets enclosed for a quarter-sized medallion. When he wanted the medallion made the size of a dime, he included less gold.

Danny O'Shay
Pocket Hunter
Trinity California Gold Frontier

Bob of Bob's Farm 1891
That ye may be fed
Trinity Gold Frontier, California

Fritz Moliter
Iron Man of Grizzly Creek
Trinity Gold Frontier, California

Long-tunnel Johnson 1899
The eternal quest
Trinity Gold Frontier, California

"He must write these letters over a period of weeks or months," Virgil laughed.

Then came the end of the Trinity Gold Frontier series and the beginning of another. George had spent World War II as a carpenter on the last Yankee square-rigger ship. He told them he'd immediately gotten the job on the Kaiulani at the beginning of World War II but wrote that it was the worst decision he ever made, as the captain was a rough, uncouth man. George vacillated between whether he wanted the captain portrayed as a scoundrel or a dignified officer. He obviously had mixed emotions over this. In the end, he went with a mix. So came the last new commemoration.

The last Yankee Square Rigger
Kaiulani
By way of Cape Horn, HG Wigsten, Master 1941

Virgil made a mold of each medallion so he could duplicate them in case George wanted more.

Red Cockroff came down, his stocking hat covered with leaves and dry twigs. With wild eyes and obviously exhausted, he plunked down on a chair. "I had quite a scare today," he said. "I decided to go down to see Old Red Barnes' place." He took out a handkerchief and wiped his brow. "I never dreamed he lived so far down in the canyon. I did find his place, but when I started up again, the sole of my boot came loose. Luckily I found some wire and wired it up."

Marcy looked at Red's boot and grinned. "Don't laugh, Marcy. The worst is yet to come," Red lamented. "I lost my way."

Virgil held back a grin.

"I knew I had to keep going back up and eventually I'd find your trail. I couldn't believe it when I'd gone a long way and still hadn't crossed it. It just had to come up, I kept thinking." Marcy handed Red a cup of coffee and he took a sip. "Well, at long last I ran across it. I never was so happy in my life!"

Marcy had noticed something wrong with Red's face and finally asked him what happened. "Oh, that." Red laughed loudly and made karate chopping motions diagonally across his face over a series of crimson scars. "Damned near killed myself!"

"How?"

"I was limbing a tree with my chainsaw and my partner yells something to me. I turned my head and just as I did, the tip of the bar caught a branch and kicked back and up, catching me right across the face." He pointed at a missing part of his nose. "It cut out this notch in my left nostril but I was damned lucky. If it was a tiny bit higher, that would have been the end of my left eye!"

"That's terrible, Red!"

"Yeah, I should've known better than taking my eyes off the bar." Red plopped down next to Virgil on a log by the sawmill and picked up a stick. His black Labrador mutt, Bowser, who had barked nonstop since they arrived, watched Red intently. His ears and tail shot up, and he barked even louder, anticipating the game. Red threw the stick and Bowser brought it back and dropped it three feet in front of Red.

"I can't reach that. Bring it to me," Red ordered. Bowser brought the stick one foot closer and Red told him the same thing. Bowser finally laid it exactly on Red's boot. They both loved the age-old game and seemed a great match.

When they went to town a few months later, a friend told them about Red's dog, Bowser. Red had started his chainsaw and the dog took it as a signal to jump up and bark. Some time back, Red had brought Bowser down to the Flat when he'd cut some trees for Virgil and Marcy had asked him if he should watch the dog. "No," Red had answered. "Old Bowser always gets out of the way. I never worry about him."

But after Red dropped this latest tree, he looked around for the dog. All he found was a throbbing heart beating out its last because the tree had fallen on Bowser and squeezed his heart right out of his body, which devastated Red.

At one point, Red decided to catch and make a pet out of a rattlesnake. He fed it and babied it until he could gently pick it up. Always the showman, he enjoyed taking the snake curled around his arm into bars where he created a lot of attention. But when they saw him later, he told them the story.

"I was in the bar and everyone wanted to see the rattlesnake show. I had her in a cage and the second I reached in, I felt something was wrong. Just as I lifted her free of the cage, I felt her stiffen when some guy came by to look at her. She nailed me right on the knuckle of the other hand. I guess she didn't like him and she hit me with a sack full of venom. "My arm swelled up like a watermelon. I went to the hospital and while lying there, I heard two doctors talking about amputating my arm. 'Oh, no!' I bellowed. After that, I knew I saved my arm because I was determined it was going to get well."

One afternoon Marcy decided to take a sponge bath in the kitchen sink, the only place besides the river to clean up between tub baths. Suddenly, two longhaired men appeared outside the kitchen, having sauntered down the path without the dogs hearing them. Marcy had barely gotten herself covered when they looked at her through the window.

"I don't want that to happen again. Can you make an early warning system, Kelly?" Marcy asked after the men departed. "You have all those radio parts."

Kelly set to work. With a photocell-based circuit and an old Radiosonde weather transmitter, he built an electronic device that was supposed to buzz down at the Flat when anyone walked along the trail just below Wind Dance Lookout. When the first buzz sounded, Marcy looked up and saw a deer. "Hey, that's great, Kelly! If it counts animals, it will count people."

But minutes later, it buzzed again. Everyone searched the hillside for movement on the trail but didn't see anything. When it buzzed again, Kelly ran up to check it, carrying a handheld radio to talk to the Flat. "I think a squirrel walked by. I see faint tracks," he relayed.

It started buzzing again and Gaines radioed for Kelly to check to see what it was. After some time, Kelly thought he'd identified the problem. "Gosh, every time a cloud goes by, it casts a shadow and triggers the thing," Kelly surmised. Everyone laughed and teased Kelly that he'd made a cloud counter.

Gaines decided to help Kelly make one that would go off only if something heavy walked on it. They dug a hole in the trail bed and put in a pressure switch triggered device framed over with a wooden platform attached to the pressure switch. Under the weight of a person, it would settle imperceptibly and trigger the switch.

The system worked great and alerted them to numerous people over the years. The ground was damp when they put it in, however, so everything was tight. When the ground dried out during the heat of summer, the wooden platform gave more underfoot.

One morning, the alarm started buzzing like crazy and didn't stop. Looking toward Wind Dance Lookout, they saw three people stopped at the alarm. The trio eventually continued down the trail and arrived at the Flat. Their visitors were young women that had come down to order a wedding ring for their brother. One wanted to know if they had a trap door up the trail a ways. "I found this section of trail that sinks down a half inch or so. I kept stepping on it," she explained.

Virgil raised one eyebrow and a slow grin crossed his face. "That's an early warning system my sons put in. But tell me, do you normally keep walking up and down on something that you suspect is a trap door?"

The young woman blushed and stammered while her companions laughed.

Kelly later installed a World War II crank-type field telephone up on the trail and the boys strung out a quarter mile of WD-1 field wire to connect it with a phone in the kitchen. He intended to add a sign that read *Telephone - to call, crank the handle to ring* but he ran out of space and the truncated message read *Telephone To Call, Crank.* So it became the telephone to call the crank and visitors got a kick out of it when Marcy answered, "This is Crank talking."

The phone was on a section of the trail that also served as the Hobo Bench Trail, however. One day the phone rang and Kelly picked it up. "Hello?" Kelly said.

A woman shrieked on the other end and Kelly heard the receiver hit the ground. In the background, he could hear her shrieking, "There *is* someone there!"

After a few seconds, a man came on the line. "I'm sorry. I thought it was just a prop and talked my girlfriend into cranking it. We really didn't mean to disturb you."

Kelly assured them it was all right and they went on their way. Over the years, the early warning systems became more elaborate and discrete as Kelly worked with the latest technological advances.

$$\sim\!\!\sim\!\!\sim$$

Gaines and Kelly's growing interest in electronic and two-way radio communication, partly inspired by their ham radio operator uncle and partly by a book Gaines had read years before, led them to stop by a new electronics shop in Weaverville. A young couple owned Cantrell's TV and Electronics. Charlotte ran the front desk and the customer service while Don happily hid in a tiny back room repairing electronic equipment.

Kelly was looking for a specific type of transistor and it had to have certain specifications. After he described it to Charlotte, she shook her head. "That's a question for Don." She turned and yelled toward the open doorway to the back room. "Don! I have a customer with a technical question."

A man with sandy-colored, curly hair appeared in the doorway. "What can I help you with?" Don asked.

Kelly explained in detail what he was looking for and what he was going to do with it. Don was visibly excited. Young teenage kids in Weaverville didn't just come in and start asking questions like that. Not only did Don find the right transistor in their stock, he started explaining all the alternate ways to build the circuit, getting more and more excited as he went on.

Gaines broke into the conversation and mentioned he wanted to get his Amateur Radio license. Now Don got really excited. "Really! I'm going to take my test next week. If I pass the Amateur Extra class license I can administer the test for the Novice class license for you!" He shifted around excitedly. "You only have to learn Morse code at five words a minute for Novice"

"I've heard about that. How exactly does that work?" Gaines asked.

"I'd give you the code test and if you passed that, I send and get the written Novice test and act as the test proctor while you take it. I can't even look at your answers or give you any kind of help. You seal the test booklet with your answer sheet in an envelope and I send it off." Another customer walked in but Don didn't even notice. "The horrible part is you have to wait six weeks to get your license and call sign. If you get something before that from the FCC, it's *really* horrible because they send out the failure notices a lot quicker! Do you have a telegrapher's key?"

The new customer was talking to Charlotte.

"Yes," Gaines said. "My uncle, Gary, is a ham and he gave me one."

"Well, you only have to receive code to pass the test as almost everyone can learn to send if they can copy. Do you have a transceiver?"

"No."

"Shortwave receiver?"

"Yes."

"Tune in and listen to the CW on there and practice between yourselves. With Novice class you can only operate on CW and don't have SSB, RTTY or SSTV privileges.

"That's a question for Don," Charlotte said to her customer. "Don, we have a question."

"The next level up is the Technician class and you get VHF FM privileges.

"Don!"

"The General class requires 13 words a minute code but you get HF SSB SSTV…"

Charlotte grabbed Don's shoulder and shook it violently. "Don!"

"Oh," Don said sheepishly and a little dazed at what undoubtedly was going to be a less than intriguing question.

Gaines and Kelly made their exit so as not to interrupt their business any longer. Later, Don let Gaines know he'd passed his test and could administer the Novice test any time Gaines felt he was ready.

For the fun of it and to help Gaines and Kelly learn the code, Joel started learning Morse code even though he had no interest in getting licensed. Kelly quickly discovered he hated Morse code, however, and dropped out of the practice sessions.

Don and Charlotte hiked down to the Flat to visit one Sunday. "How's your code speed coming along," he asked Gaines. "When do you think you'll be ready to take the test?"

"Maybe in another month," Gaines replied uncertainly.

"Where's your key? I want to send you some to see how you're doing."

Gaines found the telegrapher's key and oscillator, and a scrap of paper to copy what Don sent. Don sent for a few minutes as Gaines copied. "Let me see your paper," Don said when he had finished.

He scanned through the text counting out a few strings. "You passed your Novice code test!"

"No! That couldn't have been the test!"

"All you have to do is get one minute out of five error-free to pass and you got three minutes error-free!" Don dug in his backpack and pulled out a FCC test application form.

"You had that planned from the beginning didn't you?" Gaines accused with a big grin.

Don smirked as he filled out the FCC Form 610.

After taking the written test, Gaines finally received his license and call letters in early November. As a present, Don gave Gaines an old Heathkit DX-40 shortwave transmitter to work with the shortwave receiver Gaines already had.

A year earlier, Ted Carter had shown up with an old Briggs and Stratton gas-powered generator. He gave it to them on the condition that they call it Diane.

"Why Diane?" Marcy asked.

"Because I picked up a woman in a bar in San Francisco by the name of Diane," Ted smirked. "We were passing a dumpster and I looked in and saw this generator. I told her I knew someone who could use that generator and made her climb in with me to retrieve it. Diane with the tattooed eyelids."

"Tattooed eyelids! That's got to hurt!" Marcy said. "What did she have tattooed on them?"

"I don't know. I was afraid to look," Ted grinned.

The fall had been dry so the main hydro generator wasn't putting out any power and they could only run the small hydro generator. This plant didn't put out enough wattage to run the DX-40, however, so they employed Diane to power the transmitter while the small hydro plant powered the receiver. It was a highly anticipated event as no one had ever been able to transmit with any two-way radios from the Flat. Therefore, Gaines was skeptical as to whether he could contact Don at the 7:00 pm time they'd scheduled to try to make contact.

The old cook shack attached to the cabin was now a radio shack. The shelves made for canning jars were now occupied with electronic components salvaged from TVs and other discarded electronics found in the county dump. An extension cord connected to the transmitter ran out through a hole in the plastic film windows and about 100 feet away to be connected to Diane. A second hole was poked in the plastic window and a coax cable ran out and rose 90 feet into the air where it was tied into a homemade multi-band Dipole antenna that Joel had strung between the summer kitchen cedar and a

150-foot fir tree. Diane was to be started the minute they heard Don. Kelly and Gaines had done a test run and tuned the transmitter beforehand and everything ran well.

There was no heat in the radio shack and it was a dark, cold, cloudy day. Shivering even in a heavy coat, Gaines listened intently to the background noise on the receiver. Just above the static and white noise was a 400-hertz whine caused by the high frequency of the rewound car alternator on the small hydro plant. Right on the dot of 7:00 pm, a low-pitched tone came from the receiver. "I wonder if that's Don tuning his transmitter," Gaines said excitedly.

"It's off frequency," Kelly said.

Gaines carefully tweaked the tuning knob of the receiver until the tone became higher pitched. Then the tone died away and the steady 400-hertz whine returned to the forefront. Suddenly, a series of code tones came from the receiver and Gaines groped in the now dark radio shack for his pencil and writing pad and began copying the code. The code stopped and Gaines held up the pad to see it by the light of the receiver dial lamp. *WD6DAA de N6DON K* "It's Don!" Gaines cried. "Go start Diane!"

Kelly raced out the door into the darkness. Sitting in the dark shack, Gaines and Joel heard Kelly pulling Diane's recoil start. Diane started and slowly came up to speed. As the heavy permanent magnet rotor within the generator gained speed, Gaines flipped the switch on the transmitter, grabbed the key and began tapping out a reply. *N6DON de WD6DAA. GE DON. HOW COPY?* This was the moment of truth. Did radio signals get out of the canyon?

Kelly dashed in the door out of breath. "It's starting to snow," he gasped.

The receiver came alive with code tones. *WD6DAA de N6DON. GE GAINES, RST IS 599. K* "He copies me good!" Gaines exclaimed and started tapping out a reply.

Suddenly Diane coughed and started to die. Kelly went crashing out the door. The heavy flywheel effect of the generator kept Diane going long enough for Kelly to get to her and nurse her back to life. Kelly ran back in. "It's dumping snow now!"

Coughing and sputtering came from Diane. Gaines swore in panic and Kelly ran wide-eyed back out to fight for Diane's life. This time Diane died completely. Fortunately, Gaines was receiving and not trying to transmit but the interruptions were breaking his concentration and he was missing parts of what Don was sending. The frantic sounds of Diane's recoil start being yanked came from outside. Slowly, Diane started again but was running roughly. Gaines started transmitting.

After a while, Diane started running smoothly but Kelly didn't return. Worried that Kelly might have gotten hurt, Joel went out to check on him. In the dim light, Joel saw Kelly leaning over Diane in the madly swirling snowflakes holding his hand over the open carburetor throat to keep the snow out. Diane's air filter had disappeared in her past life. "It's sucking snow into the carburetor," Kelly shivered.

Joe went back in to report to Gaines. "The snow's sucking into the carburetor and Kelly's freezing trying to keep it out."

Gaines frowned and nodded, trying to hear Don's code and Joel's report at the same time. He tapped out *N6DON de WD6DAA. GEN IS SUCKING SN INTO CARB. KELLY IS FREEZING KEEPING IT OUT. N6DON de WD6DAA SK* Short wave radio could escape the canyon!

In time, Kelly and Joel also became licensed amateur operators and Gaines went on to challenge and conquer the Amateur Extra class exam. It was to be a long hobby, which eventually led to active parts in the local search and rescue team for all three boys.

Kelly repairing Diane

Ham radio shack

Raising the house

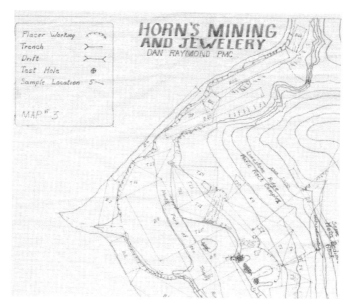

35 - Suction Dredge

In the summer of 1979, Joel and Gaines dredged a lot with the little two-and-a-half-inch Keene suction dredge. Never intended for anything but small recreational operations, the dredge did all right but soon the dredge head developed a swelling blister in the steel tube from rocks and gravel flowing through it. As the days passed, the blister swelled to the point it started to split and spray water and gravel. Also, when a dredge built on the Venturi principle starts to leak air, it loses the vacuum quite suddenly.

Finally, Joel lunged out of the water one afternoon and grabbed a screwdriver from the bank. "I've had it!" he stormed. "I saw a nugget get sucked up but it's not in the sluice box. It must have blown out the hole in this shitty head!" He swiftly unscrewed the pipe clamps that secured the head to the suction hose. "I have to weld a patch on it."

The Buzz Box had worked well over the years but over time, the damaged particleboard housing absorbed water and disintegrated so now it was just a rust colored transformer with a number of protruding wires. The arrangement of these wires determined the amperage the welder put out. The boys turned the demise of the housing into an advantage. By placing the welder in the out draft of the Hobart standby generator's cooling blower, they were able to get about 125 amps though the welder was rated for only 75. Arc welding something as thin as the steel dredge tube had become was not an easy task. Despite the ugly results, the patch on the dredge head was a temporary success.

Orders had been coming in for medallions like the ones Virgil was making for George Jorstad. George had shown the medallions around to some of the old time merchants in Weaverville, which inspired them to have medallions made, as well. The surge of orders had used up all their gold reserves and this was putting even more pressure on the dredging operations. The gold in the gravels was fairly consistent but the little worn dredge couldn't move it fast enough. When the order for Leonard and Florence Morris' 50-year wedding anniversary medallion came in and had to be completed in less than two weeks, Virgil had to do something they'd never done before. He had to buy gold from other miners around the county.

One of the miners they'd met previously ran an eight-inch Keene dredge on the claim just above Bambi Trull's claim. Gene Sapp was up at his travel trailer drying off from a day of dredging when Virgil, accompanied by the boys, drove the Jeep down the narrow access road to the benchland where Gene was camped. Virgil explained about needing gold and asked Gene if he had any to sell. Gene shook his head. "No. I have all my gold made into jewelry by a jeweler friend of mine." Seeing Virgil's obvious disappointment, Gene decided to be a little more helpful. "Jerry might have some, though."

"Jerry Trull? Bambi's youngest son?" Virgil questioned as Gene waved in the direction of Bambi's claim.

"No. Jerry Nelson. Now that Otis is gone, Jerry's working Bambi's claim for a percentage of the recovery."

Gene led them over to the downriver side of the benchland. Below them, floating in the hole the Trull kids used for swimming was a huge dredge with about 40 55-gallon drums mounted underneath for floatation. "What size dredge is that?" Joel asked in amazement.

"That's an eight-inch like mine."

"How come it's so much bigger?"

"Well, Jerry's a mechanical engineer and he built his dredge." Gene scowled a bit. "Size doesn't always mean better."

A lean blond-bearded man in a wetsuit knelt on the green-carpeted catwalk of the dredge. "Hey, Jerry! Do you have a minute? Virg here wants to talk to you," Gene yelled.

"Why?"

"He's looking to buy gold."

This got Jerry's attention and he jumped off the catwalk into the chest deep water. After he waded ashore and scrambled up the steep red bank, Gene made introductions. Virgil showed Jerry one of the medallions he hadn't yet delivered and explained how they'd run out of gold and needed to buy some. Jerry turned the one-ounce medallion in his palm. "Could you make one with my dredge on it?"

Virgil looked quizzically down at the floating behemoth before answering affirmatively.

"Could we do a deal?" Jerry asked. "If I give you a couple of ounces of gold, could you make me a medallion instead of you paying me for the extra gold?"

"Not a problem," Virgil replied.

Jerry went into his little camp trailer to get his gold. While they waited, the sound of tires crunching down the gravelly road to the camp area caught their attention. "Another Jerry," Gene said.

Jerry Miller was Gary Anderson's friend that they'd met years earlier. "A miner's convention going on here or what?" Jerry Miller laughed as he got out of his vehicle. "I got lonely dredging on Gary's claim so I came down to dredge this afternoon with Jerry Nelson."

The group talked awhile and the gold exchange was made. The convention broke up but they decided to stay long enough to watch Jerry Nelson's dredge operate. Jerry Miller waded out to the dredge and peered into one of the three sluice boxes. "Wow, Jerry! You have about seven pennyweight of gold in this box."

"Then there'll be that much in each of the other boxes," Jerry Nelson replied, putting on his facemask and wading out to start the dredge.

As the VW powered engine roared to life, the dredge shifted and settled into the pool. Great torrents of water poured out of the triple sluice boxes and a deep excitement showed in Gaines and Joel's eyes. The Jerrys put regulators in their mouths and descended into the depth of the pool. The chattering rattle of gravel and boulders coming through the dredge head and the sluice boxes said that the mining had begun.

"That's the kind of dredge we need," Joel stated on the way home.

Gaines agreed but they didn't have the money to buy a dredge like that. Soon, Gaines and Joel's enthusiasm infected them all. Virgil remembered that Ray loved dredges and thought if they drew up plans for a six-inch dredge, Ray might be better able to get the parts in southern California. "We'd pay him back in gold," Virgil said. "I'll write to him and see if he's interested."

Ray never wrote letters but Sue answered and said Ray was interested. For a week that August, Virgil and the boys worked on drawing dredge plans and making a list of materials. When the plans were completed, Virgil rolled the sheets, placed them in a mailing tube and wrote another letter to Ray. "We'll mail this tomorrow," Vigil declared.

But Ray showed up that evening, so they excitedly showed him the drawings. Ray glanced at the plans briefly. "Virg, I thought you didn't want a big dredge. I was going to bring one up a number of years ago."

"The boys are the pushers behind this," Virgil told him. "We want to pay you a percentage in gold."

"I don't care about getting paid but I could use one of the boys to come down and help with Sean and Kenny for a month. With both Kenny and Sean in wheelchairs now, there's a lot of lifting that's killing my back. I'll probably have to get surgery next spring."

"I'll go," Gaines volunteered.

"Not now," Ray said. "But after the first of the year would be a better time."

So the wheels were turning on the big dredge and that fall the boys decided to start building the long-planned new shop and their own bedrooms. The shop was to be attached to the kitchen, which they called Half Chick after the fairytale baby chick born with just one leg and one wing, because its unfinished plywood-covered back wall where the shop extension was designed to attach gave it a one-sided appearance.

Gaines laid the mortared stone foundation as Kelly and Joel hauled cement, sand and rocks again. With the sawmill working, it wasn't long before they had the walls up, the roofing laid and the tarpaper on the roof. They buttoned up the outside before it started raining. Inside, they still had to finish their bedrooms on the upper floor and the shop on the lower floor.

Rainstorms lashed over the Flat in December and January, stopping work on the house and shop. But the rains brought water to the creeks, and with the water, Joel and Marcy cleaned out the mining ditches and started sluicing for gold on the high bench deposit. The first couple of days were quite productive and they were anxious to begin their third day, but it was Sunday morning and Marcy always talked to Gary, Emy and Mama on the amateur radio on Sunday mornings.

Just as the conversation finished, a rumbling in the canyon alerted them that something was wrong. Mixed with the rumble was the sound of breaking wood and the deep grinding of shifting boulders. They all ran up to the old shop area and before them, beyond the shop where there was once a stand of Jeffrey pines, was now a shifting mass of chocolate brown mud. There were thousands of cubic yards and they stared in awe at this destruction. What had taken seconds in this mudslide would have taken them a lifetime to move.

In numbed silence, they stared. Only the sound of roots tearing loose high on the hillside above them grabbed their stunned attention. A red brown tongue of mountain liquefied, and with gathering of speed and with it energy, this earthen monster rolled through a grove of full grown white oak trees, smashing them into broken debris. The sound was terrifying and they were rooted like idiots in what appeared to be its path. Gaines' brain suddenly switched on. "Run!" he yelled.

And they did, stopping only when they knew they were safely out of its path. Turning, they saw a two-foot diameter sugar pine snap and splinter as if it were nothing more than a strand of straw. "There goes the shop!" Kelly shouted. But 20 feet uphill from the shop, the mud stream changed course. As if it had run into an invisible barrier protecting the shop, the new slide merged with the original mudflow that they'd been looking at seconds before. For a moment, the liquid earth hung. Then deep under the downhill side, a dam of broken trees broke loose and thousands of yards of brown rolled over the white rocks of the river channel and into the clear green water of the North Fork, instantly turning it mud brown.

The sliding stopped but their view of what they had always taken for granted as stable was forever changed. The lower part of the trail that had picked its way through a pretty oak forest was gone, leaving a steep slab of ugly red brown bedrock. It took them three days to cut a new trail through this solid rock. For weeks, the mud stayed a liquid quicksand-like consistency before finally setting into hard clay. At the closest, the mud advanced to within 10 feet of the shop. Many of their tools would have been lost but in the end, only Marcy's favorite pitchfork was lost forever. The horrific slide also ended the high bench mining that season. The landscape of a quarter of the Flat had changed and was now an ugly scar. But the fresh churned soil renewed its fertility and a miniature forest of seedling firs, pines and oaks like they'd never before seen sprouted that year.

Gaines didn't leave until late March to help Ray and Sue with the kids and work on the dredge. During his absence, he kept in regular contact with the family through amateur radio phone patches and told them Ray's back had become so bad he did have to have surgery. Ray lost his strength as he watched his sons slowly fade before his eyes. The happy good humor and funny jokes he always told had vanished.

Virgil, Kelly and Joel worked to put the floor in the second story, above the new shop. Before Gaines left, they'd built a tongue and groove shaper out of an old vacuum cleaner motor. They made the shaper head from a section of one-and-a-half-inch steel shaft that they shaped on a little Edelstaal lathe. They fashioned the cutter blades from the steel tines from the old Roto-Hoe, and tempered the blades in the jewelry bake-out oven.

Virgil ran all the floorboards through the shaper, which was a terrible job as it produced large amounts of fine sawdust that was hard to keep from inhaling. Finally, the construction of the floor was finished and Marcy varnished it. The new addition looked so big compared to the tiny quarters they were used to. Virgil made a tall pole ladder that they climbed for interim stairs and they put canvas over the unfinished doorway in the lower part of the house.

Through the years, they had met many fishermen who became friends. For several years, a fisherman named Gerald and his son, Vince, would walk down the river from Hobo Gulch Campground while his wife, Mary, and their small daughter, Christy hiked down the trail to wait for them to arrive at the Flat. Gerald and Mary owned a carpet store in Concord and watched construction of the house and shop over the years. "I want to put in my advertisement that I laid a carpet in the middle of nowhere," Gerald said when he saw they were moving out of the shack for good and finally moving into the new building.

They noticed a recurring theme when they talked to Gaines. He'd be scheduled to come home the next week with the dredge but it never came about. They all missed him and weren't sure when he was coming back. When they'd all but given up, he suddenly walked onto the Flat in early August. He'd shaved off his hair and for a few seconds they didn't recognize him. After four months of being away, they were thrilled to have him back. Excitedly, everyone talked at once. But when Joel asked if he had the dredge, a frown clouded Gaines' face. "Yes," he replied slowly. "But it weighs over 3,000 pounds." He rubbed the stubble on his head. "I think we can make it work."

"It weighs 3,000 pounds?" Virgil said in disbelief. "That's almost three times the weight we figured."

"Ray didn't think our plans were strong enough. You're not going to believe it when you see it, but don't say anything to Ray. It's been a pretty big strain with everything that was going on."

"Where is Ray?" Marcy asked.

"He and David are down at Trinity Oaks at the rental cabins. He wants us to meet him there tomorrow." Gaines rubbed his head. "It's been a strain," he repeated. "The dredge is in a trailer Ray pulled up with his sedan."

"He pulled the trailer up with a sedan?" Kelly questioned, knowing that Ray had a three-quarter ton pickup.

"Yes. With his back surgery, he could only sit for long periods in the soft-riding sedan. But it won't pull the trailer up the dirt road and Ray wants us to pull it up with the Jeep."

The next day in the full heat of summer, they met Ray and David at their rental cabin in Trinity Oaks. On a huge trailer, home-built sidewalls boxed in the dredge. Ray and David led the way in Ray's sedan while Virgil and the boys brought up the rear in the Jeep pulling the heavy trailer. Partway up the dirt road, the Jeep could take no more and overheated, blowing clouds of steam. Virgil stopped to let it cool.

Fifteen minutes later, the Jeep had cooled down enough to carry on but no more than a mile after that, the steam blasted from the radiator again, so once again Virgil stopped. Ray stopped also. Clearly in a great deal of pain, Ray got out of the sedan with an angry scowl. He ripped open the trunk and took out a heavy white rope, quickly tying it to the front bumper of the Jeep and the trailer hitch of his sedan. "Hey, Ray, don't tear up your car. Just give this old heap a chance to cool," Virgil told him.

But Ray wasn't listening. He climbed behind the wheel of the sedan and yelled, "Get in! We're going!"

Revving the engine, the tires spinning and spitting gravel and dust, the whole train started moving. Virgil shook his head. A quarter mile up the road, a cloud of smoke poured from under Ray's car. "You're blowing your transmission!" Kelly yelled.

Ray stopped and Virgil approached him. "Ray, why don't you just go on up to Desperation Point and wait for us?" Virgil suggested. "Relax."

When Ray agreed, Kelly unhooked the rope and Ray and David took off.

The Jeep finally arrived at Desperation Point an hour after Ray and David. They quickly unloaded the trailer so Ray could take it back with him. As usual, Ray was in a hurry and he and David quickly departed. Virgil sat down on a rock and stared morosely at the huge pile of steel parts. Gaines started explaining how it would all go together but Joel interrupted him. "No. It's not. We're going to redesign it!" Joel was emphatic. "There's no way this is going to work for us the way it's designed. There are plenty of parts here to make a much lighter system."

The monumental task of hauling the dredge down began the next morning. They took apart the pump and got it to the Flat in the first two trips. In the late afternoon on the third trip, the boys decided to haul down the engine for the dredge. Loading 400 pounds of engine on their one-wheeled cart was quite a feat. After securing it to the cart with nylon rope, they headed down the trail at a snail's pace.

One thing about the cart's design that could be hazardous was if the front man slipped and dropped the handlebars, the whole cart and load would pole-vault over on top of him. Kelly and Joel had previously found this out the hard way with 100 pounds of white rice. They'd been goofing off and Joel began shortcutting the switchbacks. Joel slipped and the whole cart pivoted right over onto him. He wasn't hurt but with 400 pounds of cast iron engine, the story would be different.

Over the years, they'd done much work on the trail but the hogback and Mattress Point section was still extremely steep and rugged. Not only was the trail steep, but the surface was covered with loose gravel. The rock was too hard and the soils too sparse to improve the trail.

The crux of the hogback was a steep descending turn around the spine of the jagged ridge. The trail surface was studded with protruding rock that fought with the tire, causing the cart to bounce and shudder. Not only was this section at the crown of a long southern facing slope that convected heat in waves, but it also caught the direct rays of the afternoon sun. Tense and sweating, Gaines and Joel fought to keep the cart under control. Kelly, with over 60 pounds of steel on his backpack, worked his way along the side of the cart to steady it on the downhill side, stumbling and sliding off the trail at times.

At the base of the steep turn was a short flat shelf at the portal of Mattress Point. The path abruptly dropped away in a rocky chute, terminating in a sharp jag against the trunk of a large sugar pine. With the cart, this was always a barely controlled slide heading straight for the trunk of the pine. At the last second, the man in the front had to negotiate the jag with a powerful thrust of his legs while nearly the full weight of the cart had pivoted onto his arms. If he failed to make the jag, the cart handles would impale him to the tree.

The brakeman in the back could never see his feet and stumbled and slid, fighting to keep the cart somewhat level and avoid having his fingers smashed or snagged by the sharp rocks along the chute. At the same time, he had to fight against the pivoting action of the cart that was lifting him off his feet. With this load, there would be no margin for error and they stopped to rest at the little shelf. "We really have to try and control the speed down the chute this time," Gaines stated.

"Ah, it will be all right," Joel said.

"The hell it will!" Gaines snapped. "If we're sliding down the chute fast, you'll never be able to make the jag and hold the 400 pounds." Joel knew Gaines was right and remained silent until they were ready to move on.

"Ok. Well, here goes nothing," Joel said, stepping off into the chute with his arms straining.

Sweating and stumbling they inched their way down the chute, coughing on the dust stirred up by their sliding feet. Kelly couldn't stand alongside the cart and steady it at this spot. Suddenly, a buzzing erupted. "Damn! What is *that*?" Gaines cried.

"Rattlesnake!" Kelly yelled.

"Where is it?"

"It's in the chute next to the tire!"

"Can we go forward?" Joel asked, arms shaking from the strain.

"No! Gaines will step right on it!" Kelly informed them.

"Well, we sure as hell can't back up!" Gaines said. "Get a stick, Kelly, and kill the bugger."

Kelly found a stick and crawled over the rocks. Taking careful aim, he swung the stick at the angry buzzing rattlesnake but the stick broke in mid-stroke and landed next to the snake, only making it angrier. Slipping and clinging to the cliff, Kelly found another stick. If he fell, he was going to take everything over the side with him, including Gaines and Joel. This stick broke, as well. Even madder, the snake crawled into the spokes of the wheel. "It's in the spokes!"

"Can we go forward *now?*" Gaines asked, his voice trembling with strain.

"No! It'll sling the snake into Joel's legs."

"Well, get that bastard out of there!"

With a rotten stick, Kelly harassed the snake until it crawled out of the spokes and slid over the side backwards. As gravity pulled it away, it remained facing them, glaring with beady eyes and buzzing loudly. "Ok. You guys can go," Kelly said.

"I want to kill that little bastard," Joel gasped between gritting teeth as they eased down the chute.

"Don't worry about it now," Gaines said. "It's going to get dark on us."

With much cursing, puffing, grunting and straining, they negotiated the terraced root section of Mattress Point. By the time they reached the Drinking Tree, darkness had closed around them. Rather than risking falling off the trail with the engine, they left it for the next morning.

When they went up the next morning, they met Uncle Doug coming down the trail.

"What's with the cart and engine I passed on the way down?" Doug asked.

"It got dark on us last night and we had to leave it," Gaines told him. "Did you see the snake at Mattress Point?"

Doug turned ashen. "What snake?" he shuddered.

The boys made trip after trip hauling the dredge down. When the pieces were all at the Flat, they began welding, grinding and fabricating. Virgil had plans to build a flatboat to float the dredge in the river but knew he wouldn't get to it this season. Still, they wanted to get the dredge in the river this year so devised an alternate plan; from cull logs from the sawmill, they'd build a raft.

It was a good concept but in reality, with all the other bugs that showed up in the dredge that summer, it was all a frustrating experience. In working configuration, the dredge weighed over 5,000 pounds and there was just not enough floatation in the raft. It did prove that with a flatboat and the bugs worked out over the winter, however, they'd have a good working dredge the following summer.

True to his word, in late August Gerald brought down his entire carpet-laying crew and laid a beautiful wall-to-wall wool carpet in the upstairs that Marcy knew would also keep the room warmer. Virgil told Gerald that when his kids got married, he'd make their wedding rings.

After Gerald and his crew left, the boys moved their beds in. There was also enough room upstairs for a big barrel heating stove grandma had given them, and a couch and chairs. One evening while they were all sitting around the stove, Kelly suddenly laughed. "Do you notice something? Look around and what do you see."

Puzzled, the rest of the family looked around. "What?" Virgil asked.

"Look at where we're sitting. We're so conditioned to sit in a certain pattern and a certain area from all the years in the little cabin that we're sitting in the same pattern now."

Sure enough, as they looked around the room, the rest of the family saw the same thing. Finally, they all laughed and began moving the couch and chairs further away.

***Cousin Nick, Virgil, Marcella, Gaines, Kelly and Joel
with new house in background***

36 - Poor Planning

The 1980 canning season was light. Although Marcy canned some blackberries, it was such a scorching summer that most of them shriveled in the heat. In addition, the apples set a puny crop, as did the acorns that year. Also, the efforts with the dredge project took a toll on the gardens and they weren't as productive as usual, and the upper garden failed completely. Uncle Doug had taken a tray of their nugget jewelry to try to sell at his workplace. The family wasn't terribly worried even though they had only a couple dollars left. What they hadn't considered was that jewelry sales plunge when the price of gold goes up. Gold had hit $800 dollars an ounce that year, so people weren't buying. Joel, almost 19 years old, took some larger nuggets Virgil was saving for jewelry and left them with Jerry Nelson to see if he could sell them. Although the price of gold was dropping by this time, there were no ready buyers.

Marcy remembered her father had said to eat cactus shoots and purslane when food was scarce. Neither grew at the Flat. Years before Red Barnes had suggested dry grass seed but it was winter and there was none. Trying to scrape together enough food for five people was a daily ordeal. The boys decided to climb digger pines to get pine nuts, which are rich in oils and contained much-needed calories. Joel brought his climbing spurs and the trio set off to the ridges and draws above the upper garden where serpentine slopes supported a large number of the silvery blue-green pines.

Digger pine cones set on the new growth yearly and take two years to mature, so the edible cones were barely a foot or so back from the tips of the branches. They found a tree that had many cones in its top branches and Joel set to climbing. Forty feet up, the trunk triple branched and Joel set out up one of the spindly limbs. It started out eight inches in diameter and at an 80-degree angle, rose branchless another 60 feet where a 20-foot section of branches and cones rose in an airy bushy crown. Craning their necks, Gaines and Kelly grew concerned as the branch started bending under Joel's weight. "It isn't going to hold you!" Gaines yelled up.

Joel paused and evaluated the situation. By this time, he was shinnying up a branch only four inches in diameter almost 100 feet above the ground. "If I could get to the branches there," he pointed, "I might be able to bend them in and cut the cones away," he yelled back.

"No! You can't bend them that much," Kelly yelled.

Joel clung to the branch, pondering. The hollow weak feeling in his stomach kept him from retreating from what seemed like an insane mission. But hunger is also a strong incentive for invention and Kelly suddenly got an idea. "What about using the 20-foot extendable pruning shears?" Kelly said.

"Yes," Gaines agreed. "Kelly, go get them."

Fatigued from clinging to the nearly vertical four-inch branch, Joel slid back down to the first fork to await Kelly's return from the half-mile roundtrip. Kelly returned with the long pole pruning shears, puffing hard from the climb. Gaines took the shears from Kelly and climbed high enough up the trunk to hand the shears to Joel where he rested cradled in the crotch of the fork. Once again, Joel climbed the long spindly branch, this time with the 20-foot shears hanging from his belt. The branch sagged and the crown quavered under his gasping efforts. He dragged himself into the first branches of the crown, braced his feet against the thin branches and took a rest.

When he had recovered his breath enough, he extended the shears and fought to get the cutting blade over the stem of the first cone, hampered by the swaying tree crown. The branch creaked ominously but Joel kept at it and the first cone fell away, hit the ground like a bomb and then rolled down the spur until it came to rest on the trunk of a downed tree. The next cone fell shortly after. "I think I got the technique down," Joel yelled to his brothers.

When they'd collected 21 cones in the one-wheeled cart, Joel came down from the tree and they returned to the Flat to begin the long task of extracting the hard-shelled nuts. Normally, the cones are left to dry until the plates open and the nuts nestled in a pair under each plate can be shaken out. But immediate hunger precluded this.

The cones were heavily covered with clear, fresh pitch. Experimenting with an assembly line process, they worked different techniques until they found the most efficient method of extraction. They set the cones on fire until the pitch had burned away and then, while still smoking hot, they split each cone into quarters with an axe and chopped the pithy core away from each quarter to release the plates and the nuts within. Then they collected the nuts and placed them in a bucket of water to determine which were edible; those that sunk were good nuts while those that floated were duds.

The pine nut shells were extremely hard and had to be cracked with a tool, such as a hammer or pliers. Everyone discovered their own favorite tool for cracking the nuts. Joel carefully cracked the shells neatly into two halves using a long handled pair of pruning shears. Marcy used pliers, Gaines used needle nosed pliers and Kelly used a hammer. Virgil collected the nuts from the piles of broken shells. Marcy remembered Red talking about how the Digger Pine Indians starved because they depended on pine nuts. "No wonder the Digger Pine Indians went extinct!" she mused as she flexed her cramping fingers.

It took a good part of the day to get one large cookie sheet full of nuts. They roasted their meager harvest on the wood-fired heating stove and then had a dinner portion of less than two handfuls each of roasted nuts for the day's effort. Day after day, they repeated the process until eventually the available cones started to give out. One morning as Marcy went out to check on their cache of digger pine cones, she caught a skunk tearing them open. She grabbed her broom and whacked him, and he ran out of the shed and up the mountain without even raising his tail in retaliation.

To provide food for the family, Joel and Gaines worked hard to catch fish but the fish were all lean, devoid of any fat. Marcy found some full cans of beer in the cellar that Doug had left and simmered the fish in it, hoping to add some nutrition. The family craved fat, starch and sugar. The caloric energy they expended to collect food was greater than the calories gathered and the weight rapidly shed from their bodies. With each day, it got harder and harder to make a meal.

Marcy got out her book by Euell Gibbons on eating wild foods and read about eating daylily bulbs and the tips of pine trees. She tried to remember where she had planted the daylilies and she and Virgil shoveled a lot of snow before they found them. When the salt ran out, they boiled down Marcy's kosher pickle juice and made green salt. It tasted horrible with its sour vinegar, dill, garlic and hot pepper flavor. Remembering the time they'd made maple syrup, they again drilled holes in the maple trees when the nights were freezing and the days were sunny. They collected the syrup and boiled it down using the forge.

After yet another disappointing trip to town to see if there had been any jewelry sales or if Joel's nuggets had sold, they came back in deep gloom. Nothing had sold and there was only enough gas left in the Jeep to make one more trip. For the first time ever, the boys talked about getting outside jobs but the economy was going into a deep recession and no one was hiring, so that option seemed a dead end. Virgil and Marcy had decided long ago that they'd never go on food stamps or welfare. Their family motto was 'Total responsibly is total freedom' and if they got to the point where they couldn't survive at the Flat, they'd move back to the city. But as things were, the city offered less. During this time, quite a few younger people in the county were trying to live the back-to-the-land life but many got by on government aid and encouraged others to do the same. But for the Horns, philosophically and psychologically, that was not an option.

As their bodies went into the autophagy stage of starvation, flesh and muscle was consumed. They also discovered that hunger breeds anger and found themselves arguing more. To keep their minds busy, the boys started clearing and burning brush. As they worked around the old cabin, they found one corner of the roof sagging. "We should just get rid of this shack," Gaines suggested to Kelly and Joel.

Although Virgil and Marcy didn't really want the cabin gone and believed it could be repaired, in their state of hunger they couldn't come up with any good counterarguments as to why it shouldn't go. Once the decision to destroy the shack was made, it came down fast. The cabin, so intimately tied to their early years at the Flat, was gone and the black smoke of its spirit drifted up on a gentle early spring breeze and floated out of the canyon. "Oh no," Marcy gasped as many memories of days gone by washed over her and tears flooded her eyes. "Our shack is gone."

One fine spring day, Virgil came to Marcy with a funny look on his face. "Ma, I know this isn't going to sit right, but can I use the plywood on the wall of your kitchen? I want to start making a flatboat for the dredge so we can start dredging as early as possible because I never want to be in this situation again," Virgil explained.

Virgil had made many fiberglass boats with his cousin, Noah, in a little boat shop in southern California. Unfortunately, just as things started getting profitable, a thief broke into the shop and stole all their equipment. They didn't have the capital to go on so they closed down the shop. "Sure, Virg, take it. Steal from Paul to give to Terry."

"It's rob Peter to pay Paul," Virgil grinned.

In the evenings, Joel took to reading Marcy's cookbooks aloud to the rest of the family and showing them color pictures of great white frosted cakes and golden brown beef roasts steaming on the table. "Will you just shut the hell up!" Gaines exclaimed. "You're making this worse."

The rest of the family agreed unanimously but food talk always seemed to come up. Gaines was talking to a ham radio operator who was griping that his wife had fed him macaroni and cheese for two nights in a row. "Well, I wouldn't complain," Gaines replied. "It sounds really good to me." None of the friends and family Gaines talked to on the amateur radio had a clue he was starving and he kept it that way.

Bit by bit, the flatboat went together and soon it was done, with the bottom painted turquoise and the gunwales trimmed in deep blue. So it sat patiently on saw horses awaiting the legal dredging season and the money to buy the high priced fuel to run it.

It was when Marcy decided to cut Virgil's hair and he took off his shirt that prompted them to burn the last of the fuel in the Jeep to check the mail. Virgil's normal weight was just 120 pounds but now his ribs pressed hard against the thin flesh of his chest. The boys and Marcy stared in horror at the dramatic evidence of what they had been closing their minds to – starvation. "My God, Virgil! You look like a refugee from a Cambodian death camp!" Joel burst out.

The rest of the family agreed and Joel got the scales for Virgil to stand on. "Eighty-seven pounds!" Gaines gasped, leaning over the scales to make sure he was seeing it right.

"We're going to check the mail tomorrow!" Marcy stated and nobody disagreed.

They had four digger pine nuts apiece to get up the trail. Arriving at the post office before the daily mail delivery, Marcy flipped through the letters and junk mail. There was nothing from Doug. Solid despair overtook them as they stood around the Jeep quietly discussing what to do. A little Volkswagen Beetle pulled into the post office parking lot and the local preacher, Gilman Welch, climbed out. They talked with him awhile and then Marcy blurted out, "Can we borrow a sack of potatoes? I'll pay you back."

Virgil and the boys looked at her in horror and she started to cry. "Damn it, Virg! I told him I wanted to borrow it! I didn't beg for it."

Gilman, a lanky old preacher who had migrated from Montana, looked on sympathetically. "We have all kinds of food. Just stop by and we'll load you up." Gilman frequently used the term 'we' because he habitually picked up people along the road who were down on their luck and tried to convert them to Jesus. His opened his home to all and usually had extra folks living there.

The daily mail truck showed up and Marcy eyed it hopefully. "We're expecting money from Virgil's brother," she explained to Gilman.

After allowing time for sorting the mail, Virgil went inside and checked their box. He stepped out of the post office grinning broadly and holding up a check from Doug. "We won't need those potatoes, Gilman. We got money," Marcy said.

"Any time," Gilman drawled.

A subject they'd discussed quite a lot beforehand was the first food they'd buy for lunch once they got some money. The consensus was white bread, peanut butter and jelly, and half-and-half. They hurried to the market to eat their fill for the first time in months.

The starvation ordeal affected them greatly. There were no fruits or vegetables left un-canned after that. Marcy felt she got something good out of the experience but Virgil and the boys wouldn't talk about it as they all realized it was a failure in the family's attitude and preconceived beliefs that had brought on the starvation.

Kelly and Gaines processing gravel from tunnel

Virgil taking sample in tunnel.

37 - Working a Mine

When the 1981 dredging season came, they set the dredge up on the river and Virgil painted a brontosaurus on the side of the sluice box. They named it the Brontosaurus 5,000, which signified the weight of the dredge while operating. As with any engineering project, flaws appeared in the design and had to be worked out. The shortage of working capital also played a role in their problems, one of which was the lack of a good air compressor. Their air compressor used a rubberized nylon diaphragm to compress the air. This diaphragm had a life expectancy of a couple hundred hours. Since Jerry Nelson had given it to them used, much of the life of the diaphragm was gone. Of the two mouthpiece air regulators Gaines and Joel were using, only one was commercially made and Joel was using it. Gaines built his out of what is commonly called the gulp valve in an automotive emission system. Of the two, the one Gaines made worked best because it allowed a greater volume of air to pass at low pressure.

Kelly tended the dredge while Gaines and Joel worked underwater. As the compressor gradually failed and the air supply declined, seeing Joel pop to the surface was usually the first sign Kelly had that anything was wrong. Verbal communication was impossible over the roar of the engine and the rattle and grinding of boulders racing through the suction head and the sluice box, so Joel would hold up his regulator and shake his head, breathing hard to catch his breath. Once Kelly shut the engine down, Gaines, unaware of the problem because his regulator had not yet registered the loss of air pressure, would surface to find out what was going on. In jest, Joel always called Gaines an air hog. Although just a simple donut-shaped piece of rubber, a replacement diaphragm was expensive so Kelly tried many different types of materials to fabricate a new one but his efforts never worked longer than 15 hours. Obviously, there was a reason for the high price. On one of Gary Anderson's visits, he noticed the problem and bought the first replacement for them, which he sent in the mail.

In spring, the waters of the North Fork are slightly milky with pure snowmelt from the Trinity Alps. Even with quarter-inch neoprene wetsuits, the boys found that the time they could spend underwater was measured in minutes. And even in those few minutes, work was slow and inefficient for they found quick movements pumped the bone aching cold water into their suits. "This isn't working!" Joel shuddered, staggering out the water and dropping his 80-pound lead weight belt with a splash in the shallows. "We're just wasting gas!"

Kelly's brow furrowed in concern. The dredge had a water-cooled engine and to keep the engine cool, he had it rigged to pump the water directly out of the river, circulate it through the water jacket of the engine and then deposit it back into the river as hot water. There was a resource here and Gaines and Kelly decided to exploit it. The water temperature was too hot to pump directly into their wetsuits so Kelly built a mixing unit that allowed him to turn a valve and mix in cold water until it reached body temperature. Gaines lashed a half-inch garden hose to each of the air hoses and the loose hose ends at the air regulator side would go down the backs of their wetsuits.

Strapping on the 80-pound weight belts, Gaines and Joel descended into the depths. Two and a half hours later, they surfaced when the first tank of gas ran out. "How does it work?" Kelly asked, exchanging the empty five-gallon gas can for a full one.

"Great!" Joel said. "The only way we can tell we're in 38-degree water is the cold around our lips."

That afternoon as Kelly sat cross-legged by the engine to keep warm in the cold wind, he saw Gaines burst from the water like a hooked fish, thrashing about on the surface, cursing and jerking at his warm water tube. As Gaines yanked the tube from the back of his wetsuit, Kelly saw it spouting geysers of steam and boiling water. In a panic, Kelly looked down and saw that a floating stick had lifted the coolant water intake out of the river. What remained in the water jacket was boiling away. A quick disconnect solved the problem and luckily Gaines was not too badly burned.

The summer swimming hole presented a prime area to dredge and they floated the dredge into position. The water in the swimming hole was 10 feet deep and they estimated that the gravel deposits in the bottom were between five and eight feet. The gravel was almost exclusively less than six inches in diameter, so very little material needed to be moved by hand. They reached six feet of gravel depth, then eight, but still no bedrock bottom. In an unusual development, the aggregate became finer the deeper they went, until they reached a fine silt layer between 13 and 20 feet down.

Gaines and Joel were now working in a huge inverted cone that was hard to climb out of. Below 20 feet, the gravel reverted to a standard riverbed composition of rocks and boulders but still no bottom. And to make matters worse, the muddy water settled into the bottom and blocked all sunlight. Holding their hands in front of their facemasks in the muddy water, neither Gaines nor Joel could discern anything but blackness. Work went on by feel and sound alone, and taut nerves due to the knowledge that as they sucked the gravel away from the bottom, the gravel wall became ever steeper until, beginning at the bottom, it collapsed in a massive slide. It was the sharp clicking sounds of boulders falling, and the building currents known as turbidity currents, that alerted them to climb out of the way before they got buried. If a long enough period passed between slides, the suction hose eventually drew the turbid water from the excavation and they could see.

At 28 feet, they became jammed in with boulders too large to suck up and too big to carry out of the hole. So for a week, they built a 30-foot boom and mast operated by a five-ton winch. Using a basket welded up from old bed frames, they lifted load after load of boulders from the excavation. They finally resumed dredging and in a moment of clear water at 33 feet of depth, while Gaines manned the suction tube, the bottom of bedrock appeared. Gaines and Joel looked at each other through a large school of rainbow trout feeding around them. With masks over their faces and air regulators in their mouths, any communication by facial expression was impossible, but a vigorous thumbs-up from Gaines confirmed to Joel that they had indeed reached bedrock!

Behind them stood a towering wall of sand and gravel from which large boulders protruded. It was not far off of vertical but had so far been stable. Then a sharp crack that carried a concussive wave alerted them to the collapse. They jerked their heads around and expelled great columns of bubbles from their regulators as they began their slow motion retreat, the only kind possible underwater with 80 pounds of lead strapped around their waists. Gaines tried to drag the stiff vinyl suction hose with him but a falling boulder pinned it to the bottom. As they repeatedly climbed up and then partially slid back down the slope, the billowing clouds of mud rose to engulf them. Safely up at the rim of the hole, they waited until the sound of falling boulders ceased and then returned to the now black water. They found the suction tube deeply buried in the landslide and no matter how hard they heaved on the tube, they could not free it. Finally, Gaines grabbed Joel's arm and pulled him upward in the hole as a signal that he wanted them to surface.

Kelly sat cross-legged on the head box of the sluice when they surfaced and Joel motioned for him to cut the engine. As the engine noise died away, Gaines pulled the regulator from his mouth. "The suction tube is buried and we can't get it loose. We have to use the boom and winch to pull it out," Gaines explained.

With bare feet Kelly leaped from the dredge boat to the pile of boulders they'd stacked up, where he swung the boom around into position over the middle of the excavation. Enough air remained in the reserve air tank for Gaines to drop down underwater and connect the chain that hung from the end of the boom to the dredge hose. He surfaced and called for Kelly to start hauling.

The winch was an old hand crank model but they'd modified it to run on a 120-volt repulsion-start electric motor. Kelly plugged the motor in and slowly the boom rose in the air until the chain came taut, then it slowed even more. "Darn! How deep is it buried?" Kelly asked, observing the heavy load on the motor.

"Probably seven feet," Joel reported.

The water was beginning to clear and Gaines peered into the depths. "It's moving; keep lifting," he said.

The hose pulled free and they resumed dredging. Two-and-a-half hours later, Gaines had sucked up the gravel that had collapsed and exposed bedrock again. He cleaned a couple square feet of bedrock, noticed that it was sloping even deeper and motioned for Joel to surface with him. Kelly saw them surface and expectantly reduced the throttle to an idle. Gaines ran his hand across his throat to indicate killing the engine. "We're at 33 feet and it might be the bottom but it's still sloping down slightly," Gaines explained once the engine had died.

Joel staggered from the water to the boulder pile and dropped his weight belt.

"There's just so much overburden," he gasped, sitting down. "But I figured out why the gravel is deposited the way it is, and so deep. The huge Thurston Gulch slide that came down during the 1964 flood blocked the main North Fork with debris. Remember Red talking about how the river started dropping and he thought the flood was crested and over?" Joel asked.

"Yeah," Gaines said.

"Well, that was when the river was blocked by the debris. Then remember that he went to bed and woke with the water in his house and barely got out before a huge sugar pine log riding on a wall of water smashed his house? Well, that has to be when the dam broke," Joel theorized.

"Well, what about the deposits?" Gaines asked.

"Those thousands upon thousands of cubic yards of debris were washed down the river and classified. The fine sand would have reached here first, followed by coarser and coarser sand and gravel," Joel continued. "It completely buried the old riverbed. That layer of fine silt is what was deposited and settled in the reservoir behind the old dam. We're 20 feet above the old river channel."

"Well, then we're going to have to move the dredge because this is just too much overburden to move," Gaines stated.

"In the last 14 years the floods have been cutting the channel back down so we'll just have to wait for the river to move all this," Joel said, agreeing that they had to move for the time being.

They resumed dredging 100 feet down the river and found the overburden much shallower. After several days of dredging, they ran the concentrates through a smaller sluice box. Then Marcy panned it down to the black sand and turned it over to Virgil.

From junk that Virgil had found in the dump, he and Gaines hand built what Virgil called a magnetic separator. With a main conveyer belt and five smaller conveyers crossing above with successively stronger magnets above each of them, the magnetic black sand was stripped away. The gold and other non-magnetic metals travelled down the belt and dropped in a bucket and then they separated out the gold flakes and small nuggets in a tiny sluice box. Finally, the concentrates went into a glass tank with a solution of potassium cyanide and water. The flour gold and microscopic gold dissolved in the cyanide solution where Virgil then electroplated the pure gold out on a stainless steel anode. Then, using a knife, Virgil peeled the gold off in flakes.

Marcella at her mother's place in southern Oregon

During fall 1981, they slowly worked to make improvements to the house and right before Thanksgiving Virgil and the boys went to town to get building materials. Desperation Point had four inches of slick slushy snow on the ground and there was two inches of the same on the Flat. They came home with a letter from the Forest Service saying they had to move out by February and that everything they owned must be off the Flat. The Bureau of Mines mineral exam in 1973, however, had declared their claim valid.

When Marcy heard the news in the letter, she started sobbing. "All our work and time! And we went by all the laws, too!" Too upset to continue her holiday preparations, she abandoned gathering canned goods from the cellar for their Thanksgiving dinner and climbed the ladder to the loft bedroom she shared with Virgil. After a good cry, she climbed back down, the open cellar door forgotten, and stepped backward off the ladder into the void.

Cast iron pans hung on nails above the cellar door and she grabbed at them as she fell, dislodging a large skillet, which followed her into the cellar and landed on her head. Despite the weight of the skillet and the eight-foot drop, the intense pain she felt radiated from her shoulder. Virgil rushed down the stairs. "Are you ok, Ma?"

"I think I broke my arm."

Joel and Gaines crowded onto the steep, narrow stairs. "Can you make it up, Ma?"

"No, I don't think so," she moaned.

Virgil helped Marcy up but she wasn't able to hold on to the steep stairs with one arm and one leg was badly bruised, as well. As gently as they could in the tight quarters, they helped her climb into the kitchen. Virgil stared at Marcy in horror. Blood poured down her face and her left shoulder sagged backward. "Well, I have something else to think about now," she grimaced.

"We'd better get on the ham radio and call search and rescue," Gaines said.

"No, don't. It's too dangerous for them to drive that snowy road," Marcy groaned.

"Can you handle it, Ma?" Joel asked.

Marcy grinned weakly as Gaines rubbed her shoulder until it started feeling better. Then she leaned back in the chair and pain shot through her like a knife. She screamed. Without further discussion, Gaines ran to the radio and eventually, with the help of various ham radio operators across the state, got a message through to George Galusha, a friend and amateur radio operator in Weaverville, and had him call the Trinity County Sheriff Search and Rescue team. Joel and Kelly raced up the trail to lead them down.

After the jolt of excruciating pain, however, Marcy's shoulder started feeling better. After a while, she cautiously moved her arm and discovered that her shoulder felt fine. "Virg, I think it went back in place. See, I can move it."

"Are you sure?" Virgil asked with obvious relief. "Yes, your shoulder isn't shoved backwards anymore."

"Gaines, run up the trail and tell them to turn around," Marcy said. "I can handle it."

It took six months for Marcy's shoulder to heal and then it was stiff, so she did yoga exercises to help heal it completely.

They worked during winter and spring on the house, which would eventually have a bathroom. But before that could happen, a septic tank had to be built. And even before that, a hole for the tank had to be dug. The boys started work digging down through the boulder field behind the house. Luck had it that no boulders larger than 300 pounds were uncovered. The hole needed to be six-feet deep, so after four-and-a-half feet, Kelly rigged a mast and boom lift system to excavate the gravel.

At six feet, the gravel changed to a stained red color and grew damper. As gold miners, this had significance and they decided to dig down a few more feet to bedrock and test for gold. At seven feet, a boulder fell from the gravel bed and just missed Kelly while he dug. It was time to put up protective shoring. They built a cage out of wood that fit down into the shaft to provide protection from falling boulders. The excavation continued but no bedrock was found. But it had to be just a bit deeper so the digging went on.

They reached eight, nine, and then a depth of 10 feet. A long debate ensued. Gaines favored calling it quits, especially since the main objective of the project was to dig a hole for a septic tank, not to dig a hole to who knows how deep. He also worried that if they found gold, the hole would never get used for the tank at all. Joel was in favor of pushing on and Kelly could go either way. Virgil and Marcy refused to get involved. Joel reasoned that if they found gold, they could dig a tunnel starting at the riverbank and this convinced Gaines to continue.

They reached bedrock at 15 feet and Joel scraped the wet red gravel from the crevices in the bedrock and placed it into the haul buckets. At the top, Virgil set up a sluice box with a hose running to it. As Gaines and Kelly hauled the buckets up, Virgil ran them through the box. When they'd cleaned all the gravel from the surface of bedrock and run the last bucket through the sluice box, Marcy panned down the concentrates. There was gold all right, in a nice amount of flakes and small nuggets. They started a tunnel at the riverbank and excavated in until they halted work in the tunnel to start dredging in the summer of 1982.

After dredging season ended, they dug the tunnel through the fall and winter. From trees downed by heavy snow the winter before, the boys cut a supply of timbers for shoring up the tunnel and building a washing plant. All the excavated material from the tunnel came out in a wheelbarrow. A long wooden ramp lead up to the top where they had a crank operated shaker screen, which funneled the classified gravel into a sluice box. They used the material excavated from the tunnel to reclaim a large broken area, placing the boulders and cobbles on the bottom and the classified washed gravel over the top.

The tunnel was 40 feet long and they learned that digging a tunnel in less than solidly cemented river bar deposit had an element of adrenaline-pumping moments. Once they shored up the tunnel with timbers, it was relatively stable, but while they used a heavy steel bar to excavate the tunnel beyond the last of the shoring, it kept them alert. They soon learned to read the gravel face and ceiling for the telltale sign of an impending collapse.

In the cool dampness of the tunnel, wearing only pants and boots, Kelly wielded the steel bar and knocked the gravel and boulders from the tunnel face. He worked by the light of an electric flood lamp clipped to one of the shoring timbers. A long electrical extension cord led out of the tunnel's portal. Joel came along behind Kelly, picking up the cobbles and boulders Kelly had knocked loose and loading them into the wheelbarrow. Suddenly Kelly stopped short. "Stop!" Kelly said, looking overhead.

Joel moved the wheelbarrow back toward the entrance, giving them room to retreat. In the tense silence, they watched the exposed ceiling. Nothing appeared wrong at first, but then one tiny grain of sand fell away, then nothing for half a minute. Then another grain of sand fell, then a tiny pebble. "It's going," Kelly predicted ominously.

Without further warning, a section of cemented boulders, cobbles and gravel calved away from the ceiling and shattered with a loud crash on the pile of rubble on the floor. For a full minute they watched, until they were satisfied that the ceiling was again stable enough to resume excavating. This was the pattern they had followed for the 40 feet of tunnel.

The gravel deposit was arranged in two layers. The first layer was on bedrock, was two feet in depth, wetter, clayed together, and obviously geologically older. All the gold was in this layer or right in the cracks of the bedrock. Above the first layer was a lighter, less clayed, sandy cemented layer. This layer contained so little gold they weren't even sluicing it, but just used it for fill instead.

Four feet beyond the last shoring, they stopped digging and cleaned the excavated area carefully. Gaines had been out running the washing plant and after this last load of pay dirt went through the plant, he shut down the gas-powered pump that was pumping water to the sluice box. Joel scrambled down to examine the first riffles. For the first 40 feet of tunnel, the gold had been in the form of fine flakes and pinhead-sized nuggets. But what Joel pulled from the riffles was nearly two pennyweight, which prompted them to clean the sluice box and discover they had truly hit a pay streak!

In excitement, they shored the last section of the tunnel and set to work excavating the next section. Three feet in, Kelly stopped with the familiar call for quiet and they watched grains of sand fall from the ceiling. Suddenly a huge section fell away, but this time the rupture extended back over the freshly installed timbers above their heads. The timbers creaked and groaned but held the killer-sized boulders at bay, letting only small cobbles and curtains of sand and pebbles rain down on them.

The tunnel went dark as the rock fall knocked the floodlight down and it went out. In a panic, Kelly and Joel fought their way past the wheelbarrow to the arch of light that was the portal. Back at a section they knew was safe, they stopped and listened toward the now pitch dark tunnel end. They listened for five minutes and several times the crash of secondary cave-ins made them jump. Eight minutes passed and all was silent. Cautiously they advanced into the darkness. In the lead, Kelly tripped over something and let out a loud curse as he grabbed his knee. "Watch the wheelbarrow," Joel cautioned belatedly.

"Thanks," Kelly said dryly.

Kelly crawled over the wheelbarrow and groped in the darkness, feeling for the floodlight. A tinny scraping sound came from the darkness. "Found it," Kelly grunted.

"Can you feel if the bulb is broken?"

Kelly didn't answer so Joel repeated his question.

"I'm not going to feel for a broken bulb that might still be plugged in," Kelly said.

Joel chuckled. "Why not? You might be able to see what you're doing if you light your eyeballs up."

"Yeah, right," Kelly muttered, not finding much humor in the situation.

Suddenly the light went on. "It just pulled the plug loose," Kelly stated. With the light back on, they could see a huge pile of boulders and gravel halfway up the tunnel sides. "Wow!" Kelly said. "It really caved this time."

Very cautiously, they started excavating the rubble. When the loose debris was gone, Joel pushed the wheelbarrow completely from the tunnel to give them a free path to safety. Kelly took the bar and swung it into the tunnel face. With a roar, a huge chunk of the ceiling crashed down leaving a dome three feet above the normal crown of the tunnel. "I don't like the looks of that!" Kelly stated darkly.

"I don't either," Joel replied. "I'm going to call Gaines to see what he thinks"

All three boys stared at the tunnel end. Joel bent down and picked up a handful of gravel and closely examined it. "It's changed. It's lost the natural cementing and there's organic matter in it," he reported. "It looks like a really large tree managed to get roots down this deep at one time and has since decayed."

Kelly was the most enthusiastic tunneler. "If we bore past this section, it might stabilize beyond," he suggested.

"If we don't get crushed before we get through it," Joel countered.

"Even if we do get past it, what happens if we're a hundred feet back and this whole section caves in?" Gaines pointed out. That sobering thought silenced them. Each one knew that would be a slow, lonely, agonizing death sentence.

Finally, Joel spoke again. "And just when we were reaching the main gold streak."

"Yet all the gold in the world will do us no good if we're dead," Gaines reminded them.

Again, a long silence hung between them for it was really dawning on them that they were staring at not only the end of the tunnel, but at the end of the whole operation, and it wasn't an easy thing to give up lightly. With wisdom beyond their years, they finally chose not to risk a very likely death and slowly walked from the tunnel. They never returned and eventually, over the years, the timbers rotted away and the tunnel caved in, at places all the way to the surface.

After receiving the District Ranger's November 1981 letter to vacate, Virgil had sent a written response informing him of the legality of their occupancy. For a year or so, they heard nothing more from the Forest Service but an era that had started in 1849 with the California Gold Rush was ending. One after another, local miners were evicted from their claims, collapsing under the relentless force of the federal government. From that time on, a dark cloud overshadowed every project as a long period of uncertainty caused by conflict with federal agencies began. Virgil decided to study all the mining laws and encouraged Gaines to study with him, which eventually lead to the decision to patent the mineral claim.

The leaves were turning colors again and the air was cold and crisp when the boys returned from town on October 27, 1988. All three grinned broadly.

"What is it? Why are you looking like that?" Marcy asked.

Joel took his hand from behind his back and handed an opened envelope to Virgil. Inside, a document from the Bureau of Land Management stated:

> *Virgil Horn and Marcella Horn are entitled to a land patent pursuant to the general mining laws...for that certain claim known as the Dan Raymond Placer Mining Claim...to have and to hold the said land with all the rights, privileges, immunities, and appurtenances, of whatsoever nature, thereunto belonging to Virgil Horn and Marcella Horn, and to their heirs and assigns, forever.*

The Dan Raymond Placer Mining Claim mineral patent had been granted. They now had real property! No more fear each trip to the post office about receiving mail from the Forest Service telling them that the adventure was over. They stared at the letter with awe for a few seconds and then Marcy gave a whoop. "We did it! We did it!" she cried and grabbed at Virgil and the boys, hugging them all.

It seemed like a million pounds had dropped off their backs and happy eyes and a huge smile lit each face. "Hey, Virg, we walked the tall grass and won," Marcy said.

He looked at her inquisitively for a moment and then remembered the time long ago when he'd told her those same words. "We sure did," he agreed, hugging her even tighter. "I guess that sign was wrong. It wasn't impossible beyond that point after all and now we really have accomplished our dream."

Photo Credits

During the years that this book encompasses, we received photographs from many of our visitors, friends and family. Unfortunately, in the case of most of these pictures, time has erased which photos were taken by whom.

We wish to thank the following people for the photos contained in this book.

Bill Jones

Dick Harms

Doug Horn

Doug Stewart

Fran & Ivan Morlan

Gary & Lonie Anderson

Gary Stockton

Gay Berrien (pages 111, 176, 184, 193, 243, and 275)

Jackie Martin

John Brooks

Larry Halter

Nick Brown

Ray Cooper

Richard Daddow

Tim Morlan

Unknown photographers

Made in the USA
San Bernardino, CA
05 July 2014